A Place in the Story

A Place in the Story

Servants and Service
in Shakespeare's Plays

Linda Anderson

DELAWARE

Newark: University of Delaware Press

Associated University Presses
2010 Eastpark Boulevard
Cranbury, NJ 08512

The paper used in this publication meets the requirements of the American National Standard for Permanence of Paper for Printed Library Materials Z39.48-1984.

Library of Congress Cataloging-in-Publication Data

Anderson, Linda, 1949 May 24-
A place in the story : servants and service in Shakespeare's plays / Linda Anderson.
    p.   cm.
Includes bibliographical references and index.
ISBN 0-87413-925-2 (alk. paper)
1. Shakespeare, William, 1564–1616—Characters—Servants.   2. Master and servant—England—History—16th century.   3. Master and servant—England—History—17th century.   4. Domestics—England—History—16th century   5. Domestics—England—History—17th century.   6. Master and servant in literature.   7. Domestics in literature.   8. Servants in literature. I. Title.
PR2992.S47A53   2005
822.3'3—dc22   2005004935

PRINTED IN THE UNITED STATES OF AMERICA

For my mother and in memory of my father

Mine honesty and I begin to square.
The loyalty well held to fools does make
Our faith mere folly; yet he that can endure
To follow with allegiance a fall'n lord
Does conquer him that did his master conquer
And earns a place i'th' story.

(Antony and Cleopatra 3.13.41–46)

Contents

Preface

THE VOLUME OF SHAKESPEARE STUDIES IS SO GREAT THAT IT SOME-times seems unimaginable that there remains an aspect of the canon that has not been exhaustively discussed. It is therefore surprising to discover how little attention has been paid to the servants in Shakespeare's plays, although all of his plays feature servants as characters, and many of these characters play prom-inent roles.[1] Over the last few decades, literary critics have be-come increasingly sensitive to the voices of the disenfranchised, and to the absence from literature of such voices. In addition to the unheard or seldom-heard voices of women and minorities, we listen, often in vain, for the voices of poor and working-class peo-ple in early modern literature. Since members of these groups were commonly unable to read or write, it is not surprising that they have often been effectively silenced. But servants, a class of workers consisting of both men and women, and occasionally including minority persons, has been given—if not its own voice—at least continual representation throughout Western lit-erature from the earliest times almost to the present.

The lack of attention paid to the role of servants in literature may stem from several causes. Modern readers, recognizing the contractual model of work for wages as a more "advanced" form of employer-employee relations, are often uncomfortable with the idea of personal service, which seems to imply "servitude" and even to verge on slavery.[2] Furthermore, servants in litera-ture often play minor roles, insignificant in terms of the themes and structures of the works they inhabit. Even when servants do play a prominent part in the action, their parts are often stereo-typed, as, for example, the intriguing slave of Greek and Roman comedy, the villainous tool of Renaissance tragedy, and the comi-cally misspeaking servant of nineteenth-century novels.

I do not intend to suggest that Shakespeare's representations of servants and service are any more realistic than his represen-tations of French queens, Scottish thanes, or Athenian workmen. To the extent that Shakespeare's servant-characters "are de-

9

scribed as faithful reflections of the servants of Elizabethan England,"[3] I think that description is largely incorrect, unless we accept that reflections can be distorted. Certainly, the servants in the plays are based on real servants and much of what they do is realistic: they carry out their employers' commands, accept punishment for failing to please their employers, complain of their treatment, dream of leaving service, etc.; they do not sail off to distant lands to astonish the infidels or thrice become Lord Mayor of London. Shakespeare's servants, however, are individuals created for particular dramatic purposes, not a representative cross section of the class of early modern servants. Various kinds of actual early modern servants are under-represented, or not represented at all; others are over-represented. Many of the real difficulties of a life in service are given short shrift; on the other hand, the question of dying for your master or mistress, which probably did not arise for most real servants, occurs quite often in the plays. Were we to extrapolate the condition of servants in early modern England from their depiction in Shakespeare's plays, we would get a very peculiar picture.

Although I have relied on the ideas and theories of many previous critics, there is no single, overarching idea or theory governing this book, because Shakespeare uses servants and concepts of service in varied and often contradictory ways; nor should any single theory circumscribe our range of reactions to his depictions of service. In *Discipline and Punish*, for example, Michel Foucault defines "service" as "a constant, total, massive, non-analytical, unlimited relation of domination, established in the form of the individual will of the master, his 'caprice.'"[4] Whether or not this is a historically accurate assessment, it is not a definition that embraces all of the ideas about service represented in Shakespeare's plays, which represent a wide range of attitudes toward service: servants who faithfully serve their employers and who are rewarded; equally faithful servants who are punished or whose faithful service leads to their deaths; servants who disobey while declaring that their disobedience is service; others who betray their employers for their own gain, and still others who quit one service for another; servants who are on intimate terms with their employers, and others who are treated as mere drudges; servants who seem quite contented with their lot, and others who complain of ill-treatment. Shakespeare's servants are male and female, good and bad, wise and foolish, obedient and disobedient, industrious and lazy, active and passive, and everything in between.

Furthermore, "service" was not merely an ideology for keeping the lower classes in line, although it certainly was that among other things. Service was also an ideal for the classes that comprised masters and mistresses, even—perhaps especially—very exalted ones. Service was a way of explaining and justifying upper-class privileges: a gentleman was, presumably, always ready to defend king or queen and country.[5] In addition to serving more exalted people (and, of course, God), aristocrats and gentry served the concept of "honor," which required them to behave in ways that might contradict their own desires and interests, and even compromise their safety. That this service to an ideal was not merely another way of enforcing good behavior—or that the establishment of such ideals could be a two-edged sword—is demonstrated by Queen Elizabeth I's difficulty in getting her hot-blooded young male subjects to stop dueling, a difficulty perhaps reflected (by servants, among others) in *Romeo and Juliet*.

Although Bruce Robbins argues that throughout the history of Western literature servants are "typically" represented as "mere appendages of their masters,"[6] this does not not seem to me an accurate description of the servants in Shakespeare's plays. Although of course the plays abound with minor roles for servants who carry messages, run errands, or simply attend their masters and mistresses, Shakespeare goes far beyond such representations. Early plays such as *The Comedy of Errors*, *The Two Gentlemen of Verona*, and *The Taming of the Shrew* show him working with the type of the clever servant inherited from Classical and Italian comedy. In later plays, however, we see a variety of servants as differentiated from one another as are his major characters. Some "servants," such as Bardolph in *Merry Wives* or the Chamberlain of *1 Henry IV*, are what we would consider employees of an establishment; even within this category there is individuation, since Bardolph is one of Falstaff's dismissed men, while the Chamberlain is in league with highwaymen. Other such "employees" include Pompey in *Measure for Measure* and Bolt in *Pericles Prince of Tyre*, both of whom are servants in brothels. In another class are Shakespeare's fools, such as Touchstone in *As You Like It*, Feste in *Twelfth Night*, and Lavatch in *All's Well That Ends Well*; here there is a range from cheerfulness to melancholy to cynicism, but all have in common the high intelligence necessary to make a living by wit, and all are notably independent and insightful characters. In contrast are such dim-witted and foolish servants as Simple in *Merry*

Wives and Lancelot in *The Merchant of Venice*. To summarize a few other individualized servants: Oswald in *King Lear* and Borachio and Conrade in *Much Ado about Nothing* are villainous; Maria in *Twelfth Night* is clever and scheming; the Gardener in *Richard II* is a political philosopher; Charmian and Iras in *Antony and Cleopatra* seem frivolous, but are faithful to Cleopatra even unto death, as Eros is to Antony; Pistol and Nym in *Henry V* are roguish servants turned roguish soldiers, while the boy who serves them is an intelligent and attractive child; Alice, an attendant to the French princess in the same play, acts primarily as an English tutor and translator; Reynaldo in *Hamlet* is sent by Polonius to spy on Laertes; Emilia, who waits on Desdemona in *Othello*, betrays her mistress but then courageously reveals Iago's plot; Pisanio in *Cymbeline* refuses to obey his master's command to kill Imogen, and thereby not only saves her life but prevents Posthumus from sinning; the Nurse in *Romeo and Juliet* is a surrogate mother to the heroine; Flavius, the steward in *Timon of Athens*, remains faithful to Timon in adversity; and Cornwall's nameless servant in *King Lear* tries to defend Gloucester at the cost of his own life. In *A Midsummer Night's Dream* and *The Tempest*, Shakespeare even depicts servants who are not human. The list is by no means exhaustive.

Servants were an intrinsic part of early modern life, and, as John Draper points out, they "were so numerous that the Elizabethans could not but be conscious of their problems and their varied status; and writers of the age are not silent on the matter."[7] Shakespeare found servant-characters and the concept of service useful in many different ways. To explore the virtues he made of the cultural necessities of servants and service is the purpose of this book.

Acknowledgments

I WISH TO THANK THE PARTICIPANTS IN THE 1993 SAA SESSION ON SERvants and service in Shakespeare, organized by Thomas Moisan. I am also grateful to the staffs of the British Library, the Folger Shakespeare Library, and the Virginia Tech Library, all of whom were extremely helpful and gracious. I owe thanks to Virginia Tech for providing me with research support. Dee Hezel, Shawn Mole, Marie Paretti, Randy Patton, and Cheryl Ruggiero all dealt with infernal machines that frequently threatened to drive me to despair; I deeply appreciate their help. I also wish to thank the editors of *The Upstart Crow*, in which journal earlier versions of chapters 7 and 9 appeared, for allowing this material to be republished. Ernest W. Sullivan, II, offered a number of helpful suggestions, for which I am very grateful. My greatest debt of gratitude is owed to Roberta Green and Janis Lull, both of whom read the manuscript with great care; this was truly service above and beyond the call of friendship, and I am profoundly grateful to both of them. They saved me from many errors; those that remain are entirely my responsibility.

Abbreviations

All's Well	*All's Well That Ends Well*
Antony	*The Tragedy of Antony and Cleopatra*
A.Y.L.	*As You Like It*
Caesar	*The Tragedy of Julius Caesar*
Coriolanus	*The Tragedy of Coriolanus*
Dream	*A Midsummer Night's Dream*
Errors	*The Comedy of Errors*
Hamlet	*The Tragedy of Hamlet, Prince of Denmark*
1 Henry IV	*The First Part of Henry the Fourth*
2 Henry IV	*The Second Part of Henry the Fourth*
Henry V	*The Life of Henry the Fifth*
1 Henry VI	*The First Part of Henry the Sixth*
2 Henry VI	*The Second Part of Henry the Sixth*
3 Henry VI	*The Third Part of Henry the Sixth*
Henry VIII	*The Famous History of the Life of Henry the Eighth*
King John / John	*The Life and Death of King John*
Lear	*The Tragedy of King Lear*
L.L.L.	*Love's Labor's Lost*
Macbeth	*The Tragedy of Macbeth*
Measure	*Measure for Measure*
Merchant	*The Merchant of Venice*
Merry Wives	*The Merry Wives of Windsor*
Much Ado	*Much Ado about Nothing*
Othello	*The Tragedy of Othello, the Moor of Venice*
Pericles	*Pericles, Prince of Tyre*
Richard II	*The Tragedy of King Richard the Second*
Richard III	*The Tragedy of Richard the Third*
Romeo	*The Tragedy of Romeo and Juliet*
Shrew	*The Taming of the Shrew*
T.G.V.	*The Two Gentlemen of Verona*
Tempest	*The Tempest*
Timon	*The Life of Timon of Athens*
Titus	*The Tragedy of Titus Andronicus*
Troilus	*The History of Troilus and Cressida*
Twelfth Night	*Twelfth Night, or What You Will*
Winter's Tale	*The Winter's Tale*

A Place in the Story

1

"The lives of other": Introduction

SERVICE IN THE EARLY MODERN ERA IS EXTREMELY DIFFICULT TO DE-
fine, since virtually any aspect of life could be, and often was, defined and described as a service relationship. Political life was
conceived of as public service; war was military service; lovers
served their ladies; domestic life consisted of a master who was
owed various kinds of service by his wife, children, and servants.
All of these kinds of service are regarded as in some degree anal-
ogous, so that the master of a household might be regarded as a
kind of king in his own household, or a lover might define himself
as his mistress's slave or soldier. The analogy between gover-
nance and service in domestic life and political life is expressed
in the subtitle of William Vaughan's *The Golden-grove, moralized in three Bookes—A worke very necessary for all such, as
woould know how to governe themselves, their houses, or their
countrey*. Vaughan also makes the analogy in the text of his work
when he states that "if servants must be obedient to their masters, aswell curteous as curst, much more ought subjects to obey
not onely their gentle, but also their cruell Princes."[1] Furthermore, the entity to whom one owes service need not be a person;
it is possible to serve one's country, or one's religion, or one's
own values.

Ideally, the Shakespearean world could be viewed as a hierarchy of service corresponding to the hierarchy of classes, in which
the upper classes serve God, king, and country by performing
valuable and dangerous services, such as diplomacy and fighting, for reasons of loyalty, patriotism, and honor, while the lower
classes perform less important services for less exalted entities,
usually for personal profit. But the correspondence between
class and service is only approximate, since a character can only
be a member of one class at any one time, whereas the kinds of
service required of a character may be multiple and conflicting:
Coriolanus may find a conflict between his service to Rome and

his personal honor; the Boatswain in *The Tempest* may find one between his service to his ship and his duty to show deference to its upper-class passengers. Such conflicts may be more common for lower-class characters than for upper-class ones, since the former must by definition serve more masters than the latter: they serve not merely their employers, but, when called upon, their king or queen and country, just as the upper-class characters do, sometimes performing the same services for the same motives. But while the lower classes are apt to have more kinds of service required of them than are the upper classes, characters of any class may experience conflicting services: it is relatively rare for a character to owe but a single service, to a single master or mistress, for a single reason. Even within a household, the question arises: are you your master's servant, or your mistress's? When the crisis comes, are you Othello's servant or Desdemona's? Or, if you happen to be unfortunate enough to be Cornwall's man, with Regan as your mistress, do you serve them, or your own conscience?

A Shakespearean character, therefore, often finds himself or herself the servant of two (or more) masters or mistresses: the individual's social or economic interests may conflict with service to a master or mistress, or patriotic allegiance may conflict with honor or spiritual duty. Furthermore, a character may perform service because of an ideal of honor or loyalty or for a reward. Service, which ideally would be a clear and well defined set of duties, and is often described as such in the conduct books, is rarely so simple in Shakespeare's plays, which are naturally concerned with drama, conflict, and complication, all of which could be found in or developed out of ideas about service. The tensions produced by the application of idealized, selfless services to real human relationships in a period of economic and social change could, in fact, be said to provide perfect dramatic material.[2]

Although service was an ideal, it was also a practical matter: in an era of limited technology, a division of labor was necessary for a class-oriented society to be maintained, as R. Morison points out: "Whan euery man wyll rule, who shall obeye? . . . An order, an order muste be hadde, and a waye founde, that they rule that beste can, they be ruled, that mooste it becommeth so to be . . . I pray you for a season, let it be as we desire, let vs imagine, we be al ryche, doth it not streight follow, I as good as he, why gothe he before, I behynde? I as ryche as he, what ned-

eth me to labour? The mayde as prowde as her dame, who myl-
keth the cowe?"³

As Morison suggests, the answer to the question of order
seems most often to have been "obedience," as the Archbishop
of Canterbury tells Henry V and his court:

> Therefore doth heaven divide
> The state of man in divers functions,
> Setting endeavor in continual motion,
> To which is fixèd, as an aim or butt,
> Obedience. . . .
>
> (*Henry V* 1.2.183–87)

As Canterbury goes on to explain, even honeybees observe and
enforce obedience, suggesting that service and hierarchy are
natural, divinely authorized paradigms, since the bees are "Creatures that by a rule in nature teach / The act of order to a peopled
kingdom" (188–89). In thus idealizing service, Shakespeare's
plays certainly legitimate hierarchy and subjection, allowing
those members of society who are more served than serving to
define their position as a natural one and to control those whose
lives consist more of serving than being served. This ideal of service, however, requires reciprocity: members of the ruling class,
as well as ordinary citizens, are conceived of as serving the commonwealth, just as all of the bees, in performing their different
functions, serve the hive; the same point is made by Menenius's
belly-fable (*Coriolanus* 1.1.94–145). We may be dubious about the
services performed by the upper classes, as some of the plebeians in *Coriolanus* appear to be, but if we accept that all members of the commonwealth must serve the commonwealth
(whoever or whatever else they serve), we have a standard for
judging the behavior of all of the plays' characters.

Furthermore, as Camille Wells Slights observes, "If the *Hom-
ily on Obedience* was central to the culture, so too was the pro-
verbial question, 'When Adam delved and Eve span / Who was
then the gentleman?'"⁴ Although the ideology of service recognized superior and inferior persons, early modern people knew
that men, not God, had created servants. In addition, the ideology of Christianity did not recognize superior and inferior souls—
not, at least, based on social class: "As seruants are the Lords
freemen, so masters are the Lords *seruants.* In this respect they
who are made rulers, and they who are vnder them, are called
fellow seruants. For howsoeuer in outward dignity there is great

difference betwixt master and seruant, yet as seruants of God they are of a like condition, and in many things may be accounted equall: especially if both be of the same faith, and so brethren in Christ."[5] Such theological exegesis may have been intended to calm dissatisfied servants, rather than to stir them up, but it is clear that, if taken seriously, it could have encouraged subversive thought as well as preparing an audience to accept drama that represented servants as possessed of independent souls, consciences, and even brains.

Although the relationship between master and servant was acknowledged as a human creation, it was nevertheless often described as being as natural and basic as that between husband and wife or parent and child.[6] This inconsistency is typical of the confusions inherent in descriptions and depictions of service. "Servant" itself was an amorphous category: unlike aristocrats and peasants, servants were made, not born, and it was likely that a person who was a servant in his or her adolescence would leave service in adulthood.[7] As Frances E. Dolan comments, "Servants were neither distinguishable nor separable as a social group."[8] Modern readers often assume that being "in service" was the lowest form of employment and modern critics, although they must know better, sometimes write as if that were true. Certainly, there are many suggestions in Shakespeare's plays that service is, in and of itself, base employment. "Servants," however, as a category, could include everyone from the lowest-paid, most over-worked, and worst-treated scullions to "serving-gentlemen" and "serving-gentlewomen," who often seem to have regarded themselves, and to have been regarded by others, as gentlemen and ladies. Such "upper" servants were often better off, by almost any standard—living conditions, work required, wealth, opportunities for advancement, power—than most people who were self-employed. Furthermore, the self-employed, especially those in "service industries," may often have been simply regarded as "public servants," at the command of anyone who paid their fees.[9] This may help to explain why Pistol, who has no hesitation about acknowledging even so poor a knight as Falstaff as "master mine" (*Merry Wives* 1.1.148), objects violently to being addressed as "mine host" (*Henry V* 2.1.29).[10]

Nevertheless, "servant" generally meant "inferior to someone," which may explain, at least in part, why none of Shakespeare's plays is "about" servants in the sense of a servant being a protagonist. Like most of today's audiences, Shakespeare's audience was apparently more interested in the lives of the rich, famous, and powerful than in the lives of the poor, obscure, and powerless, and Shakespeare catered to his audience's perceived bias.[11] However, despite the comparative unimportance of servants, it may be worth taking a close look at them and some of the attributes of service they embody.

One of the most interesting aspects of recent Shakespearean criticism has been the increased attention paid to the working-class and poor characters in the plays. Discussions of Jack Cade's rebels in 2 Henry VI; Williams, Bates, and Court in Henry V; the plebeians in Julius Caesar and Coriolanus; and, particularly, Caliban in The Tempest, have raised new questions and refocused our attention on different elements of the plays. Much of this attention has centered on such characters as subversive of the period's power structure. Few of the characters chosen as subjects for such discussion have been servants, unless they are servants rebelling against their role as servants.

It is not hard to understand why this should be so. For critics concerning themselves with subversion during this period, rebels, soldiers questioning their orders, citizens demanding a voice in the government, and enslaved natives offer ideal starting points for discussion of subversive ideas.[12] I am using the term "subversive" in Stephen Greenblatt's sense "that 'subversive' is for us a term used to designate those elements in Renaissance culture that contemporary authorities tried to contain or, when containment seemed impossible, to destroy and that now conform to our own sense of truth and reality. That is, we locate as 'subversive' in the past precisely those things that are not subversive to ourselves, that pose no threat to the order by which we live and allocate our resources."[13] Servants who fail to rebel, who do as they are commanded, who flatter their employers, who remain loyal even at the expense of their own self-interest, are harder to incorporate into our narrative of subversion. We may acknowledge that they too are oppressed, but their failure openly to resist their oppression makes them seem less interesting, though potentially more disturbing, to us than the rioters and the outlaws. Ironically, the present critical interest in how the early modern ruling class maintained power gives many critics a common interest with that ruling class: both were and are more interested in those who were unwilling or unable to serve than those who quietly assumed their places in the lower ranks of the service hierarchy. Like the ruling class of Shakespeare's era, critics today are most concerned with the masterless, the rebellious, the desperately poor, and the disorderly—the dangerous, interesting people.

This is not to say that servant-characters who are not openly rebellious, or who are not rebellious at all, have gone totally unremarked by critics, any more than obedient, reliable, faithful servants went unremarked in their own era. The household and conduct books of the time direct employers how to deal with "good" servants, although the directions, as might be expected, could be summarized in the unexciting statement, "Good servants should be treated well."[14] A large part of a servant's "goodness" as a servant was invisibility: servants who were obedient, efficient, quiet, honest, healthy, and apparently contented with their place—servants who were the equivalent of well-oiled machines—were the ideal. Employers no doubt valued their servants inversely to the amount of trouble they made, just as we most value the car or computer that requires the smallest investment of our time and money to keep running. Many of Shakespeare's servant-characters are such good, invisible servants, and it is perhaps natural that the remarks such characters inspire from both their employer-characters and critics are usually dismissive. For example, as Charles Wells points out after noting the multiple betrayals in *Antony and Cleopatra*, particularly by the ruling-class characters, "Yet surprisingly, despite this sordid catalogue of deviousness and perfidy, our overriding impression is of loyalty put to the test and holding firm. The dutifulness and dependability shown by the many servants and followers shine out all the brighter against the dark background of their 'betters'' venality. This devotion is, for the most part, taken for granted by those they wait upon, as illustrated by Pompey's off-hand remark to Menas: 'Thou hast served me with much faith: what's else to say?' (*Ant.* II.vii.57)" (139).[15]

In his book on servants in Western literature, Bruce Robbins suggests that servants are characterized by a "surprising and ... annoying sameness" and reveal "little worth investigating."[16] But however true this may be for the literary representations of servants in the novels that are Robbins's primary concern, it is hard to see these statements as accurate descriptions of Shakespeare's servants. While Shakespeare is not immune to the uses of servants as signifiers of status or as comic relief, he often represents them as acting in ways we might expect from persons with an acknowledged position in society—conscious of their own abilities, capable of independent thought and action, and even occasionally rebellious against their station in life.

Derek Cohen maintains that Shakespeare's depictions of most of the poor, including servants, are patronizing:

While the text [of *Lear*] remarks the presence of the poor in the form of servants, they are typically silent . . . Their voices, when heard, come down to us, Annabel Patterson argues, 'by way of ventrilo- quism, in the texts of the dominant culture'. They are the disguised voices of the bourgeois writer who, Patterson continues, 'must . . . utter, in order to refute them . . . claims whose force may linger be- yond his powers of persuasion.' We cannot, that is, trust Shake- speare's representation of the poor as issuing from anything but a condescendingly imagined and represented vision. Indeed . . . famil- iarity with productions of the plays tends to confirm this notion of their representation, as we accustom ourselves to a condescending lexis which discusses the poor classes, the lower order, the rabble- ment, and the working people, who are represented usually, though not invariably, as nose-picking halfwits.[17]

Since Shakespeare was not a member of the ruling class, his "ventriloquism," of course, applies as much to his representation of the rich and powerful as to his representation of the poor. In fact, as an actor and playwright (with pretensions to gentility), and as a servant himself, one of the Lord Chamberlain's Men, and later the King's Men, it is at least arguable that Shakespeare can be heard as a legitimate voice of the common—mostly poor—people, though speaking, as common people often had to and have to, in a way acceptable to the rich and powerful. Nor is it self-evidently clear that Shakespeare was unaware of the force he gave to the voices of the common people; quite possibly, he intended the claims he gave them to linger, to be appreciated by those who had ears to hear. Furthermore, modern stage repre- sentations of the poorer classes as "nose-picking halfwits" may owe at least as much to directors' and actors' beliefs that modern audiences cannot be trusted to understand and be entertained by Shakespeare's text without a good deal of added "business," as Michael Green suggests: "I need hardly say that Elizabethan comics are the unfunniest parts ever written . . . Some day I should like to run a competition to find out the unfunniest clown in Shakespeare. There's a lot of choice, from that dreadful Launcelot Gobbo to the superlatively unfunny Feste. Nobody can make me believe that even the groundlings laughed at them, un- less, as I suspect, the dire lines were enlivened by rude gestures . . . Professional directors will take great pains over the clown scenes, making extensive use of amusing business."[18] Probably few regular playgoers would be hard-pressed to recall productions where they felt that such business proceeded against the grain of their understanding of the text, and not necessarily only in "lower-order" roles. Modern productions, though, however valid on their own theatrical terms, are not reliable evidence of Shakespeare's intentions, or even, necessarily, of his accomplishments.

Lear, in fact, is arguably the worst play Cohen could have chosen to prove that servants, or the poor in general, are usually silent in Shakespeare's plays. Even leaving aside the disguised noblemen who are remarkably loquacious in their roles as the servant Caius and the poor madman (and former servant) Tom o' Bedlam, the play offers such authentic servants as Lear's Fool, Oswald, and Cornwall's servants. These constitute a varied lot, to be sure, but certainly none of them is silent, and it is hard to see any of them as "condescendingly imagined" (although "Caius" is certainly condescending toward Oswald).[19] Cohen, however, insists upon dividing Shakespeare's characters into the comic poor and weak and the tragic rich and powerful: "Beggars and the poor are almost never tragic in literature. Indeed, in much of Shakespeare they are, of course, quite the opposite. They are a staple of comedy, whose ludicrousness is usually enhanced onstage by their funny working-class or regional accents and their habits of chewing straw and belching. Poor Tom is tragic and not comic because he is Edgar and, like Lear, is not *naturally* poor. His poverty and madness are his tragedy."[20] That the poor in literature are almost never tragic would certainly come as a surprise to a number of writers other than Shakespeare, among them Dickens and Hardy. This reading, which ignores such a genuinely tragic (albeit minor) character as Cornwall's First Servant and such an arguably tragic one as the Fool, indicates a desire for neatness of pattern rather than engagement with the complexities of the play, particularly as Edgar is not really a tragic character, although he is certainly a serious and seriously abused one. Apart from the fact that Edgar is not really mad, he is kept from actual tragedy by his virtue, energy, ingenuity, and almost relentless cheerfulness. Even in his oppressed and impoverished state, Edgar simply refuses to despair or be beaten. Above all, it is his service to his father and Lear's cause, his willingness to forget his own sufferings to help others, that ultimately leads him to such limited triumph as the play makes possible.[21]

Despite some notable exceptions, Shakespearean critics have, as a rule, been as oblivious to the "good"—and even some of the bad but faithful—servant-characters as the ruling class of Shakespeare's period may have been to its good servants. What Peter Laslett refers to as the "obliteration" of the era's powerless people, including servants, has become true for their literary counterparts.[22] Part of the reason, perhaps, is what Mary Hallowell Perkins describes as the loss of "status" and "individuality" as a result of being dependent on an employer, living in someone else's house, eating someone else's food, wearing prescribed clothing.[23] Part of the reason, no doubt, is that we, like the employers of servants, unconsciously accept literary servants as labor-saving devices, although we might term them "dramatic devices." Servants are, in other words, merely useful tools or machines. We do not pay much attention to our refrigerators until they break down, although we would do so if they started talking back to us.[24] As Susan Cahn notes, the ten per cent of early modern women who never married "were largely invisible to their contemporaries, and to many historians, existing mainly as paid or unpaid domestic servants. Their contemporaries did begin to notice them if they became pregnant."[25] In the same way, critics pay attention to the same servants who occupied most of the ruling class's attention—those identified as threats to the power structure, whose resistance to that structure could be used "to ratify the exercise of power."[26] In addition, however, the whole idea of servitude tends to make us uncomfortable, and servants who seem contented with, or at least resigned to, their lot are apt to disturb us more than those who rebel.

Perkins suggests that for writers of the seventeenth and eighteenth centuries, "A good servant was merely doing what was expected of him. It was the bad servant that was worth writing about."[27] Most modern critics of Shakespeare seem to share the attitude Perkins describes. By ignoring or denigrating good servants, however, critics may be missing a truly subversive point. Since service was celebrated as an ideal for everyone, not just for servants or other lower-class people, virtuous servants can be used, and often are used by Shakespeare, to comment upon misbehaving upper-class characters, who are shown to be inferior in true nobility to those who serve them (he also, of course, uses bad servants to comment on bad servants). Although such contrasts must sometimes be inferred by the audience, they are often explicitly commented upon, frequently by the servants themselves. Such contrasts are, of course, far more dramatically effective than simply assigning all virtue and intelligence to the

upper classes and all vice and folly to the lower classes. Since
such criticisms were not directed at particular individuals or
groups, it is unlikely that they would offend the ruling class. If
any took offense, Shakespeare might say, like Jacques:

> Let me see wherein
> My tongue hath wronged him. If it do him right,
> Then he hath wronged himself. If he be free,
> Why then my taxing like a wild goose flies,
> Unclaimed of any man.
>
> (A.Y.L. 2.7.83–87)

It is unlikely, however, that the upper-class members of Shakespeare's audience, even if they saw themselves reflected in his
ignoble "noble" characters—particularly when contrasted to virtuous servants—would have been anxious to claim the resem-
blance. Furthermore, Shakespeare wrote for an audience
encompassing almost the entire social spectrum of his time—
from the monarch to the working-class citizen who could occasionally just afford a penny to see a play. This audience included
servants and many people who had been servants, as well as
people who employed servants. Although he could not write
plays that offended the ruling class, he could not be successful
without appealing to the lower classes as well. Is it too radical to
imagine that Shakespeare might have recognized that the general invisibility of servants to their employers made servants an
ideal vehicle for criticizing the power structure without offending
the members of that power structure?[28]

When Warwick uses the phrase "the lives of other" (2 Henry
IV 4.4.77), he is telling Henry IV that Prince Hal is studying his
companions to learn to take the measure of men.[29] Today, servants are other to us, because (unless we are quite rich) we do
not have them and we are unlikely ever to have been in service
ourselves. The poor who are discussed by critics are like the
homeless—we see them and pity them. The servants are like the
blue- and pink-collar working class—as a rule, we see little of
them (in large part, perhaps, because we look past or through
them), and they are likely to be less interesting to us than are the
very poor. The early modern upper classes presumably wanted
servants to be other because to empathize with them would force
a reexamination of a society that generally offered its rewards
without regard to merit; modern critics want servants to be
other because it is hard for intellectuals to accept that virtue and

intelligence may be weak and powerless. Furthermore, obedient servants—as most of Shakespeare's servant-characters are—may seem to us to be traitors to the working class: shouldn't they be rebelling, or at least protesting? By ignoring the servants in Shakespeare's plays, however, we are imposing our own limitations on the texts and thereby limiting our understanding of what these texts can tell us.

2

"What duty is": Service as
Ideal and Indignity

ALTHOUGH "SERVICE" HAD MANY MEANINGS IN SHAKESPEARE'S TIME, and retains multiple meanings today, twenty-first-century audiences are perhaps less likely than Shakespeare's original audience to accept the concept of service as an ideal. Although at least some portion of the population accords respect to military "service" and it is still common to speak of "service" in connection with religion, skepticism about the meaning of "public service" is widespread. "Service industries" are commonly regarded as those in which nothing of value is created and "service jobs" are frequently perceived as those requiring little education or training and which offer minimal rewards in terms of money, respect, or opportunity for advancement. Modern academic jargon also denigrates the idea of service: few professors appreciate having their university divisions perceived or referred to as "service departments."

Since service is traditionally defined as duty owed by an inferior to a superior, it is hardly surprising that service would be denigrated by societies that, officially, at least, declare the equality of all people and resist the idea of hierarchy. We should, however, be careful not to impose our modern resistance to the ideal of service onto people who did not necessarily share our values, or onto the art those people created. To say this is not to suggest that the ideal of service was the only idea about service current in Shakespeare's time. The Elizabethans also denigrated service, most famously in the common proverb "Service is no heritage." Nor should we ignore the fact that many servants in Shakespeare's period were oppressed or the usefulness for social control of elevating obedient service to the level of an ideal. None of this, however, means that service as an ideal is necessarily inferior to, for example, individualism; certainly, it was not any simpler a concept. "Service" was an ideal, and a means of

social control, and an insult, and a fact of life; it was also a concept that Shakespeare found useful in a variety of ways.

The Elizabethan upper classes certainly used the discourse of
service to explain and justify inequality and oppression, as propaganda for the idea that the way things were was the way God
wanted them to be: "To serve or obey well, is a great vertue, &
proceedeth of nature, which being good, is holpen by education
... Nature, and the lawes which preserve nature, bind men that
will be servants, to strict obedience."[1] The concept of service,
however, was not merely a means of keeping servants and other
"inferiors" in line, but a way of understanding the social contract,
which applied to everyone: "And common reason teacheth us,
that we are not borne for our selves onelie: for *Ortus nostri partem patria, partem amici, partem Parentes vendicant.* Our
countrey challengeth a part of our birth, and brethren and
friends require another part, and our parents (and that *optimo
jure*) do vindicate a third part."[2]

Thus, when the Duke tells Angelo that the purpose of human
life is to serve others, he is merely setting forth an early modern
commonplace:

> Thyself and thy belongings
> Are not thine own so proper as to waste
> Thyself upon thy virtues, they on thee.
> Heaven doth with us as we with torches do,
> Not light them for themselves; for if our virtues
> Did not go forth of us, 'twere all alike
> As if we had them not. Spirits are not finely touched
> But to fine issues, nor Nature never lends
> The smallest scruple of her excellence
> But, like a thrifty goddess, she determines
> Herself the glory of a creditor,
> Both thanks and use.[3]

It may, of course, be argued that the Duke himself, like Angelo,
fails to rise to this ideal of service, but the statement itself is sufficiently clear: even (perhaps especially) rulers are expected to
serve and are, in fact, endowed by Nature with their best attributes only that they may serve.

It may not be mere coincidence that toward the end of the play
the Duke says to Isabella,

> Your friar is now your prince. As I was then
> Advertising and holy to your business,

> Not changing heart with habit, I am still
> Attorneyed at your service.
>
> (5.1.390–93)

Although he has temporarily abdicated his position of authority, the Duke appears to feel that his disguise has allowed him to serve Isabella while detecting Angelo and Lucio. When he returns to his position as Duke, he indicates that he will continue to serve, though in a different capacity. Whether or not this is how we view him, it is clear that the Duke wishes to depict himself as a public servant. The Duke makes perhaps the canon's most explicit statement of this ideal—although the protagonists of the Roman plays also tend to be straightforward about declaring themselves Rome's servants—but the concept of this kind of service, owed by royalty, nobility, and gentry, as well as ordinary citizens, forms the backdrop of every play. The misdeeds of monarchs and nobles in many of the histories and tragedies are not merely personal sins but a failure to live up to a social standard that, at least in part, justifies the rulers' privileges. Even in *The Merry Wives of Windsor*, which is about as free as possible from considerations of political power, we are reminded of the failures of the nobility by Master Page's suspicions of the aristocratic Fenton's wild youth and by Sir John Falstaff's misbehavior. Possibly even more oddly, the service ideal is commented upon at the end of *The Two Gentlemen of Verona*, when, as Camille Wells Slights points out, "Valentine explicitly mentions serving the state as the gentleman's true vocation, urging the Duke to pardon the outlaws for they are 'fit for great employment'" (5.4.157).[4]

In addition to the idea that everyone is part of a hierarchy of service, the ideal depictions of early modern service emphasize that good servants are properly appreciated, cherished, and rewarded. From S. Antipholus to Prospero, Shakespeare too shows employers valuing good servants, but he also demonstrates that even such valuing could place additional burdens on servants.[5] For example, after 15 years in Bohemia, Camillo naturally desires to return to his homeland, the more so since he has been entreated to do so by his former master, the repentant Leontes, whom Camillo served best by betrayal. Polixenes, however, declines to allow Camillo to leave, and his reasons testify to the complexities of the master-servant relationship:

> As thou lov'st me, Camillo, wipe not out the rest of thy services by leaving me now. The need I have of thee thine own goodness hath

made. Better not to have had thee than thus to want thee. Thou, having made me businesses which none without thee can sufficiently manage, must either stay to execute them thyself or take away with thee the very services thou hast done; which if I have not enough considered—as too much I cannot—to be more thankful to thee shall be my study, and my profit therein the heaping friendships.

(Winter's Tale 4.2.10–20)

Clearly, Polixenes values this man who not only saved his life—and whom he promised to "respect . . . as a father" for so doing (1.2.460)—but who has also apparently done him important services since. He praises Camillo, confesses his dependence upon him, and is apparently more than willing to be generous with more tangible rewards. He will give Camillo anything except what Camillo wants: the freedom to return home. Furthermore, he makes Camillo's past services a kind of chain to keep him in Bohemia, arguing that without future services those in the past will become meaningless. Polixenes' dependence and Camillo's indispensability become a means of generating guilt that will force this good servant to remain against his will. Since Polixenes is not above trying to manipulate Camillo by using the servant's own good services against his interests, it is hardly surprising that Camillo chooses to arrange his own return to Sicilia, even though that involves a betrayal of Polixenes' interests.

Other employers, including Olivia, Orsino, Juliet, Lear, Cleopatra, Antony, Desdemona, and Othello, are also dependent upon servants. This dependency is frequently detrimental to the servants, sometimes even leading to their deaths. The threat of death also hangs over the character most often cited as the epitome of ideal service: Adam, the elderly servant in *As You Like It*. Adam has been described as a character who " 'endorses the aristocratic ideal of a static social hierarchy,'" but in fact he is more interesting than that statement would suggest.[6] As the longtime servant of the late Sir Roland de Boys, he presumably owes his service to the latter's eldest son, Oliver. But when Oliver proves wicked, Adam leaves Oliver to serve Sir Roland's youngest son, the virtuous Orlando. Although Adam remains a servant, he chooses whom he will serve, and his choice is not to serve the "static social hierarchy" in which the eldest son inherits the lion's share of his father's wealth and power, but to serve virtue, although it is poor and powerless. His choice evokes a tribute from his chosen master:

> Oh, good old man, how well in thee appears
> The constant service of the antique world,

When service sweat for duty, not for meed!
Thou art not for the fashion of these times,
Where none will sweat but for promotion,
And having that do choke their service up
Even with the having. It is not so with thee.

(*A.Y.L.* 2.3.56–62)

Adam's virtuous service wins him Orlando's reciprocal affection
and loyalty, and, since Adam declares that all he asks of fortune
is that he "die well and not [his] master's debtor" (76), this is presumably enough for him; but we cannot help but notice that he
sacrifices (at least temporarily) his life savings and collapses
from weakness in the forest, declaring that he is about to die for
lack of food (2.3.38–46; 2.6.1–2). Kenneth J. E. Graham maintains
that "it is precisely a *performance* of love that the ideal of loving
service demands" and it is exactly this ideal that Adam represents; but however admirable Shakespeare feels such service to
be, he insists that there is a price for it and that the price is often
paid, oddly enough, by the person who does the service.[7]

Ann Jennalie Cook observes that "[William Harrison in his *Description of England*] presupposed that everyone was responsible to some master or other."[8] While this is true, it is actually the
case that few members of early modern society would have had
a single master. The nobility served the king and the commonwealth; commoners served king, commonwealth, and nobility.
Servants, in addition, served their masters and mistresses. Furthermore, citizens were felt to owe service to their country and
community. And, of course, all members of the commonwealth
were assumed to acknowledge their duty to serve God. Only God
was perceived of as being served, but not serving.[9] Thus, it is not
surprising that throughout Shakespeare's plays, as in early modern society in general, virtually any relationship can be described in terms of service.[10] Though we are inclined to think of
service as something done by servants and peasants, Shakespeare often depicts rich and powerful characters as serving or
at least thinking about service.

The frequency with which Shakespeare's kings refer to themselves as servants, or are reminded of their duty to serve God or
their subjects, may seem surprising.[11] However, when kings in
Shakespeare's plays are characterized as God's servants, the descriptions are usually intended to aggrandize, rather than dimin-
ish, their prestige. Richard II says that the king is "the deputy
elected by the Lord," defines himself as God's steward, and re-

fers to God as "my master," and the Bishop of Carlisle confirms these judgments, calling Richard God's "captain, steward, deputy elect" (*Richard II* 3.2.57; 3.3.77–78, 85; 4.1.127). King John describes himself as "God's wrathful agent," who will "correct / [France's] proud contempt," while, in a lighter vein, Don Adriano de Armado, in a letter, addresses the King of Navarre as "Great deputy, the welkin's vicegerent" (*King John* 2.1.87–88; *L.L.L.* 1.1.216). However, the kings who declare themselves God's servants are often among the weakest kings in the canon, and usually depicted as ultimately serving someone other than God. Richard II, for example, ends up under Henry Bolingbroke's control, and when Henry orders Richard to be brought to him, Richard appears, asking, "To do what service am I sent for hither?"[12] From "God's wrathful agent," King John descends to taking an "oath of service to the Pope," whom he acknowledges as his overlord (*King John* 5.1.23). And then, of course, there is Richard III's declaration that he is "earnest in the service of my God," which can only be regarded as blasphemy that adds to his sins and helps ensure his destruction (*Richard III* 3.7.106).

Other royal persons declare themselves servants of other people. Royal women may declare themselves to be servants to the kings they are to marry, as do Margaret of Anjou and Katharine of Valois; Queen Margaret later tells King Lewis of France that she "Must strike her sail and learn awhile to serve / Where kings command" (*1 Henry VI* 5.3.178; *Henry V* 5.2.256–57; *3 Henry VI* 3.3.4–6). Presumably, service is an appropriate role for women, even royal women, to assume. On the other hand, it is clearly unsuitable for Charles, Dauphin of France, to say to Joan la Pucelle: "Let me thy servant and not sovereign be" (*1 Henry VI* 1.2.111). As both a king and a man, Charles should maintain his authority over a peasant girl (even if she did not display her unsuitability for authority by dressing like a man and talking with spirits); one wonders if Charles's weakness in declaring his willingness to serve Joan is intended to reflect badly not merely on him personally, but on French men in general.

Royal service, however, is not limited to God or individuals. Romans in the plays are apt to claim that kings are servants to them or other Romans (*Antony* 3.13.91–93; *Cymbeline* 3.1.61–64). John of Gaunt, the son and father of English kings, declares that England's "royal kings" are famous "For Christian service and true chivalry" (*Richard II* 2.1.51–54), which is certainly a suitable ideal of service, even if one rarely depicted in the histories. Sheldon P. Zitner maintains that the King of France in *All's Well That*

Ends Well sees himself as "a servant of his place," while Norman
Rabkin states that in his soliloquy after talking to Williams,
Bates, and Court, "[Henry V] ends by remembering his responsibility, his life of service, and sees that—'what watch the King
keeps to maintain the peace'—as the defining mark of the
King."[13] The idea of the king suffering acute anxiety because of
the responsibility of serving his people or his country also occurs
in *2 Henry IV;* in that play and in *Henry V,* the idea that the king
suffers because of his service is unattractively coupled with depictions of the king's subjects as happy in bestial oblivion.[14] It is,
of course, impossible to know either the intention or the effect of
these suggestions that the rich and powerful suffer more in their
service to the commonwealth than do the poor and powerless. It
could be intended as straightforward establishment propaganda,
although we cannot judge whether it would have been effective;
it could be intended as satire of the privileged few feeling sorry
for themselves.

The nobility, of course, owe service not only to God and their
country, but to the monarch, as the Archbishop of Canterbury
reminds the lords around Henry V: "hear me . . . you peers/ That
owe your selves, your lives, and services / To this imperial
throne" (*Henry V* 1.2.33–35). This service is often expressed in
personal terms, as if the relationship between king and nobleman were one of master and servant. Lord Hastings refers to
King Edward IV as his "master"; the same term is used by Lord
Lafew to refer to the King of France, the Lord Chief Justice to
Henry IV, Cardinal Wolsey and Archbishop Cranmer (and Queen
Katherine) to Henry VIII, and Camillo to Leontes.[15] The loyal
Earl of Kent repeatedly refers to King Lear as his "master."[16]

Noblemen and gentlemen are frequently described, or describe themselves, as servants to royalty: King John tells Prince
Arthur that "Hubert shall be your man, attend on you," while, in
the same play, Philip the Bastard, speaking to the dead King
John, says, "my soul shall wait on thee to heaven, / As it on earth
hath been thy servant still"; a few lines later, Philip vows his
"faithful services" to the new King Henry, a vow echoed by the
Earl of Salisbury on behalf of all of the nobility.[17] Richard Plantagenet, hoping to have the attaint of his father's treason lifted,
says to Henry VI, "Thy humble servant vows obedience / And
humble service till the point of death" (*1 Henry VI* 3.1.168–69).
We may think that Richard does not mean a word of this, but it is
clearly the correct formula, and it encourages Henry to create
Richard Duke of York. Horatio declares himself Hamlet's "poor

servant ever," although Hamlet responds, "Sir, my good friend; I'll change that name with you"; when his other friends, Rosencrantz and Guildenstern, offer to wait upon the prince, Hamlet replies, "No such matter. I will not sort you with the rest of my servants, for, to speak to you like an honest man, I am most dreadfully attended."[18] It is perhaps going too far to suggest that royal personages cannot have any friends, but it would appear that, on some level, even their friends are their servants.

The code of service required members of the nobility to take risks if necessary to perform loyal service; thus Henry IV's Lord Chief Justice fears that he will be punished by newly crowned Henry V for the "service" that he did for the king's late father in rebuking his wild son (2 Henry IV 5.2.6–13). An even greater risk is taken by the Earl of Gloucester, who determines to relieve King Lear, "If I die for't, as no less is threatened me" (King Lear 3.3.17–18). Gloucester, of course, endures terrible violence for his service, though not death; but Lord Hastings—who has vowed, "that I'll give my voice on Richard's side / To bar my master's heirs in true descent, / God knows I will not do it, to the death"— does suffer death for his loyal service to his dead master's children.[19] Shakespeare's history plays are largely concerned with service, good and bad, principally the service of the nobility.[20] Common men, of course, are serving (and often dying) in battle, but, except in Henry V, we do not hear much from them, and we never hear much about them.

Whereas in the history plays and many of the tragedies, public service usually has a personal, rather than a patriotic, basis, the Roman plays often depict service for Rome, or, at least, an idea of Rome. In the first scene of Titus Andronicus, Marcus says that his nephews have fought in their country's service, and Titus declares that twenty-one of his sons have died "in right and service of their noble country," later describing the family tomb as a resting place only for "soldiers and Rome's servitors" (Titus 1.1.175, 197, 353). Similarly, Coriolanus says that he got his wounds "in my country's service," Menenius says that Coriolanus has lost blood "for his country," and Brutus acknowledges that Coriolanus has "Serv'd well for Rome."[21]

Powerful nobles declaring themselves as servants, however, often may have been—or, at least, we may regard it as—largely a formality, a nod toward the ideology of service that shaped much of the official thinking of the early modern period. For those, however, who could say with Bassanio that all the wealth they had ran in their veins, service may have been a fact of life,

or even the most fortunate life they could reasonably expect.[22]
Thus, when Edmund, not only a younger son, but illegitimate,
vows his services to Nature, it may be with the understanding,
shared by the original audience, that his only alternative is to
serve as a retainer—secretary? master of horse? steward?—in
a gentleman's or gentlewoman's household. That the son of an
earl should be able to aspire to a position no higher than that of
Malvolio does not, of course, in any way justify Edmund's behavior, but it does go some way toward explaining that behavior.

While everyone in early modern society is assumed to serve
God, and Shakespeare mentions such service in passing, he
rarely spends much time on it.[23] He spends perhaps as much
time on the idea of service to the devil, as an explanation for the
bad behavior of Joan la Pucelle, Richard III, and Parolles (*1
Henry VI* 1.5.4–7; *Richard III* 4.4.71–73; *All's Well* 2.3.248). One
service apparently regarded as almost as universal as service to
God is service to one's elders, particularly one's parents, although Shakespeare explores this relationship much more than
he does theological questions of service.[24] Although by no means
all children serve their parents as they should, even rebellious
sons are usually respectful. Angry as Hamlet is with his mother,
what he says is "I shall in all my best obey you, madam" (*Hamlet*
1.2.120). Bertram is verbally deferential toward his mother, although his actions are not respectful; Prince Hal acts submis-
sively toward his father, even when defending himself; and
Coriolanus, famously, obeys his mother. Even such a truly bad
son as Richard III is polite to his mother and honors her requests, while Edmund, the worst son in the canon, is respectful
to his father even as he plots against him. Interestingly, it is the
women who are depicted as treacherous (Goneril and Regan),
insolent (Katharina), rebellious (Sylvia, Jessica, Portia, Celia, Juliet, and Desdemona), and downright disobedient (Hermia, Anne
Page, Cordelia, Imogen, and Miranda) toward their fathers. With
the exception of Lear's daughters, most of these young women
defy fathers who wish to marry them to men they do not love, or
are trying to keep them from men they do love. Because we want
true love to triumph onstage, and because the unprotesting obedience that is the service expected of these young women now
seems outdated, we seldom concern ourselves with how subversive this disobedience is. That subversive threat and the tensions
between fathers and adult sons in real life may be why, with the
exceptions of Lucentio and Florizel, the son who openly defies
his father on behalf of his own true love (or anything else) is vir-

tually absent from the plays; we see Juliet defying her parents, but not Romeo defying his. Children who fail in their obligation to serve and defer to their parents—except when motivated by love, and in a comedy—usually come to bad ends. Of course, deferring to and properly serving one's parents is no guarantee of safety, any more than faithful service always affords protection to servants.

Just as children are expected to serve their parents, servants are, sometimes and to some extent, regarded as members of the families they serve.[25] Juliet's Nurse, for example, has been with the Capulets at least since Juliet was an infant—possibly longer. She is trusted enough by Lady Capulet to be included in the discussion of Juliet's marriage; Juliet confides in her; she obviously loves her foster child. Although Juliet's mother is present in the play, the Nurse is sometimes described as Juliet's "real" mother.[26] Ralph Berry goes so far as to suggest that she tyrannizes over her employers.[27] Although the Nurse clearly holds a peculiarly privileged position in the Capulet household, she is not the only one of the Capulets' servants who acts like part of the family.[28] Even the unnamed servant who seeks Romeo's help to learn the names of the party guests—who presumably cannot be an intimate servant or a long-employed retainer, since his master is unaware that he is illiterate—feels himself to be part of the family: he refers to the party being at "our house" and responds to Romeo's inquiry as to his master by saying "My master is the great rich Capulet; and if you be not of the house of Montagues, I pray, come and crush a cup of wine" (*Romeo* 1.2.76, 80–83). He is apparently proud of his master and feels confident enough of his place in "his" house to invite guests to his master's party.

Other servants are even more familiar.[29] Lear's Fool feels free to criticize and mock his royal master, who occasionally threatens but never actually punishes him, and who becomes paternal during the storm scene, worrying more about the Fool than about himself. The Countess of Rossillion and Olivia allow their fools a good deal of familiarity, and Fiona Shaw and Juliet Stevenson comment about Celia and Rosalind that "their familiarity with [Touchstone] is obvious, and the speed with which he and Celia go into banter (only spasmodically joined by Rosalind) indicates both their mutual affection, and that Touchstone is, in part, privy to their private world."[30] Not only fools have close relationships with their employers, however. Falstaff is as thick as thieves with his men (*Merry Wives* 1.3.23–25, 36–59; 2.2.5–16). Both Dromios are familiar with their masters throughout *The*

Comedy of Errors, and Mote is extremely impudent toward Armado (for example, see *L.L.L.* 1.2.1–31). Speed is cheeky with Valentine, Pompey with Mistress Overdone, and Charmian with Cleopatra.[31]

Nor is it only employers and their servants who are familiar: servants often address other upper-class characters as though they were on terms of equality, while the gentlefolk not only fail to object, but seem to acknowledge the servants' respected place in the community. Bardolph, Pistol, and Nym, who have already robbed Slender, proceed to insult him and Parson Evans; Mrs. Quickly, on the other hand, seems intimate with Anne Page (*Merry Wives* 1.1.120–24, 149–64, 148; 2.1.153–57). Given the general disorder of Olivia's household, we should not, perhaps, be surprised to find both Maria and Fabian as impertinent toward Sir Andrew as toward Sir Toby, but Feste is not only familiar toward everyone in the household, but impudent toward Duke Orsino and Sebastian and (like Malvolio) positively rude toward "Cesario" (*Twelfth Night* 1.3.62–78; 3.2.1–28; 2.4.73–78; 4.1.1–22; 3.1.1–45; 2.2.1–16). Apemantus, like the Fool he accompanies, is perhaps a common target of abuse, but it is certainly true that the usurers' servants and the Page try to have "sport" with him (*Timon* 2.2.49–90); Angelo, however, is certainly not a figure of sport, yet Pompey is saucy with him—although, to be sure, only once (*Measure* 2.1.61). None of the upper-class figures involved in these situations suggests that the servants are acting inappropriately. Other gentlemen behave graciously toward servants. Although he describes Falstaff's men as "arrant knaves" in private conversation with his steward, Davy, Shallow specifically welcomes Bardolph and Falstaff's page, as well as Falstaff, although he also teases the page about his height (*2 Henry IV* 5.1.30, 53–56). When he finds Petruchio wringing Grumio by the ears, Hortensio refers to the servant as "my old friend" and offers to stand as surety for the man he describes as "ancient, trusty, pleasant servant Grumio" (*Shrew* 1.2.20–21, 46). Pandarus, attempting to get information from Paris's servant, addresses the man as "friend" five times in fewer than thirty lines, although the servant's refusal to esteem Cressida above Helen—and perhaps his mockery of Pandarus—finally leads Pandarus to address him as "fellow" (*Troilus* 3.1.1–38).

Even when servants are not impertinent, their attitude toward their employers is almost never abject. They are frequently privy to their masters' and mistresses' secrets and are often depicted as their most intimate friends. Commenting on her role in

Twelfth Night, Zoë Wanamaker writes, "Viola's disguise allows her to know Orsino in a way that would never have been possible otherwise. In three days he confides everything to this boy, this stranger, something he would never have done to a woman. . . . Viola is let into his mind, his confidence, his imagination, in such a way that inevitably she falls in love with him, with this extraordinary, erudite human being."[32] However, Viola's access to Orsino is not primarily predicated on the belief that she is a boy and a stranger; she is disguised as a servant, from whom Orsino has nothing to fear—who worries about being judged by his or her servants?

One reason why servants may often have been treated as family, trusted, allowed great latitude, and generally not feared, is that many servants in Shakespearean drama—as was also the case in reality—are young.[33] Although we know that Adam is elderly and Juliet's Nurse is presumably middle-aged, many of the servants, including various pages, are young. The Dromios are apparently twenty-three or twenty-four, and Iago says that he is twenty-eight, but many servants are presumably much younger than this. Brutus's Lucius is a boy, and "boy" is Lear's typical form of address to his Fool. Speed, Biondello, and Flaminius are all called "boy" (*T.G.V.* 2.1.47, 76, 89; *Taming* 1.1.239; 4.4.8; *Timon* 3.1.45) and some servants are simply nameless boys (*Much Ado* 2.3.1; *Troilus* 1.2.277; *Romeo* 1.5.11; *Macbeth* 5.3.15; *Antony* 2.7.112). The women who disguise themselves as servants invariably pass as boys. While it is possible that "boy" was used toward servants who were not, technically, boys, there is no evidence in the plays that the term is ever used derogatorily toward middle-aged or elderly servants. When Shakespeare does depict mature or elderly servants, he explicitly mentions age or the effects of age; in the absence of such evidence, we should probably assume that servants are young, not only because this would have been probable in reality, but because it reflects the equation often made in the period's prescriptive literature between servants and children.[34] Thus it makes sense for Robert Appelbaum to describe the servants in *Romeo and Juliet* as "sonlike," if only in their self-destructiveness and powerlessness.[35]

Whether or not individual servants are valued in the plays, the ubiquity and importance of servants as a class are obvious. Especially when we read or simply think about Shakespeare's plays (rather than seeing performances, in which servants and other minor characters may make more of an impression), we usually think about their major characters, most of whom are employers rather than servants. However, as Charles Wells points out, "Servants are the only category of people to appear in all thirty-seven plays, a fact which, in itself, attests to their importance in Tudor society."[36] Wells also notes the number and importance of servant-characters in the Roman plays alone: "In fact, in the Roman plays taken together, Shakespeare employs some thirty-five servants, putting into their mouths rather more than 800 lines of text. These figures do not take into account the broader category of 'follower' which, if included, would of course increase the figure very substantially. Five suicides from among this number may be cited should the importance of servants require any further statistical vindication."[37] Nor is it only the Roman plays that contain many and important servants: *Romeo and Juliet* contains five named male servants and the Nurse (who may or may not be named Angelica), in addition to torchbearers, pages, household servants, and the prince's train; of the thirteen named characters in *Twelfth Night*, six are servants, and a seventh—Viola—disguises herself as a servant; servants play major roles in *King Lear*, *Othello*, *Timon of Athens*, *Antony and Cleopatra*, *The Winter's Tale*, *Cymbeline*, and *The Tempest*, among other plays. The number and importance of servants in the plays exemplify the number and importance of servants in the society of the period, although Shakespeare's plays are a representation, not a realistic reflection, of that society.[38]

Certain categories of people are seldom found among Shakespeare's servant-characters or are found much less often than we would expect on the basis of the reality of his time. Relatively few female servants are featured.[39] Although Peter Laslett states that "Most of the servants . . . male or female, in the great house or in the small, were engaged in working the land,"[40] few agricultural servants appear in Shakespeare's plays. Shakespearean drama is also surprisingly lacking in apprentices, perhaps because Shakespeare rarely deals in detail with the lives of the working classes;[41] partially because of the lack of apprentices, Shakespeare's servants may be, as a whole, older than we would expect early modern servants to be.[42] Apart from Autolycus, there are few masterless men in the plays. And, although Joyce Green MacDonald notes that "both Henry VII and Henry VIII of England employed black household servants," Shakespeare does not represent any African or African-descended characters as servants (apart, perhaps, from some in *Antony and Cleopatra*) except for "the [unseen] Moor" reported by Lorenzo to be pregnant by Launcelot, and *Titus Andronicus*'s Aaron, who is never depicted as performing any service.[43]

In general, the servants depicted in Shakespeare's plays are not those who served for forty shillings per year and "all found." They are almost exclusively white, usually (with the exception of occasional pages) adult, and predominantly male; they are most often employed by the great and powerful and doing more than menial domestic tasks—they are "upper" servants, rather privileged persons, certainly the aristocracy of the servant class.

Perhaps the relatively privileged position of many of Shakespeare's servants helps to explain why ambition figures so little in the plays. Or perhaps staging ambitious servants was felt to be too subversive: the few servants who are depicted as ambitious to improve their lot tend to be such villains as Iago and Oswald. Or perhaps servants' ambition was regarded as uninteresting (except in villains). Although service was seen (perhaps mostly by those who received its benefits) as a good in and of itself, it was also a means of making a living and, at least occasionally, of receiving greater rewards and even of improving one's social and economic position.[44] As Alfred Harbage long ago pointed out, "We must not look for impeccable logic. It was proper to remain in one's present station, in conformity with the principle of order and degree; but it was also proper to rise in the world."[45] Although most of Shakespeare's servant-characters do not express ambition to improve their lots, some do. Female servants are apt to hope to marry as a way of leaving service, as do Margaret in *Much Ado about Nothing* and Charmian in *Antony and Cleopatra*; Nerissa in *The Merchant of Venice* and Maria in *Twelfth Night* succeed in making such marriages. Men might also hope to marry up: the obvious example in Shakespearean drama is Malvolio.[46] Most of Shakespeare's servant-characters, however, hope to rise—if such is their ambition—through service, rather than marriage—and none of them apparently aspires to parallel the rise of Dick Whittington.

Although Shakespeare rarely dramatizes servants ambitious to rise above their station, he does not ignore the cold and rather undramatic fact that most people served for reward. Even among upper-class characters, the relationship between reward and service is often made explicit. King Henry VI rewards Lord Talbot for his "truth," "faithful service," and "toil in war" by naming him Earl of Shrewsbury, and subsequently (as noted above) names Richard Plantagenet Duke of York in return for a vow of service.[47] Duke Senior promises to reward the lords who have continued to serve him in adversity, and King Henry V promises to reward good service, in response to Sir Thomas Grey's statement that even those who were his father's enemies are now dutifully and zealously serving him:

> We therefore have great cause of thankfulness,
> And shall forget the office of our hand
> Sooner than quittance of desert and merit,
> According to their weight and worthiness.[48]

While no one in the plays seems upset about the rewards given by monarchs to their upper-class "servants," Berry suggests that in at least some instances Shakespeare depicts the reward-for-service tradition negatively. Commenting on King Henry VI's reward to Alexander Iden "for his good service" in killing Jack Cade—knighthood, a thousand marks, and a position attending on the king—Berry remarks that "for all the sanctimonious 'I seek not to wax great by others' waning,' Iden hastens to claim his reward."[49] Similarly, Berry seems to view the rewards promised by Duncan and Malcolm to their supporters as rather shameful: "To avoid jealousies and perhaps future rebellions, titles will be granted with discrimination as sweeteners. Rank in this analysis is simply a means of buying off future disaffection, cash down."[50] If this is, in fact, Duncan's intention, it is obviously a mistake, since the most richly rewarded of the thanes is the one who murders him and seizes his crown. It is, however, unlikely that Shakespeare expected his audience to look askance at kings rewarding their loyal noblemen, and it may, in fact, be significant that we see Duncan and Malcolm as generously bestowing rewards "on all deservers" (*Macbeth* 1.4.42), while we see Macbeth promising a pair of murderers the opportunity to take revenge on a man he has persuaded them is their enemy. In fact, it seems likely that rich rewards for good service were felt to reflect well on both parties: the subject who is dutiful and obedient is worthy of the splendid recompense offered by the generous monarch who deserves such service. Henry VIII suggests this reciprocity when speaking of Archbishop Cranmer: "I will say thus much for him: if a prince / May be beholding to a subject, I / Am, for his love and service, so to him" (*Henry VIII* 5.3.155–57). Immediately after this statement, Henry honors Cranmer by asking him to stand godfather to the newborn Princess Elizabeth.

This does not, however, mean that all instances of reward-for-service reflect well on the parties involved in the transactions. Queen Gertrude, presumably on behalf of her husband, promises Rosencrantz and Guildenstern "such thanks / As fits a king's remembrance" for their "service" in spying on Hamlet (*Hamlet* 2.2.25–26, 31). Their service, which involves betrayal of a friend, is ignoble, and Hamlet comments on it when he refers to Rosencrantz as a "sponge . . . that soaks up the King's countenance, his rewards, his authorities," adding that "such officers do the King best service in the end" (4.2.13, 16–18). Nor can the audience be impressed by royal bounty and loyal service when Richard III promises to reward Sir James Tyrrel for murdering Richard's nephews (*Richard III* 4.2.80–81; 4.3.31–34). One wonders if it is only coincidence that we so rarely see characters who do evil service receive their rewards: some "good" servants who loyally serve evil, such as Rosencrantz and Guildenstern and Oswald, are killed before they can collect their ill-earned rewards, but even those who are not killed, such as Clarence's murderers, Banquo's murderers, and Tyrell, simply disappear from their plays, unregarded, and, as far as can be determined, unrewarded.[51] In at least one instance in the histories, a reward for service in an evil cause is revoked, when Richard III reneges on his promise to give the Duke of Buckingham "The earldom of Hereford and all the movables / Whereof the King my brother was possessed" (3.1.194–96, 4.2.88–120). Buckingham's shocked response emphasizes that he served in the expectation of reward: "And is it thus? Repays he my deep service / With such contempt? Made I him king for this?" (121–22).

Of course, it is not only members of the nobility who serve for reward, although—there being little dramatic about servants receiving their wages—we usually see less-exalted characters, not always actual servants, being rewarded for performing services in exceptional circumstances, and sometimes receiving rewards other than monetary ones.[52] For his "service" to the Greeks, the Trojan traitor Calchas asks that the captive Antenor be exchanged for Calchas's daughter Cressida, and King Agamemnon grants his request; the Duke of Vienna promises the Provost that for his "care and secrecy" he will be rewarded with "a worthier place"; and even though Prospero defines Ariel's service as payment for Prospero's freeing him from imprisonment, he continually promises Ariel freedom as a reward for good service.[53] In all of these instances, the reward reflects well on the authority figure, as a man who knows how to repay good service. Upper-class characters are also depicted as generous when they richly reward characters who do only ordinary services, as when *"Pericles gives the Messenger a reward, and knights him"* for delivering a letter from Helicanus or when Duncan sends "great largess" to Macbeth's household servants.[54] Of course, such generosity may only reflect that the generous person is in a good mood, as when Falstaff, learning from Pistol of Henry IV's death, declares, "Pistol, I will double-charge thee with dignities . . . Come, Pistol, utter more to me, and withal devise something to do thyself good"; but it may tell more about the giver, as when Prince Hal and Poins reward Falstaff's page for his witty teasing of Bardolph, or when the compassionate Silvia rewards the disguised Julia, saying, "Here, youth, there is my purse. [*She gives money.*] I give thee this / For thy sweet mistress' sake, because thou lov'st her" (*2 Henry IV* 5.3.126–27, 136–37; 2.2.82–89; *T.G.V.* 4.4.175–76). Employers also frequently reward their employees— and often increase our respect for them—through praise: Tranio tells Biondello, " 'Thou'rt a tall fellow"; Prospero says to his servant-spirit, "Thou hast done well, fine Ariel!"; and Feste is praised by Olivia, Sir Andrew, Sir Toby, and Duke Orsino.[55]

Reward does not only reflect on the givers; it seems, for example, unlikely that several major characters would praise Feste if we were not to accept him as a witty and charming fellow. Feste, however, is not only rewarded with praise: he is perhaps the most frequently rewarded servant in Shakespeare's plays. Sir Toby and Sir Andrew pay him for foolery; the Duke pays him for singing and foolery; Viola pays him for a display of wit; Sebastian pays him to get rid of him; and Malvolio promises to reward Feste for helping him.[56] Berry comments, "Feste, more than anyone else in Shakespeare, suggests the historic shift from *servant* (idealized in Adam) to today's *service industry*. Independent, detached, ruthlessly professional in his dealings, he refuses to be absorbed into the needs of his employers. He cannot be said to have a single employer, since he performs in Orsino's court as well as Olivia's household."[57] However, it is not clear whether Feste should be viewed as a precursor or if he is just better at cadging tips than most servants and freer to do so because of his position as an entertainer. And he is not quite unique: although in reality it was usually male servants who received most of the gratuities, since they were the servants who ran errands and delivered messages outside the household, Shakespeare depicts Mrs. Quickly in *The Merry Wives of Windsor* as ignoring her employer to serve herself every bit as diligently and successfully as Feste. Although technically employed as Dr. Caius's housekeeper, Mrs. Quickly is only once seen at his house, spending the rest of the play gadding about Windsor on errands for various other characters. Fenton twice gives her money, and Falstaff gives her his purse (although we have no idea how much is in it); furthermore, although her claim to have received "twenty angels" from one of Mrs. Ford's suitors is clearly false, it seems probable that Mrs. Ford and Mrs. Page have been paying her to assist in their plots (*Merry Wives* 1.4.149–50; 2.2.67–68, 120; 3.4.97). In any event it is clear that, at least in comedy, servants were not constrained to limit their services to their employers, but might be represented as collecting gratuities from all and sundry.

Costard, who also manages to make money from upper-class characters who are not his regular employers, makes the unusual criticism of one of Shakespeare's characters—Don Adriano de Armado—that he pays his servants badly.[58] This criticism, early in the play, helps define Armado as a comic butt, particularly as he later grandiloquently declares to Costard, "There is remuneration. [*He gives money.*] For the best ward of mine honor is rewarding my dependents" and as Armado's remuneration is revealed to be three-quarters of a penny, immediately contrasted with the shilling Berowne gives Costard for performing the same task.[59]

Liveries, which were part of male servants' compensation, are occasionally mentioned as reflecting on the nature of the giver.[60] When Falstaff wishes he had new liveries to give his retainers, the absence of such finery reflects his continual, comic lack of money; similarly, Valentine's jibe at the "bare liveries" of Thurio's followers suggests that Thurio is a comically down-at-the-heels gentleman (*2 Henry IV* 5.5.10–13; *T.G.V.* 2.4.41–44). On the other hand, Bassanio is described by Lancelot as a master who "gives rare new liveries," and he is apparently having new liveries made for his servants in anticipation of his trip to Belmont (*Merchant* 2.2.104–5, 110). Although some modern audiences might feel that this is wasteful and ridiculous excess, given that we know that Bassanio is in debt and has driven Antonio into debt to pay for his attempt to court Portia, there is no suggestion in the play that Bassanio is behaving badly. In fact, one assumes that not to provide new clothing for his servants would be potentially dangerous to his quest, since it could open him to the kind of ridicule to which Valentine subjects Thurio. Particularly when courting an extremely rich young woman, who is also being wooed by princes, Bassanio seems correct to ensure that he will not appear as a threadbare fortune hunter. New liveries in this situation are not idle display; they are an investment.

In general, Shakespeare rarely depicts upper-class characters who fail to pay for service. Helena, a bold woman, makes this implicit criticism of the King of France, who has rejected her offer to try to cure him: "My duty then shall pay me for my pains. / I will no more enforce mine office on you"; although the king quite logically responds, "Thy pains, not used, must by thyself be paid," he does, of course, ultimately accept her service and offer payment (*All's Well* 2.1.127–28, 148). (That the payment himself objects and decamps is irrelevant to this discussion.) Similarly, Coriolanus, defining food as a reward for service, refuses it to the Roman people on the grounds that they have not earned it:

> They know the corn
> Was not our recompense, resting well assured
> They ne'er did service for't; being pressed to the war,
> Even when the navel of the state was touched,
> They would not thread the gates. This kind of service
> Did not deserve corn gratis. Being i'th' war,
> Their mutinies and revolts, wherein they showed
> Most valour, spoke not for them.
>
> *(Coriolanus* 3.1.123–30)

Why Lucetta ungraciously declines to offer any money to Speed for delivering Proteus's letter is inexplicable, unless Proteus is correct that she felt that Speed was "a worthless post."[61] However, there can be little doubt about the motives of the new King Henry IV, who, while promising to reward the Earl of Northumberland and Lord Fitzwater for executing King Richard II's supporters, refuses to reward Sir Pierce of Exton for murdering Richard (even though Exton protests that he only acted on Henry's words), because "They love not poison that do poison need" (*Richard II* 5.6.6–18, 37–38). Henry is trying to distance himself from Exton's crime, but his shabby excuse is unconvincing.

Perhaps Henry's excuse does not even convince himself, since one is immediately reminded of Richard's murder when Henry wonders if his son's misbehavior is God's punishment for "some displeasing service" of King Henry's (*1 Henry IV* 3.2.5). Punishment for bad service (though not punishment from God) is also threatened in *Measure for Measure*: For executing Claudio "at an unusual hour" without "a special warrant," the Duke discharges the Provost of his office (although, as mentioned above, this is a plot between them, and the Provost is subsequently rewarded) (*Measure* 5.1.464–71). In an earlier play, however, it appears that bad service really does lead to a servant's dismissal. After Proteus learns that Launce offered his dog Crab to Silvia (instead of the lapdog Proteus gave Launce, which was stolen from him), Proteus says, "Go, get thee hence, and find my dog again, / Or ne'er return again into my sight. / Away, I say! Stayest thou to vex me here?" (*T.G.V.* 4.4.57–59). And Launce disappears from the play. Even extremely minor episodes may have overtones: when Justice Shallow's servant Davy asks his master, "And sir, do you mean to stop any of William's wages about the sack he lost at Hinckley fair?" and Shallow replies, "'A shall answer it," it is a reminder that all the play's characters have to answer for their behavior and, in particular, that Falstaff will have to answer for his failure to serve the ideals of knighthood (2 *Henry IV* 5.1.22–24).

Servants are sometimes forced to beg for rewards. In some instances, as when Macbeth's Porter says to Macduff and Lennox, "I pray you, remember the porter," this begging seems unimportant (although how the thanes respond in performance could tell the audience something about their characters); on the other hand, the disguised Nerissa takes the opportunity to beg Gratiano's ring "as a fee" for serving as a clerk, thus allowing her to join Portia in teaching their husbands a lesson in the play's last scene (*Macbeth* 2.3.19; *Merchant* 5.1.161–64). When Bolt begs a gratuity from Lysimachus, the Governor curses him, and the contrast between Lysimachus's attitude as he storms out of the brothel and his casual, joking attitude toward Bolt earlier in the scene, combined with his generosity toward Marina and his rejection of Bolt, indicate what a change Marina has effected in his character (*Pericles* 4.6.119–22). Coriolanus, who defines himself as a servant of his idea(l) of Rome, sees himself in the role of the servant reduced to begging for his wages, but cannot at first bring himself to do it, declaring, "Better it is to die, better to starve, / Than crave the hire which first we do deserve" (*Coriolanus* 2.3.113–14).

Coriolanus is perhaps the best-remembered character who reminds those he has served of his services and craves reward, but he is not the only one. As early as *The Comedy of Errors*, Antipholus of Ephesus is asking the Duke of Ephesus to recall his wartime service and reward him for it:

> Justice, most gracious Duke, oh, grant me justice!
> Even for the service that long since I did thee,

> When I bestrid thee in the wars and took
> Deep scars to save thy life; even for the blood
> That then I lost for thee, now grant me justice.
>
> (5.1.190–94)

Coriolanus and E. Antipholus are both asking that their heroic service be justly rewarded; Davy, however, asks that his more mundane service be rewarded by allowing him to perpetrate an injustice, when he asks his master, Shallow, "to countenance William Visor of Wo'ncot against Clement Perkes o'th' Hill." Although Davy acknowledges that Visor "is a knave," he argues that "I have served Your Worship truly, sir, this eight years; an I cannot once or twice in a quarter bear out a knave against an honest man, I have little credit with Your Worship" (*2 Henry IV* 5.1.36–48). Whereas we see the justice of Coriolanus and E. Antipholus's claims, Davy's assertion that his self-professed loyal service deserves the reward of allowing him to favor a knave over a presumably more honest man because the knave is Davy's friend is patently absurd; Shallow's apparent acceptance of Davy's argument suggests how a weak and foolish master could be influenced by a stronger-minded servant.[62]

Other pleas for rewards for service are less clear-cut: Alcibiades asks that the Athenian Senators spare the life of a friend of his who has killed a man in a quarrel, on the grounds that his friend has done the state good service in war; when his request is refused, he asks that his service, as well as his friend's, be considered. Rather than rewarding these services, however, the Senators banish Alcibiades and uphold his friend's condemnation (*Timon* 3.5.8–102). How we are to interpret this passage is debatable: on the one hand, the nameless friend is guilty, at the least, of manslaughter, and may well be guilty of murder, despite Alcibiades' attempts to mitigate his guilt; on the other, the Senators, representatives of the class that has exploited Timon's liberality, appear rigid and merciless. It may well be that justice requires the Senators to condemn Alcibiades' friend, but their treatment of Alcibiades is shown to be, at best, a mistake. A similar situation, with a different outcome, occurs in *Richard III*: Lord Stanley, Earl of Derby, bursts into the court, drops to his knees, and begs that his servant, condemned to death for killing "a riotous gentleman / Lately attendant on the Duke of Norfolk" be pardoned as "a boon . . . for my service done!"; King Edward reluctantly grants the boon, but suggests that Stanley's request is not unique:

> ... when your carters or your waiting vassals
> Have done a drunken slaughter and defaced
> The precious image of our dear Redeemer,
> You straight are on your knees for pardon, pardon
> And I, unjustly too, must grant it you.
>
> (2.1.96–102, 122–26)

Since the king acknowledges his belief that pardoning murderous servants is unjust, it seems appropriate to ask why he feels he "must" do it (evidently repeatedly). The apparent answer is that he is responding to the declaration that "service done" by his nobles requires reward, even if that reward is morally wrong.

Shakespeare's depiction of the reward-for-service system is by no means a simple one. In various plays, we see this system as source of community, oppression, and corruption. Although throughout the canon there is generally little emphasis upon money, either as an expense to employers or as a reward to servants, that may be only because such emphasis is unnecessary, since everyone knows what greases the wheels of the service system.[63] Additionally, of course, the apparent absence of reward tends to make service appear more of an ideal, and less of a quid pro quo.

Service, however, was both more and less than an ideal. Shakespeare created not only Adam, but also Iago. Service was often described as inherently base. Although good service was celebrated as an honorable calling, suggesting that someone was a servant, or servile, or a slave, was also a grave insult.[64]

That everyone in the early modern period was involved in the service hierarchy may mean that everyone—not just those on the bottom—had reason to be skeptical regarding the idealized model of service. Many of Shakespeare's characters, particularly in the early comedies, complain about their servants: both S. and E. Antipholus, as well as Adriana, complain about (and beat) both Dromios; Petruchio complains about and strikes his servants, and wrings Grumio's ears; Valentine beats Speed for failing to clean his shoes, and Proteus fires Launce; Shylock complains that Lancelot eats too much and tears his clothing. Even Oberon berates his servant Puck for failing to carry out his orders correctly (although, as Puck points out, his mistake is at least partly Oberon's fault). Falstaff despises and distrusts the troops he largely recruits from the ranks of servants and service occupations, describing them as "discarded unjust servingmen . . . revolted tapsters, and hostlers trade-fallen, the cankers of a calm world and a long peace, ten times more dishonorable-ragged than an old feazed ancient" (*1 Henry IV* 4.2.27–31). He refers to these men as "slaves" and "villains" (24, 39). Proteus, in mocking Speed by "proving" him a sheep, reveals the economic facts that underlie the supposed ideal of service: "The sheep for fodder follow the shepherd; the shepherd for food follows not the sheep. Thou for wages followest thy master; thy master for wages follows not thee. Therefore thou art a sheep" (*T.G.V.* 1.1.90–93).

It is not, however, only the upper classes who express doubts about the service ideal. Various servants and slaves, of course, complain about ill treatment, most often physical abuse. Lavatch simply repeats to his mistress, the Countess of Rossillion, the commonplace "Service is no heritage" (*All's Well* 1.3.23–24).[65]

It is left to that worst of servants, Iago, to express the resentment of those expected to put others' interests before their own:

> I follow him to serve my turn upon him.
> We cannot all be masters, nor all masters
> Cannot be truly followed. You shall mark
> Many a duteous and knee-crooking knave
> That, doting on his own obsequious bondage,
> Wears out his time, much like his master's ass,
> For naught but provender, and when he's old, cashiered.
> Whip me such honest knaves. Others there are
> Who, trimmed in forms and visages of duty,
> Keep yet their hearts attending on themselves,
> And, throwing but shows of service on their lords,
> Do well thrive by them, and when they have lined their coats,
> Do themselves homage. These fellows have some soul,
> And such a one do I profess myself.
> . . . In following him, I follow but myself—
> Heaven is my judge, not I for love and duty,
> But seeming so for my peculiar end.
>
> (*Othello* 1.1.44–57, 60–62)

Iago expresses what many—perhaps all—servants may have thought and many employers suspected: that servants who subscribed to the self-sacrificing ideal of service were fools, and that men and women of spirit would put their own interests first, while pretending to be loyal servants. Many ideals are unnatural, but service may be harder to attain than most, for why would people want to subordinate their interests to those of someone who was already more privileged, who expected to be able to order them about, and who probably would not treat them very well? Although Shakespeare depicts Iago as a diabolical villain, he allows him to express the unwelcome truth that many early modern employers may have harbored in their households, and trusted with their secrets, people who hated them. Bitterness over having to serve may take its place with thwarted ambition, racism, and sexual jealousy among Iago's multiple motives.

Iago refers to "the curse of service" (36) and the idea that service was ignoble had a long history; its advocates could point to a number of biblical references, including the stories of Cain, Ham, and Esau, that suggest that service is a punishment and a curse.[66] *The Tempest* provides some of the best examples of this idea: Prospero justifies enslaving Ariel because he freed him from imprisonment and justifies enslaving Caliban because of Caliban's attempt to rape Miranda. When Ferdinand washes ashore, Prospero accuses him of treason and promptly enslaves him, too; Ferdinand feels that his labor is "baseness," although the presence of Miranda ennobles his labors (3.1.1–7). Ironically, however, as Kay Stockholder points out, "When [Ferdinand] accepts freely the servitude Prospero forces on him, he illustrates his virtuous capacity to submit to right authority as a precondition to exercising it."[67] In the meantime, in another part of the isle, Gonzalo, in his attempt to design a perfect commonwealth, abolishes service as an institution unsuited to perfection (2.1.154).

The reactions of royal characters to the idea of service can also suggest that service is ignoble. When the Pope's legate, Cardinal Pandulph, attempts to dissuade the Dauphin Lewis from going to war (a war Pandulph had originally supported), Lewis objects on the grounds that he is not a servant:

> I am too high-born to be propertied,
> To be a secondary at control,
> Or useful servingman and instrument
> To any sovereign state throughout the world.
> ... Am I Rome's slave?
>
> (*King John* 5.2.79–82, 97)

On the other hand, to demonstrate how miserable she is, Queen Elizabeth unfavorably compares her situation with that of a servant:

> I had rather be a country servant maid
> Than a great queen with this condition
> To be so baited, scorned, and stormèd at.
>
> (*Richard III* 1.3.107–9)

Henry V accuses Cambridge, Scroop, and Grey not only of attempting to "slaughter" him, but also—apparently as another capital crime—of planning to sell "his princes and his peers to servitude" (*Henry V* 2.2.171).[68] Treating a non-servant as a servant is a means of dishonor. Queen Margaret drops her fan and orders the Duchess of Gloucester, "Give me my fan. What, minion, can ye not? *She gives the Duchess a box on the ear*," then pretends she mistook her for one of her ladies-in-waiting, saying, "I cry you mercy, madam. Was it you?" (*2 Henry VI* 1.3.138–39). Archbishop Cranmer's enemies try to shame him by making him stand at the door of the council chamber "'mong boys, grooms, and lackeys"; Henry understands exactly what the Council has tried to do, and berates them for making Cranmer "wait like a lousy footboy / At chamber door" (*Henry VIII* 5.2.18; 5.3.139–40). Clearly the idea of service as base is as powerful as that of service as an ideal.

The ambiguity in the meanings of service—ideal or indignity?—makes possible the irony of one of the greatest exemplars of the ideal of service sneering at another man at least in part because he is a servant, when Kent confronts Oswald:

> A knave, a rascal, an eater of broken meats; a base, proud, shallow, beggarly, three-suited, hundred-pound, filthy worsted-stocking knave; a lily-livered, action-taking, whoreson, glass-gazing, superserviceable, finical rogue; one-trunk-inheriting slave; one that wouldst be a bawd in way of good service, and art nothing but the composition of a knave, beggar, coward, pander, and the son and heir of a mongrel bitch.
>
> (*Lear* 2.2.14–22)

The compendium of insults that the disguised Kent directs at Oswald is masterful not only in the sense of being an overwhelming blast of invective, but also because it is so obviously an expression of contempt from a member of the "master" class toward a social inferior.[69] Kent is, of course, correct in his judgment of Oswald as contemptible, but the moral force of this judgment is weakened for modern readers and audiences by Kent's disdain for Oswald's role as a servant and his comparative poverty. We can recognize Oswald's occupation as neutral while acknowledging his behavior as a man to be despicable. Although clearly Shakespeare and his audience were also capable of making such distinctions, many of Shakespeare's characters frequently draw parallels between the baseness of being in service and base behavior.

The double meaning of "servility"—"suitable to a servant" and "less than noble"—suggests why describing someone as a servant or slave can be so grave an insult. Service is often linked with despised qualities, particularly cowardice and baseness: a Roman tribune describes "fearfulness" as "servile," and an angry Brutus mocks Cassius by saying, "Go show your slaves how choleric you are / And make your bondmen tremble" (*Caesar* 1.1.75; 4.3.44–45). Attempting to shame the plebeians into accepting Caesar's assassination, Brutus asks, "Who is here so base that would be a bondman?" (*Caesar* 3.2.29; see also 22–24); later, to shame Brutus and Cassius, Antony describes them as having "bowed like bondmen, kissing Caesar's feet" (5.1.43). Tybalt refers to the duelling Capulet and Montague servants as "heartless hinds" (*Romeo* 1.1.66).[70] The Bishop of Carlisle remarks that "fearing dying pays death servile breath," while the Duke of Vienna shows his disdain for death by addressing life: "A breath thou art, / Servile to all the skyey influences / That dost this habitation where thou keep'st / Hourly afflict" (*Richard II* 3.2.185; *Measure* 3.1.8–10).

Berry correctly points out that "terms of subordination are terms of abuse: 'slave,' 'peasant,' 'groom,'"[71] and it is because characters often use service-related terms in ways that are not strictly descriptive that the plays' language frequently blurs the distinction between actual status as a servant (or slave) and the servile, slavish, or otherwise base qualities that are assumed to characterize such persons. Context is therefore all-important in determining whether the use of such words as "slave," "villain," "knave," etc., is insulting, neutral, humorous, or even affectionate. When Berowne refers to Costard as "my good knave" and "good my knave," he presumably does not intend to be insulting, although he may intend to be patronizing; he also, however, calls Costard "slave" and "villain" (*L.L.L.* 3.1.141, 150, 149, 157, 159). On the other hand, when S. Antipholus refers to S. Dromio (out of his hearing) as "a trusty villain" and "a heedful slave," he presumably means to be complimentary (although he later calls S. Dromio "villain" as a term of abuse [*Errors* 1.2.19; 2.2.2, 17, 162]), and Sir Toby's reference to Maria as "villain" is apparently affectionate, like Doll's use of the same term toward Falstaff, Pandarus's toward Cressida, and Leontes' toward Mamillius (*Twelfth Night* 2.5.13; *2 Henry IV* 2.4.204, 219; *Troilus* 3.2.32; *Winter's Tale* 1.2.136). Aaron's disturbing habit of referring to his infant son as "slave" and "villain" also seems to fit this pattern (*Titus* 4.2.121, 177; 5.1.27, 30, 33). Because "service" is both an ideal and an indignity, the same service term can have essentially opposite meanings without necessarily confusing us: when Lear calls Oswald "my lord's knave" and soon after refers to the disguised Kent as "my friendly knave," the valence of "knave" would obviously be different, even if "friendly" were omitted (*Lear* 1.4.79, 91); Oswald, who has insulted Lear, is being reminded of his place, while Kent, who has served Lear by tripping up Oswald as punishment for incivility, is being welcomed into Lear's "family."

Commonly, however, the service terms "slave," "villain," and "knave," like the class term "peasant," are used contemptuously, most often in anger. As Berry puts it, "Shakespeare shows from the earliest plays on that people in choler turn to class terms as their first refuge. 'Churl,' 'base groom,' 'peasant' are the basic vocabulary of class invective."[72] Thus, it is not surprising that the dying Banquo's last words, addressed to the man who treacherously murders him, are "O slave!" or that Sir Humphrey Stafford calls Jack Cade "groom" and "villain" and refers to him as a "base [drudge]"; it is rather more unusual that Cade calls Sir Humphrey and his brother "silken-coated slaves," but Cade is a presumptuous fellow (*Macbeth* 3.3.24; *2 Henry VI* 4.2.120, 128, 146, 124).

There are a great number of such insults throughout the canon, most often from employers to their servants. The most notable example of class-based invective may occur in *Othello*. In the early part of the play, Iago is sometimes addressed or referred to as Othello's ancient, but once his guilt is revealed the references to him tend to emphasize his role as a servant. Although he is called "viper," "wretch," "demi-devil," "pernicious caitiff," and "Spartan dog" (5.2.293, 304, 309, 328, 372), by far the preferred epithet is "villain" (occasionally with such modifiers as "damned" and "hellish"), which refers not only to his evil nature but also to his inferior status to his accusers (243, 247, 250, 293, 322, 325, 379). The next most common epithet is even more suggestive of service as demeaning, as Iago becomes a "cursed, cursed slave" (285; see also 300) and "a damned slave" (251; see also 342). Condemned without trial or confession (378–80), Iago appears to be regarded as a suitable object for the infliction of cruelty, in part because of his servile status:

> For this slave,
> If there be any cunning cruelty
> That can torment him much and hold him long,
> It shall be his.
>
> (342–45)

Although nothing can justify or excuse Iago, it seems clear that his inferior status to most of the play's characters and, perhaps by implication, his role as treacherous servant, are used in part to justify what the Venetian aristocrats propose to do to him.

Service-based insults, however, are not limited to upper-class characters abusing lower-class characters; often, one aristocrat defames another, by implying that his or her behavior has reduced him or her to the status of a servant or slave. Thus Hamlet, trying to persuade Gertrude of Claudius's inferiority to her first husband, describes his uncle as "A murderer and a villain, / A slave that is not twentieth part the tithe / Of your precedent lord" (*Hamlet* 3.4.99–101). The Duke of York calls the Duke of Somerset "villain" and "traitor villain" (*1 Henry VI* 4.3.9, 13). Richard III comes in for masses of such abuse: Lady Anne calls him "villain" and "devilish slave"; Margaret refers to Richard as "a murd'rous villain" and calls him "the slave of nature"; Queen Elizabeth efficiently combines the epithets, calling him "thou villain slave"; finally, Richard starts calling himself "villain" (*Richard III* 1.2.70, 90; 1.3.134, 230; 4.4.144; 5.3.191, 195).

Aufidius is rather more sophisticated in his use of service imagery to disparage Coriolanus's behavior in sparing Rome. Instead of acknowledging that Coriolanus yielded to the pleas of his mother, a yielding with which the Volscians might sympathize, Aufidius claims that "at his nurse's tears / He whined and roared away your victory, / That pages blushed at him" (5.6.101–3). Aufidius thus defines Coriolanus as a man who yields to and imitates the tears of a female servant to such an extent that small boys, also in service, are embarrassed. The conjunction of "tears" and "pages" in this speech leads naturally to Aufidius addressing Coriolanus, in his next speech, as "thou boy of tears," a form of address that suggests that Coriolanus is subservient; the allusions to servants perhaps help to inspire Coriolanus's even more degrading address to Aufidius, "O slave!" (5.6.105, 109).[73]

Because service terms can be insults, neutral descriptions, or even endearments, it is not always easy to determine the intention or even the referent underlying such words as "villain" and "slave." When Timon's Steward says, "How many prodigal bits have slaves and peasants / This night englutted!" (*Timon* 2.2.170–71), it is by no means certain that he is referring to actual slaves; he may be using "slaves" as a derogatory reference to Timon's false friends and hangers-on, as is done by other characters elsewhere in the play (3.1.57; 3.6.97; 5.1.111). Similarly, when Timon says, "They have e'en put my breath from me, the slaves!

Creditors? Devils!" (3.4.105–106), it is not clear whether by "slaves" Timon means his creditors or their servants or both, particularly since "slave" is a word Timon comes to apply rather indiscriminately, using it not only of those who have betrayed him, but of Timandra's customers and Apemantus (4.3.86, 253, 378).[74]

Even greater confusion—though apparently intentional—occurs when upper-class characters mingle not only servants with slaves or "bond-servants," but servants or slaves with commoners or "peasants," as if all persons below them in social rank were merely a single class with a duty to serve them. Richard III describes Richmond's army as "A sort of vagabonds, rascals, and runaways, / A scum of Bretons and base lackey peasants" (*Richard III* 5.3.316–17), thus describing the enemy's soldiers as simultaneously servile, lazy, foreign, low-class, and criminal. Richard II shows his contempt for the common people by calling them "slaves" (*Richard II* 1.4.27). Hamlet piles epithets upon himself as if he cannot think of enough words to describe his baseness: "rogue and peasant slave," "rascal," "coward," "villain," "drab," "scullion"; while not all of these words are service-related, several of them are, and in the same speech Hamlet describes Claudius as a "slave" and a "villain" (*Hamlet* 2.2.550, 567, 571, 572, 587, 588, 580, 581). When Cornwall and Regan refer to Cornwall's rebellious First Servant as "villain," "peasant," and "slave" (as well as "dog") (*Lear* 3.7.81, 83, 99, 78), "it is," as Berry notes, "the old formula, the aristocrat's rejection of all challenge."[75]

Henry V's soliloquy after his discussion with Williams, Bates, and Court is a more complex aristocratic formula, combining as it does upper-class failure to distinguish between free commoners and slaves, aristocratic contempt for social inferiors, ostensible envy of those inferiors, self-pity for the sufferings sustained by those in authority, and a recognition that the common people play a necessary part in the life of the commonwealth. Having listed such attributes of kingship as "the balm, the scepter, and the ball / The sword, the mace, the crown imperial," "robe," "title," "throne," and "the tide of pomp," Henry declares,

> No, not all these, thrice-gorgeous ceremony,
> Not all these, laid in bed majestical,
> Can sleep so soundly as the wretched slave
> Who, with a body filled and vacant mind,
> Gets him to rest, crammed with distressful bread;

Never sees horrid night, the child of hell,
But like a lackey from the rise to set
Sweats in the eye of Phoebus, and all night
Sleeps in Elysium; next day after dawn
Doth rise and help Hyperion to his horse,
And follows so the ever-running year
With profitable labor to his grave.
And but for ceremony, such a wretch,
Winding up days with toil and nights with sleep,
Had the forehand and vantage of a king.
The slave, a member of the country's peace,
Enjoys it; but in gross brain little wots
What watch the King keeps to maintain the peace,
Whose hours the peasant best advantages.

(Henry V 4.1.258–82)

Although this speech is, of course, a specific response by Henry to his situation, it does seem to represent a mixture of attitudes common in Shakespeare's upper-class characters, who are not incapable of appreciating and even sympathizing with lower-class characters, but who nevertheless take it for granted that they are almost always superior in almost every way to those in the lower classes, all of whom are frequently perceived as being servants or slaves to their "betters." The plays themselves often subvert this belief, just as this speech, with its self-pitying tone, idealized picture of peasant life, and sneering depiction of those less fortunate than kings, undercuts itself. The attitude, however, is so common among upper-class characters that even the most virtuous and sympathetic nobles and gentlefolk are apt to display contempt by alluding to whomever or whatever displeases them as being not just "lower-class," but specifically servile or slavish. Servant, peasant, slave, coward, fool, dog—why bother making distinctions within the category of base things?

Aristocratic and royal contempt for servants, however, often reflects badly on the contemptuous.[76] Regan and Cornwall insulting the servant who heroically tries to save Gloucester is an obvious example. Although Brutus the tribune ostensibly represents the people of Rome, he is not above making disparaging descriptions of their reactions to Coriolanus's return:

                              Your prattling nurse
Into a rapture lets her baby cry
While she chats him. The kitchen malkin pins

Her richest lockram 'bout her reechy neck,
Clamb'ring the walls to eye him.

(Coriolanus 2.1.205–9)

His more famous namesake, while working out the details of
Caesar's assassination, also makes a speech about servants that
says much about him: "And let our hearts, as subtle masters do, /
Stir up their servants to an act of rage / And after seem to chide
'em" *(Caesar* 2.1.176–78); it is not Brutus's finest hour.

Cloten, the type of the cretinous aristocrat, delights in using
service terms as abuse. Although Posthumus is a gentleman and
the Princess Imogen's husband, Cloten describes him as "a base
slave, / A hilding for a livery, a squire's cloth, / A pantler—not so
eminent" *(Cymbeline* 2.3.124–26). This abuse incites Imogen to
reply in kind, presumably because Shakespeare wants us to infer
that she realizes that such abuse will most hurt Cloten:

> Profane fellow!
> Wert thou the son of Jupiter and no more
> But what thou art besides, thou wert too base
> To be his groom. Thou wert dignified enough,
> Even to the point of envy, if 'twere made
> Comparative for your virtues, to be styled
> The underhangman of his kingdom, and hated
> For being preferred so well.

(2.3.126–33)

Continuing in the same style of abuse, Cloten calls Belarius,
Guiderius, and Arviragus "villain mountaineers," and calls Belarius "slave," "villain," "villain base," and "varlet" (4.2.72, 73, 76,
81, 85, 90). When he calls Guiderius "slave," Guiderius responds
by saying, "A thing / More slavish did I ne'er than answering / A
slave without a knock," and retorts to Cloten's "villain," with
"thou double villain" (73–75, 91), before finally cutting off Cloten's
brainless head. As a king's stepson, Cloten has no claim by blood
to royalty, and his behavior is utterly ignoble; among his inglori-
ous actions are his continual suggestions that men who are much
his betters are properly his servants.

Perhaps even less intelligent than Cloten—a distinction for
which there are few contenders among Shakespeare's characters—the Duke of Suffolk defies the Lieutenant to kill him, since
their relationship has been one of master to servant:

> Obscure and lousy swain, King Henry's blood,
> The honorable blood of Lancaster,

Must not be shed by such a jaded groom.
Hast thou not kissed thy hand and held my stirrup?
Bare-headed plodded by my footcloth mule
And thought thee happy when I shook my head?
How often hast thou waited at my cup,
Fed from my trencher, kneeled down at the board,
When I have feasted with Queen Margaret?
Remember it, and let it make thee crestfall'n,
Ay, and allay this thy abortive pride.
How in our voiding lobby hast thou stood
And duly waited for my coming forth?
This hand of mine hath writ in thy behalf,
And therefore shall it charm thy riotous tongue.

                              (*2 Henry VI* 4.1.50–64)

In response, the Lieutenant says he wants to "stab" Suffolk with his words, "as he hath me" (66), suggesting that Suffolk's insults have had an effect, if not the intended effect of overawing him. Suffolk continues his service-related insults, addressing the Lieutenant as "base slave," "villain," and "lowly vassal," and referring to all of his captors as "paltry, servile, abject drudges" (67, 106, 111, 105). He at first refuses to believe that he can be killed by a "lowly vassal," then maintains that he would prefer that his head "dance upon a bloody pole / Than stand uncovered to the vulgar groom," and finally finds comfort in the thought that "Great men oft die by vile bezonians. / A Roman sworder and banditto slave / Murdered sweet Tully" (128–29, 135–37). Although he comes to accept that he will die by "servile" hands, he never changes his attitude of contempt for his executioners, nor does he refrain from expressing his disdain. Although it could be argued that Suffolk shows courage in defying his executioners, he has done much evil, as the Lieutenant reminds both him and us in a long speech (70–103); ironically, among his unvirtuous acts are multiple failures of service, Suffolk having repeatedly betrayed both king and country. In addition, Suffolk shows such ungovernable contempt for those whose duty is to serve him that we necessarily feel that his "stern and rough" "imperial tongue" (122) is part of what condemns him to death.

As represented in Shakespeare's plays, service is a two-edged sword, both source of honor, as ideal, and source of disrespect, as indignity; "the tense coexistence of such fiercely conflicting attitudes," to borrow Michael Neill's phrase, provides a natural theme for drama.[77] Service is two-edged in another sense, as well: although it is assumed that the lower classes in general, as well as servants in particular, have a duty to serve, it is also assumed that the upper classes owe service to monarch and country, and lower-class characters—even servants—may remind their "betters" of that duty. Service is both noble and ignoble, and everyone is bound to serve something or someone—often more than one something or someone. Even for the great and powerful, service is inescapable.

3

"The need we have to use you":
Uses of Servants

SHAKESPEARE'S PLAYS, OF COURSE, ARE PRINCIPALLY ABOUT KINGS, queens, princes, members of the nobility, and other "gentlefolk," rather than common people, including servants. The plays, however, are filled with servants, whose presence is necessary to demonstrate the power and wealth of the protagonists who have so many people at their beck and call, as well as for the practical reason that servants often perform necessary duties. In an age of limited technology, many tasks that are now performed or assisted by machines were necessarily done by people. In addition to their function as constant visual reminders of their employers' power, servants are useful on stage, as in real life, to perform domestic duties, run errands, and deliver information. Although servants are traditionally employed to perform dull, dirty, and disagreeable tasks on their employers' behalf, Shakespeare also consistently shows members of the upper classes delegating not only such menial tasks, but even tasks requiring intelligence and talent. The characters in Shakespeare's plays who employ servants, like their real-life counterparts, find them very helpful.[1] Beyond that, however, Shakespeare finds servant-characters useful as everything from comic relief to innocent sufferer of violence to means of commenting on upper-class characters, either directly or by contrast with a servant's own behavior.

The plays, however, do not resemble Elizabethan life in the disproportion between the numbers of male and female servants or the numbers of "high" and "low" servants represented on stage. Apart from waiting-gentlewomen, necessary to chaperone, entertain, do errands, and serve as confidantes for upper-class female characters, female servants seldom appear in the plays. The early comedies occasionally feature a kitchen maid such as Luce in *The Comedy of Errors* or a dairy maid such as Jaquenetta in *Love's Labor's Lost*, but such figures are rare. One of the exceptions, Mrs. Quickly, in describing her duties makes it clear why female servants, so ubiquitous and important a part of Shakespeare's world, play so small a part in his drama:

> *Quickly [aside to Simple]* . . . I keep [Caius's] house, and I wash, wring, brew, bake, scour, dress meat and drink, make the beds, and do all myself—
> *Simple [aside to Quickly]* 'Tis a great charge to come under one body's hand.
> *Quickly [aside to Simple]* Are you advised o' that? You shall find it a great charge. And to be up early and down late.
> (Merry Wives 1.4.89–96)[2]

While it was, obviously, a great charge for the women who were required to do all of the tasks that made the Elizabethan household run smoothly, it was not, alas, a very dramatic charge; it is, therefore, not surprising that these domestic duties failed to capture the imagination of a dramatist largely occupied with the death of princes and the course of true (mostly upper-class) love.[3]

Since, in real life, male servants waited on male employers in public and performed most duties that took servants outside the home, it is understandable that most of Shakespeare's servants are men or boys. Consequently, just as the male protagonists of the plays are the ones who do nearly all of the plotting, politicking, and fighting (though by no means all of the suffering and dying), it is usually the male servants who support their male employers in these activities. As with female servants, male servants onstage are much more likely to be "upper" servants than would be the case in reality. The plays do, however, represent male servants providing a wide range of services, many of them domestic, in addition to merely accompanying their masters. Male servants, among many other tasks, transport dirty laundry, strew rushes, help their masters dress and undress, help their masters arm and disarm, fetch needed items, act as torch-bearers, deal with horses, tell their masters what time it is, and empty the chamber pot.[4] Male servants frequently announce arrivals and are ordered to summon or escort other characters.[5]

While this evidence may suggest to some readers that Shakespeare and the Elizabethans viewed servants as mere drudges or labor-saving devices for the upper classes, it may also suggest an alternate reading: the presence of one or more servants is what establishes a socially superior character's standing in a play, just as it did in real life. And while it may be dehumanizing to regard servants as a kind of signifier of status, it also lends such individuals an importance in their relationships with their masters or mistresses. In terms of defining social roles, servants are as important as their employers, since neither can exist without the other. Furthermore, even commonplace tasks do more than merely reflect reality and forward, in small ways, the plays' plots, since such tasks are often integral to the plays' action. For example, the messages delivered and errands run by the Dromios cause much of the confusion necessary to *The Comedy of Errors*, while the information delivered by the multitude of messengers throughout the canon often dictates upper-class characters' actions.

One of the uses of servants, in the plays as in the real life of the period, was as status markers; being escorted by a large number of well-dressed and, presumably, attractive people who were doing nothing except accompanying you was a sign that you were important and rich enough to employ so many people, and that you were, therefore, a person to be reckoned with. As Stephen Greenblatt has observed, "the hallmark of power and wealth in the sixteenth century was to be waited on by others."[6] With rare exceptions, royal persons do not go unaccompanied: "*Enter Prince Escalus, with his train*"; "*Enter the King of France, with letters, and [two Lords and] divers attendants*"; "*Enter King Richard, John of Gaunt, with other nobles and attendants.*"[7]

Queen Margaret emphasizes the importance of multiple attendants as evidence of status when railing about the behavior of the Duchess of Gloucester:

> Not all these lords do vex me half so much
> As that proud dame, the Lord Protector's wife.
> She sweeps it through the court with troops of ladies,
> More like an empress than Duke Humphrey's wife.
> Strangers in court do take her for the Queen.
>
> (*2 Henry VI* 1.3.75–79)

This quotation also suggests, of course, that aristocrats, as well as royalty, are often accompanied by attendants.[8] Even such non-aristocratic women as Helena may travel with attendants, since women would be especially vulnerable to the dangers of traveling unescorted (*All's Well* 1.3.250–52; 5.1.1.s.d.). On the other hand, Orsino's order that "some four or five attend" Cesario, who is merely carrying a message from the court to Olivia's house, is obviously a display of the power and wealth of a prince who can afford to send four or five men and a boy to do his wooing for him.

The absence of servants can be as significant as their presence. The importance of servants as status markers is perhaps most immediately obvious in *King Lear*, in which, as Rolf Soellner notes of Lear's entrance at act 2, scene 4, "On the stage, Lear is already visibly reduced in status by being accompanied merely by the Fool and one gentleman (as the stage direction has it), even though theoretically he still has his hundred men."[9] Similarly, Richard II measures his fall from greatness by the loss of his retainers, as he demonstrates when he sees himself in the "flattering glass": "Was this face the face / That every day under his household roof / Did keep ten thousand men?"[10] It is not only numbers of servants or the absence of such numbers that is significant, however; the lack of one or two personal servants can indicate that a protagonist is isolated. Even in his sufferings, Lear has his Fool and "Caius"; Macbeth has Seyton, Antony Enobarbus, and Timon his Steward. Desdemona, Lady Macbeth, and Cleopatra all have ladies-in-waiting. While not all of these characters may be confidant(e)s—and while a confidential servant may be a curse, rather than a blessing, as Iago is to Othello—their presence does suggest that the protagonists, however exalted, are connected to society through human relationships. On the other hand, Coriolanus would be difficult to envision as a "lonely dragon" if he had a loyal servant.

Coriolanus, however, is a soldier of Republican Rome, not a member of a royal family. The Shakespearean protagonist most surprisingly alone is Hamlet, Prince of Denmark. Although Ralph Berry asks us to "Consider his affable relations with all social classes,"[11] Hamlet (as opposed to *Hamlet*) is remarkably lacking in servants. He does not seem to have a retinue, or even, apparently, a personal servant, as we would expect a prince to have. Horatio, of course, acts as his confidant, but Hamlet's lack of servants serves to emphasize his isolation: he seems less "dreadfully attended" than dreadfully unattended.[12] When Claudius and Gertrude wish to spy on the prince, they find it necessary to import Rosencrantz and Guildenstern, who of course prove utterly incompetent. Oddly enough, the dead Yorick is arguably the most vivid, if not the most important, actual servant in the play.[13] Hamlet's lack of servants has inspired critics to see him as incorporating within himself the equivalent of the confidential servant of other tragedies, although just which servant and which tragedy depends on the critic: James R. Andreas maintains that "In a sense, Hamlet is his own Iago," while Jonathan Bate parallels Hamlet with Titus Andronicus, arguing that "Where Lear has his Fool and then the company of Poor Tom, Titus and Hamlet play their own fools"[14] Even where confidential servants are lacking, some commentators find that their functions are so necessary that the protagonists incorporate these functions within themselves.

Other than the Prince of Denmark, royalty, of course, had many common servants, but an important aspect of royalty was the ability to employ members of the aristocracy as servants. The tasks that these aristocrats do could as easily be done by ordinary servants, but being served by aristocrats advertises the power of their employer, and the aristocrats recognize that serving a monarch is part of their duty. Tasks that would shame an aristocrat if done for someone else are honors when performed for the monarch. Thus, King Henry VI can make the Duke of Exeter his "messenger," as did his father before him, and Claudius shows his power by ordering the King of England to have Hamlet executed (3 Henry VI 1.1.272; Henry V 2.4.75–76; Hamlet 4.3.62–69). Royal personages can also demonstrate their power by commanding aristocrats to perform tasks that the royals could easily do for themselves; thus, the Princess of France orders Lord Boyet to open a letter for her (L.L.L. 4.1.56–57). Those who aspire to the monarchy also treat aristocrats as servants, most notably Richard, Duke of Gloucester, who, throughout Richard III, has various lords and knights running his errands and sends a bishop to order strawberries for him (3.4.31–34). Similarly, throughout the plays, aristocrats at the top of the ladder command the services of aristocrats below them.

The ability to command powerful servants confirms the power of their employers; God Himself, after all, employs angels as servants and the principal classical gods and goddesses employ the services of minor deities (Romeo 2.2.28; Tempest 4.1.70–71, 76–77). Oberon's power as king of the fairies is demonstrated by his employment of a messenger who can "put a girdle round about the earth / In forty minutes" (Dream 2.1.175–76). Just as the audience recognizes the power of a king who can command dukes and earls, it accepts Prospero's power because he has a servant (or slave) who "perform[s] . . . the tempest" (Tempest 1.2.195) of their play's title, who can make himself invisible or appear in altered form, whose powers, in fact, appear almost unlimited.

In contrast, the inability of a formerly powerful person to employ a person of high degree as a servant can also be significant. Thus, Dollabella measures the fall of Antony's fortunes by Antony's use of his schoolmaster as a messenger to Caesar, noting that Antony "had superfluous kings for messengers / Not many moons gone by"; however hyperbolic this statement may seem, Antony himself echoes it: "Authority melts from me of late. When I cried 'Ho!', / Like boys unto a muss kings would start forth / And cry, 'Your will?'" (*Antony* 3.12.5–6; 3.13.91–93).

The existence of servants as a class allows some upper-class characters to take on the appearance of servants for their own purposes. In the final scene of his play, Titus Andronicus enters "*like a cook*" (*Titus* 5.3.25 s.d.), presumably to continue the charade of his madness by abasing himself before Saturninus and Tamora, thereby disarming them and ensuring the success of his revenge.[15] On a lighter note, Prince Hal and Poins disguise themselves as drawers so that they can spy on Falstaff (2 *Henry IV* 2.2.161–68; 2.4.15–18, 232 s.d.). Women are at least as likely as men to disguise themselves as servants; Julia disguises herself as "Sebastian" to follow Proteus; Nerissa accompanies Portia in the guise of a nameless servant; Viola takes service in Orsino's court under the name and appearance of "Cesario." That Shakespeare's comic heroines frequently dress as men or boys is a commonplace, but it is not always noticed how useful the servant role is to some of these heroines. While Nerissa's disguise is simply an echo of her mistress's, impersonating servants allows Julia and Viola not only to conceal their identities, but to receive the protection of their masters and establish intimate relationships with these men. The male servant's disguise is so useful and allows the young women who assume it so much more freedom than would otherwise be available to them that it is not surprising that it was a popular device in the drama and ballads of the period.[16]

Derek Cohen argues that "The slave and the servant's function, as often as not, is to do the dirty work, clean up the mess, of the master or mistress."[17] While there is clearly a good deal of truth in this generally, it is by no means entirely accurate as a description of the servant-characters in Shakespeare's plays. Caliban, whom Cohen specifically mentions, is forced to carry logs; Iago is ordered to fetch the luggage; but—remembering that, for the most part, menial servants are vastly underrepresented in Shakespeare's plays—we should not be too surprised to find that what we might think of as leisure activities and even artistic productions often depend on servants rather than their employers.

One of the great distinctions between the upper and lower classes is the leisure enjoyed by the former, a distinction so important and obvious that the ruling class has been described as "the leisure class." For the upper classes of Shakespeare's time, however, even leisure could not be enjoyed in the absence of servants. Feasts and parties required a host of servants to prepare, serve, and clean up after dinner.[18] Hunting and hawking usually required skilled specialists to help the lords and ladies locate game, take care of the hawks, hounds, and horses, and, presumably, butcher the killed animals and transport the meat home (*L.L.L.* 4.1.7–10; *Shrew* Induction.1.15–28; *2 Henry VI* 2.1.1 s.d.).[19] Some upper-class characters employ professional entertainers or "fools," although Touchstone, Feste, and Lavatch often seem to spend more time entertaining other people or themselves than their employers. It is not only such professional entertainers, however, on whom employers rely for amusement; any rank of servant from slave to lady- or gentleman-in-waiting may be called upon to amuse an employer. Antipholus of Syracuse describes Dromio of Syracuse as "A trusty villain . . . that very oft / When I am dull with care and melancholy, / Lightens my humor with his merry jests" (*Errors* 1.2.19–21; we see S. Dromio doing this at 2.2.50–107 and 3.2.73–154). Puck describes himself as a kind of jester to Oberon, and Thersites—whose exact status is questionable, but who is treated as a servant or slave—is described as a privileged fool and seen entertaining Achilles (*Dream* 2.1.44; *Troilus* 2.3.40–67, 89–90). Groups of servants may also be asked to extemporize a performance, as the unnamed Lord in the Induction of *The Taming of the Shrew* requires his servants to "manage well the jest" that he dreams up upon spying the sleeping Christopher Sly (Induction.1.44). Richard II's queen asks her attendants to suggest sport to drive away care, although she proceeds to reject all of their suggestions, which include bowling, dancing, storytelling, and singing (*Richard II* 3.4.1–19).

The suggestion of singing raises a question about servants and music in the plays, since the other suggestions regarding amusements are framed as group amusements—"we'll play at bowls," "we'll dance," "we'll tell tales"—presumably with the queen joining in. The final suggestion, however, is framed differently: "Madam, I'll sing." The queen's objection to the role of auditor is unusual, since Shakespeare's upper-class characters are often eager to listen to their servants make music.[20] Although musical ability was an appropriate upper-class accomplishment, few of Shakespeare's upper-class characters produce their own music except in extraordinary circumstances. The exiled lords in *As You Like It* presumably lack the usual retinue of servants and are therefore driven to the expedient of singing for themselves.[21] Simonides reports that the temporarily servantless Pericles is "music's master" (*Pericles* 2.5.30), although we do not hear or see him play or sing. His daughter Marina, who "sings like one immortal," is in an even worse situation: enslaved, she is driven to teaching singing and other graces for the profit of the bawd who owns her; at Lysimachus's command, she also sings to Pericles in an attempt to cure him of his melancholy (5.Chorus.3; 5.1.82 s.d.). Arviragus and Guiderius also lack servants, and, further, when they chant their funeral song, are no more aware that they are princes than that "Fidele" is a woman, their sister, and still alive (*Cymbeline* 4.2.261–84).[22]

Singing on the part of other upper-class characters often seems to suggest either great distress or "ungentle" behavior. Ophelia sings only when she is mad, and her songs are some of the strongest evidence of her madness; Desdemona sings when deeply upset by Othello's treatment of her; King John sings in his death-agony; Edgar sings while disguised as an insane former serving-man; and Parson Evans sings when "full of cholers . . . and trempling of mind."[23] Mercutio sings a snatch of bawdy song as part of his ungentlemanly taunting of Juliet's Nurse, and Falstaff sings in a tavern (*Romeo* 2.4.132–37; *2 Henry IV* 2.4.33–35). Pandarus also sings, but his gentility, too, is questionable (*Troilus* 3.1.114–26). Finally, Sir Toby and Sir Andrew join Feste in singing in *Twelfth Night*, but their behavior is problematic, since not only are they being overly familiar with a servant (or servants, if the reluctant Maria is to be counted as one of their party), but they are riotously keeping Olivia's household (if not the entire neighborhood) awake in a most ungentlemanly, if rather engaging, manner (*Twelfth Night* 2.3). Similarly, Silence sings snatches of drinking songs (probably drunkenly) in the midst of feasting with Shallow and Falstaff (*2 Henry IV* 5.3.16–76).

That such characters sing informs us about their attributes and situations, and what they sing is as important as that they sing: most of the songs sung by these characters are not original lyrics by Shakespeare, but ballads or other songs that would have been familiar to his original audience. Because these songs were familiar, Shakespeare could use them to focus attention on the characters' states of mind and behaviors, rather than on the songs themselves, although the use he makes of the songs is not always consistent. It is appropriate that Desdemona sings a song about a woman forsaken by her lover, but inappropriate that Parson Evans sings lines from "Come live with me and be my love," which he comically muddles together with a verse from the Psalms. Ophelia's choice of songs is both appropriate and inappropriate: her songs recall her father's death and her "desertion" by Hamlet, but her insistence on singing rather than conversing and her choice of a bawdy song make her madness obvious. Similarly, Sir Toby and Sir Andrew sing songs appropriate to their behavior as revellers, but this behavior—and perhaps the fact that they are harmonizing with a servant—shames their social position.[24]

Upper-class characters in these plays, however, are much more likely to command music than to make it themselves, and many of the plays' songs, particularly most of Shakespeare's original songs, are the province of servants. Music is sometimes performed by hired musicians, who are effectively common servants of anyone who will pay their fee, but is more often performed by a group of an individual employer's servants at his or her command.[25] Individual servants also frequently sing at their employer's command or that of other members of the upper class.[26] Fools sometimes burst into song without being ordered to do so, but this is presumably accepted behavior from professional entertainers (All's Well 1.3.70–79; Lear 1.4.163–66; 3.2.74–77). Most of the songs performed to order are designed to match the mood and situation of the people who order the singing; love songs and drinking songs are most common. Understandably, this music is suited to its hearers, not necessarily its performers; unlike songs sung by members of the upper classes, servants' songs are not generally intended to reveal their characters.

In contrast to members of the upper classes, however, servants sometimes sing when they are happy, for their own pleasure and, occasionally, for the pleasure of nonemployers. Lear's Fool sings in answer to the disguised Edgar's singing, and Feste does the same with Sir Toby, apparently for the sheer fun of it (Lear 3.6.25–28; Twelfth Night 2.3.102–12). Feste, who says he "take[s] pleasure in singing" (2.4.68), sings and plays music apparently for his own amusement at several other points in his play (3.1.1 s.d.; 4.2.72–79, 121–32; 5.1.389–408).[27] Other servants who sing primarily for their own pleasure include Iago, Autolycus, Caliban, Ariel, and Stephano.[28] Stephano, one of the few servants in these plays who anticipates radically changing his status, comments on the difference between the employing and serving classes in terms of music. As a butler, he sings; but, when he contemplates becoming king of the island, he states, in response to Ariel's music: "This will prove a brave kingdom to me, where I shall have my music for nothing" (*Tempest* 3.2.146–47). Throughout the plays, as perhaps in the real life of the period, the ability to produce music is less valued than the ability to command it. In *Merchant*, the scapegrace Lorenzo confirms the authority Portia has vested in him by his easy mastery of her musicians, in obvious contrast to the difficulty he has in controlling Launcelot (5.1.51–53, 66–68; 3.5.41–61). As the music he has commanded plays, Lorenzo makes one of the play's most famous speeches, which ends with an explanation of the relation between music and moral character:

> The man that hath no music in himself,
> Nor is not moved with concord of sweet sounds,
> Is fit for treasons, stratagems, and spoils;
> The motions of his spirit are dull as night,
> And his affections dark as Erebus.
> Let no such man be trusted. Mark the music.
>
> (5.1.83–88)

Whether having music in oneself means possessing the ability to make music or merely the ability to appreciate music is unclear, but it appears to be the latter. The emphasis is clearly on consumption, rather than production; the attitude is that of the aristocratic patron, rather than the artist.

Presumably reflecting either class reality—that a gentleman was expected to be in command of language, but not necessarily of the tools of the visual arts—or theatrical reality—that language and music played large parts in Renaissance drama and the visual arts (other than costuming) very small ones—little is said in the plays about architecture, painting, or sculpture (always excepting "that rare Italian master, Julio Romano"). However, characters do occasionally write, recite, and discuss poetry (distinct from the blank or rhymed verse Shakespeare may have given them to speak). The status of such poetry in the plays is quite different from the status of music. Poetry seems generally to be perceived of as the means by which upper-class young men open their hearts to the young women they love.[29] Unlike music, poetry does not seem to be a commodity that can be ordered from the professionals, and this is arguably unfortunate, since the running joke throughout the canon is that these well-born, intelligent, honorable, and usually well-educated lovers are very bad poets. The idea of gentlemen-amateurs being unable to write good love poetry is one that seems to develop in tandem with Shakespeare's development of romantic comedy, although it occasionally appears in noncomedic plays as well.[30] No one comments on the quality of Valentine's love verse, but the princess and her ladies criticize their lovers' attempts at poetry in *Love's Labor's Lost*, and several characters mock Orlando's verses.[31] Even Falstaff, when wooing, is reduced to doggerel (*Merry Wives* 2.1.14–18).

Several of these gentlemanly poetasters redeem themselves by recognizing and commenting upon the badness of their love-poetry. Longaville and Dumaine are dubious about their verses' "power to move" and clarity (*L.L.L.* 4.3.51–53, 117–18). Hamlet criticizes his own poetry, as does Benedick (*Hamlet* 2.2.120; *Much Ado* 5.2.35–41). Berowne swears off trying to write poetry, vowing to use only simple language in his future wooing (*L.L.L.* 5.2.403–14). Henry V, on the other hand, sensibly refuses even to attempt versifying, recognizing that his talents lie elsewhere (*Henry V* 5.2.134–47).[32] Orlando alone maintains that it is merely the inadequacy or malice of his readers that makes his verses appear bad, which we may interpret as testimony either to his lack of education or his sensitivity about that lack.

In contrast to his general depiction of gentlemen as incapable of writing passable verse even when given time to consider and revise and stimulated by love, the ultimate inspiration (*L.L.L.* 4.3.320–21), Shakespeare consistently portrays servants as capable of producing serviceable oral verse extemporaneously. Not surprisingly, the Fools, as professional entertainers, are among Shakespeare's most competent and confident rhymesters: Touchstone is critical of Orlando's verses, which he parodies (*A.Y.L.* 3.2.99–110); Lear's Fool rhymes at will (*Lear* 1.4.116–25, 138–45, 316–20; 2.4.76–83; 3.2.27–34, 81–94); and Feste seems to be able to supply song lyrics whenever he needs them (*Twelfth Night* 4.2.121–32). This talent is not limited to the professionals, however. Armado's page, Mote, is a clever versifier (*L.L.L.* 1.2.95–102, 3.1.89–90). Maria composes a rhymed "fustian riddle" that nevertheless is effective in misleading and entrapping Malvolio (*Twelfth Night* 2.5.95–98, 103–7). Iago composes a clever, scurrilous, and apparently extemporaneous rhyme on the characters of women in response to a request from Desdemona

(*Othello* 2.1.119–60). Even Pistol recites a scrap of appropriate, if undistinguished, verse (*Merry Wives* 1.3.94–97). While some of the verse produced by servants may be no better than that produced by their social superiors, the servants' oral rhymes usually produce the impression that their authors are witty, whereas the written verse produced by their social superiors is either obviously mediocre at best or criticized by its readers or the writers themselves in ways that suggest that it is below the expected standard for educated gentlemen.

One of the oddities of the plays with regard to servants is that they are frequently given orders by people not their employers, and they usually fulfill these commands without question. It is not surprising that Sir Toby gives orders to Maria (*Twelfth Night* 2.3.14): he is her mistress's kinsman, he lives in the house, and they have a personal relationship that culminates in marriage. Within the context of the play, it is understandable that Feste sings for Orsino, since we have been told that he is given to sneaking away from Olivia's house, and throughout the play we see him cadging money from the play's upper-class characters (*Twelfth Night* 1.5.1–4, 16–18, 38–39; 2.4.1–14, 42–67). There is, however, less apparent logic when Hortensio sends orders to his wife by means of Lucentio's servant, Biondello, or Proteus sends Valentine's servant, Speed, to deliver a love note to Julia (*Shrew* 5.2.90–91; *T.G.V.* 1.1.95–96). And then there's Simple, in *The Merry Wives of Windsor*, who appears to be every man's servant. It is natural enough that his ostensible master, Slender, orders him, "Go, sirrah, for all you are my man, go wait upon my cousin Shallow," but subsequently Evans sends Simple to deliver a letter to Mrs. Quickly (on behalf of Slender), Caius sends Simple to deliver a letter back to Evans, and Evans sends Simple to look for Caius (1.1.252–53; 1.2.1–9; 1.4.101–2; 3.1.1–10). It begins to make sense that the first lines addressed to Simple are a complaint that he has been absent from his master (1.1.184–85); throughout the play, Simple is continually waiting on characters other than Slender. Nor is Simple the only servant in the play to take orders from characters other than his or her employer: Mrs. Ford asks information of and gives an order to Robin, who is officially Falstaff's servant, although on loan to Mrs. Page (3.3.18–19, 31), while Shallow orders Mrs. Quickly to interrupt Fenton and Anne Page, and Quickly does so (3.4.22–23, 29–30, 34–35). In reality, people such as Shallow and Evans would almost certainly have been accompanied by servants most of the time; while it may have been the case that people occasionally gave orders to other people's servants (such as using them, as Caius does Simple, to reply to a message), the obvious reason for most such extra work allotted to onstage servants is a practical theatrical one: Simple's errand-running eliminates the need for extra actors to play servants to other characters.[33]

Shakespeare also uses servant-characters for purposes more intrinsic to the plays. Particularly in the early plays, servants are often the butt of humor. Servants who make mistakes, or are perceived by their employers as making mistakes, are often beaten or otherwise physically abused or threatened; these punishments, and the servants' complaints about their treatment, are apparently intended to be funny, but such "comic" violence decreases dramatically after the early comedies. (See, for example, *Errors* 1.2.77–94; 2.1.44–84; 2.2.7–54; passim; *Shrew* 1.2.5–42; 4.1.1–2, 64–75, 131–55; 4.3.31–35; 5.1.43–59. Violence toward servants is discussed at greater length in chapter 10.) Servants are also represented as foolish in their inability to speak correctly or to understand what is said to them. For instance, Grumio sometimes reverses the subjects and objects of his sentences, an extremely low form of humor that Shakespeare soon abandons (*Shrew* 1.2.31–33; 3.2.205–6); Juliet's Nurse assumes that Romeo's "I protest" is a "gentlemanlike offer," without giving him a chance to say what he means (*Romeo* 2.4.168–75). Servants are also sometimes represented as boastful and cowardly, as Sampson and Gregory are (*Romeo* 1.1.1–59). Some servants are simply not too bright, like Lance, who assumes that because his dog is ten times bigger than Proteus's lap dog, it would make a greater gift for Sylvia, or the servant who praises the lack of bawdry in Autolycus's ballads while unwittingly revealing that the songs are actually risqué (*T.G.V.* 4.4.42–56; *Winter's Tale* 4.4.181–200). On occasion, it is impossible to be certain whether a servant is being witty or foolish, as with Peter's double entendre reply to the Nurse's rebuke for allowing Mercutio to insult her (*Romeo* 2.4.152–57).[34]

Mary Hallowell Perkins notes that "The servant's enormous appetite and his propensity for sleeping were stock jokes," but this description does not seem to apply to any of Shakespeare's servant-characters later than Lancelot Gobbo.[35] Some servants are unquestionably comic relief, but after the early plays it becomes questionable whether servants are perceived as intrinsically funny. Do Falstaff and the Host tease Simple because he is a servant or because he is simple? (*Merry Wives* 4.5.1–53). The suggestion that he is dim-witted because he is a servant seems a bit—sorry—simple, given that nearly every major character in the play (except the young lovers) is made a fool of; although Simple is certainly an idiot, he is no more ridiculous than his master, Slender. Other servants are sometimes, but not always, foolish. Juliet's Nurse is frequently comic, especially in her verbosity, her outrage at Mercutio's mockery, and her misunderstandings of what is said to her (*Romeo* 1.3.12–58; 2.4.143–206). But she is also clever enough to be intentionally comic, as when she teases Juliet by delaying her report of Romeo's reply (2.5.25–64).

The assumption that servants are inherently comic may be more common among modern critics than it was among Shakespeare's contemporaries, and this assumption can lead to misjudgments. Despite Russ McDonald's assertion, it is not clear that in Shakespeare's plays "characters . . . who cannot read, such as Capulet's servant in the second scene of *Romeo and Juliet,* are treated as comic butts."[36] Launce accuses Speed of being unable to read, calling him "jolt-head" and "illiterate loiterer," but Speed proves that he can read, so the joke goes nowhere (*T.G.V.* 3.1.287, 291). Upon learning that the Page cannot read, Apemantus remarks, "There will little learning die then that day thou art hanged" (*Timon* 2.2.85–86), but this is a mild comment coming from Apemantus, who scorns everyone. Furthermore, he does what the Page asks and tells him which of the letters he is carrying goes to which recipient. Similarly, Romeo helps Capulet's illiterate servingman after a brief exchange that derives its humor as much from Romeo's self-absorption as from the servingman's illiteracy (*Romeo* 1.2.57–63). Before meeting Romeo, the servingman has rather wittily played with the idea that a tool is useless in the hands of a person not trained in its use (38–44). As far as he is concerned, writing is simply a tool he cannot use; therefore, he concludes, "I must to the learned." He is polite toward Romeo, but not at all awed by him. Romeo reads him the names of more than a dozen people invited to the Capulets' party, some of whose wives, daughters, sisters, and nieces are also invited, and he apparently memorizes the list at a single hearing. He then invites the man who did him this favor to the party at "our house," and exits with a cheerful "Rest you merry!" (76, 80–83). The servingman is not at all embarrassed by his inability to read, nor does Romeo seek to make him embarrassed about it. Obviously, the servant is made illiterate not so that Shakespeare can joke about ignorant servants, but so that Romeo can find out about Rosalind attending the Capulets' party. Nor, because a couple of servants in the canon are illiterate, should it be assumed that this is the normal condition for servants, particularly "upper" servants. Stephen J. Greenblatt refers to "the lower-class and presumably illiterate Stephano and Trinculo,"[37] but it is not clear that we should assume that the King of Naples would employ "lower-class" servants or that these men are any more likely to be illiterate than are Malvolio or Touchstone. Since many members of Shakespeare's audience were presumably illiterate and probably did not see anything particularly funny about that condition, it would perhaps not have been the most apposite topic about which to make jokes.

Obviously, some servants are used for comic relief or are simply comic characters; in fact, there are so many funny servants in the plays that only a couple of examples can be discussed in any detail. In general, Shakespeare's comic servants, like his servant-characters in general, are neither rustic nor particularly low-class: they may be emigrants from the countryside (although their backgrounds are rarely explored), but as servants they are members of great, rich households, who live in urban, cosmopolitan settings. If they are women, they are usually described as gentlewomen and are the companions of their mistresses; if they are men, they are often jesters, stewards, gentlemen-in-waiting, or footmen. They are, at least within their own class, comparatively privileged persons and, while they may be stupid, or ignorant, or drunk, it is rarely suggested that any of these conditions is directly related to their position as servants, any more than the connection is made for servants who are particularly clever and witty.

One of the most famous examples of "comic relief" in the canon is *Macbeth*'s Porter. As has long been noted, the Porter scene gives Macbeth "time to change and wash his hands," as well as providing comic relief.[38] The Porter, despite having been "carousing till the second cock" (2.3.23–24), is capable of imagining himself the "porter of hell gate" (1–2), in which role he admits three sinners, about whom he makes appropriate jokes. As any number of commentators have pointed out, what the Porter says is not only clever and entertaining, but relates to the crimes we have just seen Macbeth and Lady Macbeth commit.[39] He imagines a sinner who is a thief, another who "committed treason," and a third who "hanged himself on th'expectation of plenty." All of these, in various ways, mirror what we have just seen Duncan's murderers do: they steal his life and his kingdom, thereby committing treason, and destroy themselves in the hope of being monarchs. After opening the gate to Macduff and Lennox (and asking them for money), the Porter gives his speech on lechery, which no doubt amused the original audience as much as it continues to amuse audiences (and students) today. That act 2, scene 3, of *Macbeth* is often referred to as "the Porter scene," although the Porter's entire contribution to the play consists of only about thirty-five lines of prose, is testimony to how memorable an impression one lowly, comic servant, considerably the worse for drink, can make in the midst of a terrible tragedy.

Malvolio's contribution to his play is, of course, much greater than the Porter's, not only because his role is much larger, but because he is not simply comic relief, but intrinsic to the plot and meaning of his play. Many critics (and directors) see Malvolio as abused.[40] It is, however, improbable that this is how Shakespeare intended us to see Olivia's steward, or that it is how the original audience saw him.[41] Critics have noted how Shakespeare cleverly makes Malvolio integral to the completion of the main plot,[42] with which he is also connected early in the play, as he seeks to frustrate "Cesario's" attempt to see Olivia and then follows Orsino's servant to deliver Olivia's ring; throughout the middle of the play, of course, he is the central figure in the subplot. In the last fifty years or so, however, that subplot has been frequently interpreted as appalling, rather than comic. There is little likelihood that argument will persuade anyone to find something funny, but there are arguments for "the mistreated Malvolio" that can and should be refuted.

Even critics who are sympathetic toward Malvolio frequently acknowledge M. C. Bradbrook's judgments that he is "self-opinionated and self-satisfied," as well as lecherous.[43] Critics argue, however, that he is a capable servant who is oppressed by those arbitrarily placed above him in the early modern social hierarchy.[44] Defenses of Mavolio's competence are odd, given that he fails at every task he is assigned, and frequently irritates his mistress, even when he has not been tricked into doing so. A simple list of his activities, omitting his gulling, is as follows: In his first speech, he contradicts Olivia, even though her "Doth he not mend?" directs him how he should respond, apparently because he cannot overcome his desire to try to put Feste in a bad light; he follows that with a speech impugning her taste: "I marvel Your Ladyship takes delight in such a barren rascal" (*Twelfth Night* 1.5.70–74, 80–81). Rebuked by his mistress and sent to dismiss Orsino's messenger, he soon returns to report that he is unable to do so (105–6, 136–46). Sent to deliver a ring to the departed messenger, he returns it in a manner that earns Viola's accurate description of him as "churlish" (2.2.23). Critics have pointed out that, in trying to break up the revellers' late-night drinking party, Malvolio is (he says) following Olivia's orders and doing his job as her steward.[45] While this may be true, he is as rude as he dares be, and he does not actually disperse the revellers: he merely redirects their energies from singing to plotting against him. Finally, he wrongly accuses Olivia of wronging him; granted, he is led to believe that, but his self-love is as much to blame as Maria's forged handwriting. Given all of this, and given the fact that Olivia's household is clearly disfunctional, with servants wandering off, quarreling among themselves, and socializing with their social superiors, it is hard to imagine how anyone can describe Olivia's steward as competent. Malvolio is completely ineffectual in keeping order, which is virtually his job description, and it is probably intended to be part of his character's humor that he thinks so well of himself despite his obvious incompetence.

Certainly, we see "class tensions" in the conflict between Malvolio and Sir Toby and Sir Andrew, and we are likely to feel, at least, that we *should* side against the unearned and undeserved privilege represented by the drunken knights.[46] Sir Toby, however, never—at least before Maria's plot—threatens Malvolio's position with Olivia, nor, given his standing with his niece, is it likely that he could do so. Malvolio, on the other hand, is depicted as using his influence to threaten the livelihoods of all three of the other servants we meet in Olivia's household (1.5.70–86; 2.3.120–23; 2.5.7–8). Donald Sinden, who played Malvolio in the RSC's 1969 production of *Twelfth Night*, notes of his portrayal of the character in the drinking scene: "I cannot openly attack Sir Toby or Sir Andrew, but I can attack Feste and Maria, my minions, and through them the other two, so I address Feste."[47] To the extent that the play is about the misuse of power, Malvolio is the major offender, and it is therefore just that the audience find him the play's comic butt: bullies deserve whatever mockery they get.

Malvolio is one of Shakespeare's relatively rare servant-characters who is mocked for being a servant: "Art any more than a steward?" (2.3.113–14). Toby's question, of course, is intended as a reminder to Malvolio to remember his place, but with regard to Malvolio we might want to consider it as a serious question, for Malvolio seems to be one of those people who is only his job and whose only dreams are of improving his position. He is hated by his "inferiors" and scorned by his "superiors." We may not want to align our sympathies with Toby and Andrew, but Malvolio also attacks Maria, although she is shown trying to quiet the revellers; "Cesario," who is simply doing "his" job; and Feste—and what Shakespearean character other than a villain or an imbecile gets on the wrong side of a professional fool?[48] Malvolio does not become admirable or lovable because he is opposed to a drunk and a cretin or because his enemies attack him on the basis of his position—which, in any event, is not their primary mode of attack, although it is his. Malvolio is funny because he is a servant, but only because he is a particular kind of servant: arrogant but incompetent, a bully who, properly, gets his comeuppance.

Servants are not important only because they are amusing. They can be used to foreshadow behavior of upper-class characters, as in *The Merchant of Venice*, when Lancelot Gobbo's departure from Shylock's household foreshadows Jessica's elopement, or in *Romeo and Juliet*, when the servants' fighting in the first scene foreshadows the later fighting by the families they serve.[49] Critics have also suggested that servants can appear as agents of chance or destiny, Capulet's illiterate servant being a popular example.[50] Conversations among groups of servants can also influence our attitudes, as do Timon's servants discussing their master's fall and Aufidius's servants discussing his reconciliation with Coriolanus.[51] Shakespeare also uses servants as structural elements in the plays. James Edward Siemon observes that "the degree to which the pattern of *Winter's Tale* represents only a readjustment of the terms of the basic comic pattern is suggested by the recurrence here of the device by which the wily slave is the efficient cause of the dramatic resolution . . . In *Winter's Tale* this ancient device is fully exploited in the schemes of Leontes' servants Camillo and Paulina, who provide for Hermione's preservation and for the return of Perdita to the kingdom, and whose own union suggests the force of the ancient pattern."[52] Richard G. Moulton maintains that the entry of Antony's unnamed servant as the assassins are bathing their hands in Caesar's blood "is the 'catastrophe,' the turning-round of the whole action."[53] Servants can be constructed to act as foils for their employers or other social superiors, as the Fool does for Lear or Francis the drawer does for Prince Hal,[54] or as scapegoats, as Parolles does for Bertram. Critics, however, while agreeing that servants are important in a play, may disagree about which servant is important and how: whereas Janet Adelman states that "in *Othello* . . . the tragedy consists precisely in the relationship between [Othello] and his tricksy servant," Carol Thomas Neely maintains that "the play's central theme is love—specifically marital love—that its central conflict is between the men and the women. . . . Within *Othello* it is Emilia who most explicitly speaks to this theme, recognizes this central conflict, and inherits from the heroines of comedy the role of potential mediator of it."[55]

Critics have also argued that various servants are intended to influence or substitute for the play's audience. Robert F. Willson, Jr. finds that "When [Cornwall's] First Servant stands up to his master (lines 75ff.) and attempts to put an end to the cruel proceedings, he acts for us as surely as any character in [*King Lear*]"; Robert Egan sees Kent as "an embodiment of the particular empathetic anxiety which . . . must be central to any audience's experience of *King Lear*"; Mildred E. Hartsock indicates that the principal purpose of the Gardener's speech after the exit of Richard II's queen (*Richard II* 3.4.102–7) is to encourage the audience to sympathize with Richard's plight; and Phyllis Rackin maintains that when the Groom visits Richard II in prison, the deposed king "receives the benefit of patriotic sentiments—not only from an imagined subject in the play but also from real ones in Shakespeare's audience."[56] Other servants obviously speak for us, including the nameless servants who lead away Gloucester and carry off their dead colleague's body at the end of act 3 of *King Lear*; Timon's Steward, as he foresees and laments his master's inevitable destruction; the Gentlewoman and Doctor in the last act of *Macbeth*, as they tremble before their knowledge of horror; and Enobarbus, in his commentary on his master and mistress.[57]

Shakespeare depicts his upper-class characters as dependent on their servants in any number of ways. Although we rarely see the undramatic facts of early modern life that were supported by servants, we frequently see servants delivering messages, running errands, and carrying out other orders. On occasion, we see servants performing actions that would do credit to a lady or gentleman. In *Henry V*, the Princess of France takes English lessons from Alice, her waiting-gentlewoman, who also interprets between Henry and the Princess (3.4, 5.2), while the nameless Boy who serves Pistol translates between English and French for his master and Monsieur Le Fer (4.4). Although it appears that some members of the English or French royalty and nobility are bilingual—or they would be unable to carry on the conversations necessary in 2.4 and 5.2—it is servants who are represented as knowledgeable when the clash of languages is foregrounded. Orsino sends servingmen to do his wooing for him, and Juliet sends her Nurse on errands to Romeo. Polonius sends Reynaldo to spy on Laertes. Oberon relies on Puck and Don John on Conrade and Borachio to accomplish their schemes, which perhaps suggests that employers' confidence in their servants is not always well placed. Some dependencies are more general; Thomas Moisan notes "Lucentio's clear intellectual dependence upon his servant Tranio."[58] Davy and his master, Justice Shallow, bear out Nicholas Ling's contention that "A crafty servant ruleth his master."[59] Lear needs Kent and the Fool, Othello becomes increasingly dependent on Iago, and Macbeth, toward the end of his play, seems to rely upon the mysterious Seyton.[60] Even Prospero, despite his power, seems dependent on both Ariel and Caliban.[61]

Probably the most servant-dependent of all Shakespeare's protagonists are Antony and Cleopatra. As a triumvir and a queen, they are always surrounded by servants, soldiers, and other followers.[62] A number of critics have commented on Antony's need to be surrounded by people to reinforce his sense of self, admire him, obey him, even reassure him that he exists, simply by looking at him.[63] That many of Antony's followers remain with him even after it is clear that his fortunes are waning suggests something about his character; as Charles Wells writes, "Only the most remarkable of men can inspire such allegiance."[64] In the end, however, Antony is deserted by all of his servants and must deal with his fall from greatness and its meaning alone except for Cleopatra, who seems rather more concerned with her grief than with Antony's dying.

Less attention seems to have been paid to Cleopatra's dependence on her servants, although it is much greater than Antony's and endures even beyond her death. Although Cleopatra is frequently discussed as the embodiment of "the East," the transcendent love goddess, the seductive destroyer of a great man, or as some combination of these, she seems not to have been much discussed as a mistress or employer of servants.[65] This oversight is odd, since Cleopatra, the only (legally) royal person in *Antony and Cleopatra*, is not only surrounded by servants but shares more scenes with servants than she does with Antony (who, sincerely or not, also describes himself as her servant, 1.3.70).[66] Servants are her confidantes, her informants, her tools, and her means of self-expression. Her interactions with servants—not exclusively those she employs, but others whom she can command or who offer her service, such as Enobarbus and Dolabella—do much to characterize her throughout the play.

Partly because she is a woman, but more, perhaps, because she is a queen, Cleopatra takes very little action. Even when she approaches Antony after his first defeat, she is led by Charmian and Eros, and must be repeatedly urged by them and Iras to speak to Antony, which she does only after ordering the servants to "stand by" and "sustain" her (3.11.25–45). Ordinarily, when she wants something done, she requires someone else to do it for her: "That Herod's head / I'll have; but how, when Antony is gone, / Through whom I might command it?" (3.3.4–6). Although Antony's temporary absence leaves her unable to fulfill her supposed desire for Herod's head, this statement also demonstrates her power: if Antony were present, she could command him. More often, though, she commands things to be done by servants. Some of the orders she gives are for trivial things (the ink and paper she orders at 1.5.68 and 79); others are given for their effect on her hearers, as when she orders her lace cut, or declaims, "Give me to drink mandragora" (1.3.71; 1.5.3); still others are significant, as when she orders her servants to help heave Antony aloft into her monument or arrange her suicide (4.15.30–31;[67] 5.2.191, 194–96, 280, 283). She expects things to be done for her, and they are; her passivity shows her power: she might say, like the biblical Centurion, "I say to this *man*, Go, and he goeth; and to another, Come, and he cometh; and to my servant, Do this, and he doeth *it*" (Authorized King James Version of the Bible, Matthew 8.9). Her most active scenes in the play occur when a servant appears to defy her.[68]

On the other hand, the need to retain the position of nearly unmoving mover requires Cleopatra to rely on others. Enobarbus's description of Cleopatra's barge, usually interpreted as showing the effect of her "magic," in fact suggests her need for servants to make her magic happen (2.2.196–223). She also needs servants to provide her with information, such as Antony's whereabouts and condition (1.2.83; 1.3.1–2; 1.5.40–55; 2.5.23–60; 4.15.6–9), whose fault the lovers' initial defeat in battle is (3.13.2–12), and Caesar's plans for her (5.2.197–203),[69] and to deliver her messages and otherwise do her bidding (1.2.88–90; 1.3.2–5; 4.14.22–34, 118–32; 5.1.52–68).

Cleopatra's servants perform many other functions, some predictable, some less so. She accepts both their flattery and their sympathy, but she also engages them in idle conversation and looks to them for companionship in amusements, at least when Antony is away (3.3.2–4, 43–44; 4.15.42; 1.5.9–17; 2.5.1–23). Charmian even apparently believes that she can get away with teasing her mistress (1.5.69–75). Cleopatra also uses her servants as an audience, and since she can command them and has no need to manipulate them, what she says to them is often much more reliable and representative of her true thoughts and feelings than what she says to Antony or Caesar. Although we see her teasing and manipulating Antony in act 1, she can appear lovesick before her servants in his absence (1.5.19–35, 56–64; 2.5.109–12, 117–21; 4.4.36–38).[70] She also uses her attendants as audience for commentary on how fallen majesty is treated, how the depth of her sorrow causes her to despise comfort, and how the earth's greatness is lost when Antony dies (3.13.38–40; 4.15.2–6, 61–70, 78–87).

Cleopatra's servants tend to tell her what she wants to hear, whereas Antony's followers and servants are more willing to tell him unpleasant truths, at least early in the play. After Cleopatra excuses the unfortunate messenger who brings her news of Antony's marriage to Octavia, she shows her dependence on her servants:

> *Cleopatra*
>   In praising Antony, I have dispraised Caesar.
> *Charmian*   Many times, madam.
> *Cleopatra*
>   I am paid for't now. Lead me from hence;
>   I faint. Oh, Iras, Charmian! 'Tis no matter.
>   Go to the fellow, good Alexas. Bid him
>   Report the feature of Octavia: her years,
>   Her inclination. Let him not leave out
>   The color of her hair. Bring me word quickly.
>   [*Exit Alexas.*]
>   Let him for ever go!—Let him not, Charmian.
>   Though he be painted one way like a Gorgon,
>   The other way's a Mars. [*To Mardian.*] Bid you Alexas
>   Bring me word how tall she is.—Pity me, Charmian,
>   But do not speak to me. Lead me to my chamber.
>   (2.5.109–21)

She concludes this scene by asking her servants for their physical support, their help in obtaining information, and their silent pity, all of which, presumably, they give her; her underlying trouble, however, is beyond any aid they can give.

When Antony rages at her after his defeat at Actium, Cleopatra frantically seeks help from her servants, and they offer it to her in the form of advice:

> *Cleopatra*
> Help me, my women! Oh, he's more mad
> Than Telamon for his shield; the boar of Thessaly
> Was never so embossed.
> *Charmian*   To th' monument,
> There lock yourself and send him word you are dead.
> The soul and body rive not more in parting
> Than greatness going off.
> *Cleopatra*   To th' monument!
> Mardian, go tell him I have slain myself.
> Say that the last I spoke was "Antony,"
> And word it, prithee, piteously. Hence, Mardian,
> And bring me how he takes my death. To th' monument!
>   (4.13.1–10)

This advice, of course, leads directly to Antony's suicide—although that was perhaps inevitable—and it may be that Shakespeare is attempting to relieve Cleopatra of some of the blame for the deception by making it her servant's idea. That Cleopatra is in a state of apparent panic is, perhaps, also intended to excuse her, although, ultimately, she must be held responsible. As queen, she should be the person to exercise good judgment, and if she has become excessively dependent on her servants, that may be understandable, but it is not really, by early modern standards for authority, excusable.

Cleopatra's interactions with Charmian and Iras following Antony's death show their mutual love and concern. After her women revive her from her faint and after she testifies to her love for Antony, Cleopatra turns her attention to Charmian and Iras:

>   How do you, women?
> What, what, good cheer! Why, how now, Charmian?
> My noble girls! Ah, women, women! Look,
> Our lamp is spent, it's out. Good sirs, take heart.
> We'll bury him; and then, what's brave, what's noble,
> Let's do't after the high Roman fashion,
> And make death proud to take us. Come, away,
> This case of that huge spirit now is cold.
> Ah, women, women! Come. We have no friend
> But resolution, and the briefest end.
>   (4.15.82–91)

Although these lines express concern for her women, they also seem to suggest that Cleopatra assumes that Iras and Charmian will accompany her into "the secret house of death," as, in fact, they do without demur or discussion.[71] Cleopatra may be urging Iras to do so by including her in the fate Cleopatra foresees for them if they live—"Thou an Egyptian puppet shall be shown / In Rome as well as I"—and by praising Iras's resolution not to see such humiliation (5.2.208–26). Even if she is attempting manipulation, though, it is arguable whether she does so for selfish motives or because she believes that "the briefest end" is best for her women as well as for herself.

Cleopatra's fond leaving-taking of her ladies, Iras's death (whatever its cause, but especially if, as seems probable, it is the result of grief), and Charmian's running commentary as Cleopatra prepares for death all affirm the affection between Cleopatra and the remaining characters who presumably know her best. This love indeed appears stronger than death, since Charmian continues to serve Cleopatra even after her mistress's death, praising her, closing her eyes, and straightening her crown (314–19).[72] She then follows her dead mistress and in her final speech defends her queen's decision to die (326–327). Iras and Charmian's deaths testify to Cleopatra's worth more strongly, perhaps, than anything else in the play.

Jonathan Gil Harris notes "the gulf that separates Roman (mis)characterizations of [Cleopatra] and the 'real' Cleopatra presented to us in, for example, her exchanges with Mardian, Charmian, and Iras."[73] Since at least two Romans, Enobarbus and Dolabella, serve and praise Cleopatra, however, the Roman-Egyptian dichotomy is clearly not absolute. Elizabeth Story Donno notices that the Roman view of Cleopatra is not monolithic: "It is left to others—Philo, Pompey, Scarus, and especially *Antony himself*—to present the unflattering side of Cleopatra's nature. For Enobarbus, she is simply a 'wonderful piece of work.'"[74] Since even Caesar praises Cleopatra after she is safely dead, and Antony's expressions about her run the gamut, there is also no simple distinction to be made between perceptions of Cleopatra in terms of employers and servants, but Cleopatra's interactions with those who serve her do suggest different aspects of her character. Antony and Caesar, those she cannot command (except, in Antony's case, insofar as he cedes that power to her), she tries to manipulate. Servants, whom she can command, allow her to be honest, although her honesty may express less-than-admirable qualities. Servants allow her to show her power as queen and create her magical effects; the corollary, however, is that she is dependent upon her servants: without their service, her title becomes meaningless and she is essentially powerless. When defied by a servant, even when this defiance is in the service of truth, she becomes active, but her activity only ineffectually displaces her anger at Antony, Caesar, and herself onto someone helpless. Her dependence on her servants shows her, at various points in the play, weak, passive, ill-advised, and lacking in self-control and magnanimity. At the end of the play, however, Cleopatra is able to use her dependence on servants to make an ass of Caesar and show herself like a queen, an enchantress, and "a lass unparalleled" (315).

Although Shakespeare's drama rarely suggests an upper-class vulnerability to loss of power, it depicts employers' dependence on and vulnerability to their servants. The plays frequently imply that servants are necessary for far more than menial services and may be their employers' superiors even in such sophisticated artistic pursuits as music and poetry. Given that Shakespeare was himself at least technically defined as a servant, it should not be surprising that his work often represents employers as mere consumers of culture or inept amateurs, while their servants, like Shakespeare himself, are frequently artists and thorough-going professionals, or that it is faithful service that allows great persons to establish and maintain that greatness.

4

"The mere word's a slave": Language and Service

WHAT WE CALL "SHAKESPEARE" CONSISTS PRIMARILY OF THE LAN-
guage of Shakespeare's characters, and that language is imbued
with metaphors of service. Insofar as language shapes the characters' reality and our perceptions of the plays, all of these plays
exist in a world largely defined by the idea of service.[1] Many of
the characters are themselves largely defined in terms of employer-servant relationships: they employ servants, or they are
servants, or sometimes both. Their relationships toward higher
powers are defined in terms of service: like the fallen soldiers
commemorated by the war memorials so common in English
towns, they serve (among many other entities) God, king, country, and honor. Service, however, is not confined to the human
realm. Anything from a body part to an abstraction to an inanimate object can be discussed as serving a character or even described as a servant; abstractions can also be described as
things to be served. Service is so prevalent a concept and metaphor that it is also the occasion of a good deal of wordplay
throughout the canon.

As Philip the Bastard notes, much talk about service is merely
the common coin of "worshipful society":

> "My dear sir,"
> Thus, leaning on mine elbow, I begin,
> "I shall beseech you"—that is Question now;
> And then comes answer like an Absey book:
> "O, sir," says Answer, "at your best command;
> At your employment; at your service, sir."
> "No sir," says Question, "I, sweet sir, at yours. . . ."
> (*King John* 1.1.205, 193–99)

The Countess of Rossillion takes a similarly realistic view of protestations of service:

> *First Lord*   We serve you, madam,
>> In that and all your worthiest affairs.
>
> *Countess*
>> Not so, but as we change our courtesies.
>
> <div align="right">(<i>All's Well</i> 3.2.108–10)</div>

Olivia goes further, objecting when the mannerly "Cesario" calls "himself" her servant, pointing out that "Cesario" is Orsino's servant *(Twelfth Night* 3.1.97–99). Despite Olivia's rather literal-minded objection, however, mannerly protestations of service in the plays—as when "Cesario" and Sir Andrew Aguecheek describe themselves as each other's servants *(Twelfth Night* 3.1.71–73)—if meaningless, are also depicted as harmless and often amusing, but the expectations founded on a belief in true service can have serious consequences. This is perhaps best illustrated in *Timon of Athens;* in the play's first scene, the Poet tells the Painter,

> You see how all conditions, how all minds,
> As well of glib and slippery creatures as
> Of grave and austere quality, tender down
> Their services to Lord Timon.
>
> (1.1.56–59)

In the next scene, Ventidius offers to return Timon's talents "doubled with thanks and service" and Alcibiades tells Timon, "My heart is ever at your service, my lord" (1.2.6–7, 75). Near the end of the play, the Poet and the Painter, having heard that Timon has gold, go to the forest, ostensibly to offer Timon their "service" (5.1.71, 74). Since few characters in the play are faithful to Timon, despite their protestations, one is almost inclined to sympathize with Apemantus when he describes the courtesies exchanged between Timon and his guests as merely "serving of becks and jutting-out of bums" (1.2.233). Timon has believed in an ideal of service for love, and the destruction of that ideal by the faithlessness he discovers in those he regarded as his friends and dependents destroys him.

Polite offers of service may be the most common use of the word throughout the plays, but they are not usually the most serious: those, generally, would be the references to the service owed by subjects to their sovereigns, which occur frequently and with a number of implications.[2] The most conventional concept—that all subjects owe unquestioning duty to the monarch—is exemplified in Feeble's declaration that "No man is too good to serve's prince" (2 *Henry IV* 3.2.237–38). Although Feeble's name (as, presumably, his appearance) suggests that he is a comic character, his brave declaration contrasts him with his draft-dodging colleagues, as well as with the corrupt and cowardly Sir John Falstaff, and touches him with nobility.[3] A more reciprocal relation is suggested in the Duke of Gloucester's statement to Queen Elizabeth: "First, madam, I entreat true peace of you, / Which I will purchase with my duteous service" (*Richard III* 2.1.63–64). Since we already know Richard's character and his feelings about the queen, we also know that this reasonable-sounding statement is mere hypocrisy. And while the soldiers Bates and Williams "determine to fight lustily for" their king, they insist that if they serve him in what ultimately proves to be a bad cause, they are absolved of guilt because they are only doing their duty, while "the King himself hath a heavy reckoning to make" (*Henry V* 4.1.189, 134–35). The soldiers' discussion of their duty depicts them as thoughtful and properly concerned with the condition of their souls, as well as brave and loyal; furthermore, their consideration of their service and its consequences has a profound effect on King Henry, who remembers the crime that brought his family to the throne and earnestly prays to God that He will not avenge the deposition and murder of Richard II on the morrow.

The immediate service that Henry V requires of Bates, Williams, and their fellows on St. Crispin's Day, of course, is military. Both military affairs in general and the actions of soldiers are referred to as "service" throughout the canon.[4] Military institutions and activities being among the relatively few fields of human action that have retained the term "service," modern audiences do not find it surprising that Shakespeare's great military characters frequently refer to themselves as "servants." What or whom they serve, however, and how they serve, varies from play to play. When Lord Talbot describes himself as "Servant in arms to Harry King of England" (1 *Henry VI* 4.2.4), he is identifying himself as part of the traditional hierarchy of personal service, with the monarch as its earthly head. Similarly, the Duke of York's last words are "Commend my service to my sovereign" (*Henry V* 4.6.23).[5] Soldiers in the service of Rome seem to find her a difficult mistress and are much less likely to remain faithful than are the soldiers who identify themselves as the personal servants of a monarch. Charles Wells quotes Paul Cantor as stating that "with the transition from Republic to Empire, we see, in the Roman plays, 'the relationship of master and servant replace the relationship of city and citizen . . . [putting] a new emphasis on personal fidelity as a virtue.'"⁶ That is indeed what we would expect to see, but it is actually hard to see that such a change takes place. Titus Andronicus sees himself and his sons as serving Rome, rather than a particular emperor (*Titus* 1.1.193–97, 353–54; 3.1.72–80); in fact, he becomes the enemy of the emperor. Although the conspirators in *Julius Caesar* suggest that the cause they serve is "Rome," they in fact seem more concerned that they not become servants of Caesar (1.2.79–175; 3.2.13–33). The older Antony identifies himself as serving neither Rome nor Octavius Caesar, but says to Cleopatra, "I go from hence / Thy soldier, servant, making peace or war / As thou affects" (1.3.69–71);⁷ he himself dies deserted by those who served him. Finally, Coriolanus, who—in a Republican Rome—should exemplify the citizen, continually identifies himself as a servant and is so described by others.⁸

Othello's penultimate speech links his personal tragedy with violence and service. He begins his final self-justification by declaring, "I have done the state some service, and they know't" (5.2.349). As a mercenary general, he has performed this service by enacting violence on the enemies of Venice. He goes on to speak of his personal tragedy, but his conclusion, in addition to setting the stage for his "bloody period," seeks to remind his hearers of the one aspect of his life of which he remains proud:

> Set you down this;
> And say besides that in Aleppo once,
> Where a malignant and a turbaned Turk
> Beat a Venetian and traduced the state,
> I took by th' throat the circumcisèd dog
> And smote him, thus.
>
> (361–66)

Othello seems to be suggesting that his killing of the Turk was not merely a personal reaction to injustice, but another form of loyal service to Venice and that his violence is another part of his self-justification. Despite his acknowledged folly and sin on a personal level, on a professional level he remains the loyal servant of the Venetian state, as evidenced by his violence in defense of its citizens and national honor. He dies a self-confessed murderer, albeit, he insists, an "honorable" one, but he wants his reputation as a good servant remembered and reported as well.⁹

One of the major human enterprises referred to as service

throughout the plays is love. Most traditionally, romantic love is envisioned as a form of service performed by a male servant-lover for his beloved lady, although other equations of love with service also occur.[10] Lovers who define themselves as servants are particularly common in some of the earlier comedies.[11] In *The Two Gentlemen of Verona,* Sylvia and her admirers refer to her as the "mistress" and her lovers as her "servants" (2.4.1–8, 35, 98–111, 116). Even in serious situations, as when Proteus, having rescued Sylvia from the outlaws, seeks a reward, the pretence of a mistress-servant relationship is maintained:

> Madam, this service I have done for you—
> Though you respect not aught your servant doth—
> To hazard life and rescue you from him
> That would have forced your honor and your love:
> Vouchsafe me for my meed but one fair look;
> A smaller boon than this I cannot beg,
> And less than this, I am sure, you cannot give.
>
> (5.4.19–25)[12]

The young lovers in *Love's Labor's Lost* maintain the same poses: Rosaline says that if she knew Berowne were really in love with her, she would make him "shape his service wholly to my hests"; echoing the lords they speak of, Maria says, "Dumaine was at my service" and refers to him as "my servant," while Katharine says that "Longaville was for my service born" (5.2.65, 277–78, 285). At the end of the play, the princess and her ladies impose services on their lovers. Dumaine promises Katharine, "I'll serve thee true and faithfully till [the expiration of the twelvemonth and a day]" and Berowne demands of Rosaline, "Mistress, look on me . . . Impose some service on me for thy love" (5.2.821, 827, 830). *Troilus and Cressida* also follows these conventions of courtly love: Diomedes says to Cressida, "to Diomed / You shall be mistress, and command him wholly"; however, Troilus objects that Diomedes is "unworthy to be called her servant" (4.4.119–20, 125). Diomedes later tells his servant, "commend my service to [Cressida's] beauty" (5.5.3). Even the appalling Bertram, while trying to seduce Diana, declares, "I love thee / By love's own sweet constraint and will forever / Do thee all rights of service," while Lafew says of Bertram's wife that her "dear perfection hearts that scorned to serve / Humbly called mistress" (*All's Well* 4.2.15–17; 5.3.18–19). The convention, however, is not limited to comedies. Charles the Dauphin says to

Joan la Pucelle, "Let me thy servant and not sovereign be," while Richard, Duke of Gloucester, having vowed his love for Lady Anne, calls himself her "poor devoted servant" (*1 Henry VI* 1.2.111; *Richard III* 1.2.209). Chiron declares himself "as able and as fit as [Demetrius] / To serve, and to deserve my mistress' grace" (*Titus* 2.1.33–34), though this idea of serving a mistress rapidly turns into a plan to rape Lavinia.

Shakespeare, however, does not hesitate to play with the convention of mistresses and their male servant-lovers. Although Ferdinand, who refers to Miranda as his "sweet mistress" and addresses her as "most dear mistress" and "noble mistress" (*Tempest* 3.1.11, 21, 33), may seem the epitome of the courtly lover, he does not actually serve his mistress; Prospero sets him to moving logs simply as a way of keeping the two lovers apart and testing Ferdinand's patience and endurance. Both young people pass the test with honors (Miranda, interestingly, by disobeying Prospero), but carrying logs from one place to another is a peculiar task for a lover and one that is hard to see as a tribute to the beloved mistress.[13] However, Miranda represents a more obvious change in the traditional pattern of service in love when she declares that she intends to be Ferdinand's servant (85), thus transforming the mistress to a master and reversing the gender of the servant. Occasionally, female characters such as Julia and Viola actually disguise themselves and serve men they love. More often, women simply declare that they are or intend to be servants of men; although these statements are usually made in passing and seem innocent, such statements are often made by women who are represented as strong-willed and evil, including Margaret of Anjou, Helen of Troy, and Goneril (*1 Henry VI* 5.3.177–78; *Troilus* 3.1.155; *Lear* 4.6.273). The Shakespearean woman most insistent upon defining herself as the servant to the man she loves, however, is the humble but resolute Helena, who says of Bertram, "My master, my dear lord he is, and I / His servant live and will his vassal die" before their marriage and refers to him as "My dearest master" afterward (*All's Well* 1.3.155–56; 3.4.9). Addressing Bertram, she is even more subservient, saying, "I dare not say I take you, but I give / Me and my service, ever whilst I live, / Into your guiding power" and "Sir, I can nothing say / But that I am your most obedient servant" (2.3.102–4; 2.5.72–73). This abasement presumably stems from the class difference between the Count of Rossillion and a poor physician's daughter; it may also be expected to remove some of the curse from a woman who shows herself utterly determined to get what she wants, even when she knows that he does not want her. The only general conclusion to be derived seems to be that when women serve men or declare themselves willing to do so, something odd is to be expected.

Love may also motivate characters to perform—or at least propose—services other than those normally expected between lovers or spouses. Antonio so loves Sebastian that he volunteers to become his servant, while Sir Toby Belch is so taken with Maria's trick on Malvolio that he offers to become her bondslave (*Twelfth Night* 2.1.33–34; 2.5.186–87). Less hyperbolically, Helena finds a declared servant in her landlady:

> *Widow*   Gentle madam,
> You never had a servant to whose trust
> Your business was more welcome.
> *Helena*   Nor you, mistress,
> Ever a friend whose thoughts more truly labor
> To recompense your love.
>
> (*All's Well* 4.4.14–18)

The suggestion in this passage is that Helena, who has found no love in her husband, has formed a bond of affection with the Widow. Similarly, King Lear, having been rejected by his two eldest daughters, finds that the Earl of Kent "in disguise / Followed his enemy king and did him service / Improper for a slave" (*King Lear* 5.3.223–25). Gratitude, rather than love, can sometimes lead to professions of service, as when Titus promises Tamora, disguised as "Revenge," that if she does him "some service," by killing "Rape" and "Murder" (the disguised Chiron and Demetrius), he will act as her "wagoner," provide her with horses, and later "dismount, and by [her] wagon wheel / Trot like a servile footman all day long" (*Titus* 5.2.44–55). Paulina tells the Lords who have expressed horror at her announcement that Hermione is dead:

> I say she's dead. I'll swear't. If word nor oath
> Prevail not, go and see. If you can bring
> Tincture or luster in her lip, her eye,
> Heat outwardly or breath within, I'll serve you
> As I would do the gods.
>
> (*Winter's Tale* 3.2.203–7)

These hyperbolic offers of service are perhaps made so extreme because they are intended to conceal and deceive. Titus recognizes Tamora despite her disguise, and Paulina presumably knows that Hermione is alive, but wishes to conceal that knowledge. For these two upper-class characters, offering service is apparently a kind of ultimate bluff, even though both expect their hearers to reject the offers made in their speeches. It is perhaps easier to accept the desperate Mariana's offer to Isabella that if she will kneel to plead for Angelo's life, "I'll lend you all my life to do you service," although, as the Duke points out, the injury Isabella believes Angelo has done her is so great that it is "against all sense" to think she could forgive him (*Measure* 5.1.440–41). Miraculously, however, she does show mercy to the man she believes has wronged her, although there is no indication that Mariana's offer of service has any influence upon her decision.

"Serve" and "service" can also have sexual meanings.[14] Falstaff constructs an elaborate, double-entendre-laden analogy between sex and military service when talking to Doll Tearsheet: "to serve bravely is to come halting off, you know; to come off the breach with his pike bent bravely, and to surgery bravely; to venture upon the charged chambers bravely—" (2 *Henry IV* 2.4.49–53). Falstaff's intention is to irritate Doll, which he succeeds in doing, and the way he does it—by finding witty parallels between two kinds of "service"—is typical of his humor. More directly, Edgar, in his disguise as a former servingman, claims that he "served the lust of my mistress' heart" and Aaron advises Chiron and Demetrius to "serve [their] lust" on Lavinia; later, Demetrius says, "I would we had a thousand Roman dames / At such a bay, by turn to serve our lust" (*Lear* 3.4.85–86; *Titus* 2.1.130; 4.2.41–42). Presented with Marina, Lysimachus says, "Faith, she would serve after a long voyage at sea" (*Pericles* 4.6.43–44). These are simply straightforward and unpleasant suggestions that lust is an appetite that insists upon being served. Other statements, such as Goneril's to Edmund—"To thee a woman's services are due / My fool usurps my body"—or Bertram's to Diana—"I love thee / By love's own sweet constraint and will forever / Do thee all rights of service" (*Lear* 4.2.27–28; *All's Well* 4.2.15–17)—while carrying a sexual suggestion, are less coarse.

The association of sex and service generally seems to occur in deplorable circumstances, such as rape, seduction, and adultery, as the examples above suggest. Possibly this is the case because of the association of "service" and prostitution. In *Measure for Measure*, for example, Pompey Bum addresses Mistress Overdone as "You that have worn your eyes almost out in the service" and Lucio says that the Duke "knew the service" (1.2.109–10; 3.2.116–17). As J. W. Lever notes of these passages, Pompey and Lucio suggest that "Prostitution is 'the service' as if it were a public service maintained for the good of the state."[15] Gower also refers to Marina's "unholy service" in the brothel (*Pericles* 4.4.50).[16]

"Service" also commonly occurs in other unsavory contexts. Ironically, it is often associated with traitors, who have, by definition, rejected the object of their proper service. Calchas asks the Greek leaders to ransom his daughter in recompense for "the service I have done you" (*Troilus* 3.3.1). Nicanor says that his "services are . . . against" the Romans (*Coriolanus* 4.3.4–5). Similarly, Edmund, false to his father, brother, and king, is praised by Oswald for his "loyal service" to Cornwall and his allies (*Lear* 4.2.7). Revenge may also be described as service; Coriolanus, in fact, links the two words, offering his "revengeful services" to Aufidius and the Volscians (*Coriolanus* 4.5.94). Coriolanus, of course, is a notoriously blunt fellow; other characters imply revenge without actually using the word. This can be done in comic mode, as when Mrs. Ford asks Mrs. Page, "Shall we tell our husbands how we have served [Falstaff]?" or in more serious circumstances, as when the Earl of Warwick threatens the Duke of Suffolk, "Unworthy though thou art, I'll cope with thee / And do some service to Duke Humphrey's ghost" (*Merry Wives* 4.2.200–201; *2 Henry VI* 3.2.230–31). Another blunt fellow, Philip the Bastard, also sees revenge as part of his function as a servant, and a part that survives the death of his master, King John:

> Art thou gone so? I do but stay behind
> To do the office for thee of revenge,
> And then my soul shall wait on thee to heaven,
> As it on earth hath been thy servant still.
> (*King John* 5.7.70–73)

Because service was such a controlling metaphor for Shakespeare's society, it was not applied only to the duties human beings owed to each other or God or the state. Virtually anyone or anything could be defined as serving virtually anyone or anything else. Animals, aspects of nature, actions, abstractions, and many other things were defined and described in terms of service. Even when such references seem mere conveniences, they are indicative of the extent to which the idea of service pervaded the culture of the period.[17] Often, however, such references are more than conveniences: they are a way of making connections where no obvious connections seem to exist, or a way of representing a hierarchy among elements that do not seem to have such a relationship. They are a way of allowing characters to elevate, explain, excuse, or execrate themselves or other characters.

Although it may seem degrading to human servants, the idea of animals as servants is one of the less surprising associations made by Shakespeare's characters. Since we still have animals working for us, though to a much smaller degree than did people in Shakespeare's society, and since we still refer, for example, to a dog's "master," this association is not too distant from our own perception.[18] Thus, though we recognize the anthropomorphizing of the Constable's statement that "our steeds for present service neigh!" (*Henry V* 4.2.8), and Launce's definition of his relationship with his dog Crab as that of master and servant (*T.G.V.* 4.4.1–2, 28–29), we also recognize that these characters are simply describing domesticated animals in terms of a familiar domestic relationship (although Crab is certainly a most unsatisfactory servant). Even when Macbeth describes a wild animal as a servant in stating that the wolf is the "sentinel" of "withered murder" (*Macbeth* 2.1.53–54), the association is obviously appropriate.[19]

Other references, however, are effective because of their apparent inappropriateness, as when Antigonus addresses the infant Perdita:

> Some powerful spirit instruct the kites and ravens
> To be thy nurses! Wolves and bears, they say,
> Casting their savageness aside, have done
> Like offices of pity.
>
> (*Winter's Tale* 2.3.186–89)

A baby whose only hope of nurturance depends upon fierce, predatory animals acting as her nurses is obviously in desperate circumstances, yet the possible service of these animals, as Antigonus recognizes, seems to be Perdita's only hope, since her own father has become more savage than any beast. One of the most powerful associations of animals with service is Romeo's description of worms as Juliet's "chambermaids" (*Romeo* 5.3.109). Because he believes her to be dead and resting in her final chamber, the metaphor is apt, but the dreadful difference in the attendance to be expected from these "chambermaids" and ordinary ones brings home the horror of death and decay as few other statements could.

The preceding examples are not directly derogatory toward human servants, but people can be equated with animals that serve. Brutus tells Sicinius that in order to turn the plebeians against Coriolanus, the tribunes must tell them that Coriolanus would like nothing better than to turn the people into animals that are rewarded only for their service:

> We must suggest the people in what hatred
> He still hath held them; that to 's power he would
> Have made them mules, silenced their pleaders, and
> Dispropertied their freedoms, holding them
> In human action and capacity
> Of no more soul nor fitness for the world
> Than camels in their war, who have their provand
> Only for bearing burdens, and sore blows
> For sinking under them.
>
> (*Coriolanus* 2.1.244–52)

Although we never actually hear the tribunes make this accusation to the people, it is obviously a more powerful metaphor than even to accuse Coriolanus of wishing to enslave the plebeians. Slaves are human; mules and camels are drudges even in the animal world, and to suggest that this is how Coriolanus perceives the plebeians and how he would treat them is obviously an effective argument against granting him power.

Since not only human beings and animals, but all of nature is part of one great pattern created by God, all parts of creation can be seen as performing their orderly functions in a grand hierarchy.[20] This idea is most notably stated by Ulysses in his famous speech on degree, which includes lines suggesting that even celestial objects observe "office":

> The heavens themselves, the planets, and this center
> Observe degree, priority, and place,
> Insisture, course, proportion, season, form,
> Office, and custom, in all line of order.
>
> (*Troilus* 1.3.85–88)

Given the assumption of hierarchy as extending throughout nature, it is understandable that aspects of nature are conceived of as servants; thus King Henry refers to sleep as "Nature's soft nurse" (2 *Henry IV* 3.1.6), Lear describes lightning flashes as

"Vaunt-couriers of oak-cleaving thunderbolts" (*Lear* 3.2.5), and Romeo describes the lark as "the herald of the morn" (*Romeo* 3.5.6). On the other hand, natural phenomena are sometimes described as serving human beings. The morning after their wedding night, Juliet, not wanting Romeo to leave, projects her love for him onto Nature, telling him that the light they see is "some meteor that the sun exhaled / To be to thee this night a torchbearer / And light thee on thy way to Mantua" (*Romeo* 3.5.13–15). Descriptions of natural objects serving human beings may be used to suggest that these people are righteous or powerful, as when Troilus says, "The seas and winds, old wranglers, took a truce, / And did [Paris] service" (*Troilus* 2.2.75–76), or the Messenger states that "Menecrates and Menas, famous pirates, / Makes the sea serve them" (*Antony* 1.4.49–50).

Such descriptions of natural phenomena as servants to people are not necessarily flattering to the characters referenced, however; when, for example, Cleopatra calls dung "the beggar's nurse and Caesar's" (*Antony* 5.2.7–8), the effect is not complimentary to Caesar. Timon refers to gold as "this yellow slave," but the effects he attributes to this "slave" are entirely negative; later in this scene, Timon declares that "man" is gold's "slave" (*Timon* 4.3.34–45, 395). In a more naturalistic vein, Apemantus points out that such natural objects as the air, trees, water, and animals will not act as Timon's servants (*Timon* 4.3.223–33). This is particularly ironic, of course, since in the first scene, the Poet and the Painter have discussed how all human beings in Athens serve Timon (1.1.56–99). While the idea of various aspects of nature serving people is not surprising, Edmund's declaration— "Thou, Nature, art my goddess; to thy law / My services are bound" (*King Lear* 1.2.1–2)—is clearly intended to be shocking, since this vow of loyalty is also a denial of service to such proper subjects as God, king, and virtue.[21]

Man-made objects, such as a gown or coat may also be described in terms of the service they have seen or can perform (*T.G.V.* 4.4.160–62; *Winter's Tale* 4.3.66–67).[22] Camillo describes the possibility of anchors doing good service for Florizel and Perdita (*Winter's Tale* 4.4.573–75). Other references to inanimate objects as serving are more meaningful, as when Titus says that, because Lucius's napkin is wet with its owner's tears, it "Can do no service on [Lavinia's] sorrowful cheeks," or when Timon's servant Servilius describes the change in his master's fortunes by a change in the service done by his doors: "Now his friends are dead, / Doors that were ne'er acquainted with their wards /

Many a bounteous year must be employed / Now to guard sure their master" (*Titus* 3.1.146–47; *Timon* 3.3.38–41). Some objects are described as specific kinds of servants, as when Egeus describes "bracelets of [a lover's] hair, rings, gauds, conceits, / Knacks, trifles, nosegays, sweetmeats" as "messengers" (*Dream* 1.1.33–34). Descriptions in terms of service may seek to establish an emotional connection, as when Bolingbroke describes England as not only his "mother" but also his "nurse" (*Richard II* 1.3.307) or when Queen Elizabeth addresses the Tower as a "rude ragged nurse" which she hopes will "use [her] babies well" (*Richard III* 4.1.101–2).

Perhaps because war was a common and honored type of service, weapons are particularly likely to be described as servants or at least as serving. Such different characters as Friar Laurence and Ulysses refer to swords as lacking their masters, while King Henry IV and Leontes refer to knives having masters (*Romeo* 5.3.142; *Troilus* 1.3.76; *1 Henry IV* 1.1.17–18; *Winter's Tale* 1.2.156–57). King Philip describes cannon balls as "messengers of war," while Helena addresses bullets as "leaden messengers" (*John* 2.1.260; *All's Well* 3.2.109–12). Edward, Earl of March, having wondered if his and his brother Richard's "words will serve," is answered by Richard: "And if words will not, then our weapons shall" (*2 Henry VI* 5.1.139–40). A servant at Pompey's banquet uses a metaphor of a weapon incapable of serving to describe Lepidus's inadequacy: "Why, this it is to have a name in great men's fellowship. I had as lief have a reed that will do me no service as a partisan I could not heave" (*Antony* 2.7.11–13).

One common way of identifying people as servants is to refer to them as wearing livery, although not all references to livery refer to service, since the word may mean simply a distinctive form of dress (*Dream* 1.1.70; 2.1.111–14) or, as it used several times with regard to Bolingbroke, inheritance (*Richard II* 2.1.202–4; 2.3.129; *1 Henry IV* 4.3.62–67). Many references to livery demonstrate the poverty or prodigality of servants' employers (*2 Henry IV* 5.5.10–13; *T.G.V.* 2.4.41–44; *Merchant* 2.2.103–5; *Henry VIII* 1.1.22–23). Other references are more significant: Jack Cade uses livery to represent both fraternity and subjection, promising his followers that, when he is king, he will "apparel them all in one livery, that they may agree like brothers and worship me their lord" (*2 Henry VI* 4.2.73–74). When Prospero alludes to Caliban, Stephano, and Trinculo as wearing livery—"Mark but the badges of these men, my lords, / Then say if they be true" (*Tempest* 5.1.270–71)—he is presumably alluding not to their real badges denoting service, but to the stolen clothing they are wearing. They have removed or covered up their true livery, but this is a venial sin compared to their plan to murder Prospero and become rulers of the island. The falsity of their attire symbolizes their evil intentions and rejection of their proper role as servants.

"Livery" can also refer to characteristics other than clothing that represent a person's service to an abstraction: Lafew comments that "A scar nobly got, or a noble scar, is a good livery of honor," while Isabella says that Angelo's supposed virtue is "the cunning livery of hell" (All's Well 4.5.99–100; Measure 3.1.9). Claudius refers to youth's livery, which he contrasts with the more sober dress of "settled age"; his nephew states that "the stamp of one defect" in a man may be "nature's livery" (Hamlet 4.7.78–82; 1.4.31–32). Hamlet's second reference to livery seems not to have been interpreted as servants' livery, but his statement that "the monster custom" gives "a frock or livery" to both bad habits and "actions fair and good" suggests that custom is a kind of Janus-faced master whose service, for good or evil, becomes easier the longer it is practiced (3.4.168–72).

Actions are also characterized as serving, as when the king tells Helena that his "performance" will serve her "will," or when Antony excuses his departure to Cleopatra by claiming that "The strong necessity of time commands / Our services awhile" (All's Well 2.1.204; Antony 1.3.42–43). Macbeth declares his devotion to Duncan by describing service as its own reward and his duties as Duncan's servants:

> The service and the loyalty I owe,
> In doing it pays itself. Your Highness' part
> Is to receive our duties; and our duties
> Are to your throne and state children and servants,
> Which do but what they should by doing everything
> Safe toward your love and honor.
>
> (Macbeth 1.4.22–27)

Troilus also connects actions and service, though in a very different way, in his explanation to Cressida: "This is the monstrosity in love, lady, that the will is infinite, and the execution confined, that the desire is boundless and the act a slave to limit" (Troilus 3.2.80–82). In contrast to Macbeth's conception of actions as ideal, self-rewarding servants, Troilus's "act" is a poor slave, unable to perform the behests of unfettered will and desire.

Shakespeare's characters often describe words or speech as "serving" in the sense of "being sufficient" (*Richard III* 3.5.62–63; *Coriolanus* 3.2.98–99). A comic elaboration of this meaning of "serve" is Lavatch's "answer that will serve all men" (*All's Well* 2.2.13); a serious one is Canidius's comment that Caesar "shakes off" Antony's "offers / Which serve not for [Caesar's] vantage" (*Antony* 3.7.33–34). A more direct description of speech as performing a useful function is Sebastian's statement that Antonio's "counsel now might do me golden service" (*Twelfth Night* 4.3.8). Characters may also describe words or speech as base servants in order to change other characters' attitudes, as when the king tells Bertram that Helena's lack of "honor" is no bar to marrying her, because "the mere word's a slave" (*All's Well* 2.3.137), or when Richard III urges Ratcliffe not to dwell on news of allies' betrayals, since "fearful commenting / Is leaden servitor to dull delay" (*Richard III* 4.3.51–52).[23] Images of service are used to make language more vivid: phrases may be described as acting like servants, as in Lady Macbeth's "Letting 'I dare not' wait upon 'I would'" (*Macbeth* 1.7.45); rather than saying "let us talk seriously," Celia uses the image of servants dismissed from their positions: "But, turning these jests out of service, let us talk in good earnest" (*A.Y.L.* 1.3.25–26). Written language may also be described in terms of service: Proteus refers to Julia's handwriting as "the agent of her heart" (*T.G.V.* 1.3.46); Benvolio refers to a "letter's master" (*Romeo* 2.4.11); and Hamlet offers an interesting insight into class prejudice against legible handwriting:

> I once did hold it, as our statists do,
> A baseness to write fair, and labored much
> How to forget that learning, but, sir, now
> It did me yeoman's service.
>
> (*Hamlet* 5.2.33–36)

Much less common are sentiments such as Queen Elizabeth's line, "And make me die the thrall of Margaret's curse" (*Richard III* 4.1.45), which suggests that she is enslaved by the older woman's language.

Although the most famous Shakespearean statement of body parts as serving is Menenius's "belly fable" (*Coriolanus* 1.1.94–153), the service Menenius describes is ostensibly that of varied members serving a commonwealth, rather than any hierarchical employer-servant relationship. Some later lines, "The service of the foot, / Being once gangrened, is not then respected / For what before it was" (3.1.315–17),[24] are more suggestive of an individual, specifically Coriolanus, as the servant of the commonwealth, and parallel Brutus's description of Antony as being "but a limb of Caesar" (*Caesar* 2.1.166). Although the tribune's description is intended to justify sacrificing Coriolanus for the good of his collective master and Brutus's description is intended to spare Antony as being a servant too negligible to kill, both statements make their points by defining men as mere body parts, insignificant compared to the bodies they serve.[25] Description of service being performed by individual body parts, rather than their possessors, is particularly typical of the Roman plays. Philo says that Antony's eyes "turn / The office and devotion of their view / Upon a tawny front," and Antony says to Caesar, "So the gods keep you / And make the hearts of Romans serve your ends!" (*Antony* 1.1.4–6; 3.2.36–37). Titus describes his service to Rome as if it were done by his hands alone:

> Give me a sword, I'll chop off my hands too,
> For they have fought for Rome, and all in vain;
> And they have nursed this woe in feeding life;
> In bootless prayer have they been held up,
> And they have served me to effectless use.
> Now all the service I require of them
> Is that the one will help to cut the other.
> 'Tis well, Lavinia, that thou hast no hands;
> For hands to do Rome service is but vain.
>
> (*Titus* 3.1.72–80)

Titus describes his hands as servants, which he commands and which have done service for him as well as for Rome, but his language suggests that they are somehow separate from him even before he literally severs one of them. He blames his hands for sustaining his life and for failing to serve him effectually, and proposes to punish these inadequate servants by chopping them off, although he admits he will need the help of one hand "to cut the other."[26]

References to body parts as servants, however, are not limited to the Roman plays. Prospero says that "these lords . . . scarce think / Their eyes do offices of truth" (*Tempest* 5.1.154–57). Tongues are also described in terms of service. Bertram suggests that his tongue is a particular kind of servant to his heart or feelings, saying of Lafew's daughter, "I stuck my choice upon her, ere my heart / Durst make too bold a herald of my tongue" (*All's Well* 5.3.46–47). Bolingbroke says that before he would withdraw his challenge to Mowbray, he would bite off and spit out his tongue, which he describes as "the slavish motive of recanting fear" (*Richard II* 1.1.193). While Bertram's statement is merely poetic description, Bolingbroke's suggests that withdrawing his challenge would be so ignoble that it could only be attributed to fear, an emotion he characterizes as servile, and that he would discard with contempt a part of his body that would so dishonor him by failing to serve him properly.[27]

Not only body parts, but expressions or effusions from the body can be defined in terms of service. Buckingham tells Richard that "ghastly looks / Are at my service, like enforcèd smiles" (*Richard III* 3.5.8–9). Salisbury says that "The color of the King doth come and go / Between his purpose and his conscience / Like heralds 'twixt two dreadful battles set" (*John* 4.2.76–78). The Countess of Rossillion describes a tear as a messenger (*All's Well* 1.3.148), and Julia expands this metaphor by naming a master for such servants, when she declares that Proteus's tears are "pure messengers sent from his heart" (*T.G.V.* 2.7.77). This description, however, contrasts with one provided earlier by her own waiting-woman. Julia has said that she is certain of Proteus's love because he has given her "A thousand oaths, an ocean of his tears, / And instances of infinite of love," but Lucetta has warned her that "All these are servants to deceitful men" (2.7.69–70, 72). Julia and Lucetta agree, therefore, that tears are servants, but their disagreement about the service being provided symbolizes their contrasting feelings about Proteus's trustworthiness.

Shakespeare's characters also mention more abstract human qualities, such as "reason," "stomach" (in the sense of "appetite" or "inclination"), "sense," and even "indiscretion" as serving them or other characters, and Iago ironically professes regret that he "[lacks] iniquity . . . to do [him] service" (*Measure* 5.1.67–70; *Shrew* 1.1.37–38; *Hamlet* 3.4.72–77; 5.2.8; *Othello* 1.2.3–4). In contrast, Laertes speaks to Ophelia of "The inward service of the mind and soul," as though the intellectual properties were comparable to religious service occurring within the "temple" of the body (*Hamlet* 1.3.12–13). More elaborate metaphors often convey more specific meanings. Bertram's last words to his mother as he takes leave of her express more dutifulness than he will ever show to her: "The best wishes that can be forged in your thoughts be servants to you!" (*All's Well* 1.1.75–76). The philosophical Player King, dubious about his wife's protestations against remarrying, remarks that "Purpose is but the slave to memory"; on the other hand, the pragmatic Lady Macbeth describes memory as "the warder of the brain" (*Hamlet* 3.2.186; *Macbeth* 1.7.66).[28] Juliet expresses her impatience over her Nurse's slowness in bringing news from Romeo by exclaiming, "Love's heralds should be thoughts" (*Romeo* 2.5.4). Valentine's verse letter describes his thoughts as his slaves, heralds, and servants to express not only his love for Sylvia but also his frustration at being unable to be with her, as his servant thoughts are (*T.G.V.* 3.1.140–49). Macbeth uses the idea of servitude to excuse what he describes as his and his wife's inadequate entertainment of Duncan: "Being unprepared / Our will became the servant to defect, / Which else should free have wrought" (*Macbeth* 2.1.17–19); if their will had been free of servitude, he suggests, their hospitality would have been much more bountiful.

Macbeth's statement clearly applies only to this particular situation, but other such metaphors of service, although lacking any explicit indication that they are situational, are clearly not intended as statements of the speaker's belief that a mental or emotional state invariably serves something else. For example, Edgar, on seeing the mad Lear bedecked with weeds, says, "The safer sense will ne'er accommodate / His master thus" (*Lear* 4.6.81–82). Presumably, the rational Edgar is not really suggesting that the body is the mind's master, but since the body is dressed in accordance with the mind's decisions, as the master is dressed by his servants, the metaphor, in this instance, determines the meaning. Finally, in a kind of grand summation of human qualities as servants, Florizel enumerates various possible aspects of humanity, physical, mental, and social, and dedicates them all to the service of his beloved Perdita:

> were I crowned the most imperial monarch,
> Thereof most worthy, were I the fairest youth
> That ever made eye swerve, had force and knowledge
> More than was ever man's, I would not prize them
> Without her love; for her, employ them all,
> Commend them and condemn them to her service,
> Or to their own perdition.
>
> (*Winter's Tale* 4.4.372–78)

For Florizel, a position bestowed upon him, his existence as "the fairest youth," and attributes he might possess, different as these are—and the somewhat elliptical syntax indicates Florizel's difficulty in marshalling his ideas—become a collective "them" to be dedicated to his mistress's service. The individual elements are subsumed under the general idea that everything Florizel can imagine being should serve Perdita.

Even abstractions are characterized as serving characters, although, since any abstraction will serve, not all such service is desirable. Richard II's queen addresses "mischance" as a messenger, saying, "O, thou thinkest / To serve me last, that I may longest keep / Thy sorrow in my breast"; in the following scene, her husband declares that by abdicating he has, among other things, made "sovereignty a slave" (*Richard II* 3.4.92, 94–96; 4.1.252). Although both king and queen suggest that they retain their roles of command, being served by mischance and enslaving sovereignty are not enviable powers. Both Richard and his queen continue to define themselves as recipients of service, although they may no longer be able to choose their servants; their statements suggest their belief that fortune continues to serve monarchs, although ill fortune may replace good fortune in the role. Gloucester's statement that "the superfluous and lust-dieted man . . . slaves [the heavens'] ordinance" (*Lear* 4.1.66–67) suggests a different type of unfortunate service: evil men have the power to enslave even the heavens' laws, although such power is obviously deplorable.

More common are statements that favorable abstractions serve characters or wishes that they may do so. To describe Timon's wealth and generosity, the Second Lord says, "Plutus, the god of gold, / Is but [Timon's] steward" (*Timon* 1.1.289–90). To emphasize his authority, King Henry IV declares, not that he himself will punish rebellion, but that punishments are among his servants, saying that if Hotspur "will not yield, / Rebuke and dread correction wait on us, / And they shall do their office" (*1 Henry IV* 5.1.110–12). Archbishop Cranmer prophesies of the infant Elizabeth and her successor: "Peace, plenty, love, truth, terror, / That were the servants to this chosen infant, / Shall then be his, and like a vine grow to him" (*Henry VIII* 5.5.48–50).

Wishes for profitable service by abstractions tend to occur, as one might expect, in doubtful situations, as when a kingdom, a battle, or a life may be lost unless some power intervenes. When the newly proclaimed King Edward IV tells Montgomery and his other followers, "If fortune serve me, I'll requite this kindness" (*3 Henry VI* 4.7.78), his promise to reward his followers' loyalty is dependent on the service of fortune. In the midst of a fierce battle with the Volscians, Lartius says to Martius, "Prosperity be thy page" (*Coriolanus* 1.5.24).[29] Such expressed hopes are appropriate when the issue is in doubt and perhaps when human activity can influence the outcome. The idea that "fortune favors the brave" suggests that courageous people may deserve service from whatever powers control the outcomes of uncertain situations. When the situation seems hopeless, however, such a wish for service when no effective service seems possible may be unsuitable. Although it is no doubt well intended, the young lord's statement to the ailing King of France—"Health at your bidding serve your majesty!" (All's Well 2.1.18)—is a reminder that the king's powers do not extend so far as to command health, and it is therefore not surprising that the king fails to acknowledge this wish.

Characters who describe themselves as serving abstractions may do so to suggest good fortune, as does Falstaff when he declares himself "fortune's steward" (2 Henry IV 5.3.133); more often, however, characters who describe themselves or others as serving abstractions do so to suggest their unhappiness or desperation. The Duchess of York expresses her grief for the death of her sons by telling some of her remaining family members, "I am your sorrow's nurse" (Richard III 2.2.87), while Richard II describes his hopelessness upon learning that his lords have betrayed him by saying, "A king, woe's slave, shall kingly woe obey" (Richard II 3.2.210). Similarly, the desperate Florizel says that he and Perdita "profess / [Themselves] to be the slaves of chance" (Winter's Tale 4.4.542–43). On the other hand, a character may demonstrate fortitude or endurance by refusing service to an abstraction, as Pompey does in declaring that fortune will never make his heart "her vassal" (Antony 2.6.53–56). Similarly, Hamlet praises Horatio for not being "passion's slave" (Hamlet 3.2.70–73).

Abstractions are also depicted as servants by characters who use generalizations to interpret a situation or persuade other characters to change their behavior. In explaining how Parolles manages to thrive, despite his obvious vices, Helena uses a metaphor of service: "full oft we see / Cold wisdom waiting on superfluous folly" (All's Well 1.1.106–7). The Duke of Norfolk tells King Henry that "danger serves among" the rebellious cloth-workers, driven to desperation by Wolsey's taxation (Henry VIII 1.2.37). Proteus, for whom his "love" justifies any behavior, declares that "love / Will creep in service where it cannot go" (T.G.V. 4.2.19–20). Earlier, he has counseled patience to Valentine, declaring that "Time is the nurse and breeder of all good" (T.G.V. 3.1.244). The Duke of Burgundy, attempting to reconcile the French and

English kings, describes Peace as "Dear nurse of arts, plenties, and joyful births" (*Henry V* 5.2.35).

Characters who are suffering, physically or emotionally, tend toward considerations of endurance or the end of suffering, often phrased in terms of slavery. The Prince of Verona, faced with mystery as well as tragedy, counsels stoicism until blame can be assigned: "let mischance be slave to patience" (*Romeo* 5.3.221). Characters without hope philosophize that their situation is the common lot of humanity, a condition that includes the enslavement of an aspect of life ordinarily perceived as free: thought. The deposed King Richard, analyzing his state, comments that "Thoughts tending to content flatter themselves / That they are not the first of fortune's slaves, / Nor shall not be the last" (*Richard II* 5.5.23–25). The dying Hotspur refers to "thoughts, the slaves of life, and life, time's fool" (*1 Henry IV* 5.4.81).[30] Both Richard and Hotspur declare not only that their thoughts are enslaved, but that the enslavement is to something other than themselves. At the end of their lives, they perceive that they have lost, or never had, the service even of their own thoughts. A more profound metaphor for powerlessness is hard to imagine.

Because the concept of service is so ubiquitous, and because the words "service" and "serve" and other service-related words can be used in so many ways, there exist many opportunities for irony, puns, and other kinds of wordplay. Shakespeare makes use of many such opportunities, as well as allowing characters to equate different kinds of service both humorously and to make serious points.

After the Earl of Warwick offers to allow Gloucester's brother, King Edward, to "remain the Duke of York," Gloucester responds, "I'll do thee service for so good a gift" (*3 Henry VI* 5.1.28, 33). Since Edward is already king, Gloucester's offer of service is clearly ironic. Similarly, the Boy who serves Bardolph, Nym, and Pistol expresses his contempt for their cowardice and petty thievery, specifically for the theft by Nym and Bardolph of a fire shovel: "I knew by that piece of service the men would carry coals" (*Henry V* 3.2.44–46). In a multiple pun, the Boy suggests not only that the theft of the shovel demonstrates that his masters would accept degrading employment, but also that he knows this because the theft is the extent of their military service.

Perhaps more common than simple sarcasm, and certainly more dramatic, is a character mentioning service in a straightforward sense, and a second character taking up the word but using it to refer to a different type of service. Frequently, this change is used as a rebuke:

Rivers
Were you well served, you would be taught your duty.
Queen Margaret
To serve me well, you all should do me duty,
Teach me to be your queen, and you my subjects.
Oh, serve me well, and teach yourselves that duty!
(*Richard III* 1.3.250–53)

Bertram   I love thee
By love's own sweet constraint and will forever
Do thee all rights of service.
Diana   Ay, so you serve us
Till we serve you.
(*All's Well* 4.2.15–18)

Apemantus You three serve three usurers?
All the servants Ay. Would they served us!
Apemantus So would I—as good a trick as ever hangman served thief.
(*Timon* 2.2.94–98)

Lucius's servant   Ay, but this answer will not serve.
Flavius
If 'twill not serve, 'tis not so base as you,
For you serve knaves.
(*Timon* 3.4.58–60)

Because "service" has multiple meanings, its use may lead to confusion, as it does for Sir Richard Grey's widow when she asks King Edward IV to restore her husband's lands to her:

King Edward
I'll tell you how these lands are to be got.
Lady Grey
So shall you bind me to Your Highness' service.
King Edward
What service wilt thou do me if I give them?
Lady Grey
What you command that rests in me to do. . . .
King Edward
An easy task. 'Tis but to love a king.
Lady Grey
That's soon performed, because I am a subject.
(*3 Henry VI* 3.2.42–45, 53–54)

As King Edward goes on to explain, the service he has in mind is more than the love that subjects owe their sovereign, but it is not surprising that Lady Grey does not immediately perceive the king's intentions toward her. Although the confusion in this instance is about a serious subject, such linguistic confusion is comic in itself and adds a humorous aspect to this scene as the king tries to distract Lady Grey from her fixation (real or pretended) on the service loyal subjects owe their monarch. Such ringing of the changes on "service" is an obvious source of comedy and thus natural fodder for such a "shrewd knave" as Lavatch:

> *Lafew*
> Whether dost thou profess thyself, a knave or a fool?
> *Lavatch*
> A fool, sir, at a woman's service, and a knave at a man's.
> *Lafew*
> Your distinction?
> *Lavatch*
> I would cozen the man of his wife and do his service.
> *Lafew*
> So you were a knave at his service, indeed.
> *Lavatch*
> And I would give his wife my bauble, sir, to do her service.
> *Lafew*
> I will subscribe for thee, thou art both knave and fool.
> *Lavatch*
> At your service.
>
> (*All's Well* 4.5.22–34)

In his play on "service," however, Lavatch is not merely exercising his wit. He extends his discussion of service, claiming that he can serve the prince of darkness, but concluding that so great a prince should be served only by the nobility. He thus uses another concept of service to suggest that while poor folk like himself are fit for heaven, most of those who live surrounded by "pomp" will be damned (36–55). Since his audience is a nobleman, it is not surprising that Lafew announces that he is "aweary" of Lavatch and orders him to make sure Lafew's horses are tended well (56–59), thus reminding Lavatch of his role as a servant. Nevertheless, Lavatch clearly demonstrates that his wit is superior to Lafew's.[31]

One kind of pun often made by characters is to link some form of "service" meaning actions performed by people with "service" meaning "the serving of food." The Clown in *The Winter's Tale* describes Antigonus's struggle with the bear as "land service" (in contrast with the naval service of the sinking ship, which he also describes); in a pun that combines horror and comedy, however, Antigonus is also "land service" because he becomes the bear's dinner (3.3.92–103). Achilles, in his question to Thersites, "Why, my cheese, my digestion, why hast thou not served thyself in to my table so many meals?" (*Troilus* 2.3.41–42), combines contempt and compliment: Thersites is addressed as a dish of food whose purpose is to serve Achilles' "digestion," but clearly Achilles has missed Thersites' failure to serve himself in. A more serious, though still punning point is made by Isabella in pleading with Angelo not to execute Claudio: "He's not prepared for death. Even for our kitchens / We kill the fowl of season. Shall we serve heaven / With less respect than we do minister / To our gross selves?" (*Measure* 2.2.89–92). In this speech, Claudio becomes an out-of-season dish unfit, in his present state, to be served to God. The multiple meanings of "serve" and "service" allow characters to link such different ideas as military service, entertainment, and paying homage to God with serving food; such puns are clever and amusing, but also frequently reveal a fresh and surprising way of analyzing a situation.

Not all of the wordplay on "service" in the plays depends on the use of that word, nor is all of it intended as ammunition in verbal battles. Puns on various aspects of service are sometimes made purely for their own sake, for the fun of playing with language and ideas; often, this wit is demonstrated by servants. After Egeon refers to E. Dromio as E. Antipholus's bondman, E. Dromio says, "Within this hour I was his bondman, sir; / But he, I thank him, gnawed in two my cords. / Now am I Dromio and his man, unbound" (*Errors* 5.1.289–91). Launce considers the woman he loves: "And yet 'tis a milkmaid. Yet 'tis not a maid, for she hath had gossips. Yet 'tis a maid, for she is her master's maid, and serves for wages" (*T.G.V.* 3.1.268–70). Non-servants may also demonstrate such playfulness, perhaps particularly with regard to servants. Julia says to her waiting-woman, Lucetta, "Let's see your song. How now, minion?" (*T.G.V.* 1.2.88); Berners A. W. Jackson, editor of the Pelican edition of the play, glosses "minion" as "hussy (with pun on 'minim,' a half-note)."[32] Since one of Launcelot Gobbo's reasons for seeking to serve Bassanio is that he "gives rare new liveries," Bassanio's response— "thou hast obtained thy suit"—may be a pun combining Launcelot's request to serve and the clothing that symbolizes service, especially since Bassanio then orders that Launcelot be given "a livery / More guarded than his fellows'" (*Merchant* 2.2.103–6, 133–36, 146–47). Granted, neither of these employers' jokes is side-splitting, but neither is particularly witty elsewhere. A more entertaining character, Mercutio, makes a servant-related jest below his usual level of wit by intentionally misunderstanding Tybalt's reference to Romeo as "my man" as "manservant"; in this instance, however, Mercutio's primary goal is not amusement: he simply wishes to continue provoking Tybalt—who, however, ignores this jibe (*Romeo* 3.1.55–58).

Characters who are not servants sometimes define themselves in that role either jokingly or seriously. After Antonio gives Sebastian his money, Sebastian says he will be Antonio's "pursebearer" (*Twelfth Night* 3.3.47); after "Brook" offers Falstaff "all, or half" of a bag of money "for easing me of the carriage," Falstaff says, "Sir, I know not how I may deserve to be your porter . . . I shall be glad to be your servant" (*Merry Wives* 2.2.164–71). Although each of these statements is lighthearted, it is also a kind of expression of gratitude and acknowledgement that the person receiving the money is indebted to the donor, as servants owe service to their employers. Describing oneself as being in service can have much more significance, however. Each of the principal antagonists in *Richard II*, when at a low point in his fortunes, describes himself as a servant. Bolingbroke defines his exile as a term of indentured servitude during which he expects to gain nothing: "Must I not serve a long apprenticehood / To foreign passages, and in the end, / Having my freedom, boast of nothing else / But that I was a journeyman to grief?" (1.3.271–74). After Bolingbroke rejects such servitude and returns to England, King Richard learns that his subjects have flocked to his cousin's service and finds his only consolation in defining both himself and Bolingbroke as servants: "Strives Bolingbroke to be as great as we? / Greater he shall not be; if he serve God, / We'll serve Him too, and be his fellow so" (3.2.97–99). By rejecting his service to foreign passages and grief, Bolingbroke also rejects his service as an obedient subject. His success in attracting allies leaves Richard with a much reduced role: a king with (almost) no obedient subjects, like an employer with no servants, is merely "the name, and not the thing." In the face of Bolingbroke's disobedience, therefore, Richard retreats to the role of God's servant, a role shared by kings and commoners, and declares himself at least Bolingbroke's equal in that role. Although both Bolingbroke and Richard define themselves as servants, for Bolingbroke the role is a temporary disgrace, and to be resisted; for Richard, the role is a permanent refuge, which none can take from him and which makes him the equal of his more powerful adversary. Defining oneself as a servant, therefore, can be either a degradation or a comfort.

Characters frequently refer to other, non-servant characters as servants, or, more often, as slaves, in order to insult them or show in what contempt they hold them.[33] It is also possible, however, to define a non-servant as a servant in a complimentary way. Romeo in soliloquy compares Juliet to a serving-woman whose beauty exceeds that of her mistress and urges her to discard her virginity like a servant's discarded livery:

> Arise, fair sun, and kill the envious moon,
> Who is already sick and pale with grief
> That thou her maid art far more fair than she.
> Be not her maid, since she is envious;
> Her vestal livery is but sick and green
> And none but fools do wear it. Cast it off.
>
> (*Romeo* 2.2.4–9)

He goes on to compare her to a celestial servant:

> Oh, speak again, bright angel, for thou art
> As glorious to this night, being o'er my head,
> As is a wingèd messenger of heaven.
>
> (2.2.26–28)

The servants with whom Romeo equates Juliet are exceptional beings, to be sure, but exceptional beings in this period are not debarred from serving. The move from the conventional characterization of Juliet as the sun to the description of her as a maid whose beauty makes her mistress envious and the depiction of her as one of God's most beautiful servants provides Romeo with some of his most memorable images.

Because "service" is used to describe so many relationships and activities, it is understandable that various kinds of service are compared or equated, not merely in puns, but in more developed form.[34] Having discovered Viola's true identity, Orsino releases her from her service to him, and, as a reward for her service, proposes to reverse their roles: "since you called me master for so long, / Here is my hand. You shall from this time be / Your master's mistress" (*Twelfth Night* 5.1.324–26). Whereas Orsino equates the relationships of employer-servant and mistress-lover, Diomedes confuses them to create a double entendre by praising Cressida's beauty and then adding "to Diomed / You shall be mistress, and command him wholly"; Troilus's objection that Diomedes is "unworthy to be called her servant" may or may not refer to the idea of lovers as their mistresses' servants (*Troilus* 4.4.119–20, 125). Orsino's equation of services allows him to make a graceful proposal of marriage, while Diomedes' reference to Cressida as his "mistress" allows either an innocent or a bawdy interpretation.

Henry V seems particularly fond of comparing (or confusing) various kinds of service. He does so as a kind of threatening joke to Montjoy, suggesting that the French soldiers will soon be in the condition of dismissed servants, stripped of their livery:

> And my poor soldiers tell me, yet ere night
> They'll be in fresher robes, or they will pluck
> The gay new coats o'er the French soldiers' heads
> And turn them out of service.
>
> (*Henry V* 4.3.116–19)

Henry makes a much more significant, though questionable, equation of services when trying to persuade Williams that the king is not answerable for the deaths of his soldiers who die in his battles while not in a state of grace. Henry compares his soldiers to a son serving his father or a servant serving his master, concluding that "The King is not bound to answer the particular endings of his soldiers, the father of his son, nor the master of his servant; for they purpose not their deaths when they propose their services" (4.1.155–58). Henry, of course, overlooks the fact that the father and employer presumably do not expect the proposed services to include risking death, whereas the king knows that some of his men must inevitably die in battle. Since neither Williams nor Henry's other hearers dispute this equation of services, it is hard to tell whether they accept Henry's equation as logical or whether they simply overlook it in focusing on his later argument that "every subject's soul is his own" (177). That Shakespeare could depict Henry making such an unopposed equation in a serious argument, however, indicates that what we see as such different relationships as father-son, employer-servant, and king-soldier could be accepted by Shakespeare's audience as essentially the same.

Characters may also refuse to equate services, as when Coriolanus objects to Brutus's suggestion that he knows what service is:

> *Brutus*   But since he hath
>   Served well for Rome—
> *Coriolanus*   What do you prate of service?
> *Brutus*   I talk of that that know it.
> *Coriolanus* You?
>
>   (*Coriolanus* 3.3.89–92)

As the editor of the Arden edition points out in his note on these lines, "Cf. IV.vii.31, where Aufidius remarks, 'The tribunes are no soldiers'. Brutus's service is of the civic kind, unacknowledged by Coriolanus."[35] This refusal to equate services is perhaps a family failing, since in the next act Volumnia emphasizes the superiority of Coriolanus's kind—as well as quality and quantity—of service to that of the tribunes when she confronts them: "Hadst thou foxship / To banish him that struck more blows for Rome / Than thou hast spoken words? . . . More noble blows than ever thou wise words, / And for Rome's good" (4.2.20–24). Although it is possible that Coriolanus and Volumnia are objecting to the tribunes' failure to serve Rome by acting in the city's best interests, there is a strong suggestion that neither character equates political service with military service. In this play, the leading characters—all of them aristocrats and all of the men warriors (except the elderly Menenius)—extol the kind of service that their class is trained to provide, and the virtue, courage, most associated with that service. The plebeians and their representatives are generally depicted as lacking courage and military ability. Although not all of Shakespeare's other plays equate various kinds of services, *Coriolanus* seems anomalous in representing characters who explicitly rank one particular type of service above another, rather than classifying various functions and duties as equivalent parts of the overall category of service.

   Just as social life in the early modern period was imbued with the concept of service, Shakespeare's plays are permeated with the language of service. Rather than finding the hierarchical and rather rigid structures of the era's service a handicap, Shakespeare was able to make use of various kinds of and ideas about service to create descriptions, surprises, and humor that entertain and enlighten audiences and readers not only about servants and employers, but even the larger concept of service. The language of service in these plays is as pervasive in its effects as the service hierarchies of the era were in theirs.

5

"If I last in this service":
Loyalty and Disloyalty

IN AN ESSAY ON *KING LEAR*, JOHANNES ALLGAIER WRITES:

> In love man becomes unselfish, sometimes to the extent of laying down his life for his friends. One may look at love therefore as an abandonment of self to the object of one's love, as a suspension of self-interest, as it were. But from this it follows that some sense of selfhood, some consciousness of one's own worth and integrity, some "pride" perhaps, is a necessary requirement for love, for how can one abandon or suspend something of which one is not in possession or over which one has no control? Our reflection has yielded a paradox, namely, that one must love oneself if one wishes to love one's neighbor. But surely logical pedants need not shrink from accepting such a paradox as a reflection of reality when modern psychology, and physics, for that matter, can do no better.[1]

While we may find it easy enough to accept Allgaier's argument with regard to characters (or persons) of more or less equal social class, such as Lear and his daughters, who are Allgaier's primary focus, modern critics, reacting against the use of the doctrine of service to oppress the "lower" classes, often find it impossible to believe in such self-sacrificing love on the part of servants, suggesting that depictions of such love are merely propaganda by the servant-employing classes. Nevertheless, it is obvious that, for whatever reasons, Shakespeare often depicts servants for whom faithful service is an important part of their selves, a part they refuse to abandon, sometimes even at the cost of their lives. It seems a kind of snobbery to accept such love from a Juliet or an Antony, but not from an Adam or a Charmian. Loyalty in the plays, however, is not merely a question of doglike devotion by self-sacrificing innocents; bad servants, as well as good ones, can be loyal. Servants are also depicted as leaving

116

their employers for various reasons, and some servants are depicted as treacherous.

Servants' loyalty seems most justified toward those upper-class characters who express affection for and take actions to help their servants. While it is quite true that we do not see employers willing to die for their servants as some servants in the plays are willing to die for their employers, expressions of concern by the employers are not always negligible; after all, servants were expected to sacrifice for their employers, while the reverse was not true, or at least not to the same extent.[2] Many masters and mistresses in Shakespeare's plays, however, distinguish themselves by their solicitude toward and care for those who serve them;[3] among these are the Countess of Rossillion and Brutus.[4] In some situations, it could be argued that employers are more concerned about their own reputations than their servants' welfare (although this is not necessarily the case), as when King Lear defends the character of his knights against his daughter's accusations; Antony shows generosity to his servants; or Prospero expresses his affection for Ariel (*King Lear* 1.4.262–65; *Antony and Cleopatra* 4.5.12–17; *The Tempest* 1.2.207, 216; 3.3.83–84, passim.). In others, there is no advantage to be gained by dissembling, as when Marina weeps for her nurse's death (*Pericles* 4.1.11).

Some employers go much farther: Orlando seeks food for the starving Adam, although he evidently feels he is risking his life in so doing (*A.Y.L.* 2.6.6–7; 2.7.88–108). In the final scene of *Cymbeline*, the Roman general Lucius begs not for his own life, but for that of his page, "Fidele" (5.5.84–93).[5] In *Richard III*, the Earl of Derby, on his knees, begs that his servant, condemned to death for killing "a riotous gentleman / Lately attendant on the Duke of Norfolk" be pardoned as "a boon . . . for my service done"; King Edward reluctantly grants Derby's request, while suggesting that it is not unique (2.1.101–2, 96, 122–26).[6] Although Lucius and Derby both beg for their servants' lives, the effect is quite different. "Fidele" (as Lucius points out to Cymbeline) has done nothing wrong, whereas Derby's servant has committed at least manslaughter, if not murder. Although it arguably humanizes both masters to plead for the lives of their retainers, the granting of Derby's request, as the king points out while doing it, leaves an unmistakeable whiff of corruption.

A happier instance of a master's regard for and generosity toward a servant occurs in the first scene of *Timon of Athens*.

Faced with the Old Athenian's objection to Lucilius as a son-in-law, Timon says:

> This gentleman of mine hath served me long;
> To build his fortune I will strain a little,
> For 'tis a bond in men. Give him thy daughter.
> What you bestow, in him I'll counterpoise,
> And make him weigh with her.
>
> (1.1.151–55)

Ann Jennalie Cook sees this act of generosity as "intended to show almost from Timon's first appearance that he is gravely flawed in the exercise of his benevolence"; however, it was apparently not unknown for a master to arrange an outstandingly good marriage for a servant: Philip Gawdy writes to his brother Bassingbourne in 1602: "fame blewe into myne eares a wonderfull reporte of an extraordinary marriage you made for yowr man. . . ."[7] Furthermore, the author of *A Refutation of the Apology for Actors* seems to assume that generosity to good servants is only to be expected: "*Dionisus* the *Sciclian* tyrant demanded of *Diogenes*, with what persons wee should deuide our goods: who answered, with aged persons that should counsaile vs, good seruants which should obey vs, friends that should comfort vs, and the poore that shoold pray for vs."[8] Timon's concern for his servants is one of his most attractive characteristics; later in the play, touched by his Steward's sincere expressions of sorrow for his plight, Timon praises his Steward and attempts to cheer him up.[9]

Servant-employer relationships in the plays are varied and variable: not all members of the employing classes are depicted as employing servants; those who do employ servants may have either very distant or very intimate relationships with them, or anything in-between. The one intimate servant-employer relationship rarely depicted by Shakespeare is that of sexual relations.[10] He does hint at abuses and affairs, but, unlike some other early modern dramatists, rarely does more than that. Richard of Gloucester, in the process of slandering his brother, the late King Edward IV, tells the Duke of Buckingham to accuse Edward of "hateful luxury / And bestial appetite in change of lust, / Which stretched unto their servants, daughters, wives" (*Richard III* 3.5.80–82); however, we have no reason to assume this accusation to be true. The Shepherd, on finding the infant Perdita, says, "though I am not bookish, yet I can read waiting-gentlewoman in the scape" (*Winter's Tale* 3.3.70–71)—not a bad hypothesis, given the evidence he has, although the audience knows it to be incorrect. In *King Lear*, Edgar is disguised as a former servingman who, he says, "served the lust of my mistress' heart, and did the act of darkness with her" (3.4.85–87); although it cannot be certainly stated that this mistress is the servingman's employer, and not just his paramour, it seems probable. Similarly, it has been speculated that Oswald is, or aspires to be, sexually involved with his mistress, Goneril. However, Edgar's account is fiction, and there is no evidence of such intimacy between Goneril and Oswald, so even here there are only hints. The play most obviously pushing the boundaries of class with regard to sex may be *Twelfth Night*, in which Olivia falls in love with "Cesario," employed as one of Orsino's serving-gentlemen (1.5.293–302; 3.1.108–164; 3.2.4–6; 3.4.203–19), and ultimately marries "him" in the form of Sebastian; Olivia's uncle, Sir Toby Belch, marries Olivia's waiting "gentlewoman," Maria (5.1.362–64); and Olivia's steward, Malvolio, is temporarily convinced that Olivia intends to marry him (2.5.23–28, 38–39, 160–75). However, there is no evidence of sexual relations in the play, and the relationships are "justified," in terms of class, since Sebastian is not a servant of any kind; Viola is not a serving-gentleman, since she is not a gentleman at all; Maria is at least as good a lady as Toby is a knight; and no one except Malvolio is actually in love with Malvolio.

Although sexual relationships between servants and employers are almost unknown in Shakespearean drama, other familiar and even loving relationships are common.[11] As noted earlier, servants in Shakespeare's plays tend to be "upper" servants, who live in proximity to their employers and whose status is not far below theirs.[12] Thus, it is not peculiar that we often see servants acting as their employers' confidant(e)s. The French gentlewoman Alice serves that function for Princess Katharine in *Henry V*; Alice is, in fact, apart from King Henry in the wooing scene, the only character in the play who speaks to Katharine or listens to her.[13] It is a critical commonplace that Juliet has a closer, more maternal, relationship with her Nurse than with her mother.[14] Although both of Juliet's parents are present, the Nurse is the person in whom she confides and from whom she seeks advice, and the Nurse openly expresses a mother's fondness for Juliet:

> God mark thee to his grace!
> Thou wast the prettiest babe that e'er I nursed.
> An I might live to see thee married once,
> I have my wish.
>
> (*Romeo* 1.3.60–63)

The Nurse also warns Romeo not to "deal double" with Juliet,
and is apparently deeply touched by Juliet's "death" (2.4.162–67;
4.5.14–15, 17–18, 23, 30, 49–54). Although Juliet rejects the Nurse
when the Nurse counsels her to forget Romeo and marry Paris,
there is no evidence that the Nurse realizes that Juliet no longer
trusts her, and her affectionate teasing as she attempts to wake
Juliet suggests that her love for the child is unchanged
(3.5.214–43; 4.5.1–11). Another, unnamed, Nurse and the named
but never-appearing "Cornelia the midwife" of *Titus Andronicus*
are entrusted with Tamora's dangerous secret that she is carrying Aaron's child, rather than her husband's; both confidantes
pay for their knowledge with their lives.[15] Emilia also pays with
her life for her loyalty to Desdemona.[16] Servants in *Much Ado* are
not only aware of, but assist with, the plots in the play. Hermione's last speech to Leontes before being sent to prison demonstrates the affection between the queen and the ladies who serve
her:

> Who is't that goes with me? Beseech Your Highness
> My women may be with me, for you see
> My plight requires it.—Do not weep, good fools;
> There is no cause. When you shall know your mistress
> Has deserved prison, then abound in tears
> As I come out.
> ... My women come, you have leave.
>
> (*Winter's Tale* 2.1.117–22, 125)[17]

While many of the confidantes in the canon are women, men
also entrust their secrets to servants or are comforted by them.
While Ursula and Margaret help Hero entrap Beatrice, Don John
relies on Borachio and Conrade to conceive of and enact the plot
against Claudio. Similarly, in *Twelfth Night,* Orsino so quickly
forms a close relationship with "Cesario" that it occasions comment from another of the Duke's gentleman attendants, Valentine; Orsino himself admits, "Cesario, / Thou know'st no less but
all. I have unclasped / To thee the book even of my secret soul"
(1.4.12–14). Antipholus of Syracuse describes his slave, Dromio of
Syracuse, as "A trusty villain, sir, that very oft / When I am dull

with care and melancholy, / Lightens my humor with his merry jests" (*Errors* 1.2.19–21). Loyalty can even be found on the supernatural level: Oberon trusts his henchman Puck to aid in the plot against his wife and the plot to assist Helena, and Ariel, although he complains about Prospero's oppression, nevertheless reports Caliban's plot to kill Prospero (*Dream* 2.1.148–74, 249–67; *Tempest* 3.2.117; 4.1.139–41).[18]

Romeo necessarily conceals his intent to commit suicide from his servant Balthasar, but the two nevertheless apparently have a close relationship. After hearing Romeo's response to Juliet's death, Balthasar has advised his master, "I do beseech you, sir, have patience. / Your looks are pale and wild, and do import / Some misadventure" (*Romeo* 5.1.27–29). His concern, of course, is well founded, since misadventure is exactly what Romeo intends toward himself. Later, at the Capulets' tomb, Romeo threatens to kill Balthasar if the servant does not leave; Balthasar promises to do so, and Romeo's tone changes: "So shalt thou show me friendship. Take thou that. [*He gives him money.*] / Live, and be prosperous; and farewell, good fellow"; but Balthasar continues to show active friendship, despite Romeo's threats, saying in an aside: "For all this same, I'll hide me hereabout. / His looks I fear, and his intents I doubt" (5.3.41–44). He, like Paris's page, is unable to do his master any good, but both servants' intentions are admirable.

As has often been noted, *King Lear* is largely about service, and by no means all of this service is done by servants.[19] Cordelia and the Earls of Kent and Gloucester faithfully serve Lear, while Edgar, though rejected by his father, loyally serves him; even these upper-class characters, however, often represent themselves as servants: Kent disguises himself as "Caius," Gloucester continually refers to Lear as his "master," and Edgar pretends to be a servingman who has been stricken with madness. In addition, a number of servants are more loyal than family members: although two of Lear's daughters betray him, his Fool and at least one gentleman remain true to him, and one of Cornwall's servants, while declaring that he does it as good service, attempts to prevent Cornwall's torture of Gloucester (3.1.15–17, 52–55; 3.7.75–78).[20]

If we would prefer not to attribute servants' loyalty to love for their employers, Camille Wells Slights provides another possible explanation in a description of the relationships in *As You Like It*:

The nucleus of the emergent society is a relationship produced by nurture, not nature. In growing up together Celia and Rosalind have formed ties "dearer than the natural bond of sisters" (I.ii.276). Their artificial sisterhood is stronger than the blood relationship of Celia to her father and stronger than the natural brotherhoods of Orlando and Oliver and of Duke Frederick and Duke Senior. Similarly, bonds of personal love and loyalty unite Touchstone with Celia, Adam with Orlando, and Duke Senior with his men. These relationships function most prominently not by satisfying private emotional needs but by providing a means of achieving social identities.[21]

Relationships as a means of achieving social identities may in fact work better across class boundaries than within them; certainly, it is true that servants in Shakespearean drama are often more faithful and trustworthy than other characters.

One of the great exemplars of faithful service in the canon is Adam in *As You Like It.* Adam begins the play as the hero's confidant; he attempts to act as a peacemaker, to reconcile the quarreling brothers who are the sons of his old master; thwarted by Oliver's evil temper, he warns Orlando of Oliver's plot against his life, he also offers Orlando his life savings, and goes with him into the Forest of Arden as his servant. Slights's comment on this situation is "More important in reviving Orlando's spirits than Adam's offer of his five hundred crowns of savings is his request to 'let me be your servant' (II.iii.46). Adam's proposal to follow allows Orlando to lead" (203). Many commentators, including Mark Thornton Burnett, have testified to Adam's virtue and the sympathy his role evokes;[22] however, Burnett comments that "Adam's conduct is virtuous only from a particular vantage-point," since "in order to follow Orlando, Adam must be unfaithful to Oliver, which suggests that loyalty, a quality to be earned, can never be taken for granted" (*Masters and Servants*, 84). Although Adam can be viewed as changing loyalties, it is clear that in the first scene he is attempting to reconcile Orlando and Oliver: "Sweet masters, be patient! For your father's remembrance, be at accord" (1.1.60–61). Although Adam refers to Oliver as his "master" (25), he retains his loyalty to his "old master" (80), who was Orlando's father as well as Oliver's; furthermore, we might feel that Oliver's sneer to Adam as Orlando exits—"Get you with him, you old dog" (78)—(a response to a loyal, aged servant that, as Adam rather pathetically notes, Oliver's father would never have made) would fully justify Adam's departure with Orlando, even if Oliver did not later validate it by his attempts against Orlando's life.[23] Ralph Berry, in fact, describes this line as "in effect Oliver's dismissal of Adam" (*Shakespeare and Social Class*, 62). Adam chooses to serve his old master's virtuous son, rather than his villainous son, a choice Shakespeare surely must have meant us to applaud.

Oddly, however, Burnett goes on to state, "But Adam's 'constant service', despite being marked out for praise, is recognized as a transient phenomenon. Almost as soon as he enters Arden, Adam declines and presumably dies, which suggests that the virtues of his 'antique world' are unsustainable . . . In *As You Like It*, it is only suggested that service is unstable—the ubiquitous male domestic servants against whom Adam's exceptional qualities are measured never make an appearance" (84–85). This is ingenious, but unconvincing. There is no evidence that Adam dies in Arden, and in fact the point of Orlando's reciprocal service to his servant and the Duke's hospitality would largely be lost if Adam were not saved to rejoice with the others at the play's happy ending. That he does so silently is surely less surprising than that Celia also loses her voice in the latter part of the play; silence, after all, was part of a good servant's repertoire, whereas, as Rosalind points out, it was traditionally not characteristic of women (3.2.246–47). As for Adam being the only male domestic servant in the play, such a suggestion overlooks not only Touchstone, who loyally follows Celia into Arden (1.3.130–31), but the Lords who serve the exiled Duke; despite the Lords' exalted social status prior to their exile and the fact that they are having to be domestic in a forest, their principal function throughout the play is to demonstrate the survival of loyal service, even if such is temporarily ejected from Duke Frederick's court. The Lords and Touchstone parallel Adam in their determination to serve their employers despite the personal cost to themselves, and we come to see Arden as (among other things) a place in which faithful service flourishes and is properly respected and rewarded by those to whom such service is tendered.

Even servants who are not depicted as being intimate with their employers often express sympathy for the sorrows of their masters and mistresses. In the Induction to *The Taming of the Shrew*, the Second Servingman tells Sly that his madness "makes your servants droop" (Induction 2.27). When Marcade brings the Princess of France the news of her father's death, he begins his message by saying, "I am sorry, madam, for the news I bring / Is heavy in my tongue" (*L.L.L.* 5.2.715–16). Similarly, the servingman who must tell the Duke of York that his sister has died hesitates, saying, "But I shall grieve you to report the rest" (*Richard II* 2.2.95). Timon's Steward declares, in an aside, "I bleed inwardly for my lord," and even as he later attempts to bring Timon to his senses, he weeps—not, he says, for the first time (*Timon* 1.2.205; 2.2.136–86). Sometimes, however, sympathy for employers expresses itself in anger, rather than tears: this is the case with Timon's servant Flaminius and Posthumus's servant Pisanio when they are offered bribes to betray their masters (*Timon* 3.1.40–49; *Cymbeline* 1.5.48–89). Bribes, however, are not the only way to anger servants: the most famous example of servants angered on their employers' behalf is perhaps the quarreling Montague and Capulet servants in the first scene of *Romeo and Juliet*, but another example occurs when Coriolanus makes a slighting reference to Aufidius's Third Servant's master; although Coriolanus may only mean to call the servant foolish, the servant responds, "How, sir? Do you meddle with my master?" (*Coriolanus* 4.5.49–50), a response that earns him a beating.[24]

It is hardly surprising when, in *Richard II*, one of the queen's ladies sympathizes with her or one of the king's favorites attempts to comfort her (3.4.21; 2.2.1–4, 14–27, 33, 67).[25] Such generous sympathy, however, is not limited to "upper" servants, but can be seen even in servants whose jobs make intimacy unlikely; *Richard II* offers further examples. A Gardener, after having been cursed by the queen for speaking the truth, says, "Poor queen, so that thy state might be no worse, / I would my skill were subject to thy curse"; he then promises to plant "a bank of rue . . . In the remembrance of a weeping queen" (3.4.102–7). Finally, a Groom of the stable enters Richard's prison, becoming the last character to sympathize with the fallen king (5.5.67–97). Although he has only a dozen lines, his appearance adds poignancy to the end of the play, suggesting that Richard still has support among the common people, but that his supporters are powerless to help him. The Groom's exit line is "What my tongue dares not, that my heart shall say."[26]

The importance of loyalty in the plays has, of course, been commented upon. Madeleine Doran emphasizes the importance in the romances of "the active goodness of loyal men and women," but, although she mentions Pisanio and Paulina, she does not note that this loyalty is at least as representative of servants as of non-servants.[27] John Mortimer observes that Horatio and Kent "are the characters [Shakespeare] writes most sympathetically: the honest man, the good man, whose life is dominated by friendship to a fallible superior."[28] This is certainly true (although Mortimer's failure to mention any good women is unfortunate), but it is, arguably, equally true of Lear's Fool, of Adam in *As You Like It*, of Eros, Charmian, and Iras in *Antony and Cleopatra*, and of Emilia in *Othello*—the complete list would be a long one.

Clearly, in many of Shakespeare's plays, servants are more loyal and have closer relationships with their plays' protagonists than do members of the protagonists' families. Interestingly, however, it is not only virtuous servants who are loyal; in some instances, bad servants also display loyalty. Typically, such servants agree to do evil—to commit crimes or sins or both—in the service of their employers, with the promise of a reward for the accomplishment of their service. Servants who fit this pattern include Sir James Tyrrel in *Richard III*, Rosencrantz and Guildenstern in *Hamlet*, and Thaliard, Leonine, and Bolt in *Pericles*.[29]

By far the most notable and noted of loyal bad servants, however, is Oswald in *King Lear*. Oswald is Goneril's Steward, and loyally serves her, neglecting service to the king her father at her command, carrying her messages, even protecting her secrets from her sister Regan. Kent, who originally serves his royal master by disobeying him, has a visceral hatred of Oswald, to the extent that he describes him as the kind of servant who can make a vice of loyalty (*Lear* 2.2.74–81). Oswald's loyalty to his evil mistress makes him incapable of seeing or understanding another viewpoint; thus, when he reports events to Goneril's husband, he is astonished at Albany's reception of his news:

> I told him of the army that was landed:
> He smiled at it. I told him you were coming;
> His answer was, "The worse." Of Gloucester's treachery
> And of the loyal service of his son
> When I informed him, then he called me sot
> And told me I had turned the wrong side out.
> What most he should dislike seems pleasant to him;
> What like, offensive.

(4.2.4–11)

Although Oswald reports Albany's statement that the Steward's values are exactly the reverse of what they ought to be, it is clear that he does not understand what he is reporting. Phyllis Rackin provides an interesting explanation of how evil and stupidity interact in Oswald's character:

Oswald's fault throughout has been that he is completely the creature of the social and political hierarchy, unaware of any values beyond worldly status or any code beyond manners . . . Since he is
nothing but clothes, he is inhuman—no less so than the unclothed
creature that Lear beholds in the storm. If the poor, bare, forked animal needs clothes to distinguish him from the beasts, the thing made
by a tailor lacks even the natural affections that distinguish the
beasts from inanimate things. The opportunism that makes Edmund
brutal and enables him to betray his own father still lacks, it seems,
the sheer deadliness of the pragmatism with which Oswald responds
to the sight of the blinded Gloucester:

> A proclaim'd prize! Most happy!
> That eyeless head of thine was first fram'd flesh
> To raise my fortunes. Thou old unhappy traitor,
> Briefly thyself remember: the sword is out
> That must destroy thee.

Oswald sees a human being as a "prize": he is capable of reducing
the whole purpose of Gloucester's creation to mechanistic and ego-
tistical terms. Gloucester, to Oswald, is an economic advantage pure
and simple.[30]

Oswald's loyalty to Goneril and her party (and to his own advantage, which is virtually the motto of that party) leads directly to
his death, but with his last breath he asks his killer to deliver the
letter he carries to Edmund. Thus, he fully deserves the epitaph
Edgar pronounces over his body: "I know thee well: a serviceable
villain, / As duteous to the vices of thy mistress / As badness
would desire" (4.6.255–57).

While Oswald's loyalty does not make him an admirable character, it does suggest what an important aspect of service loyalty
is, and why disloyalty is seen as such an extreme violation of the
obligations of service. Servant characters who obey their employers without considering any higher ethical imperative also
reflect on those employers: since Rosencrantz and Guildenstern
have virtually no existence without Claudius (they have little
enough even with him), we blame the king, as much as or more
than his sponges, for the evil that they do; since it is Richard III
who empowers Tyrrel to murder the princes, Richard shares
Tyrrel's guilt for the murders. Oswald attempts to kill Gloucester
because "Preferment falls on him that cuts him off," but also because, as he tells Regan, he wants to "show / What party I do
follow" (*Lear* 4.5.40–42). Because they establish that "party,"

Goneril and Regan are guilty not only of their own crimes, but also of the crimes that follow from the corruption of such servants as Oswald.[31]

Loyalty in service is no guarantee to servants that their employers will reward, appreciate, or even remember them. In *Troilus and Cressida*, Ulysses describes "desert in service" as one of the "subjects . . . / To envious and calumniating Time" (3.3.172–75). Even without the passage of time, however, servants are forgotten, or fear being forgotten, by their employers; other upper-class characters, audiences, or, latterly, critics—sometimes more than one of these groups—also forget servants, no matter how deserving.

"Forgetting" of service and servants can, of course, be intentional, as is Richard III's reaction to the Duke of Buckingham's demand for his reward for his service in bringing Richard to the throne (*Richard III* 4.2.88–120). Less obvious "forgettings," however, are often more interesting. Since Timon declares to his Steward "I have forgot all men" (*Timon* 4.3.478), it would not be surprising if, as he insists, he had forgotten the Steward and the rest of his former servants. However, it is clear that he has not really forgotten his servants; he simply misjudges them: "I never had honest man about me, I; all / I kept were knaves, to serve in meat to villains" (482–83). Since we have earlier seen how loyally Timon's men have served him, we know this judgment to be false, although Timon admits a change of heart only toward the Steward (487–506). As Timon admits, he would "fain . . . have hated all mankind" (504), finding it easier to generalize about the nature of humanity than to acknowledge the need to make individual judgments.

Another, less deserving, Steward seems to be genuinely forgotten by his employer in *Twelfth Night*, when Olivia, reminded of Malvolio, says,

> alas, now I remember me,
> They say, poor gentleman, he's much distract.
> A most extracting frenzy of mine own
> From my remembrance clearly banished his.
>
> (5.1.279–82)

These lines are often overlooked by commentators who see Malvolio as the center of the play and who believe that Olivia values him greatly; obviously, Olivia is far more concerned with her own emotions than with the condition of her Steward.[32]

A more serious "extracting frenzy," of course, affects the aged King Lear when the Earl of Kent, who has served him so faithfully, attempts to "bid [his] king and master aye good night":

> *Kent* [*kneeling*]   O my good master!
> *Lear*
>   Prithee, away.
> *Edgar*   'Tis noble Kent, your friend.
> *Lear*
>   A plague upon you, murderers, traitors all!
>   (*Lear* 5.3.239, 272–74)

Eventually, Lear recognizes Kent, but he seems incapable of realizing that Kent was disguised as Caius and is thus unable to appreciate the service Kent has done him. Although one hesitates to say that Kent's service—and the other services done in this play that is so much about service—are in vain, it is certainly true that the service done by Lear's servants, supporters, and loyal daughter cannot save him (or anyone in the play), and that the acknowledgment that is all the reward Kent seeks—he has earlier told Cordelia, "To be acknowledged, madam, is o'erpaid" (4.7.4)—is lost, like so much else in the play.[33]

Kent is not the only character who hopes, at or near the end of his life, to receive an acknowledgment for good service. Othello, having murdered his innocent wife and destroyed his happiness, returns, just before killing himself, to the one area of his life which he has not sullied: "I have done the state some service, and they know't" (*Othello* 5.2.349). Similarly, the Duke of York's last words, reported to Henry V by the Duke of Exeter, are "'Commend my service to my sovereign'" (*Henry V* 4.6.23). Though York is dying and knows it, he wants his master to know what he has done in battle, and he wants his service noted and presumably remembered and praised. Exeter's testimony of his tearful response to York's last words helps direct the audience's response, and Henry's reaction—"I blame you not; / For, hearing this, I must perforce compound / With mistful eyes, or they will issue too" (32–34)—proves that he appreciates loyal service and is, therefore, the sort of king who deserves such service.

Even critics who are carefully considering a text are apt to overlook servants. For example, when Molly Easo Smith states that "Alarbus's death and mutilation graphically illustrate the nature of all subsequent deaths in the play as enactments of private revenge conducted without royal or legal approval," she is ignoring Aaron's murder of the Nurse, which is not revenge, and Saturninus's execution of the Clown whom the Andronici employ as a messenger to the emperor, which is certainly done with royal approval (4.2.144–48; 4.4.39–40).[34] Not unnaturally, critics as well as actors and audiences are likely to concentrate on protagonists and forget the protagonists' servants, even when the servants play important roles. As Michael Neill comments, at the end of *Othello*, "it is quite usual to imagine two bodies stretched out side by side under a canopy—and this is how it is commonly played. But if Emilia's 'lay me by my mistress' side' (5.2.235) is (as it surely must be) a dramatized stage direction, there should be three."[35] "Significantly," Neill adds, "eighteenth- and nineteenth-century promptbooks reveal that Emilia's request was invariably denied" (407 n. 66). Neill feels that having three bodies on the bed suggests "something adulterous," reminding us of Iago's suspicions of Othello and Emilia and helping "to account for the peculiar intensity of Lodivico's sense of scandal" at the sight of the bodies on the bed (407). The sense of "wrongness" at Emilia's inclusion, however, may be as much class-based as sex-based: although Emilia arguably echoes Othello's error in placing loyalty to Iago above loyalty to Desdemona, and although she dies heroically attempting to rehabilitate Desdemona's good name, she is nevertheless Desdemona's servant, and her request to lie by her mistress violates the decorum of the social hierarchy.[36]

Although the majority of the servants in Shakespeare's plays are loyal to their masters and mistresses, even when these employers are unfair, unfortunate, or wicked, some servants consider changing service, actually do change service, or are forced out of service.[37] Such incidents are widely variable in their effects, although they frequently reflect badly on the employers, only rarely suggesting evil in the servants. Change of service is often represented as the best or only choice a servant has.

Servants sometimes seem to be passed from one employer to another with a casualness that suggests that they are thought of as property, but which may also be a testimony to dramatic necessity.[38] Thus Prince Hal says that he has "given" a page to Falstaff, Falstaff gives a page (perhaps the same one) to Mrs. Page, Titania gives her human page to Oberon, and Posthumus gives Pisanio to Imogen (2 *Henry IV* 2.2.66–68; *Merry Wives* 2.2.106–26; *Dream* 4.1.58–60; *Cymbeline* 1.1.171–76). Imogen herself, in her disguise as the page Fidele, becomes part of the spoils of war: her master Lucius having successfully begged for Fidele's life, Cymbeline immediately takes "him" into service as his page (*Cymbeline* 5.5.119–20). One of Henry VIII's grievances against the Duke of Buckingham concerns a man who was the king's "sworn servant" until "the Duke retained him his" (*Henry VIII* 1.2.191–92). Henry has rather poor luck with his servants, since, a bit later, Gardiner promises Cardinal Wolsey that, although he is the king's secretary, he will "be commanded / Forever by Your Grace, whose hand has raised me" (2.2.118–19). Gardiner's statement highlights a difficulty of changing services: retaining loyalty to one's former employer can mean disloyalty to one's new employer.

One common reason for changing service is because a servant perceives himself to be badly treated, a perception and condition particularly common in the early comedies.[39] After Petruchio wrings Grumio's ears, for example, Grumio says that such treatment is "a lawful cause for me to leave his service" (*Shrew* 1.2.29), although he does not do so. Lancelot Gobbo does not accuse Shylock of physically abusing him, but he claims to be "famished in [Shylock's] service" and is attracted to Bassanio's service because Bassanio "gives rare new liveries" (*Merchant* 2.2.101–5).[40] A more serious reason for changing employers is given by the Boy who serves Bardolph, Nym, and Pistol, who finds his masters' cowardice and dishonesty repugnant: "I must leave them and seek some better service. Their villainy goes against my weak stomach, and therefore I must cast it up" (*Henry V* 3.2.50–52).[41] The elderly servant Adam has a similar motive for changing service, and acts upon it. Revolted by Oliver's wickedness and admiring Orlando as the "memory" of his revered old master, Adam forsakes his home of sixty years to follow (and financially support) a virtuous master, thus testifying to his own virtue (*A.Y.L.* 2.3.2–3). Pisanio agrees to betray Posthumus and Imogen and serve Cloten, but it is clearly Cloten's threat to kill Pisanio, rather than his money and promises of further reward, that produce this result; furthermore, Pisanio declares (to himself) that he has given Cloten only useless information, and that he has no real intention of changing service (*Cymbeline* 3.5.80–163). In this instance, the proposed new master is the evil character (although Pisanio has earlier criticized the judgment of his master Posthumus), and the servant remains the exemplar of virtue.

Servants are sometimes forced to change services, rather than choosing to do so. The Boy in *Henry V* becomes the servant of Bardolph, Nym, and Pistol only after the death of his original master, Falstaff. Pompey leaves the service of Mistress Overdone after the Provost offers him the choice of serving his full sentence of imprisonment and receiving "an unpitied whipping" or of serving Abhorson as the hangman's helper. Not surprisingly, Pompey chooses the latter option; his change of occupation, however, does nothing to extinguish his natural flippancy, which may suggest that the change is not too great a punishment (*Measure* 4.2.6–16, 49–51; 4.3.21–33).

Shakespeare also depicts servants who are forced out of service with no suggestion that they will be able to find another position. Although servants in the plays are rarely dismissed for incompetence, this appears to be the fate of Lance after he loses the lapdog Proteus intended as a gift for Sylvia; Proteus tells him never to return unless he finds the dog, and Lance exits, never to reappear (*T.G.V.* 4.4.57–59).[42] We are never told why Autolycus, who formerly served Prince Florizel, is now "out of service," although it seems that he was deservedly "whipped out of the court" for some misdeed (*Winter's Tale* 4.3.13–14, 85–87). As the authorities of the period feared, this masterless man has indeed turned to crime, but Shakespeare represents his crimes as petty, and Autolycus himself as a cheerful and charming rogue.[43]

The fall of a great house could also mean destitution for the dependents of that house. Shakespeare (or his collaborator, Thomas Middleton) devotes a scene, in the midst of the tragedy of Timon, to the tragedy of his servants, who are ruined along with their master when he goes bankrupt. Although they describe themselves as "undone, cast off . . . all broken implements of a ruined house," forced to "part / Into this sea of air" (*Timon* 4.2.2, 17, 22–23), Timon's servants waste little time in self-pity. Rather, they regret their lost fellowship, since they will no longer constitute a household, and mourn the fall of their beloved master. Their concern for Timon contrasts sharply with his apparent lack of concern for them (other than his Steward). If Timon had heeded the advice of his Steward, he would not have been ruined; if, instead of fleeing to the woods, he concerned himself with the fate of his servants, he would see that some people, if "only" servants, are motivated by compassion, generosity, loyalty, and friendship (a fact that Timon denies at 4.3.482–83, suggesting that he never really understood the men who served him). Since act 4, scene 2 does nothing to forward the plot—except for the Steward, all of the nameless characters in it disappear at the end of the scene, never to be referred to again except in Timon's erroneous disparagement of them—it would appear that Shakespeare and Middleton include the scene to contrast the behavior of servants with that of the great, even with that of the play's protagonist. The playwrights seem to be suggesting, as so often in the plays, that wisdom, moderation, and virtue are more likely to be found among servants than among their employers.[44]

In the plays, however, being forced out of service is not necessarily a bad thing. When Falstaff finds that he has more followers than he can afford, the Host hires Bardolph as a tapster; Bardolph says, "It is a life that I have desired," although Pistol regards the change as base (*Merry Wives* 1.3.4–20). The Arden edition notes of Falstaff's statement, "a withered servingman [makes] a fresh tapster" (16–17) that "Falstaff completes his sentence by deliberately varying, or misquoting, another proverb, 'an old servingman a young beggar' (Tilley S255)," but there seems no reason to think that Bardolph will fail to flourish in the Host's service. On the other hand, the future for Pistol and Nym—fired, ostensibly for refusing to carry Sir John's letters to Mrs. Page and Mrs. Ford (1.3.80–83)—looks bleak.

If *Lear* is, in part, an exploration of loyal service, *Antony and Cleopatra* can be viewed as an exploration of disloyalty; as Janet Adelman points out, "We are given, for instance, a series of servants who desert their masters and masters who desert their servants, each of whom comments by implication on the rest."[45] Servants who desert or betray their employers include Menas, Alexas, Canidius, Enobarbus, Decretas, Dolabella, and possibly Seleucus. Adelman concludes, "Servants and masters desert, in short, with every reason and under every circumstance; the pattern is repeated with endless variation. Our impression is simultaneously that nothing changes and that nothing is the same" (47). As Adelman suggests, however, the disloyalty in this play is by no means limited to servants; furthermore, several servants are loyal even to the point of dying for or with their employers. *Antony and Cleopatra* depicts a world coming apart; thus, it is not surprising that many of the people in that world cannot maintain their loyalties, although it is even more admirable that some people do remain loyal.

The Tempest is also intensely concerned with disloyalty, but in a somewhat different sense: the disloyalty is not as widespread—if only because there are fewer servants—but it is much deeper. The disloyalty in *Antony and Cleopatra* seems to occur largely because of circumstances: the men who desert Antony, for example, do not dislike him, nor do they object to being in service; they only fear to remain on the losing side. In *The Tempest*, on the other hand, both Ariel and Caliban ardently desire freedom; in addition, Caliban passionately hates Prospero. (Ariel is not given Caliban's opportunities to speak of his feelings out of Prospero's presence.) Even Stephano and Trinculo celebrate their release from service and see life on a desert island as liberty and exaltation in rank (of course, they are quite drunk). Berry comments: "Master and man: that is the relationship to which *The Tempest* returns again and again. Ariel and Caliban are servants, yearning for their freedom"; however, Berry also sees a difference: "Ariel has always been a servant, first to Sycorax and then to Prospero. Caliban was once independent" (*Shakespeare and Social Class*, 180, 182). In fact, we do not know that Ariel was *always* a servant—we might speculate that he was free before Sycorax imprisoned him for refusing to serve her. There is, however, a real difference in their service roles: Ariel, who has been promised that his term of service will be limited, is in the position of an indentured servant; Caliban, who has received no such promise, is a slave.[46] Their situations, as much as their natures, may define both their reactions to service and Prospero's interactions with them. Ariel, hoping to shorten his period of service, flatters and cajoles his master, who, like an honest employer, eventually honors his promise to free his servant. Caliban, having no expectation of freedom, curses and plots to murder his master; Prospero's response is problematic, for, as Stephen J. Greenblatt points out, "Shakespeare leaves Caliban's fate naggingly unclear."[47] Presumably, Shakespeare knew whether he wanted Caliban to end up as free (and alone on the island) or enslaved (but still part of the community)—after all, someone had to decide whether the actor playing Caliban exited and, if so, when and how—but he did not embody his intention in the script. It is more than a little ironic that *The Tempest*'s one enslaved character is the character least bound by the text at the end of the play.

Shakespeare having left the question open, some productions leave Caliban "masterless." During the last twenty years or so, critics and historians have been much interested in the idea of "masterlessness"; it seems possible that contemporary critics may be more interested in this state than was Shakespeare, who depicts relatively few masterless men, other than Cade's rebels, for whom it may be only a temporary state.[48] Apart from these rioters, the principal examples are Pistol and Nym, sacked by Falstaff in the first act of *The Merry Wives of Windsor;* Edgar in *King Lear;* Autolycus in *The Winter's Tale;* and Stephano, Trinculo, and (perhaps) Caliban in *The Tempest*. In other plays, including *Richard II* and *Timon of Athens*, we see or hear of servants losing their jobs, but we see little or nothing of them in a masterless state.[49]

In *The Merry Wives*, after hearing Pistol and Nym report that Falstaff intends to seduce his and Ford's wives, Page assumes that Falstaff's former followers are worse out of his service than when they were in it: "Hang 'em, slaves! I do not think the knight would offer it. But these that accuse him in his intent towards our wives are a yoke of his discarded men—very rogues, now they be out of service" (2.1.163–66). However, we are aware, though Page is not, that Pistol and Nym were "very rogues" while they were serving Falstaff and were, in fact, employed to be rogues: they stole under their master's protection and shared the proceeds with him (2.2.11–16). It is when they are out of his service that they tell the truth, revealing Falstaff's plot to Ford and Page; to be sure, they have an ulterior motive—revenge—for their honesty, but, nevertheless, they cannot be said to behave worse out of service than in it, although that may be as much a reflection on their former master as on them.

Edgar is an anomalous figure, since he is not, and never has been, a "servingman," as he claims. Not only is his "masterlessness" a disguise, it is part of a complex, multiply layered disguise, since Edgar is pretending to be a former servingman who is now "poor Tom," the wandering madman. As in *Merry Wives*, the depiction here is of a masterless figure who is less harmful than when he was in service, since Edgar/Tom describes his servingman persona as a compendium of deadly sins: "False of heart, light of ear, bloody of hand; hog in sloth, fox in stealth, wolf in greediness, dog in madness, lion in prey" (*Lear* 3.4.91–93). Again, as in the case of Nym and Pistol, the man in service is represented as a greater sinner than the masterless man. In fact, of course, Edgar (like Malcolm in *Macbeth*) describes himself as beset by sins that are strangers to his nature, nor is he masterless: soon after this speech, he takes it upon himself to serve the father who has rejected him, but whom he has not ceased to love, and continues in that service until Gloucester's death.

More typical of the period's fear of the masterless man is the case of Autolycus, formerly servant to Prince Florizel, who has apparently dismissed him. Autolycus appears to be thriving, but his success is due to the fact that he has turned to crime: specifically, he is a cutpurse, although he also peddles "trumpery" and steals anything that comes to hand (*Winter's Tale* 4.3.23–31;

4.4.599–621). Despite his light fingers, however, Autolycus is depicted as an amusing, essentially harmless rogue, more trickster than criminal; it may be significant that he continues to refer to Florizel as his "master" (4.4.713, 837; 5.2.152), and it appears that by the end of the play he is likely to be accepted back into a position of service at the court.

Whereas the servants who leave their employers in Antony and Cleopatra generally do so to take service with the winning side, Stephano and Trinculo plan to forsake service and rule the island.[50] Caliban is, in one sense, never a masterless man, given that he attempts to leave Prospero's service by immediately pledging himself to Stephano; in another sense, he is the epitome of the masterless man as early modern nightmare: rebellious, disloyal, profane, and murderous. Like Cade's followers, Caliban, Trinculo, and Stephano no sooner rebel against the conventional system—although, given that Stephano and Trinculo believe all of their companions and employers to be drowned, "rebel" is perhaps too strong a word—than they set up a hierarchy of their own: Stephano will be the king of the island, and Trinculo and Caliban will be viceroys (Tempest 3.2.107–9).[51] That what they propose is a ridiculously abbreviated hierarchy is less significant than that its establishment echoes the hierarchies that popular literature described as existing among rogues and vagabonds; according to this literature, the state of "masterlessness" never really existed, since hierarchies appeared as if they were natural growths, even among persons without employers.[52] Lack of employment did not mean lack of service. Shakespeare's contemporaries may have been shocked—as well as amused—by the idea of a drunken butler as a king, served as viceroys by a jester and a "debauched fish," but the arrangement was not inconceivable; what was apparently unthinkable—or at least unstageable—was that three masterless servants would establish a democracy or go their separate ways or fail to acknowledge hierarchy and service.[53] That would, apparently, have been far more shocking than simply proposing a change in who served whom, and Shakespeare never depicts such a revolutionary situation.

Although Shakespeare rather seldom depicts disloyal servants, he reports disloyalty and hints at the possibility of disloyalty fairly often.[54] For instance, Green reports that when the Earl of Worcester broke his staff of office, "all the household servants fled with him / To Bolingbroke" (Richard II 2.2.58–61; see also 2.3.26–28); however, we later see a Gardener who sympathizes with the queen and a Groom who remains loyal to Richard. Ophelia refers to "the false steward, that stole his master's daughter" (*Hamlet* 4.5.176–77), but that reference is all we are given. We hear Timon express his hope that Athenian slaves and servants will rebel against the Senate and steal from their masters, his desire that maids will betray their mistresses by sleeping with their masters, and his belief that gold "Will lug [the gods'] priests and servants from [their] sides" (*Timon* 4.1.4–6, 10–12; 4.3.32), but we do not see any of this actually happening. Prince Hal suggests that Francis, the apprentice drawer, flee his service, but there is no evidence that Francis seriously considers doing so (*1 Henry IV* 2.4.39–78). The tyrant Macbeth says of his thanes, "There's not a one of them but in his house / I keep a servant fee'd" (*Macbeth* 3.4.132–33), but it is not clear that his spies provide him any useful information.[55] Philip the Bastard tells King John, "Your nobles will not hear you, but are gone / To offer service to your enemy" (*King John* 5.1.33–34), but the traitors' service has no effect on the battle, and the revolted nobles soon return to John's service and are forgiven.

Few of Shakespeare's employers suspect their servants of disloyalty, but Orsino comes to suspect "Cesario" when he realizes that Olivia loves his servant; however, "Cesario" is true to Orsino, as the Duke eventually realizes. In other plays, the betrayals are real, but unimportant. Prince Hal bribes Bardolph and Falstaff's page not to tell their master that the prince has arrived in London (*2 Henry IV* 2.2.152–56); however, the servants might consider (in addition to the money) that they have a duty to obey their prince, and the page, being the boy that the prince "gave" Falstaff, might feel that the prince is as much his master as Falstaff is. But Falstaff is unlucky in his page (or pages), since Robin, his page in *The Merry Wives of Windsor,* also (or again) betrays him to Mrs. Page for the promise of "a new doublet and hose," although Falstaff has threatened to dismiss him for disloyalty (*Merry Wives* 3.3.22–30). *The Merry Wives* also features Mrs. Quickly, arguably as disloyal a servant as Shakespeare ever created: she plots against her master's interests and makes money for herself in her machinations with Anne Page's various lovers. She is helped by John Rugby, who keeps watch for Caius's return; Quickly promises him a posset and praises his honesty, willingness, kindness, and secretiveness (*Merry Wives* 1.4.1–14). Quickly promises Evans (via Simple) to help Slender (1.4.31–32, 86–87); manipulates Caius and lies to him (1.4.34–35, 65–81, 108, 114–15, 119); and promises to help Fenton, although she also lies to him (1.4.129–49). Other betrayals by servants have good effects, even though they may not be so intended: Parolles repeatedly betrays his master Bertram, first to Diana, then to "the enemy," and finally to the King of France (*All's Well* 4.3.209–97; 5.3.240–67); although Parolles betrays Bertram out of braggadocio and cowardice, the result is to help Bertram realize his mistakes and lead him to a happy ending. Similar positive effects are produced by Camillo's multiple betrayals: he betrays Leontes in order to save the innocent Polixenes (*Winter's Tale* 1.2.431–45; see chapter 9). He subsequently betrays Polixenes by helping Florizel and Perdita flee to Sicilia and then betrays the young lovers by informing Polixenes where they have gone; although he expresses a desire to keep Florizel from ruining himself, his principal motive is to satisfy his "woman's longing" to see Sicilia again (4.4.511–17, 666–71), but the upshot is that all of the play's major characters arrive in Sicilia, where they can forgive and be forgiven. Dolabella's betrayal of Caesar's plans to Cleopatra, though it does not lead to a happy ending (to quote Hemingway, "there can be no happy ending"), leads to the only appropriate ending: as Charmian affirms of Cleopatra's (and her servants') suicide: "It is well done" (*Antony* 5.2.326).

Other betrayals are indefensible and have tragic consequences. Edmund betrays his brother, father, and king because he believes that serving Cornwall will lead to wealth and power, which it does, but only briefly and at a terrible cost (*Lear* 2.1.113–18; 3.5.10–26). Similarly, Aaron, having cuckolded his "master," Saturninus (*Titus* 4.3.70–75), and fathered a baby by Tamora, murders the two women who know his secret and ultimately loses his own life trying to save his child.[56]

Few serious betrayals turn out profitably for the disloyal servants. Menas leaves Pompey when Pompey refuses to follow his advice to murder his enemies treacherously, although Pompey's professed willingness to accept the fruit of such treachery prevents us from accepting him as the moral figure he would like to appear; Pompey's moral ambiguity may suggest why Menas, almost alone of those who have deserted to Caesar's party, seems to flourish there.[57] More often, serious betrayals end badly for the traitors, but serve to testify to the glory or nobility of the traitors' employers. This is ultimately true for Enobarbus, even though, after his desertion, Antony sends his treasure after him "as if rewarding him for playing a part he has assigned to him, as if he is still serving Antony in betraying him."[58] In fact, Enobarbus does in a sense continue to serve Antony because Antony is at his best in adversity, which gives him the opportunity to rise

above what common men can and will do. As the ultimate
Roman, the embodiment of the Roman code of enduring until endurance becomes triumph, Antony, faced with Enobarbus's betrayal, shows himself, as one of Caesar's soldiers says, "a Jove"
(*Antony* 4.6.30). Similarly, the traitorous lords in *Henry V* testify
to the desire of the king's subjects to serve him:

> *Grey*
>   Those that were your father's enemies
>   Have steeped their galls in honey, and do serve you
>   With hearts create of duty and of zeal. . . .
> *Scroop*
>   So service shall with steelèd sinews toil,
>   And labor shall refresh itself with hope,
>   To do your grace incessant services.
>   (*Henry V* 2.2.29–31, 36–38)

Given that the speakers, along with the Earl of Cambridge, intend to kill the king, such speeches are deeply ironic, but, when
the conspiracy is revealed and the traitors realize that they are
condemned, they express what presumably is to be taken as sincere repentance for their treason:

> *Scroop*
>   Our purposes God justly hath discovered,
>   And I repent my fault more than my death. . . .
> *Cambridge*
>   God be thankèd for prevention. . . .
> *Grey*
>   Never did faithful subject more rejoice
>   At the discovery of most dangerous treason
>   Than I do at this hour joy o'er myself,
>   Prevented from a damnèd enterprise.
>   (151–52, 158, 161–64)

Not only their testimony that they regret their betrayal of their
duty to serve Henry, but his reaction, establishes him as a worthy king; he begins by saying, "God quit you in his mercy!" before
spelling out the harms that would proceed from his assassination, and continuing:

> Touching our person seek we no revenge,
> But we our kingdom's safety must so tender,
> Whose ruin you have sought, that to her laws
> We do deliver you. Get you therefore hence,

> Poor miserable wretches, to your death,
> The taste whereof God of his mercy give
> You patience to endure, and true repentance
> Of all your dear offenses!
>
> (166, 174–81)

Henry's renunciation of personal vengeance, his care for his kingdom, and his concern for the souls of his treacherous lords all distinguish him as a monarch worthy of loyal service. Since the traitors' plot does no actual harm, its only effect is to further testify to Henry's status as a righteous and heroic king.

One of the few disloyal servants who apparently survives betraying an employer is the Duke of Buckingham's Surveyor in *Henry VIII*. His namelessness befits his role as a tool of Cardinal Wolsey, who uses him (and, subsequently, several of the Duke's other servants) to bring about Buckingham's fall (*Henry VIII* 2.1.11–27). The Surveyor's symbolic function is emphasized when Buckingham, in his last speech before being led to the block, compares his fall with that of his father, concluding that "both / Fell by our servants, by those men we loved most—/ A most unnatural and faithless service!" (121–23). Buckingham, however, does not merely hear an echo of family history, but sees a universal lesson:

> Heaven has an end in all. Yet, you that hear me,
> This from a dying man receive as certain:
> Where you are liberal of your loves and counsels
> Be sure you be not loose; for those you make friends
> And give your hearts to, when they once perceive
> The least rub in your fortunes, fall away
> Like water from ye, never found again
> But where they mean to sink ye.
>
> (124–31)

The Surveyor (and Buckingham's other servants) disappear from the play with no one even commenting on whether they were rewarded for testifying against their master or executed for conspiring with him. These servants' only importance is in their effect on their master's fate: they enact the early modern anxiety, as expressed by Buckingham, that trusted servants will turn against their employers; otherwise, they barely exist as characters. This is not surprising in terms of this play, which largely centers around betrayals and consequent falls, since the other betrayals are not committed by servants: Katharine is betrayed by her husband, and Wolsey by someone even closer—himself (3.2.209–28). Of course, Wolsey's fall can also be viewed as that of a servant who has betrayed his master and gets only what he deserves; he refers to himself as a servant and the king as his master and finally describes himself as "Weary and old with service" (3.1.166–67; 3.2.246–48, 271–76, 364), but as Leonard Tennenhouse observes, "Wolsey's populist energy serves only his own ambitions."[59] Wolsey, however, exits the play maintaining that he is a loyal servant betrayed by others, his error consisting of serving the wrong, ungrateful, master: "Had I but served my God with half the zeal / I served my king, he would not in mine age / Have left me naked to mine enemies" (3.2.456–58).

The epitome of disloyal Shakespearean servants is, obviously, Iago; he is not only disloyal in himself (while appearing to be "honest"), but the cause that disloyalty appears to be in other men and women.[60] He is an artist of disloyalty: critics who find Othello excessively credulous should remember that Iago successfully deceives every important character in the play. Roderigo, to be sure, is a dolt, but the same can hardly be said for Desdemona, Cassio, and Emilia. The danger of Iago's scheme lies not only in what he does but in how he does it. While encouraging all of the play's characters to trust him, he also manages to encourage them to suspect each other and, on occasion, nonexistent others.[61] The villain of the piece burnishes his reputation for honesty by lying about honest characters and accusing them of betrayal.

Iago combines many of the attributes and actions most repugnant to early modern moralists. He plots with another man, whom he ultimately stabs to death from behind while his unfortunate accomplice lies wounded in the dark. He is a coward who boasts of his soldiership, a liar who glories in his reputation for honesty, and a servant who is entirely out for his own profit. An open enemy, like Brabantio or the Turks, would not threaten Othello; it is Iago's hypocrisy that makes him dangerous. Similarly, it is significant that Iago compares the false ideas he has conjured up in Othello's mind to the most domestic of murderer's weapons: "The Moor already changes with my poison / Dangerous conceits are in their natures poisons" (*Othello* 3.3.341–42). The horror of Iago's crime is not simply that it leads to four deaths, but that it poisons Othello's nature and changes him from a man who was "once so good" to someone who can hardly be recognized by his wife, his servants, and the men around him (5.2.299; 3.4.101–2, 126–27, 134–35; 4.1.247–48, 271–89; 4.2.102–8).

By the end of the play, Othello feels himself transformed by Iago's poison, for, when Lodovico asks, "Where is this rash and most unfortunate man?" his response is, "That's he that was Othello" (5.2.291–92).[62] Othello is "Fall'n in the practice of a cursèd slave" (293): a straightforward attack could never have brought him to become a murderer; the machinations of a stranger could never have deceived him. Only the treachery of a man he trusted, a man whose job was to be trustworthy toward him, could have corrupted Othello. While Shakespeare's contemporaries often worried about lazy and negligent servants, Shakespeare reveals that the real danger lurks within the servant who appears to be attached to his master by love, but who in fact hates his master and plots treacherously to destroy him.

Frances E. Dolan sees Iago as rebelling against the constraints of service (a view certainly supported by what Iago himself says): "While self-interest is too dangerous a livery to wear, the master's livery should also not shape the servant too much, because, in Iago's view, a servant's 'soul' exists only in resistance. Iago makes service bearable by so redefining the verbs 'serve,' 'follow,' and 'attend' that they are no longer recognizable."[63] On the other hand, it can be argued that Othello's livery does define Iago, in the sense that the servant shapes himself and his obvious abilities only to the destruction of the master, with no obvious benefit for himself, unless we accept as his motive his desire to obtain revenge on Othello, either for promoting Cassio over him or for seducing Emilia. However, the fact Iago claims two very different grounds for his revenge tends to suggest that revenge is not really his motive. Emily C. Bartels argues that "Iago's attempts to demonize and disempower Othello respond, then, not to racial or sexual difference that proves the Moor an inferior outsider but to a political status that makes him the authorizing insider and that threatens to keep Iago in the margins of power."[64] Clearly, Othello is the authority figure in Iago's life, but early modern servants were far more likely to profit when their employers succeeded than when they failed. Although it could be argued that Iago foresees that, with Cassio dead and Othello disgraced, Iago would rule in Cypress, there is no textual evidence to suggest that he has such a promotion in mind and, with both Othello and Emilia alive, such a plan is very unlikely to succeed. It appears that Iago embodies the employing classes' ultimate apprehension regarding their servants: the servant who so hates his employers that he is willing to destroy himself provided that he may first destroy them.[65] This may explain

Iago's refusal to answer when Othello asks "Why he hath thus ensnared my soul and body?" (5.2.310). He has repeatedly declared his hatred for his master and given multiple motives therefore; there is no reasonable likelihood that his plot will advance him in the world, or even that he will survive the working-out of his scheme. Although Iago has defined himself as the rational man who knows how to love himself (1.3.314–35), he acts on passion, and that passion is hatred for Othello and Desdemona. An honest answer—if we could expect such from Iago—to Othello's question about his motive would be subversive almost by definition, and yet would almost certainly sound anticlimactic. A rebellious servant is frightening because plausible, but also because defeat by a servant is ignoble. More effective, certainly, to leave Iago the defiant demi-devil. On the other hand, though he destroys his master and several other people, he does not, in the end, prevail, and it is one of the play's ironies that the man who declares, "not I, for love and duty" (1.1.61), is ultimately defeated by his wife's love and duty toward her mistress.

6

"Good counsel": Servants' Advice and Commentary

DESPITE THE PLETHORA OF MESSENGERS AND NAMELESS ATTENDANTS in his plays, Shakespeare presents his audience with many varied and individualized servants, from noblemen who define themselves in terms of their service, to waiting ladies and gentlemen, to nurses, fools, and clowns; these servants sometimes gossip about their employers and sometimes flatter them, but often provide them with useful information, comment seriously and intelligently about their behavior, counsel and comfort them, and argue with them. Rarely is what a servant says to or about his or her employer pointless; when Shakespeare gives servants a voice, they usually say things that matter and often they are demonstrably correct in what they say. Servants frequently direct the audience's view of their employers' actions, demonstrating to us (and often directly to their employers) that the main characters are behaving foolishly, or dangerously, or villainously.

As Lawrence Stone points out, "Among the middle ranks, servants—children of other families—were everywhere ... Even the rich, with ample house-space, were constantly spied upon and interrupted by their domestic servants."[1] Servants' ubiquity meant that they were likely to know a lot about not only their employers' households but the households of those with whom their employers had contact, since the contact would likely include servants; that servants were always around everywhere also meant, of course, that employers knew a lot about their servants—their virtues and their faults. In this area as in others, Shakespeare is presumably not attempting a realistic depiction of servant-employer relations; rather, he highlights particular aspects of those relations to fulfill particular dramatic purposes.

Throughout the canon, employers show exceptional trust in their servants. S. Antipholus, in a strange town where he goes under threat of death, entrusts what is apparently a considerable sum of money to his bondsman (*Errors* 1.2.8–10); the Duke of York orders his servingman to get a thousand pounds from his "sister Gloucester" and is about to give his servant his ring as proof that the order comes from him when the servingman reports that the Duchess is dead (*Richard II* 2.2.90–92); and, while it is clear that Timon is exceptionally careless about money, it is equally clear that not only has he trusted his Steward, but that he was perfectly right to do so (*Timon* 2.2.136–49). Nor is the trust between employers and servants confined to monetary matters. Orsino trusts his servants Valentine and "Cesario" to woo Olivia for him, and Romeo and Juliet trust their servants to arrange their meetings. The Earl of Derby sends a messenger to Hastings with an oral proposal that they flee Richard of Gloucester (*Richard III* 3.2.1–18); the Countess of Auvergne plots with her Porter to capture Lord Talbot (*1 Henry VI* 2.3.1–3, 32 s.d.); and Sir Pierce of Exton confides in his servant his plan to murder Richard II and takes servants with him to kill Richard (*Richard II* 5.4.1–11; 5.5.105–7).

As these last two examples (not to mention the entire plot of *Othello*) suggest, it is not always a testimony to employers' virtue or wisdom that they trust their servants. However, it is very often the case, in the comparatively rare instances in which employers distrust their servants, that this suspicion reflects badly on the employer.[2] Macbeth doubts and curses the servants who bring him the news of the approach of Malcolm's army (*Macbeth* 5.3.11–19; 5.5.33–41). Othello doubts not just Cassio's honesty, but Emilia's (*Othello* 4.2.1–24). The great example of a master mistrusting his servants—and that mistrust testifying to his own sin—is, of course, Leontes. He begins by accusing Camillo of being dishonest, a coward, negligent, or a fool (*Winter's Tale* 1.2.241–48). Soon, he comes to mistrust all of his servants:

> if I
> Had servants true about me, that bare eyes
> To see alike mine honor as their profits,
> Their own particular thrifts, they would do that
> Which should undo more doing.
>
> (1.2.307–11)

In all of these instances, the servants are completely trustworthy; it is their employers who are at best mistaken and at worst corrupt. Throughout Shakespeare's plays, servants are usually reliable, and their employers are usually intelligent enough to realize it.

Given this level of trust and the fact that servants were ubiquitous in early modern society, it is hardly surprising that Shakespeare frequently depicts servants as sources of information for their employers, and occasionally about their employers. Often this information takes the form of a simple announcement: a servingman brings Portia news of her wooers; a servant informs Leontes of the return of Cleomenes and Dion; servants announce the arrival of gifts for Timon and an invitation to hunt (*Merchant* 1.2.121–24; *Winter's Tale* 2.3.193–97; *Timon* 1.2.181–89). Servants can provide their employers' friends with information: Pandarus quizzes Troilus's man as to his master's whereabouts; Benvolio reports that Romeo's man has told him that Romeo did not come home the previous night; and Grumio confirms to Hortensio that Petruchio is only interested in money (*Troilus* 3.2.1–3; *Romeo* 2.4.3; *Shrew* 1.2.76–81). Earlier in *Romeo and Juliet*, Romeo questions a Capulet servingman as to Juliet's identity, but the servant either does not know or will not say; eventually, the Nurse tells Romeo who Juliet is, and later identifies the guests for Juliet—including Romeo, although she has to inquire his name (*Romeo and Juliet* 1.5.42–44, 113–18, 129–38). Some information suggests that servants have more intimate knowledge of the household than do their employers, as when the Countess of Rossillion is told by her steward, Rinaldo, that Helena loves Bertram (*All's Well* 1.3.104–18).

Servants can also be sources of background information, as when Pompey tells Mistress Overdone about the proclamation concerning brothels, Alexander imparts the latest war news to Cressida,[3] or young Richard, Duke of York, claims that his uncle Richard's nurse told him that Gloucester had teeth at two hours of age (*Measure* 1.2.93–103; *Troilus* 1.2.1–36; *Richard III* 2.4.27–34). (Since little Richard's grandmother objects that the nurse was dead before the boy was born [31–34], this may be an example of a servant being used as a scapegoat for some other rumorer, in which case young Richard is indeed a "parlous" boy.) Such reports, of course, ensure that audience members, as well as the characters onstage, receive information. Some information provided by servants is more unusual than news or gossip. Although Friar Laurence can explain much of the tragedy at the Capulets' tomb, it is left for Romeo's man and Paris's page to explain how their masters came to be there and how Paris came to be killed (*Romeo* 5.3.271–85). Richard III asks a page if he can recommend "any whom corrupting gold / Will tempt unto a close exploit of death" and the child responds that he knows a man whom gold will "tempt . . . to anything" (*Richard III* 4.2.32–41); that a page is expected to recommend a murderer and is able to do so suggests the utter depravity of Richard's court. An entirely different effect is created when the servant leading Lord Talbot says, "O my dear lord, lo, where your son is borne!" (*1 Henry VI* 4.7.17); not only is this scene an emblem of English courage and loyalty, but the servant's line and presence foreshadow that Lord Talbot, too, is about to die. Occasionally, servants resist giving information: not only does Thersites refuse to give Ajax the information he seeks, but Paris's impudent servant mocks Pandarus (*Troilus* 2.1.20–55; 3.1.1–42). Pandarus is mannered and pretentious, while Ajax is a cretin, and the servants are obviously mentally quicker than their social superiors, but the servants' cheekiness also reinforces Ulysses' judgment that "neglection of degree" (1.3.127) is widespread—and has infected the Trojan camp as well as the Greek.

The intimacy in which masters, mistresses, their children, and their servants lived, and the lack of privacy in most Elizabethan homes, combined with the facts that servants naturally had both opinions and tongues and that good servants presumably recognized their own value, seem inevitably to have led to a great deal of familiarity between many employers and servants, not all of it necessarily unwelcome. Various writers agree that servants can be useful counselors to their employers.[4] Nevertheless, writers on the servant question are clearly concerned about the dangers of allowing servants too much freedom of expression. Such familiarity is sometimes felt to be a threat, not only to employers' authority, but perhaps even to their identity.[5] Servants in this period were the recipients of contradictory messages: they were recognized as potentially valuable counselors, but also forbidden either to flatter or to "answer againe," both actions that were held to violate their duty to their employers.[6] Clearly, early modern servants often must have had to make difficult choices between duties toward their God and their employers, between their consciences and their worldly self-interest, between their dignity as men and women and their inferior position as servants. Although writers on "the servant question" obviously recognize these conflicting duties, they content themselves merely with mentioning the possibility of conflict and stating that service to the higher authority, God, must always take precedence; such writers do not explore these conflicts, probably because to do so would be to suggest too many instances in which disobedience to employers, and perhaps to other earthly authorities, such as monarchs and magistrates, would be the virtuous choice. These potentially revolutionary conflicts, however, are explored in many of Shakespeare's plays, in which servants sometimes offer advice and sometimes give in to the temptation to flatter their employers, but are perhaps most often represented as critical of their master's or mistress's behavior, their comments clearly validated by the obvious errors of their employers and the outcome of the employers' behavior, which is usually unaffected by the servants' brave and intelligent commentary.

Servants in the plays seem more likely to offer unasked-for advice than to have advice requested of them. King Lear, for example, receives advice not only from his daughters and nobility, but also from—among others—one of his attendant knights, who advises him of his neglect by Goneril's servants and of the Fool's "pining away"; the Fool himself, who advises him—too late—that giving away the kingdom was a mistake; Gloucester, who reminds him of Cornwall's "fiery quality"; and Kent as "Caius," who advises him to take shelter (Lear 1.4.56–73, 102–7, 115–97, 227–28; 1.5.14–44; 2.4.47–54, 89–92; 3.2.60–67). Though she says it sarcastically, Goneril is surely right in at least one sense when she comments, "This man hath had good counsel" (1.4.321). Certainly, he has had plenty of counsel, and most of it seems good, although he can make little use of it.

Asking advice may be a way of flattering a social inferior, as it appears to be when Regan tells Gloucester that she and Cornwall have descended unexpectedly upon his house to "have use of your advice" and "your needful counsel to our businesses"; although Gloucester is a nobleman, his response—"I serve you, madam"—expresses his acknowledgement of his role as servant to a superior (Lear 2.1.122–31). Other requests for advice may be serious, as when Julia asks Lucetta for counsel, Lucentio asks Tranio for counsel and assistance, and Bertram asks Parolles to advise him (T.G.V. 2.7.1; Shrew 1.1.158–59; All's Well 2.3.295).

Servants' advice, though often practical, is not always welcome. Dromio of Syracuse advises his master to stay in Ephesus, at least for one night, since he perceives that the Ephesians "speak us fair; give us gold"; his master, however, refuses (Errors 4.4.151–58).[7] A messenger advises Adriana, "O mistress, mistress, shift and save yourself!" and tells her that unless she sends "some present help" E. Antipholus and E. Dromio will kill Pinch. Her response is "Peace, fool!" but the messenger continues to advise her to "begone" (5.1.168–184). The Duke of Gloucester's servant suggests that they should rescue the Duchess from the sheriffs, but Gloucester forbids the attempt (2 *Henry VI* 2.4.18–19). The First Huntsman in the Induction to *The Taming of the Shrew* tries to persuade his master that Bellman is as good a dog as Silver, but is told that he is a fool (Induction.1.21–25). When Speed advises Valentine to join the outlaws, his master's response is "Peace, villain!" although Valentine ultimately—and, to be sure, under threat of death—takes the advice (*T.G.V.* 4.1.39–41). Although Juliet asks for the Nurse's counsel, the actual advice—that Juliet forget Romeo and marry Paris—is even less appreciated, and is not, of course, followed (*Romeo* 3.5.205–30).[8] Leontes, who does not seek advice from his courtiers, nevertheless receives it from Camillo, Antigonus and other lords, and, especially, Paulina (*Winter's Tale* 1.2.278–98, 320–22; 2.1.127–73; 2.3.52–127; see chapter 9); that he rejects the unanimous advice of so many good and loyal royal servants makes his tragedy all the more senseless and inevitable.

Some servants, like Paulina, take the liberty of giving personal advice to their employers to change their mood or behavior, as Nerissa does to Portia (*Merchant* 1.2.1–32), Conrade does to Don John (*Much Ado* 1.3.1–24), and Timon's Steward professes to have done to his master (*Timon* 2.2.128–77). Although such very familiar advice usually has little, if any, effect on an employer, there are exceptions. Cleopatra regains her self-control after Charmian pleads for the messenger the queen is mistreating, and later approachs Antony at the urging of her ladies and Eros (*Antony* 2.5.76–82; 3.11.25–43). Lychorida counsels Pericles, stricken by the news of Thaisa's death, to practice "patience" and to "be manly and take comfort" for the sake of his newborn daughter, and he does so (*Pericles* 3.1.19–27). Such advice, of course, is not always good: in large part, it is the willingness of employers to talk familiarly with their servants and take advice from them that allows Iago to deceive Othello.

Not all advice passes from servants to their employers. Occasionally, employers give their servants advice. After beating S. Dromio, S. Antipholus gives him advice on how to avoid being beaten again; Petruchio, having wrung Grumio's ears, tells him, "Sirrah, begone, or talk not, I advise you"; and Olivia, having rebuked Feste, advises him how not to offend his listeners (*Errors* 2.2.26–46; *Shrew* 1.2.43; *Twelfth Night* 1.5.107–8). Since all of this advice amounts to "Do not anger your employer," however, it is presumably included only for comic value. In a couple of instances, characters who are overwrought become convinced that an employer and one or more servants are plotting against them.

This is the case with Adriana, who suspects that her husband and his slave are in league to fool her; ironically, the man she mistakes for her husband has accused his slave of plotting with her (*Errors* 2.2.159–60, 167–69, 202–4). Of course, no one is plotting; everyone in the play is simply very confused. When Master Ford exclaims, "Oh, you panderly rascals! There's a knot, a ging, a pack, a conspiracy against me" (*Merry Wives* 4.2.111–12), his situation is somewhat different. In one sense, he is right, for, although Mrs. Ford is not betraying him with Falstaff, and the Fords' servants John and Robert are not onstage when Falstaff gets into the buck-basket, the servants do learn that they unknowingly smuggled a man out of Ford's house, but they do not inform their master of this fact (4.3.100–107). Since Mrs. Ford is virtuous, no harm is done, but these situations suggest how close the bond between employer and servant could be perceived to be, as well as the potential for divided loyalties in households with both a master and a mistress, which of course was the typical household structure.

Servants are not limited to advising only their own employers. Maria, for example, gives good advice to Feste and Sir Toby (*Twelfth Night* 1.5.16–18, 30; 2.3.72–74, 85); and, although Mrs. Quickly has promised to try to win Anne Page for her master, Dr. Caius, she nevertheless advises Fenton to speak to Mrs. Page—and praises herself when he takes her advice and Mrs. Page seems not entirely unsympathetic (*Merry Wives* 1.4.109–19; 3.4.77, 95–97). Sometimes, however, servants who give advice to persons who are not their employers do so only for their own satisfaction. Fabian advises Sir Andrew to fight "Cesario" as a means to win Olivia (*Twelfth Night* 3.2.17–28, 38), but only because he and Sir Toby think that such a duel would be amusing. Camillo advises Florizel and Perdita to disguise themselves and flee to Sicilia, but only because he plans to betray them to Polixenes and thus satisfy his desire to re-visit his homeland (*Winter's Tale* 4.4.544–78, 626–71).

Servants' advice is usually well meant—Fabian and Camillo presumably intend no real harm, and do none—but such advice is not always good. Lucentio asks Tranio for his advice and help in winning Bianca, both of which Tranio offers (*Shrew* 1.1.158–59, 179–218). Throughout most of the remainder of the play, Tranio pretends to be Lucentio, in which role he outbids Gremio for Bianca's hand, persuades Hortensio to forswear Bianca, and tricks an old man into playing Lucentio's father (2.1.361–95; 4.2.22–31, 73–122). He is very clever, but also—in his deceit and violation of hierarchy—very naughty. When he denies knowing Lucentio's father Vincentio, Vincentio becomes so angry with him that Lucentio has to take responsibility for his servant's actions and beg Vincentio to forgive Tranio (5.2.121–22). Tranio is clearly the direct descendant of the clever slave of Roman comedy, but he is also a potentially dangerous figure: dressed in his master's clothes, he is a plausible gentleman, and therefore a threat to a system in which servants were expected to know—and remain in—their place. Delinquency is not the only reason that servants give bad advice; honest ignorance or stupidity are also possible explanations why Polonius tells Claudius that Hamlet has run mad for love of Ophelia or Panthino believes that spending time at the Emperor's court will be good for Proteus (*Hamlet* 2.2.86–151; *T.G.V.* 1.3.29–33).[9]

Antony and Cleopatra may receive as much advice from servants as any two employers in the canon. Sometimes Cleopatra rejects this advice, as she does several of Charmian's suggestions and Enobarbus's presumably facetious advice on what they should do after their first defeat in battle (1.3.6–12; 1.5.7; 4.15.2; 3.13.1). In other instances, she accepts her attendants' advice to comfort Antony and to retire to her chamber (3.11.25–44; 4.4.35). After Antony threatens to kill her, she actively seeks her servants' help and accepts Charmian's advice, with catastrophic results (4.13.1–9). Both Cleopatra and Antony might serve as bad examples for the authorities of Shakespeare's era, who felt that employers ought not be too familiar with their servants or allow servants too much influence. Caesar argues that Antony has forgotten the Roman virtues of discipline and hierarchy and allows equality or superiority not only to an Egyptian woman, but also to servants and slaves, describing his fellow triumvir as one who "sit[s] / And keep[s] the turn of tippling with a slave" (1.4.18–19). Enobarbus, responding to Cleopatra's threat to "be even with" him for trying to keep her out of the war, tells her that Antony "is already / Traduced for levity, and 'tis said in Rome / That Photinus, an eunuch, and your maids / Manage this war" (3.7.1, 12–15).[10] Whether this accusation is true or a Roman fiction, act 3, scene 7 shows that both Cleopatra and Antony are deaf to the reasoned arguments of Antony's supporters: his right-hand man Enobarbus, his lieutenant-general Canidius, and his nameless "worthy soldier" all plead with him (and Enobarbus argues with her) in vain, leaving Canidius to conclude that they are all "women's men" (71), the plural perhaps suggesting that he agrees that Charmian and Iras, as well as Cleopatra, are managing Antony's army.[11] Both Cleopatra and Antony listen to advice from their attendants, but they sometimes ignore good advice and sometimes follow bad, and it is part of the Roman case against Antony that he has become, like Cleopatra, overly dependent on and familiar with servants.

With the exception of Iago, who goes beyond simply giving advice, Parolles is probably the worst adviser in the canon. Although Parolles vehemently objects to the imputation that Bertram is his master, it is obvious that he is the "count's man" (All's Well 2.3.186–95).[12] He advises his master to "steal away bravely" to the Florentine war, and, although "There's honor in the theft," Bertram's flight—taken more to escape marital duty than to win martial glory—angers the king, whom the young count has already irritated by his reluctance to marry Helena (2.1.29–30, 35; 3.2.28–32; 5.3.8–11). Bertram's abandonment of Helena also offends his mother to such an extent that she declares herself ready to disown him (3.2.66–68). Once they arrive in Italy, Parolles becomes Bertram's go-between in his attempt to seduce Diana, or, as Mariana puts it, "a filthy officer he is in those suggestions for the young earl"; Diana even suggests that Parolles is responsible for Bertram's dissipation: "Yond's that same knave / That leads him to these places" (3.5.17–18, 83–84). Given that Parolles is described by Helena, the Countess, the First Lord, and Lafew as "a notorious liar," "a coward," "a very tainted fellow, and full of wickedness," "an hourly promise-breaker," "a fool and a knave" (1.1.102–3; 3.2.87; 3.6.10; 5.2.54), it is hardly remarkable that he gives Bertram bad advice. While modern audiences generally find Parolles amusing, he must have embodied a considerable worry for early modern parents of immature young men who might be led astray by plausible, gentleman-like servingmen of bad character.[13]

One piece of advice Parolles gives Bertram, although seemingly minor, is a key to his character; Bertram, typically, has been sulking while the brothers Dumain are preparing to depart for the war, and after they exit, Parolles urges Bertram to follow them:

Use a more spacious ceremony to the noble lords; you have restrained yourself within the list of too cold an adieu. Be more expressive to them, for they wear themselves in the cap of the time; there do muster true gait, eat, speak, and move under the influence of the most received star; and, though the devil lead the measure, such are to be followed. After them, and take more dilated farewell. (2.1.51–58)

Although the lords may well deserve more ceremony at their leave-taking, Parolles' reasons for offering such courtesy are not that the Dumains are noble men and honorable soldiers, but that they are fashionable gentlemen. Parolles advises Bertram to respect show, rather than substance, "though the devil lead the measure." Although all ends well, and although everyone in the play except Bertram sees through Parolles almost immediately, Parolles is a caveat regarding the danger of flattering followers, particularly to foolish youth.

Comparatively few of Shakespeare's servants are flatterers, apart from those who surround such evil masters as Richard III. Rosencrantz and Guildenstern flatter Claudius, but Hamlet refuses to let them "play upon" him and derides them as "sponges" (*Hamlet* 3.2.349–71; 3.3.8–23; 4.2.10–22). Kent states that his reason for despising the "superserviceable" Oswald is the latter's lack of "honesty":

> Such smiling rogues as these,
> Like rats, oft bite the holy cords atwain
> Which are too intrinse t'unloose; smooth every passion
> That in the natures of their lords rebel,
> Being oil to fire, snow to their colder moods,
> Renege, affirm, and turn their halcyon beaks
> With every gale and vary of their masters,
> Knowing naught, like dogs, but following.
>
> (*Lear* 2.2.74–81)

Kent, who proudly defines himself as "no flatterer" is criticized by Cornwall, who describes him as a plain knave who "harbor[s] more craft and more corrupter ends" in his plainness than would twenty flatterers (2.2.103, 96–105), while Oswald responds by accusing Kent of "flattering [Lear's] displeasure" (2.2.119). Cornwall's opinion, that of a particularly proud and evil lord who will later become enraged when opposed by one of his own servants, seems anomalous; though Oswald does not deny Kent's words and may merely be turning Kent's own accusation back upon him, it appears that the suggestion of flattery as a motivation for a servant's behavior is felt to be an insult.[14]

Though few of Shakespeare's servant-characters are flatterers, many of them are critics. While some, like Touchstone, Feste, Lavatch, and Thersites, are critical of everything and everyone, others concentrate their commentary on the upper classes. Some servants criticize "their betters" because they feel badly treated; thus, Juliet's Nurse twice refers to Mercutio as "scurvy knave" after he mocks her (*Romeo* 2.4.150–51, 159). Grumio, whose ears have just been wrung by his master, keeps up a steady stream of commentary on the upper-class characters (*Shrew* 1.2.128–29, 137–38, 142, 159, 176). A disgruntled sentinal, ordered to stand guard, comments, "Thus are poor servitors, / When others sleep upon their quiet beds, / Constrained to watch in darkness, rain, and cold" (*1 Henry VI* 2.1.5–7). Servants, however, need not be hurt or offended to be critical: Mote and Costard mock the linguistic affectations of Armado, Holofernes, and Nathaniel, while Francis and another drawer at the Boar's Head feel free to comment on the behavior of Prince Hal, Poins, and Falstaff (*L.L.L.* 5.1.36–75; *2 Henry IV* 2.4.1–20). Touchstone makes sport of knightly pretensions to honor, court manners, and the elaborate conventions surrounding challenges (*A.Y.L.* 1.2.57–77; 3.2.62–66; 5.4.39–50, 66–102).[15] Lavatch speaks slightingly of the court (*All's Well* 2.2.4–13) and tells Lord Lafew, "I can serve as great a prince as you are," continuing,

> I am a woodland fellow, sir, that always loved a great fire, and the master I speak of ever keeps a good fire. But sure he is the prince of the world; let his nobility remain in 's court. I am for the house with the narrow gate, which I take to be too little for pomp to enter. Some that humble themselves may, but the many will be too chill and tender, and they'll be for the flowery way that leads to the broad gate and the great fire.
>
> (4.5.36–37, 47–55)[16]

The allusion, being biblical (Matthew 7:14), is unassailable, but the suggestion that the nobility, with their pompous and pampered lives, belong with the Prince of Darkness, while such humble servants as Lavatch will follow the strait and narrow way to heaven, is subversive (though quite Christian). Understandably, Lafew announces himself tired of Lavatch, whom he pronounces "A shrewd knave and an unhappy" (56, 63).

As some of the preceding examples show, servants sometimes comment on aristocratic characters who are not their employers, as the servants on Pompey's ship do on the drunken Lepidus:

> *Second Servant* Why this it is to have a name in great men's fellowship. I had as lief have a reed that will do me no service as a partisan I could not heave.
> *First Servant* To be called into a huge sphere, and not to be seen to move in't, are the holes where eyes should be, which pitifully disaster the cheeks.
>
> (*Antony* 2.7.11–16)

The servants' comments are intelligent and even philosophical, but that even another man's servants can see Lepidus's unsuitability to be a triumvir, that they gossip about it and pity him, emphasizes how hopelessly inadequate he is. The situation of Aufidius's household servants when confronted by Coriolanus is rather more complex. Having failed to eject Coriolanus from the house, they summon their master, only to see the two former enemies swear friendship. The servants then begin extravagantly praising Coriolanus, even at the expense of their master (*Coriolanus* 4.5.154–74, 209–21). What this scene means is arguable. Perhaps the servants are merely echoing Aufidius and the other Volscian aristocrats, who are now making much of Coriolanus. Perhaps this is a demonstration that the Volscian lower classes are as fickle as those of Rome. The servants' new attitude certainly foreshadows the reaction of the Roman citizens in the following scene: both groups of men have originally undervalued Coriolanus, but change their minds when Coriolanus changes allegiance. Aufidius's Third Servant also foreshadows his master's new status, when he tells his fellows, "our general is cut i'th' middle and but one half of what he was yesterday" (206–8). In their capriciousness and enthusiasm for war, Aufidius's servants may seem foolish, but they have a better grasp of what Coriolanus's arrival will mean to their master than he himself does.

Various of Shakespeare's other servants also comment on their employers' affairs, often criticizing their employers' foolishness or villainy out of their employers' hearing. Examples include Mistress Quickly calling Caius an ass (*Merry Wives* 1.4.119), the Boy in *Henry V* describing Nym, Bardolph, and Pistol as cowards and thieves (3.2.27–52; 4.4.69–76), Lance describing his master as "a kind of a knave" and his colleague Speed's master as "a notable lubber" (*T.G.V.* 3.1.263; 2.5.40),[17] and Pisanio criticizing Posthumus's "too ready hearing" and "low" mind in believing Imogen to be false (*Cymbeline* 3.2.1–11). Even the servants of the great feel competent to judge their masters' behavior. The Third Watchman in *3 Henry VI* disparages King Edward's judgment (4.3.16–19), while the Gardeners in *Richard II* criticize the way their lord and master has governed his kingdom (3.4.29–91).[18] The Nurse who brings Aaron his infant son and the information that Tamora expects him to kill the child adds her own comments that not to do so will bring disaster upon them all; she also makes several demeaning remarks about the baby (*Titus* 4.2.55–71). While it is unlikely that anything could have saved the Nurse—princes' secrets being notoriously dangerous to their keepers—Aaron's reaction to her racist disparagement of his offspring—"Zounds, ye whore, is black so base a hue?" (72)—reminds us that free speech was not a right accorded to servants. Nevertheless, they do talk, and in some plays, including *Twelfth Night* and *King Lear*, they talk a good deal, often to considerable purpose. Our views of Antony and Cleopatra throughout their play are influenced by the comments of their followers, from Philo describing his general as "a strumpet's fool" to Charmian declaring that Cleopatra's suicide "is well done, and fitting for a princess / Descended of so many royal kings" (*Antony* 1.1.13; 5.2.326–27).[19]

While early modern gentlefolk would certainly not have approved of their servants criticizing them, it appears that "answering again"—actually disputing with their masters and mistresses—was what really irritated employers. However, despite the many contemporary statements that servants should be not only obedient but silent,[20] many of Shakespeare's servants do "answer again," taking it upon themselves to dispute with their masters or mistresses. Furthermore, such wrangling servants are often shown to be justified by their employers' foolishness, heedlessness, or bad behavior.

Occasionally, servants answer back because of personal concerns, such as ill-treatment by their employers. This is the case with E. Dromio (*Errors* 1.2.45–52, 63–65; 3.1.11–18; 4.4.29–39), Grumio (*Shrew* 1.2.28–35), and the Messenger who brings Cleopatra the news of Antony's marriage to Octavia (*Antony* 2.5.63–75, 101–3). More often, what might appear to be a dispute is merely familiar teasing between employer and employee, as when Lucetta and Julia verbally spar over Proteus's love-letter or Speed mocks Valentine's love for Silvia (*T.G.V.* 1.2.66–141; 2.1.1–169).[21] Armado sometimes invites his page, Mote, to be familiar with him, although he is not always pleased with Mote's responses (*L.L.L.* 1.2.1–121; 3.1.1–64). Such lengthy verbal duels between employers and employees are the source of much of the humor in Shakespeare's early comedies, but such disputes are not limited to these plays. Perhaps the play most characterized by such teasing is *Twelfth Night*, in which the disorderly household presided over by Olivia harbors several disputatious servants. Even ignoring teasing between, for example, Maria and Feste, we find Maria mocking Sir Andrew, Malvolio quarreling with "Cesario," and Feste contradicting Olivia, Orsino, "Cesario," and Sebastian (1.3.62–78; 2.2.1–16; 1.5.35–69; 2.4.67–78; 3.1.1–59; 4.1.1–22; 5.1.9–38).[22] In a similar vein, Charmian needles

Cleopatra by praising Julius Caesar over Antony (*Antony* 1.5.66–76). Emilia does not hesitate to answer back to her mistress, Desdemona, or—more seriously—to her master, Othello (*Othello* 4.3.10–106; 5.2.134–74).

Other servants risk making serious and less personal complaints, often violating their duty to conform their words to their masters' desires in order to serve a higher duty. The most extreme example of a master-servant dispute, perhaps, is that between the armorer Thomas Horner and his apprentice, Peter Thump, in which the servant accuses the master of high treason, proving his claim by killing his employer in single combat (*2 Henry VI* 1.3.27–36; 2.3.47–105). Although few servants win such decisive victories over their employers, servants are often proved to be right when they take issue with their masters' behavior. Examples include the Messenger who, after bringing news of the English losses in France, adds his opinion that the factionalism of the English nobility is to blame (*1 Henry VI* 1.1.69–81) and Canidius, Enobarbus, and the Soldier, all of whom try to persuade Antony to fight on land rather than at sea (*Antony* 3.7.27–49, 61–67).[23] Among the most argumentative servants in the canon are those who appear in *King Lear*. Both Kent and the Fool are distinguished by their penchant for answering back to their master, despite commands to be silent, threats, and punishment.[24] Their insights are invariably correct, and their loyalty to their rash and imperious master ranks them among the most virtuous characters in the play. Thersites may be even more argumentative than Kent and the Fool, and it hard not to favor him over the dim-witted Ajax or the proud and selfish Achilles, but Thersites is a malcontent. Although his judgments of the heroes seem correct—if harshly phrased—he does not recognize any duty except to himself. He is scurrilous toward the knaves and fools who surround him, and he is a coward who abases himself as not worth killing when he meets a Hector or a Margareton in battle (*Troilus* 5.4.26–35; 5.7.13–23). He is an anomaly, who acknowledges no master, fears no beating (he seems to encourage Ajax to beat him), and tells the truth because the truth is disgusting and delights him.

The ubiquity of servants in the plays no doubt reflects their ubiquity in the life of the period, but so many servant-characters "answer again," or intelligently critique their employers in the latter's absence, that Shakespeare must have felt that this useful dramatic contrivance was acceptable to his audience; had it not been, it would have been easy enough to put these or similar critiques into the mouths of the main characters' family or friends.[25] That these critiques are given to servants suggests that neither the playwright nor the audience believed that employers had monopolies on intelligence and virtue. It may also suggest that both Shakespeare and his audience were interested in and willing to explore the conflicts entailed by conflicting services. Finally, it may indicate that Shakespeare—whose career as one of the Lord Chamberlain's Men and later one of the King's Men officially classed him as a servant—delighted in creating dramatic representations of the fact that servants' inferior social position did not destine them to other kinds of inferiority. Although Lavatch tells Parolles that "many a man's tongue shakes out his master's undoing" (All's Well 2.4.23–24), this is not the case in Shakespeare's plays, where free-speaking servants are more likely to be clever and virtuous than otherwise.

7

"A losing office": Messengers

READERS WITH EVEN THE SLIGHTEST KNOWLEDGE OF SHAKESPEARE'S plays recognize that these works teem with messengers, but the lack of critical commentary on these characters suggests that most scholars have assumed that messengers are merely dramatic devices for providing necessary information to the audience.[1] A close examination of the messengers throughout the canon, however, indicates that Shakespeare used messengers for many other purposes than merely retailing information. Socially superior characters sometimes demonstrate intelligence and apprehension by recognizing what a messenger is about to say from a messenger's look or manner, even before the message is reported in words. Messengers often express fear that they will be punished for bringing bad news, and how employers treat the bearers of ill tidings demonstrates their magnanimity and self-control or, alternatively, their cruelty, unfairness, and loss of control. Some messengers express views about their social superiors that influence audience opinion about these "superiors." Messengers are not important, however, simply because their interactions with social superiors help to characterize the upper-class characters. Even though most of them are nameless, messengers have their own importance, frequently representing the opinions of common people, who are shown to be more insightful and humane than those who employ them. Although they generally play small parts in terms of their number of lines, the messengers in Shakespeare's plays are by no means unimportant or interchangeable characters. In the voices Shakespeare gives them, we can frequently hear echoes of the voices of the powerless people of his time; the words of Shakespeare's messengers, and the reactions they evoke, often raise disquieting questions about the intelligence and ethics of the rich and powerful.

Clearly, messengers are useful to a dramatist in various ways.

A messenger can be used to report what would be difficult or impossible to stage, as in Biondello's description of Petruchio and Grumio's approach and apparel and Grumio's report of Petruchio and Katharina's journey, which include descriptions of the appearance and behavior of horses (*Shrew* 3.2.43–85; 4.1.47–75). Either in response to questions or by volunteering information, messengers can be used to inform the audience, as well as on-stage auditors, about absent characters or characters who have not yet appeared, off-stage plot developments, and other necessary questions of the play.[2] Even the failure of such upper-class characters as Antony and Achilles to listen to messengers can help to characterize them, whether the audience draws its own conclusions about this behavior or accepts the opinions of other characters (*Antony* 1.1.18–64; 1.4.7; 2.2.76–79; *Troilus* 2.3.78).

In several instances, Shakespeare's messengers deliver their messages even before they speak them. Bearers of bad news broadcast their messages in their appearance, allowing upper-class characters who are both intelligent and apprehensive to "read" the messengers' looks. The Earl of Northumberland explicitly describes Morton, who has come to report the rebels' loss at Shrewsbury and Hotspur's death, as a text:

> Yea, this man's brow, like to a title leaf,
> Foretells the nature of a tragic volume.
> So looks the strand whereon the imperious flood
> Hath left a witnessed usurpation. . . .
> Thou tremblest, and the whiteness in thy cheek
> Is apter than thy tongue to tell thy errand.
> Even such a man, so faint, so spiritless,
> So dull, so dead in look, so woebegone,
> Drew Priam's curtain in the dead of night
> And would have told him half his Troy was burnt;
> But Priam found the fire ere he his tongue,
> And I my Percy's death ere thou report'st it.
>   (2 *Henry IV* 1.1.60–63, 68–75)

The messenger's appearance, Northumberland tells us (in a reversal of the more usual procedure of getting news from messengers about the upper classes) is as clear to read as a title page, and as natural and obvious as the furrows of a wave-washed beach. Northumberland suggests that the messenger's looks are not merely appropriate for a bearer of disastrous tidings, but part of a tradition stretching back to ancient times. Northumberland might not be so insightful an interpreter, however, were it not for his situation. It is only upper-class characters apprehensive of bad news who are able to read a messenger's appearance. Northumberland has been awaiting news of a battle's outcome; two other characters who interpret a messenger's appearance as heralding bad news, King John and Macbeth, have been experiencing setbacks and are aware of their own guilt and their enemies' hatred (*John* 4.2.106–8; *Macbeth* 5.3.11–12).[3] These upper-class characters' ability to interpret a messenger's looks, therefore, may testify less to their intelligence than to an apprehension of deserved disaster.

A messenger's fearful appearance is understandable, since messengers who deliver bad news in these plays are sometimes greeted with curses and threats and occasionally met with violence.[4] The treatment meted out to messengers is sometimes used to demonstrate important differences among upper-class characters. When a messenger reports that the Volscians have beaten the Romans "to their trenches," Cominius responds, "Though thou speakest truth, / Methinks thou speak'st not well," and forces the messenger to justify the time it took to deliver his message (*Coriolanus* 1.6.10–21). When Martius appears to announce that Corioles has been taken, Cominius's first thought is "Where is that slave / Which told me they had beat you to your trenches? / Where is he? Call him hither"; Martius, however, defends the messenger: "Let him alone; / He did inform the truth" (1.6.39–42). Martius, whose only concern is the accuracy of the messenger's report, is represented as more admirable than Cominius, who criticizes the report first as unwelcome and later as detrimental to a patrician's or Rome's reputation; Cominius is not unconcerned with the truth, but it is not his only concern. His more complex reaction to the messenger may help to suggest why he is a more successful political figure than is Coriolanus, but his reactions toward the messenger do not suggest that his greater political acumen will necessarily lead to better treatment for the plebeians than they might have expected from Coriolanus. A similar contrast occurs when the tribunes are told that a slave has reported that the Volscians are laying waste "Roman territories" (4.6.39–44). Brutus's response is "Go see this rumorer whipped"; Menenius's reaction, however, is more sensible:

> But reason with the fellow
> Before you punish him, where he heard this,
> Lest you shall chance to whip your information

And beat the messenger who bids beware
Of what is to be dreaded.

(50, 54–58)

When a messenger enters to report that "some news" has inspired the nobility to assemble, Sicinius responds like his fellow tribune: "'Tis this slave—/ Go whip him 'fore the people's eyes—his raising, / Nothing but his report" (61–64). Particularly since the slave's news is quickly confirmed, it is obvious that Menenius's response is more intelligent than that of the tribunes, who wish to deal with the messenger in much the same way that they have dealt with Coriolanus, by rejecting what threatens them, whatever the potential cost to Rome. Ironically, it is a patrician, not the representatives of the common people, who seems willing to spare a poor but honest man from unmerited punishment.

In *Henry VIII*, a messenger's behavior, rather than his appearance or news, is what gets him into trouble. A messenger from King Henry enters the dismissed Queen Katherine's apartments at Kimbolton to report the arrival of Lord Capuchius. However, the messenger, intentionally or not, offends Katherine by failing to kneel in her presence and by addressing her as "Your Grace," rather than "Your Highness." Before he can get more than four words out, Katherine rebukes him: "You are a saucy fellow. / Deserve we no more reverence?" (4.2.100–101). He is also rebuked by Katherine's gentleman usher, Griffith, for his "so rude behavior" (103). The messenger kneels, addresses Katherine properly, and apologizes, explaining that "My haste made me unmannerly," but Katherine is not appeased, saying to Griffith, "this fellow / Let me ne'er see again" (105, 107–8). That the usually gentle queen is so offended by the messenger's breach of etiquette could be explained by her physical condition: the stage direction at the beginning of the scene specifies that Katherine is "sick." However, Katherine has just forgiven her enemy, Cardinal Wolsey, whose death Griffith reports to her. It is more probable, therefore, that her reaction to the uncivil messenger stems from the injury to her pride caused by King Henry's rejection of her, rather than her physical pain. Katherine has lost her husband and title, and she is dying, but she insists upon being treated as a queen, and her response to the messenger demonstrates that her spirit is undefeated.

Reactions to a messenger's bad news can be used not only to emphasize differences among characters, but also to demonstrate how a protagonist's nature changes in the course of a play.

As noted earlier, Antony begins *Antony and Cleopatra* by refusing to listen to Caesar's messengers; by the second scene, however, he is not only willing to listen, but encourages a reluctant
messenger who is aware that "the nature of bad news infects the
teller" by saying,

> When it concerns the fool or coward. On.
> Things that are past are done with me. 'Tis thus:
> Who tells me true, though in his tale lie death,
> I hear him as he flattered.
>
>   (1.2.101–5)

When the messenger again hesitates to report his "stiff news,"
Antony finishes the report himself, acknowledging his faults and
revealing that he knows what is said of both him and Cleopatra:

> Speak to me home; mince not the general tongue.
> Name Cleopatra as she is called in Rome;
> Rail thou in Fulvia's phrase, and taunt my faults
> With such full license as both truth and malice
> Have power to utter. O then we bring forth weeds
> When our quick minds lie still, and our ills told us
> Is as our earing.
>
>   (1.2.106, 111–17)

At this point in the play, Antony appears to deserve the departing
messenger's reference to him as "noble" (118).[5] When, however,
Antony has Caesar's messenger whipped and offers the life of a
freed bondman as an exchange for this violation of protocol
(3.13.101–3, 150–54), it is obvious that his character has deteriorated. The Antony who, if unable to renounce his faults, at least
acknowledged them honestly has become a man who acts out his
anger toward Caesar, Cleopatra, and himself by torturing helpless social inferiors.[6]

Richard III's treatment of Catesby and Ratcliffe as messengers also demonstrates a deterioration in his character:

> *King Richard*   Catesby, fly to the Duke.
> *Catesby*
>   I will, my lord, with all convenient haste.
> *King Richard*
>   Ratcliffe, come hither. Post to Salisbury;
>   When thou com'st thither—[*To Catesby*] Dull, unmindful villain,
>   Why stay'st thou here, and go'st not to the Duke?

Catesby
  First, mighty liege, tell me your Highness' pleasure,
  What from Your Grace I shall deliver to him.
King Richard
  Oh, true, good Catesby. Bid him levy straight
  The greatest strength and power that he can make,
  And meet me suddenly at Salisbury.
Catesby   I go.   *Exit.*
Ratcliffe
  What, may it please you, shall I do at Salisbury?
King Richard
  Why, what wouldst thou do there before I go?
Ratcliffe
  Your Highness told me I should post before.
King Richard
  My mind is chang'd.

                              (*Richard III* 4.4.442–56)

Richard, who until this point in the play has controlled every situation, is clearly no longer even in control of his own mind, and although his failure of memory at this point has no immediate effect, it foreshadows his loss of kingdom and life. Similarly, his striking of the Third Messenger later in the scene (507 s.d.) shows a new inability to disguise his feelings and control his behavior that indicates his end is near; unable to strike Richmond, Buckingham, or the other lords who have deserted him, he displaces his anger onto a helpless messenger (as earlier onto Catesby), ironically one who is bringing him good news. These interactions with messengers represent Richard's first obvious failures (although we later learn what we may already have suspected, that he has failed to convince Queen Elizabeth to woo her daughter for him). Because his previous successes have resulted from his intellectual superiority and ability to conceal his feelings, his memory lapses and emotional outbursts at this point, even with his underlings, demonstrate that Richard is no longer Richard, at least no longer the dominating Richard of the earlier part of the play.[7]

Macbeth also reacts violently toward a messenger who appears immediately after he has declared his faith that the spirits have pronounced him invincible and, twice in nine lines (*Macbeth* 5. 3. 2–10), announced his fearlessness:

    The devil damn thee black, thou cream-faced loon!
    Where got'st thou that goose look? . . .

Go prick thy face, and over-red thy fear,
Thou lily-livered boy. What soldiers, patch?
Death of thy soul! Those linen cheeks of thine
Are counsellors to fear. What soldiers, whey-face?

(11–12, 14–17)

His lines after ordering the messenger "Take thy face hence" show a very different attitude than his opening speech: "Seyton!—I am sick at heart / When I behold—Seyton, I say!—This push / Will cheer me ever, or disseat me now. / I have lived long enough" (19–22). It is apparently the recognition of the messenger's fear at least as much as the report of the English advance, which Macbeth has been preparing for, that disheartens and distracts him; the anger he displaces onto the messenger, who has done nothing wrong and who cannot reasonably be blamed for his involuntary change in color, indicates that Macbeth is controlling himself only with difficulty and prepares us for his inability to complete his thought, his uncertainty, and his recognition that even if he wins the battle, he has lost what makes life worth living.

Macbeth's reaction to the messenger who appears immediately after his speech on the meaninglessness of existence also shows his failing control both of his situation and himself. Although the king demands a quick report, the messenger understandably hesitates; since what he has to report is an impossibility, he may fear being either believed or disbelieved. When he does finally declare that he saw Birnam Wood moving, Macbeth lashes out at him: "Liar and slave!" (5.5.35). Typically, the messenger defends the truth of his report (36–38). Macbeth's response is a mixture of doubt, despair, and determination:

> If thou speak'st false,
> Upon the next tree shall thou hang alive,
> Till famine cling thee. If thy speech be sooth,
> I care not if thou dost for me as much.
> I pull in resolution, and begin
> To doubt th'equivocation of the fiend
> That lies like truth. "Fear not, till Birnam Wood
> Do come to Dunsinane," and now a wood
> Comes toward Dunsinane. Arm, arm, and out!
> If this which he avouches does appear,
> There is nor flying hence nor tarrying here.
> I 'gin to be a-weary of the sun,
> And wish th'estate o'th' world were now undone.

Ring the alarum bell! Blow wind, come wrack,
At least we'll die with harness on our back.

(38–52)

Although Macbeth still professes to doubt the truth of the messenger's report, he realizes what it means if true: he has been tricked and is now trapped in a situation in which his only options are fight or flight, neither of which can save him. His acknowledgment in the final line that death is imminent, however, is a tacit admission that he believes the messenger, who, without understanding the import of his report, has told Macbeth that he is doomed.

The most memorable instance of actual violence against a messenger is Cleopatra's treatment of the messenger who brings her news of Antony's marriage to Octavia.[8] Cleopatra's reaction to the messenger does not show a change in her character, since throughout the play she displays a regal unconcern for controlling her passions, or, as Laura Quinney puts it, "she is from the beginning what she will be."[9] Cleopatra's treatment of the messenger, however, does reveal important aspects of her character and situation. After striking the messenger, threatening him with torture, and finally drawing a knife on him, Cleopatra reverses Antony's transformation, regaining most of her self-control, and even some of her humor, and acknowledging her fault (2.5.80–85). When the messenger returns, she continues to threaten and curse him, but she refrains from further violence. She cannot, however, bring herself to thank or reward the messenger, although his protests at her treatment of him—"I have done my duty," "Should I lie, madam?" and "Take no offence that I would not offend you. / To punish me for what you make me do / Seems much unequal" (90, 95, 101–3)—are clearly justified.

The messenger's return in act 3, scene 3 to report on Octavia's appearance provides a comic coda to the scene in which he is beaten, but it too is not without a point. Clearly, the messenger has learned that it is the better part of valor to give Cleopatra what she wants; without, perhaps, entirely deviating from the truth, he describes Octavia in less-than-glowing terms,[10] and is rewarded. Similarly, throughout this scene Cleopatra's household servants tell her what she wants to hear: Alexas flatters her (2–4), and Charmian repeatedly echoes Cleopatra's self-serving judgments and praises the messenger's perspicacity (16, 23–24, 27, 44, 46–47, 51). Cleopatra, we see, gets the service she demands and deserves, foreshadowing, perhaps, the poor service she will later receive from her navy and the augurers who before the last battle "say they know not, they cannot tell, look grimly, / And dare not speak their knowledge" (4.12.5–6).

The messenger abused by Cleopatra is one of the few in the canon who we know makes a return appearance. Since most messengers are nameless, it is frequently impossible to determine whether a given messenger appears more than once in a play; in addition, since most messengers have few lines and would probably not have been costumed in such a way as to allow the audience to remember them as individuals, it is unlikely that Shakespeare usually intended to represent individual messengers' opinions or attitudes changing in the course of a play. One other exception to this general rule, the herald Montjoy, does change his mode of address in each of his appearances. This change, however, says less about the character of his messages' recipient than about the characters of the French King and nobility for whom he speaks. Montjoy opens his first meeting with Henry V with the contemptuous greeting, "You know me by my habit" (*Henry V* 3.6.114); when Montjoy next appears, again asking if Henry will pay ransom rather than fight, he addresses the king as "King Harry" (4.3.79, 126). At his final appearance, however, after the French defeat at Agincourt, Montjoy addresses Henry as "great King" (4.7.69, 80). Henry's gracious responses to Montjoy's original cheekiness, complimenting and rewarding the herald (3.6.139, 158), suggest his forbearance and magnanimity, but the more important aspect of the herald's changed demeanor is its indication of the changed attitude of his employers, who have been forced to acknowledge Henry's greatness.[11]

Since the innocent bearers of bad news are so subject to threats and violence from their employers, it is understandable that they sometimes hesitate to report what they know, as the messenger to Cleopatra does, and sometimes ask for pardon before making their reports. The Dauphin's messengers, despite their particularly protected status as ambassadors, seek reassurance from Henry V that there will be no reprisals for rendering their message "freely" (*Henry V* 1.2.237–40). Similarly, the Post who returns to Edward IV from King Lewis of France declares that he dares not relate his news until he receives the king's "special pardon" (*3 Henry VI* 4.1.84–88). Nor is it only royal servants who fear their employers' anger: after reporting Juliet's death, Balthasar says to Romeo, "Oh, pardon me for bringing these ill news, / Since you did leave it for my office, sir" (*Romeo* 5.1.22–23). In all of these cases, the messengers are spared their employers' anger, which may suggest the wisdom of asking pardon, but probably also demonstrates that these employers are in command of themselves and their situations (or want to appear so), since the two kings are about to lead victorious assaults against their enemies, while Romeo declares that he is about to wrest control of his fate from the stars.

Other fearful messengers use various strategies to avoid their employers' wrath. Messengers who deliver written messages commonly refer the recipients to these, avoiding oral report.[12] A messenger from Northumberland, for example, is quizzed by Hotspur, who obtains information about his father's supposed state of health; but when Hotspur asks about Northumberland's military plans, the messenger says, "His letters bears his mind, not I, my lord" (1 Henry IV 4.1.20). Since Northumberland's letters indicate that he and his forces will not be present at the approaching battle (31–38), the messenger may be claiming ignorance in an attempt to avoid Hotspur's anger. Other messengers also prefer to let the written word deliver bad news. Gower brings the Lord Chief Justice word that the king and Prince of Wales are near and adds, "The rest the paper tells"; the Chief Justice's terse response after reading the letter—"I have heard better news"—may suggest that Gower is discreet, rather than ignorant, since when he is subsequently questioned regarding troop movements, he appears well informed (2 Henry IV 2.1.132–33, 164, 170–73).

The same tactic is used even by messengers who are delivering news to characters who are their equals or otherwise unlikely to punish them. In The Merchant of Venice, Salerio acts as a messenger from Antonio to Bassanio. Before opening his letter from Antonio, Bassanio inquires after his friend, but Salerio replies only that Antonio is "Not sick, my lord, unless it be in mind, / Nor well, unless in mind. His letter there / Will show you his estate" (3.2.234–36). After Bassanio reads the letter, he turns to Salerio for confirmation of the news of Antonio's losses, which Salerio gives him, adding a report of Shylock's eagerness for revenge (272–83). Salerio is, therefore, obviously aware of Antonio's "estate," which is desperate, but he is reluctant to break this news to Bassanio. In As You Like It, when Silvius acts as a messenger, he is actually duplicitous. Although he knows that Phoebe planned to write "a very taunting letter" in which she would be "bitter . . . and passing short" (3.5.133, 137), he tells the letter's recipient, "Ganymede":

I know not the contents, but as I guess,
By the stern brow and waspish action
Which she did use as she was writing of it,
It bears an angry tenor. Pardon me;
I am but as a guiltless messenger.

(4.3.9–13)

Since "Ganymede" is not Silvius's master and is unlikely to be a very intimidating figure, it is improbable that even the "tame snake" Silvius (71) fears Ganymede's wrath; Silvius's reluctance to take responsibility for the "bad news" he bears may therefore be, like Salerio's, evidence of kindheartedness.

Messengers who have no written message may adopt other self-protective strategies, such as attributing their news to rumor (*Coriolanus* 4.6.67–71; *John* 4.2.119–24). The messenger who reports Alcibiades' approach to the senators, when queried as to the accuracy of his estimate of the army's numbers, says that he has given the lowest possible estimate, although he then adds that an attack is imminent (*Timon* 5.2.1–4). Finally, the servant who reports Mamillius's death to Leontes prefaces his news by saying, "Oh, sir, I shall be hated to report it!" and delays using the word "dead"—substituting "gone"—until Leontes asks for clarification (*Winter's Tale* 3.2.143–45). Throughout the plays, messengers recognize the force of Northumberland's statement to the messenger who brings him word of Hotspur's defeat and death: "the first bringer of unwelcome news / Hath but a losing office, and his tongue / Sounds ever after as a sullen bell / Remembered tolling a departing friend" (2 *Henry IV* 1.1.100–103).[13]

Despite their fears, and despite the attempted bribery by such upper-class characters as Northumberland and Cleopatra for favorable, though false, news (2 *Henry IV* 1.1.88–90; *Antony* 2.5.69–73), messengers throughout the canon are shown as remarkably loyal to the truth. Even messengers who occasionally deliver incorrect information, such as Lord Bardolph in 2 *Henry IV*, apparently believe the truth of their own reports (1.1.51–54). Servants who are acting as messengers sometimes make mistakes, such as delivering messages or letters to the wrong person (*Errors* passim; *L.L.L.* 4.1.53–58; 4.2.88–90, 126–39), but messengers rarely lie about the actual facts of what they know, although—as noted earlier—they may try to conceal the extent of their knowledge.[14]

Shakespeare's messengers, however, do more than simply report information truthfully and worry about the consequences of such reporting. When Viola disguises herself as "Cesario" and takes service with Orsino, she becomes aware, and makes us aware, of some of the complications inherent in the messenger's role as she attempts to deliver a message from her master to Olivia:

> *Viola*   Most radiant, exquisite, and unmatchable beauty—I pray you, tell me if this be the lady of the house, for I never saw her. I would be loath to cast away my speech; for besides that it is excellently well penned, I have taken great pains to con it. Good beauties, let me sustain no scorn; I am very comptible, even to the least sinister usage.
> *Olivia*   Whence came you, sir?
> *Viola*   I can say little more than I have studied, and that question's out of my part. . . . Most certain, if you are [the lady of the house], you do usurp yourself; for what is yours to bestow is not yours to reserve. But this is from my commission. I will on with my speech in your praise, and then show you the heart of my message.
> *Olivia*   Come to what is important in't. I forgive you the praise.
> *Viola*   Alas, I took great pains to study it, and 'tis poetical. . . . Good madam, let me see your face.
> *Olivia*   Have you any commission from your lord to negotiate with my face? You are now out of your text.
>
> (*Twelfth Night* 1.5.166–75, 183–91, 225–27)

Although Viola's intended message—most of which she does not get to deliver—is perhaps longer and more complicated than those of most messengers, her conversation with Olivia does depict difficulties inherent in the typical messenger's role. Messengers who are not simply delivering letters must learn and remember information and report it accurately to the correct person or persons while dealing with such distractions as interruptions, questions, or other reactions by their auditors. Messengers must do all of these things while respecting the wishes of both the message's originators and recipients. Finally, the messenger is expected by his employers to act merely as a tool for the transmission of information who does not express thoughts or feelings of his own.[15]

Shakespeare's messengers, however, are not only frequently unable to control their physical appearance, as noted earlier, but also unable or unwilling to suppress their intellectual and emotional reactions to the knowledge they possess. The expressions of thoughts and feelings that they append to their messages may lack realism, but they offer Shakespeare an opportunity to influence the audience's reactions to reported information. Although messengers' opinions rarely matter to the upper-class characters, the audience recognizes that the reactions of such truthful, generally disinterested characters are often more reliable than those of their employers.

It is not surprising that upper-class characters who are acting as messengers or ambassadors feel free to append their own opinions to their assigned messages (*John* 2.1.54–78; *1 Henry IV* 4.3.34–39); ordinary messengers, however, also frequently express unasked-for opinions. Some such opinions correspond with those of the messengers' employers, as when the messenger who reports to Claudius the approach of "young Laertes, in a riotous head" calls Laertes' followers "rabble" and criticizes their presumption in seeking to overthrow tradition by choosing their own king (*Hamlet* 4.5.101–11). Similarly, the messengers bringing news of Jack Cade's rebellion tell King Henry that "[Cade's] army is a ragged multitude / Of hinds and peasants, rude and merciless" and "The rascal people, thirsting after prey, / Join with the traitor" (*2 Henry VI* 4.4.32–33, 51–52). Although it is possible to interpret these messengers as expressing their personal views, they could be trying to curry favor with their powerful, though temporarily besieged, employers. It is not only royal messengers who have opinions, however; the messenger who brings Cade the news of Lord Say's capture describes two reasons why the rebels hate Say: he "sold the towns in France" and taxed the people excessively (*2 Henry VI* 4.7.18–21). Again, it is impossible to know whether the messenger should be viewed as expressing his own views or attempting to ingratiate himself with Cade.

Other messengers are depicted as willing to risk voicing extremely derogatory opinions about the behavior of their own employers and the ruling class in general.[16] An example is the messenger who reports the English losses in France to the leading English lords and then rejects the Duke of Exeter's convenient suggestion that "treachery" must have caused the losses:

> No treachery, but want of men and money.
> Amongst the soldiers this is mutterèd,
> That here you maintain several factions;
> And whilst a field should be dispatched and fought,
> You are disputing of your generals.
> One would have ling'ring wars with little cost;
> Another would fly swift, but wanteth wings;
> A third thinks, without expense at all,

By guileful fair words peace may be obtained.
Awake, awake, English nobility!
Let not sloth dim your honors new begot.
Cropped are the flower-de-luces in your arms;
Of England's coat one half is cut away.

(1 Henry VI 1.1.69–81)[17]

Soon another messenger appears to describe how the English were beating the French until an English knight disgraced himself and doomed his army:

Here had the conquest fully been sealed up,
If Sir John Falstaff had not played the coward.
He, being in the vaward, placed behind
With purpose to relieve and follow them,
Cowardly fled, not having struck one stroke.
Hence grew the general wrack and massacre. . . .

(130–35)

That mere messengers (and soldiers, if the first messenger is to be believed) hold and express such opinions suggests that even the common people can see what is wrong with the government of England. The noblemen's failure to react to such criticism of themselves and their peers by the common people indicates not only the absence of strong authority but also that the ruling class tacitly acknowledges the truth of these accusations of factionalism and cowardice. The lords cannot deny that they are to blame for England's failures, and the common people know this and are saying so even to their faces. The harm done to England by "the vulture of sedition" is demonstrated throughout the play and explicitly echoed by an upper-class character, Sir William Lucy (4.3.47–53; 4.4.13–46), but the first characters to alert us to the corruption and failure of authority are these nameless messengers.[18]

In the sequel to 1 Henry VI, the nobility's dissension continues to destroy England's military capability and a Post continues the pattern of a common man offering advice, as well as news, to his employers:

Great lords, from Ireland am I come amain
To signify that rebels there are up
And put the Englishmen unto the sword.
Send succors, lords, and stop the rage betimes,

> Before the wound do grow uncurable;
> For, being green, there is great hope of help.
>
> (2 Henry VI 3.1.282–87)

This advice is immediately followed by another flare-up of the quarrel between York and Somerset, the continued plotting of Suffolk against Gloucester, and a long soliloquy by York detailing his plans to overthrow King Henry. All of this indicates that the Post's advice, though good, is unlikely to be followed, but that is no reason for critics to overlook it.[19] Because the *Henry VI* plays are largely devoted to representing the harm done to England by her weak and self-serving rulers, the views expressed by these messengers are dramatically unnecessary except insofar as they show that the common people recognize what is wrong, although they are powerless to correct the situation. These anonymous messengers, speaking, as they do, the truth on behalf of the common people and desiring only the good of England, provide a contrast to the corrupt nobility of the plays.

Messengers, however, are not necessarily serious characters. Messengers between lovers, or messengers who perform their duties on behalf of lovers, are by far most common in the comedies, and are themselves generally comic. Costard, for example, is employed to deliver love letters from Armado to Jaquenetta and Berowne to Rosaline, but he gets them mixed up (*L.L.L.* 3.1.128–29, 161–67; 4.1.53–59; 4.2.88–90, 126–39). Proteus sends Valentine's servant, Speed, to deliver a love note to Julia; although Speed performs his errand, Proteus concludes that he "must go send some better messenger" (*T.G.V.* 1.1.95–99, 147). Proteus is particularly luckless, however, since later in the play, when he wants to deliver a ring and a letter to Sylvia, the messenger he chooses is Julia herself, disguised as "Sebastian," and this messenger's conversation with Sylvia only bolsters Sylvia's belief that Proteus is a cad (*T.G.V.* 4.4.84–176). Oddly enough, one of the few competent messengers in a love affair that ends happily (although some critics have expressed doubts of its future) is the ridiculous Launcelot Gobbo, who carries messages between Jessica and Lorenzo (*Merchant* 2.3.5–7; 2.4.9–20; 2.5.39–41). Equally competent, and much less silly, is Oliver, who carries a message from the wounded Orlando to Rosalind; more typical of love-messengers is Silvius, who carries Phoebe's love letter to "Ganymede" and the answer back to Phoebe (*A.Y.L.* 4.3.76–157; 3.5.133–36; 4.3.7–75). Although Silvius is an adequate messenger, we know his errand to be a foolish one, since Phoebe, for more than one reason, is no match for "Ganymede," and Silvius looks silly doing it, since he himself is in love with Phoebe.

Twelfth Night is a riot of love-messengers, and, while some of them are able enough, none is really successful in fulfilling an employer's wishes. Since Orsino and Olivia do not meet until the final scene of the play, Orsino's futile courtship is conducted exclusively by messenger, first by the appropriately named Valentine and then by "Cesario" (1.1.22–31; 1.4.15–36; 1.5.164–283; 2.4.79–86, 123–24; 3.1.84–164). Since Olivia cannot leave the house to pursue "Cesario" through the streets, she sends Malvolio, an unnamed servant, and the Clown, who encounters Sebastian rather than Viola (1.5.295–302; 3.4.58–60; 4.1.1–16). *The Merry Wives of Windsor* is even more overrun with ridiculous, incompetent, and ineffectual love-messengers, although in fact love plays little part in most of the relationships proposed in the play. Parson Evans sends Simple to deliver a letter to Mrs. Quickly regarding Slender's suit to Anne Page, with the result that the unfortunate Simple nearly gets skewered by the volatile Dr. Caius (1.2.1–11). Pistol and Nym regard carrying love letters from Falstaff to Mrs. Page and Mrs. Ford as employment too base for them, and Falstaff dismisses them from his service, delegating his page Robin to carry the letters and act as go-between for Falstaff and Mrs. Page (1.3.70–78; 2.2.106–8, 117–18). Nym and Pistol then deliver their own messages to Ford and Page, igniting Ford's jealousy, which Robin's presence at the Pages' home increases, as Ford perceives that the boy could carry messages between Falstaff and the wives (2.1.104–39; 3.2.28–29, 33). Mrs. Quickly, described by Pistol as one of "Cupid's carriers," is arguably the apotheosis of the comic love-messenger (2.2.128). She carries messages between the wives and Falstaff (2.2.32–125; 3.3.176–81; 3.5.25–54; 4.1.1–5; 4.5.98–120; 5.1.1–8); promises to do what she can for Slender (1.4.31–32, 86–87); falsely promises Caius that he will marry Anne (1.4.119–22); carries a ring from Fenton to Anne (3.4.98–99); and replaces Anne as the Fairy Queen (5.5.36 s.d.). She freely offers opinion, information (not always accurate), and advice, but notes that even she does not know whom, besides herself, she is serving (3.4.102–7).[20]

A few love-messengers, although comic in themselves, are involved in more troubled and troubling affairs. Parolles is described not as a messenger in his errands between Bertram and Diana, but as a "filthy officer," "knave," and "vile rascal" (*All's Well* 3.5.17, 84–86). There is no love and no affair between Bertram and Diana, and Parolles' endeavors on Bertram's behalf are clearly doomed to failure—even if Parolles himself had not betrayed his master (4.3.209–35). Although the word "bawd" is not used by the women discussing him, they obviously think him a despicable person—and they are quite right, of course. Pandarus, who presides over the doomed love affair of Troilus and Cressida, is twice called "bawd," by his niece and by himself; Troilus refers to him as "broker-lackey," and curses him with "Ignomy and shame" (*Troilus* 1.2.283; 5.10.37–39, 33–34). And although Juliet's Nurse might seem a more sympathetic figure, she plays a similar role in a similarly doomed relationship, and is similarly called "bawd"—three times, by Mercutio, who is joking, but who may be thought to speak wiser than he is ware of (*Romeo* 2.4.128). Although she objects to Mercutio's vulgarity, the Nurse, like Pandarus, is excessively eager to bring together two young people; though both characters might argue that they are serving the lovers, they appear at times to be serving their own vicarious desires in a most unseemly fashion, and it is not surprising that both characters are mocked. One also remembers Kent's description of Oswald, who is Goneril's steward but often acts as a messenger, as "one that wouldst be a bawd in way of good service" (*Lear* 2.2.19–20), with its suggestion that service can be taken too far.

In contrast to such comic characters, messengers are sometimes represented as not only more intelligent and patriotic than their employers, but as more moral and humane. Messengers not only risk their own safety to warn of approaching danger (2 *Henry VI* 4.4.27–37; *Hamlet* 4.5.101–112; *Coriolanus* 5.4.35–39), but sympathize with the suffering caused by their news and with those whose suffering is their news (2 *Henry IV* 1.1.105–6; *Richard III* 2.4.39). Occasionally, messengers are allowed to express their humanity at greater length, as is the case with the mysterious messenger—from whom?—who arrives (too late) to warn Lady Macduff to flee. As Kenneth Muir notes, "He is a welcome reminder that all have not been corrupted by Macbeth's tyranny."[21] Similarly humane is the messenger who brings Titus Andronicus the heads of his sons and his own severed hand:

> Worthy Andronicus, ill art thou repaid
> For that good hand thou sent'st the Emperor.
> Here are the heads of thy two noble sons,
> And here's thy hand, in scorn to thee sent back—
> Thy grief their sports, thy resolution mocked,

That woe is me to think upon thy woes
More than remembrance of my father's death.

(*Titus* 3.1.234–40)

In these few lines, the messenger demonstrates that an ordinary servant is morally superior to the Emperor and his court, who make the grief and mutilation of an elderly national hero the subject of their mockery. The messenger not only recognizes and comments on the inappropriateness and injustice of this behavior by his social superiors, but makes it clear to us that there are humane people remaining among Rome's citizens, however depraved the Empire's rulers have become.[22] A similar contrast between messengers and their employers appears in *Timon of Athens* when a messenger reports to the senators, "I met a courier, one mine ancient friend, / Whom, though in general part we were opposed, / Yet our old love made a particular force / And made us speak like friends" (5.2.6–9). Whereas the Athenian nobility has rejected the generous Timon and is about to descend into civil war, two messengers, though employed on opposite sides, are able to retain their friendship.

Such criticism, explicit or implied, of the upper classes is not easy to reconcile with critical views such as that of Leonard Tennenhouse: "Like the courtier, the dramatist also aimed at ingratiating himself with those in power. An Elizabethan playwright's economic survival depended upon his winning favor through the medium of theatrical performance in a more literal way than did the courtier's. But it was also true that the dramatist had no hope of obtaining membership in the privileged class to which his patrons and censors belonged; he represented their class to them from the viewpoint of the outsider and subject."[23] While Elizabethan playwrights were at the mercy of the ruling class, it is clear that Shakespeare's plays frequently show that class in an extremely unflattering light. Since, however, passages such as those quoted above seem not to have offended Shakespeare's patrons and censors, it would appear that the playwright ingratiated himself less by consistent flattery of the ruling class as a whole than by care not to offend particular members of it.[24] It is also possible that "the outsider and subject" Shakespeare was engaging in a bit of clever class camouflage in placing criticism of the nobility in the mouths of messengers. Messengers, after all, are almost invariably insignificant characters, rarely even deemed deserving of a name. Like modern detective-story writers who realized that the best disguise for a criminal was as a

postman, a waiter, or some other necessary but "invisible" func-
tionary, Shakespeare may have recognized that criticism from a
"mere" messenger, while it would have dramatic effect, would be
ignored or viewed as innocuous by the ruling class of his society,
just as it is ignored by the ruling class in the plays. Ironically,
many critics continue to imitate the plays' upper-class characters in continuing to overlook these messengers and ignore what
they say and its importance to the drama's effect on the audience.

8

" 'Tis proper I obey him, but not now":
Conflicts of Service

THEORETICALLY, SINCE GOD HAD ESTABLISHED THE HIERARCHIES OF earthly life and determined who would command and who obey, there should be no conflicts among services.[1] This supposed unity of service, particularly the unity between service to God and the monarch, is frequently demonstrated in the history plays, for example when Bolingbroke, via a herald, declares Mowbray "A traitor to his God, his king, and [Bolingbroke]," while Mowbray responds (also via a herald) by claiming that Bolingbroke is "To God, his sovereign, and to [Mowbray] disloyal" (*Richard II* 1.3.108, 114). Later in the play, King Richard makes the same equation of service to God and to himself: "Revolt our subjects? That we cannot mend; / They break their faith to God as well as us" (3.2.100–101). Henry V's battle cry—" 'God for Harry! England and Saint George!' " (*Henry V* 3.1.34)—also suggests this unity.

Nevertheless, there were conflicts of various kinds: between God and monarch, God and employer, king and employer, king and one's kindred, king and one's own honor, employer and another social superior, employer and one's own desires, etc.[2] Shakespeare also dramatized conflicts of service based on class conflicts and conflicts peculiar to women. The ideal of unified service was presented in conduct literature, but popular literature, including Shakespeare's plays, often depicted a less theoretically correct but more complex—and more dramatic—world.

Perhaps the canon's best known contrast between service to God and monarch is Cardinal Wolsey's lament to his protégé Thomas Cromwell: "Had I but served my God with half the zeal / I served my king, he would not in mine age / Have left me naked to mine enemies" (*Henry VIII* 3.2.456–58). Since service to the king should also have been, by definition, service to God, these lines may have been intended to highlight Wolsey's failure as a

royal servant. For instance, Polonius (ironically) sees his duty to
God and to his "gracious king" Claudius as being perfectly com-
patible (*Hamlet* 2.2.43–45). Had Wolsey actually been serving
King Henry's interests, rather than his own ambition, he would
also have been serving God, and the conflict he suggests would
not have existed. The disguised Henry V suggests a correspondence between service to God and service to the king when he
says to some of his soldiers, "Methinks I could not die anywhere
so contented as in the King's company, his cause being just and
his quarrel honorable"; however, Williams retorts, "That's more
than we know," and Bates expands upon his companion's idea:
"Ay, or more than we should seek after" (*Henry V* 4.1.126–30).
Both soldiers imply that congruence between service to God and
service to the king cannot be assumed, and Williams goes on to
suggest that the inevitable deaths in the morrow's battle could
"at the Latter Day . . . be a black matter for the King" (137, 145).
The soldiers argue that they have no choice but to serve the king,
but they refuse to accept the conventional assurance that God is
necessarily on Henry's side. Even more subversive, and therefore only hinted at, is the suggestion that serving an evil king
could put a person in opposition to God. This idea, although obvious, was probably too dangerous to be explored in any depth.[3]
However, when the king is evil or commands subjects to do evil
deeds, the conflict is evident. The principal example of an evil
king in Shakespearean drama is, of course, Richard III; thus, it is
not surprising that, on their way to the block, two of his accomplices give speeches that comment on their failure to serve God
and the evil ends that service to Richard have brought them to.
William, Lord Hastings, suggests that the choice to serve a man,
rather than God, has brought about his fall:

> Oh, momentary grace of mortal men,
> Which we more hunt for than the grace of God!
> Who builds his hope in air of your good looks
> Lives like a drunken sailor on a mast,
> Ready with every nod to tumble down
> Into the fatal bowels of the deep.
>
> (*Richard III* 3.4.96–101)

The Duke of Buckingham suggests that he is being properly punished for flouting God by swearing a false oath:

> This is the day wherein I wished to fall
> By the false faith of him whom most I trusted. . . .

That high All-Seer which I dallied with
Hath turned my feignèd prayer on my head
And given in earnest what I begged in jest.
Thus doth he force the swords of wicked men
To turn their own points in their masters' bosoms.

(5.1.16–17, 20–24)

Although neither character directly says "the king is evil" (and Richard, technically, is not king when he condemns Hastings), the conflict between serving God and serving earthly authority is obvious and is highlighted in Buckingham's speech by the phrases "false faith" and "wicked men." For this particular conflict, at least in print, there is only one permissible answer, and characters who make the wrong choice have to be shown as paying the price.

For the most part, similar political correctness prevails when a conflict arises between service to monarch and service to employer. The apprentice Peter Thump defeats and kills his master, a situation that may have disturbed members of the original audience and certainly disturbs some modern critics.[4] Thomas Horner, however, is clearly a villain, and it is hard to imagine— even if it had been possible to stage loyalty to an employer trumping loyalty to the crown—that anyone would have wanted to see an apprentice depicted as committing, or even concealing, treason on behalf of such an employer.

So dominant is the concept of service to the monarch, that even when a character fails in allegiance to the crown because of family loyalty, that motive may be hidden, as it is for the Earl of Cambridge in *Henry V*, who plots against Henry on behalf of his brother-in-law, Edmund Mortimer, the Earl of March. The failure to explain the reason for Cambridge's perfidy makes him appear simply another traitor, motivated by greed for power or money or by resentment of Henry. An exception to the rule—an instance when family loyalty supersedes that to the monarch with no apparent ill consequences to the traitors—occurs in *Richard II*. The Earl of Worcester rejects his service to his king to side with a kinsman, in this instance his brother, the Earl of Northumberland, as Northumberland's son reports to him: "[Worcester] hath forsook the court, / Broken his staff of office, and dispersed / The household of the King" and "is gone to Ravenspurgh / To offer service to the Duke of Hereford," "because Your Lordship was proclaimèd traitor" (*Richard II* 2.3.27–28, 31–32, 30). Immediately after reporting his uncle's defection

from the king's service, Hotspur also offers his service to Bolingbroke (2.3.41–44). Although the Percy family prospers in the
short term, however, they continue to be rebellious even after
Hereford ascends the throne as Henry IV, and ultimately all die
in battle or as convicted rebels. Occasionally, however, rebels
prosper. When Richard II seizes the banished Hereford's property, Edmund of Langley, Duke of York and uncle to both Richard
and Hereford, is inspired to declare:

> Both are my kinsmen;
> Th'one is my sovereign, whom both my oath
> And duty bids defend; t'other again
> Is my kinsman, whom the King hath wronged,
> Whom conscience and my kindred bids to right.
> (*Richard II* 2.2.111–15)

York ultimately chooses to serve Hereford rather than his king,
even preferring Hereford over his own son, the Duke of Aumerle,
when Aumerle sides with Richard. York thus rebels against his
king in favor of a wronged kinsman, and then, when that kinsman
seizes the throne, remains loyal to him in preference to his own
son (and the deposed, rightful king); the result is that both he and
his son wind up alive and in the king's favor. Hereford's insurrec-
tion, of course, is the rare successful rebellion, and Shakespeare
is, on the whole, following his historical sources. Beyond that, it
is rather difficult to see what, if any, principle can be found here
except that it is a fine idea to end up on the winning side.[5]

Another conflict of service that sometimes occurs in the plays
is between a character's service to the monarch and his (only
rarely her) own honor. For example, after being sent to broker a
marriage between King Edward IV and the French king's sister,
only to learn, upon his arrival at the French court, that Edward
has suddenly married Lady Grey, the Earl of Warwick tells King
Lewis and Queen Margaret that Edward is "No more my king,
for he dishonors me," and adds:

> Shame on himself! For my desert is honor;
> And to repair my honor lost for him,
> I here renounce him and return to Henry.
> My noble Queen, let former grudges pass,
> And henceforth I am thy true servitor.
> (*3 Henry VI* 3.3.184, 192–96)

Although Warwick ("the Kingmaker") helped put Edward on the
throne, he now feels that he has been shamed by his king and

master to such an extent that his lost honor requires that he align himself with his and Edward's greatest enemy, an alliance that will allow Warwick to avenge himself on Edward. The demands of his honor must be served before his king. This same idea is directly voiced by Mowbray when King Richard II orders him to abandon his intention to fight a duel with Bolingbroke:

> Myself I throw, dread sovereign, at thy foot.
> My life thou shalt command, but not my shame.
> The one my duty owes; but my fair name,
> Despite of death that lives upon my grave,
> To dark dishonor's use thou shalt not have.
> *(Richard II* 1.1.165–69)

One of the rare examples of a woman elevating service to honor over service to the crown precipitates the situation that so infuriates Warwick. Edward IV attempts to seduce Lady Grey, suggesting to her that, if she yields to him, he will restore the lands seized from her late husband; when she refuses, he tells her, "Why, then, thou shalt not have thy husband's lands," and she replies, "Why, then, mine honesty shall be my dower, / For by that loss I will not purchase them" (*3 Henry VI* 3.2.71–73). Much as she wants the property for her children, Lady Grey refuses to value wealth or even the king's favor over her honor. The upshot is that Edward marries her. Conduct books, which were written primarily by and for the middle and working classes, are not concerned with how personal honor may conflict with service, but drama, which is often concerned with the affairs of the ruling class, finds the issue not only relevant, but extremely useful as a way of complicating the conventional, simple concept that all subjects owe obedience to the monarch under all circumstances.

Still another potential conflict of service is obedience to one's duty or orders when they conflict with the wishes of another member of the upper class. In *Richard III*, Sir Robert Brakenbury, Lieutenant of the Tower, is continually faced with such conflicts. In the play's first scene, he tries to obey King Edward IV's order "that no man shall have private conference" with George, Duke of Clarence, without offending either Clarence or Richard, Duke of Gloucester (1.1.84–104). Later in the same act, Brakenbury surrenders custody of Clarence to the two murderers, who have been given a warrant by Richard (1.4.90–95).[6] After Richard becomes de facto king, Brakenbury finds himself required to forbid Queen Elizabeth, the Duchess of York, the

Marquis of Dorset, and Richard's wife from visiting the princes in the Tower, despite the boys' relatives' protests (4.1.13–27). Again, he is anxious to avoid responsibility for offending them, pleading, "I am bound by oath, and therefore pardon me" (27). Brakenbury's conflicts reflect the final convulsions of the Wars of the Roses: although the Yorkists are now unchallenged in their power, their royal authority is tainted by guilt, so that even their servants cannot obey royal commands without condemning other members of the royal family. Similarly, although the Jailer describes Paulina as "a worthy lady / And one whom much I honor," he cannot accede to her request that he "Conduct [her] to the Queen," because, he explains, "To the contrary I have express commandment" (*Winter's Tale* 2.2.5–8). He is also concerned about the punishment he may incur if Hermione allows Paulina to take the baby Perdita to Leontes, although he finally accepts Paulina's statement that the innocent baby cannot justifiably be kept prisoner; nevertheless, Paulina offers to shield him from Leontes' anger (2.2.56–66). This is a problem that often seems to be the lot of jailers: the Provost in *Measure for Measure* allows the man he thinks is a Friar to delay Claudio's execution (4.2.157–202; 4.3.69–91); in this instance, unlike Brakenbury and Leontes' Jailer, the Provost disobeys the established authority he is sworn to serve, instead doing what he believes is right. There is no real conflict, however, since the Friar is the disguised Duke; thus, the Provost (unwittingly, to be sure) is able to obey the "Friar," satisfy his conscience, and still serve his real master. It is one of the few times in the canon that such a conflict finds so neat a resolution.

Another conflict that occasionally arises, particularly for domestic servants, is whether to serve husband or wife when the two are at odds.[7] Since few of Shakespeare's plays feature long-established marriages in which the husband and wife require different services, this is not a common conflict; when recent marriages are depicted, the spouses are usually shown as bringing their own servants to the marriage, almost in the way that such royal couples as Oberon and Titania have their own retinues of servants. One comic example of the difficulty of trying to serve both a master and a mistress occurs in *The Comedy of Errors*, in which E. Dromio, who is trying to serve a mistress and (at different times) two masters, receives most of the play's beatings. A less physical, but deadlier, conflict is discerned by Carol Thomas Neely in a servant's attempt to remain loyal to both a man and a woman—not, technically, a husband and wife, but definitely a couple: "Enobarbus, caught between Antony and Cleopatra, Roman power and Egyptian desire, comedy and tragedy, dies embodying the play's oppositions."[8] In *The Winter's Tale*, members of the court must decide whether to obey Leontes or support Hermione; although several members of the court declare their belief in Hermione's innocence, only Paulina ultimately risks the king's wrath by defying him and remaining in Sicilia. Similarly, Emilia defies her mistress's husband (and her own husband) to testify to Desdemona's virtue. One very obvious instance of this conflict occurs in the most domestic of Shakespeare's plays, *The Merry Wives of Windsor*, when two of the Ford family's servants, John and Robert, participate in the wives' plot to punish Falstaff and cure Ford. Although they may not know what's going on the first time they are ordered to carry the buck basket to Datchet Mead, they certainly know, after dumping Falstaff into the Thames, that they smuggled a man out of the house and that their master is looking for a man in his house, but they do not tell him what they know (4.2.100–107). They are loyal to their mistress, but at the very least they are part of a plot to make a fool of their master, and they may simply be betraying him. Since Ford is foolishly jealous, and his wife is virtuous and clever, the servants' loyalty is well placed for the purposes of the comedy, but one wonders if for some of the men in the original audience this episode did not represent another of their great fears: that their wives would betray them with the help of their servants.

One of the most common conflicts of service is that between service to an employer and one's own desires and welfare. Here again, of course, the theory of service would suggest that there should be no conflict, if only because servants are expected to want only what's best for their employers. Shakespeare, however, was not writing theory, and his characters, even when they are servants or serving, often represent or comment upon the difference between what their duty requires them to do and what they as human beings desire. As noted earlier, Wolsey serves his own ambition rather than either God or king. Iago betrays his master and mistress for his own reasons, though critics are still arguing over exactly what those reasons are. Various of Antony and Cleopatra's servants, including Enobarbus, desert to Caesar out of fear of being on the losing side, while Camillo forsakes Leontes' service out of fear of what will happen to him if he does the king's bidding or what Leontes will do to him if he disobeys. Women who disguise themselves as servants to men they love

are apt to find this conflict particularly painful. Viola, disguised
as "Cesario," faithfully serves Orsino in his attempt to woo
Olivia, although she sees her service as "a barful strife" because
"Whoe'er I woo, myself would be his wife" (*Twelfth Night* 1.4.41–
42). A more elaborate explanation of this dilemma is made by
Julia, disguised as "Sebastian," when she delivers a love letter
and a ring from Proteus to Silvia:

> How many women would do such a message?
> Alas, poor Proteus! Thou hast entertained
> A fox to be the shepherd of thy lambs.
> . . . This ring I gave him when he parted from me,
> To bind him to remember my good will;
> And now am I, unhappy messenger,
> To plead for that which I would not obtain,
> To carry that which I would have refused,
> To praise his faith which I would have dispraised.
> I am my master's true-confirmèd love,
> But cannot be true servant to my master
> Unless I prove false traitor to myself.
>
> (*T.G.V.* 4.4.89–91, 96–104)

Unlike Viola, Julia chooses service to herself over service to Proteus, telling Silvia how her master wrongs Julia (140); although
this is another violation of the ideal of service, Proteus is such a
cad that it is impossible to feel any sympathy for his plight as the
master of a disloyal servant. Clearly, Shakespeare is not following the conduct books in presenting an ideal of service; rather,
he is demonstrating how difficult an ideal it is and how complicated it is to apply to the realities of life.

Because service is often the means by which classes come into
contact with one another, conflicting services can lead to conflicts between classes. Class conflict in Shakespeare often results when characters, particularly lower-class characters,
confront the question of the multiple services they owe and
choose to serve a person or an idea that differs from the one to
which class conventions dictate they owe service.

One of the simpler examples of such class conflict occurs in 2
Henry VI. Jack Cade and his rebellious followers reject the idea
that they owe service to anyone but themselves. Although a tool
of the Duke of York (3.1.355–59), who likewise rejects his proper
service to the king, Cade either does not know or refuses to accept this position: he denies William Stafford's assertion that the
Duke of York taught him to claim royal descent (4.2.149–50) and

never indicates any intention of serving York. Cade appeals to his followers' desire to serve none but themselves, suggesting that— once the rebels have "recovered [their] ancient freedom" and thrown off their "slavery to the nobility" (4.8.24–27)—food and drink will be cheap or free, there will be no money, all things will be in common, and all men will "agree like brothers" (4.2.63–67, 71–74; 4.6.1–4; 4.7.17). In order to achieve this state, he declares, they must kill not only all the lords and gentlemen, but also all the lawyers and clerks (4.2.75–106, 179).

But Cade makes it clear that he is not opposed to service as a concept; he simply wants to stop serving and be served himself: the men who wear his livery and agree like brothers will be expected, he says, to "worship me their lord" (4.2.74) and the rest of the population will serve him: "The proudest peer in the realm shall not wear a head on his shoulders unless he pay me tribute. There shall not a maid be married but she shall pay to me her maidenhead ere they have it. Men shall hold of me *in capite*; and we charge and command that their wives be as free as heart can wish or tongue can tell" (4.7.115–20). Cade's rebellion fails when Thomas, Lord Clifford, succeeds in recalling the rebels to their proper service by invoking the magical name of Henry V, appealing to their patriotism, and mentioning that "Henry [VI] hath money" to pay them for fighting the French (4.8.32–51). Although the rebels' grievances are expressed in terms of class antagonism, none of them can really imagine a classless world, a world without some people serving others: Cade seeks an England in which he commands service rather than giving it, while his supporters define themselves as followers, whether exclaiming "We'll follow Cade, we'll follow Cade!" or "A Clifford! A Clifford! We'll follow the King and Clifford!" (4.8.32, 51).

Derek Cohen describes the rebels as "fools and dolts, easily misled by a villain who promises them anarchy."[9] Obviously, however, Cade is not promising real anarchy, or at least not permanent anarchy; he simply intends to eliminate the present commanders of service so that he can command service himself, and his followers clearly regard him as a leader worth serving. The rebels are certainly depicted as ridiculous at times, as well as very dangerous, but they are not fools or dolts because they fail to conceive of a new paradigm in which no one owes service to anyone else.[10]

Although class conflict is less violent in *Henry V*, class consciousness is certainly present, despite Henry's attempts, in some of his speeches, to obscure class distinctions in various ways. He exalts the common soldiers: "there is none of you so mean and base / That hath not noble luster in your eyes" (3.1.29–30) and promises that their service will eliminate class distinctions:

> We few, we happy few, we band of brothers.
> For he today that sheds his blood with me
> Shall be my brother; be he ne'er so vile,
> This day shall gentle his condition.
>
> (4.3.60–63)

He identifies himself as a man, rather than as a king, and forswears the privileges of his status, in particular the privilege of being ransomed:

> I think the King is but a man, as I am. The violet smells to him as it doth to me; the element shows to him as it doth to me; all his senses have but human conditions. His ceremonies laid by, in his nakedness he appears but a man.
>
> (4.1.102–6)

> Come thou no more for ransom, gentle herald.
> They shall have none, I swear, but these my joints,
> Which if they have as I will leave 'em them,
> Shall yield them little, tell the Constable.
>
> (4.3.122–25)

> Know'st thou not
> That I have fined these bones of mine for ransom?
>
> (4.7.67–68)

But the common soldier Williams, although persuaded by Henry that "every man that dies ill [in battle], the ill upon his own head, the King is not to answer it" (4.1.186–87), remains dubious about the king's motives and honesty:

> *King* I myself heard the King say he would not be ransomed.
> *Williams* Ay, he said so, to make us fight cheerfully; but when our throats are cut, he may be ransomed, and we ne'er the wiser.
> *King* If I live to see it, I will never trust his word after.
> *Williams* You pay him then! That's a perilous shot out of an elder-gun, that a poor and private displeasure can do against a monarch! You may as well go about to turn the sun to ice with fanning in his face with a peacock's feather. You'll never trust his word after! Come, 'tis a foolish saying.
>
> (4.1.190–201)[11]

Williams recognizes that the king may be lying in order to inspire his lower-class soldiers and that, if he is, there is nothing the soldiers can do but recognize and resent it. But this class consciousness comes nearer conflict when Williams and Henry exchange gloves and vow to fight out the quarrel after the battle. Although Williams is, of course, unaware that his opponent is the king, Fluellen—a character who is a kind of repository of the best of chivalric values—makes it clear that in his opinion service to one's own honor outweighs class distinctions:

> *King*   What think you, Captain Fluellen, is it fit this soldier keep his oath?
>
> *Fluellen*   He is a craven and a villain else, an't please Your Majesty, in my conscience.
>
> *King*   It may be his enemy is a gentleman of great sort, quite from the answer of his degree.
>
> *Fluellen*   Though he be as good a gentleman as the devil is, as Lucifer and Beelzebub himself, it is necessary, look Your Grace, that he keep his vow and his oath. If he be perjured, see you now, his reputation is as arrant a villain and a Jack-sauce as ever his plack shoe trod upon God's ground and his earth, in my conscience, la!
>
> (4.7.128–40)

Because Williams's honor is important to him, he puts himself, even though unwittingly, in a potentially perilous position, since, as Henry points out, "It was ourself thou didst abuse" (4.8.49). Williams's reply goes to the heart of Henry's dissembling: "You appeared to me but as a common man—witness the night, your garments, your lowliness. And what Your Highness suffered under that shape, I beseech you take it for your own fault and not mine; for had you been as I took you for, I made no offense" (4.8.50–55). By serving the code of martial honor, Williams has violated the class code; he is forgiven because Henry chooses to be "generous," but Henry's deception has exposed the discrepancy between the two kinds of service Williams owes: there is no way a man in his position could act without offending against either honor or class; his services in this situation are mutually exclusive—he cannot serve both, yet he must serve both. It is hardly surprising that Henry "excuses" Williams his offense against class without answering him; because both Williams's services are correct, though conflicting, there can be no logical solution to his dilemma.[12]

A more serious instance of class conflict occurs in act 3, scene 7 of *King Lear*, when Cornwall's servant rebels during his master's blinding of Gloucester. One might assume that this rebellion could be any human being's response to Gloucester's plea, "He that will think to live till he be old, / Give me some help!" (72–73), but the First Servant, Cornwall, and Regan all phrase their speeches in terms that emphasize service and class:

> First Servant Hold your hand, my lord!
>   I have served you ever since I was a child.
>   But better service have I never done you
>   Than now to bid you hold.
> Regan How now, you dog?
> First Servant [to Regan]
>   If you did wear a beard upon your chin,
>   I'd shake it on this quarrel.—What do you mean?
> Cornwall My villain? [He draws his sword.]
> First Servant [drawing]
>   Nay, then, come on, and take the chance of anger.
>   [They fight. Cornwall is wounded.]
> Regan [to another Servant]
>   Give me thy sword. A peasant stand up thus?
>   [She takes a sword and runs at him behind.]
> First Servant
>   Oh, I am slain! My lord, you have one eye left
>   To see some mischief on him. Oh! [He dies.]
>
>   (75–85)

Although the Servant is obviously violating the conventional idea of service in opposing his master, he does not claim that he does not owe service, or that as a moral human being he is not bound to obey immoral commands or stand by idly while wicked deeds are done; instead, he appeals to a higher ideal of service. He is still, he says, serving his master, but he argues that in this situation opposition is better service than passive obedience would be. For the Servant, two kinds of service are possible, and he chooses the less conventional kind. Regan and Cornwall seem less disturbed by the attempt to thwart their wishes than by the fact that the attempt is made by a servant. They make no effort to argue with him or even threaten him; they seem astonished that a "dog," a "villain," a "peasant," would dare to defy them, and they deal with his rebellion in the quickest possible way by treacherously killing him. Cornwall commands his remaining servants to "throw this slave / Upon the dunghill" (99–100) and that, for Cornwall and Regan, would be the end of the matter, but that the Servant has given Cornwall his death-wound, thus serving in his rebellion the ends of justice, if not those of his evil master.[13]

Although upper class, Caius Marcius Coriolanus is a servant of Rome, by both his own description and his enemies'. Class conflict results in *Coriolanus* because the hero resents having to declare that he serves the plebeians, as well as "Rome"; he is uncomfortable with the identification made by the people and their representative, the tribune Sicinius:

> *Sicinius*
>   What is the city but the people?
> *All Plebeians*   True,
>   The people are the city.
>
> (3.1.202–3)

Although even the tribunes, who hate Coriolanus, acknowledge his valuable services (2.3.235–37; 3.1.315–17; 3.3.89–90), they and the plebeians reject him because he performs these services for the wrong reasons:

> *Second Citizen* Consider you what services he has done for his country?
> *First Citizen* Very well, and could be content to give him good report for't, but that he pays himself with being proud.
> *Second Citizen* Nay, but speak not maliciously.
> *First Citizen* I say unto you, what he hath done famously he did it to that end. Though soft-conscienced men can be content to say it was for his country, he did it to please his mother and to be partly proud, which he is, even to the altitude of his virtue.
>
> (1.1.28–38)[14]

That their distrust of Caius Marcius's motives is well-founded is proven by the man himself, who tells his mother "I had rather be their servant in my way, / Than sway with them in theirs" (2.1.202–3) and who distinguishes between serving his country and a people he despises:

>   What must I say?
> 'I pray, sir'—Plague upon't! I cannot bring
> My tongue to such a pace. 'Look, sir, my wounds!
> I got them in my country's service, when
> Some certain of your brethren roared and ran
> From th' noise of our own drums.'
>
> (2.3.50–55)

Ironically, the plebians are willing to let Coriolanus be their master if he will publicly acknowledge himself their servant, but they will not let him remain even "a petty servant to the state" (2.3.179) if he persists in acting like their master.

Coriolanus's conflict is not a simple class conflict, of course, although class has much to do with it. As David G. Hale points out, he "tries to reconcile the demands of obedience to his mother and obedience to the concept of honor which he learned from her."[15] Volumnia wants Coriolanus to claim the highest of aristocratic offices—the consulship—but in order to attain that height, he must abase himself by professing himself the servant of the plebeians:

> Your voices! For your voices I have fought;
> Watched for your voices; for your voices bear
> Of wounds two dozen odd. Battles thrice six
> I have seen and heard of; for your voices have
> Done many things, some less, some more. Your voices!
> Indeed, I would be consul.
>
> (2.3.126–31)

Zvi Jagendorf sums up the complexity of Coriolanus's dilemma: "Volumnia cannot entertain the possibility that her son may fail. The hero's birthright is to take all. But the possibility of 'nothing' may not be ignored, especially when that absurdity, the aristocrat-laborer, must receive his hire and salary from that political oddity, the plebeian employer."[16] Ultimately, Coriolanus cannot bring himself to say that the services he has performed have been done for people whom he cannot respect, and Rome's greatest servant is dismissed.

Yet, despite his unwillingness to define himself as the Roman people's servant, Coriolanus is a man who insists on defining himself in terms of service even after he has been expelled from Rome. He refuses to see himself as a masterless man; instead, he seeks to serve Aufidius and the Volscians:

> My birthplace hate I, and my love's upon
> This enemy town. I'll enter. If [Aufidius] slay me,
> He does fair justice; if he give me way,
> I'll do his country service.
>
> (4.4.23–26)

> Wife, mother, child, I know not. My affairs
> Are servanted to others.
>
> (5.2.83–84)

Hail, lords! I am returned your soldier,
No more infected with my country's love
Than when I parted hence, but still subsisting
Under your great command.

(5.6.72–75)

Although Coriolanus is certainly a character who serves his own
pride, honor, and mother, he seeks to serve something beyond
these things as well, first the idea of Rome, then the idea of
Rome's enemy. His tragedy may occur because he cannot serve
ideas without doing and professing service to actual people, but
he is also entrapped in a situation he himself describes as "double worship," that of attempting to serve multiple masters, even
though he recognizes

> when two authorities are up,
> Neither supreme, how soon confusion
> May enter twixt the gap of both and take
> The one by th'other.

(3.1.145, 112–15)

Unable simultaneously to serve an ideal Rome, the less-than-
ideal plebeians, his honor, and his mother's ambition for him, Coriolanus is dismissed from service by his plebeian employers;
later, trying to reconcile his service to the Volscians with his duty
to his family, he is destroyed. His conflicting services are irresolvable and are the cause of his tragedy.

A much less serious instance of class conflict is presented in
the dialogue between the Boatswain and Alonso, Antonio, Sebastian, and Gonzalo in the first scene of *The Tempest*. The Boatswain would ordinarily owe and show deference to his social
superiors, but he has neither the time nor the inclination for such
deference to characters whose presence interferes with his more
important service of trying to prevent the ship from running
aground (and thereby saving the upper-class characters' lives,
although for the Boatswain that is merely a concomitant benefit).
The Boatswain is not merely irritable, for his speeches to his
master and the crew show no animosity: "Here, Master. What
cheer?" "Heigh, my hearts! Cheerly, cheerly, my hearts! Yare,
yare!" (2, 5–6). His statements to the nobility, however, are in a
very different vein. He begins with a moderate request—"I pray
now, keep below" (11)—and continues with an explanation—
"You mar our labor. Keep your cabins! You do assist the storm"
(13–14). So much the Boatswain might say to anyone who inter-

fered with him at such a time; but when Gonzalo remonstrates with him, he reacts by declaring social rank absurd in this situation: "Hence! What cares these roarers for the name of king? To cabin! Silence! Trouble us not" (16–18). Gonzalo's attempt to recall him to a knowledge of his duty to higher ranks—"Good, yet remember whom thou hast aboard" (19–20)—produces a statement that stresses both the meaninglessness of social hierarchy in the face of natural disaster and his own rejection of social duties that interfere with his services to himself and his ship, which services are now one:

> None that I more love than myself. You are a councillor; if you can command these elements to silence and work the peace of the present, we will not hand a rope more. Use your authority. If you cannot, give thanks you have lived so long, and make yourself ready in your cabin for the mischance of the hour, if it so hap.—Cheerly, good hearts!—Out of our way, I say.
>
> (20–28)

It is, of course, arguable that the Boatswain is doing the nobility who so annoy him the best service in his power by attempting to save their lives along with his own and his ship. But certainly they—with the possible exception of Alonso, who does not return to trouble the Boatswain further but goes off to pray (54)—do not accept this form of service. When Sebastian, Antonio, and Gonzalo reappear, they are confronted with a series of rhetorical questions—"Yet again? What do you here? Shall we give o'er and drown? Have you a mind to sink?" (39–40)—and depart after cursing the man who is trying, however discourteously, to save them (41–42, 44–46, 56–58).[17] Whether the Boatswain's "Work you, then" (43) is addressed to the nobles (in which case, he is suggesting that gentlemen should work with their hands) or to his sailors (in which case, he is ignoring his "betters"), it is clearly disrespectful. Antonio's "We are less afraid to be drown'd than thou art" (45–46) may be a final attempt to assert class superiority, but it is a feeble one. The Boatswain may well be an "insolent noisemaker" (44–45), but he is clearly sensible in deferring deference in favor of his more important service. As Curt Breight has noted, the Boatswain's attitude is "refreshingly subversive," and it seems likely that at least some elements of Shakespeare's original audience would have appreciated it.[18]

The services demanded by the conventions of class in Shakespeare's plays seem relatively straightforward, at least to the characters attempting to uphold such conventions: the lower classes should defer to the wishes of the upper classes, and servants should obey their masters and mistresses. But class service is only one of a number of types of service represented in the plays, and often it is not the most important. Where class service conflicts with other services that are also clearly correct and necessary, such as survival, honor, and ethics, the result is frequently class conflict; and our sympathies are often with those characters who reject class service in favor of less conventional services.

The other great service conflict that underlies many of Shakespeare's plays is that of gender. Again, the services imposed by the conventions of the period would appear to be simple and obvious: women defer to men; female servants defer to their (usually female) employers. In *Broken Nuptials in Shakespeare's Plays*, Neely suggests that Shakespeare's drama represents relationships between women as almost invariably supportive: "Intimacy, mutual aid and instinctive sympathy are characteristic of most female relationships delineated by Shakespeare. Women's sympathy for and identification with each other cross boundaries of age, class, role, and value, existing between Julia and Sylvia, Beatrice and Hero, Desdemona and Emilia, Cleopatra and her waiting women, Hermione and Paulina. But at the same time, female friendships consistently support and further women's bonds with men. Unlike male friendships, they are not experienced or dramatized as in conflict with heterosexual bonds."[19] However, while Neely's description is accurate for many such relationships, the situation is sometimes more complex than she suggests. The relationships between ladies and their serving-women are often complicated by the servants' conflicts between duty to their mistresses and duty to their husbands or lovers. Although this conflict is usually invisible to the employer, who assumes that her servant is completely loyal to her, Shakespeare makes the audience aware that the serving-woman who also has a relationship with a man is likely to be caught in an irreconcilable dilemma: if the demands of her mistress conflict with those of her husband or lover, she is bound to honor both, although she cannot honor both. Such dilemmas, however, are shown to have importance far beyond individual characters: the choices made by the women trapped in such conflicts of service are often integral to the action of their plays.

Of course, many servingwomen are apparently not faced with such conflicts, since they are not represented as being involved in love relationships with men. Examples of such heart-whole and fancy-free women include Alice in *Henry V*, Lucetta in *The Two Gentlemen of Verona*, Ursula in *Much Ado about Nothing*, Lady Macbeth's Gentlewoman, and the nameless Lady who refuses to allow Cloten to bribe her into allowing him access to Imogen (*Cymbeline* 2.3.79–87). In such comedies as *Love's Labor's Lost* and *The Merchant of Venice*, relationships with men can even serve to unite mistresses and serving-women when both are simultaneously in love with men who are also friends. On the other hand, a mistress's love relationship can divide her from her female servant, as happens in *Romeo and Juliet*,[20] and even a serving-woman as loyal to her mistress as Charmian can consider, if only jokingly, the idea of marriage as freedom from service, as she hopefully instructs the Soothsayer: "Find me to marry me with Octavius Caesar, and companion me with my mistress" (*Antony* 1.2.30–32).

Religious texts, legal handbooks, conduct books, and popular entertainments—nearly all, of course, written by men, most of them probably members of the servant-employing, rather than serving, classes—mandate absolute obedience from women and servants toward their husbands and employers.[21] The writers of such works declare, not only that God and the state command such obedience, but that husbands and masters are themselves like God and the monarch in relation to women and servants.[22] However, whereas various writers, particularly religious controversialists, were willing to suggest that there are instances when a man should resist church and state, few writers were willing to suggest that servants should resist their employers, and even fewer to explore the possibility of women resisting their husbands or opposing their ideas and feelings to those of men. Although such writers were willing to grant liberty to the consciences of free men to oppose and even overthrow church and state, granting the same liberty to servants and women apparently brought resistance a little too close to home.[23]

Although prose writers seem to have largely ignored the possibility of these potentially conflicting services, Shakespeare makes repeated and varied use of such conflicts. The one unchanging factor seems to be that the serving-woman involved yields to the demands of her husband or lover (whom she presumably hopes is her husband-to-be), thereby at least neglecting the interests of her mistress, and sometimes even betraying her. In the serving-women's defense, however, it can be said that Shakespeare never creates any of them villainous; although their

choices may be wrong and may lead to tragedy, there is no textual evidence that they intend harm to their ladies, and in the
most serious cases they remain ignorant of the evil intended by
the men whose interests they choose to serve. This may not
speak very highly of their intelligence, but it does testify to their
basic virtue. Although their men apparently expect them to put
male interests ahead of those of their mistresses, they apparently recognize that the women are too virtuous and loyal to their
mistresses knowingly to commit any act that would endanger
them.

On the other hand, at least one serving-woman takes the lead
in a scheme that disturbs her mistress's household: Maria in
Twelfth Night is the guiding intelligence of the plot to humiliate
Malvolio. Although this plot does not cause Maria's mistress,
Olivia, any harm and in fact hardly concerns her in her love-be-
sotted state,[24] it does have the effect of further disrupting her admittedly already disorderly household and it does represent a
challenge to her authority in its attack on her steward. Furthermore, Maria and her fellow-plotters (all, except Sir Andrew, who
takes no real part, servants or dependents of Olivia) apparently
have no compunction about lying to Olivia to convince her that
Malvolio is "possessed" and potentially dangerous (3.4.9–13;
5.1.280, 284–91). Maria's declared motive for this violation of trust
is personal: she detests Malvolio, who is rude to her (as he is to
nearly everyone in the play) and threatens to get her into trouble
with Olivia, and whose pretentiousness and self-satisfaction she
professes to find intolerable (2.3.120–23, 146–52). Although these
are the obvious reasons for what she refers to as "my revenge"
(152), she can hardly be unaware that such a plot will meet with
the enthusiastic approval of Sir Toby, who also has reason to de-
test Malvolio. Whether or not we accept Toby's declaration that
Maria "adores" him (178–79), she does find that humiliating Malvolio is the way to Toby's heart (2.5.176–202) to such an extent
that, according to Fabian, he marries her "in recompense" of the
plot (5.1.362–64). Although we have no way of knowing whether
Maria's primary motive for plotting against Malvolio was to
please Toby and encourage him to propose marriage, she does
accept him. Whatever we might speculate about her feelings or
hopes for future happiness, this marriage presumably has the effect of elevating her social status from waiting-gentlewoman to
knight's lady.[25] Since it does not appear that Olivia holds a grudge
(and since Malvolio rejects her offer to allow him to judge the
plotters), it seems that Maria's foregrounding of her own and

Toby's interests over those of her mistress will be forgiven and forgotten, as is suitable to comedy, if somewhat irregular, given the violation of hierarchy Maria has perpetrated.

Margaret, one of Hero's waiting-gentlewomen in *Much Ado*, is both like and unlike Maria. Her lines express no animosity toward her mistress, although an actress could perhaps convey such a motivation wordlessly.[26] Such motivation is unnecessary, however, if we believe Borachio's statement that he is "much . . . in the favor of Margaret" (2.2.13). It is, however, difficult to construct a plausible explanation of what Margaret could imagine she is doing when she follows Borachio's instructions to enter Hero's empty room between midnight and 1 a.m., dress in Hero's garments, look out Hero's window, and listen to Borachio address her as "Hero," though presumably she does not imagine that they will be overheard (3.3.142–49; 4.1.83–84; 5.1.227–34).[27] Margaret may be absolved of evil intent by Borachio's insistence that he alone is guilty, while Margaret has always "been just and virtuous" (5.1.257–58, 297) and Leonato's enigmatic statement that although "Margaret was in some fault for this," it was "against her will, as it appears / In the true course of all the question" (5.4.4–6). What is easier to explain, but much harder to justify, is Margaret's silence when Don Pedro and Claudio shame Hero during the first wedding scene: as one of Hero's waiting-gentlewomen, she must be present, and she alone (excepting the plotters themselves) must realize the truth. Presumably, she says nothing because she is frightened about what will happen to her, or perhaps to Borachio, or both, if their transgressions are revealed. Nevertheless, this silence, which threatens to destroy Hero's life and the lives of those who love her, seems an unforgiveable betrayal, which is presumably why, except for Leonato's suggestion that Margaret was under some unexplained duress, this comedy cannot afford to explore the issue.

Although *Much Ado* is not, of course, in any sense "about" Margaret's character, it seems just possible that we are expected to see her (and Maria) as somewhat parallel to the clever slaves of Plautine comedy, whose principal loyalty is to themselves. Such slave-characters plot to gain their freedom; these female characters may also resent their servitude and plot to get married, which will get them as much freedom as was available to women of the period.[28] Ralph Berry describes Margaret as "a character who does not 'know her place,'" which may be an accurate assessment from an employer's viewpoint; however, Margaret may in fact be (or at least be interpreted as) a character who knows her place and her feelings about that place all too well and also knows what she needs to do to advance beyond that place: find a husband.[29]

Margaret is certainly much interested in the subject of marriage: though her number of lines is small, she devotes many of them to chaffing both Hero and Beatrice on the subject (3.4.28–36, 49–56, 67–85), and she quibbles with Benedick about it, posing marriage as her only alternative to a life "belowstairs" (5.2.4–10).[30] In addition, she is obviously intelligent: she holds her own in repartee with the two principal wits of the play, both of whom acknowledge her acuity (3.4.62–63; 5.2.11–12). Finally, the play suggests that she is not altogether trustworthy (although in this play, in which nearly every character is involved in deception, that may not distinguish her greatly). Margaret is the servant whom Hero chooses to lure Beatrice into the trap to make her love Benedick; this indicates that not only does Hero trust Margaret's power to deceive the clever Beatrice, but that Hero thinks that Margaret will be accepted as the kind of servant who would betray Beatrice's private conversation. Beatrice later suggests, however jokingly, that Margaret is a wanton who will betray her husband when she has one (3.4.43–45). Perhaps as a result of her guilty conscience, Margaret also seems obsessed with misinterpretation, renunciation of faith, and conversion (3.4.31–33, 46, 52–53, 74–85), concluding her speeches in act 3, scene 4 (which she dominates) with the declaration that her tongue does not run "a false gallop" (87). Given Margaret's intelligence, deviousness, probable desire to be married, and (especially) failure to divulge what she knows, it is not easy to assume that she is entirely innocent; one is forced to wonder if Leonato's statement that Margaret served Borachio's interests "against her will" is true, or if this is simply a final example of Margaret's somewhat unscrupulous cleverness in serving her own interests, rather than those of her employers.

The most serious (although also, in some ways, the most innocent) betrayal of a mistress by her serving-woman is, of course, Emilia's betrayal of Desdemona. The handkerchief she appropriates from Desdemona is a principal, perhaps the principal, element in Iago's plot to destroy Othello and Desdemona.[31] Furthermore, she compounds her crime by lying when Desdemona asks her if she knows where the handkerchief might have been lost (3.4.23–24). On the other hand, it *is* only a handkerchief, and her speech when she discovers it seems designed by Shakespeare to minimize her guilt:

I am glad I have found this napkin.
This was her first remembrance from the Moor.
My wayward husband hath a hundred times
Wooed me to steal it, but she so loves the token—
For he conjured her she should ever keep it—
That she reserves it evermore about her
To kiss and talk to. I'll have the work ta'en out,
And give't Iago. What he will do with it
Heaven knows, not I;
I nothing but to please his fantasy.

(3.3.306–15)

Although Iago has apparently been urging Emilia to steal the handkerchief, she has not done so: given Desdemona's attachment to it, perhaps she has not had the opportunity, and given her failure to return it, she may seem to be quibbling here, but the fact is that she does find, rather than steal, the "napkin." Emilia cannot possibly know the importance Othello attaches to it (although she does know the importance Desdemona attaches to it) or the use Iago plans to make of it. Furthermore, the man who requires her to obtain it is her husband, whom she is bound to obey. Most importantly, however, she does not, apparently, intend to filch the original at all: she plans to have it copied and give the copy to Iago.

Her conversation with her husband, who enters immediately after this speech, goes even further to absolve her from guilt. In the course of this brief dialogue (316–36), Emilia, who apparently hopes to please her husband with the handkerchief, is met with scorn; she attempts to learn why he wants it, but he refuses to tell her. Apparently, she never actually gives it to him; rather, he snatches it from her. When, remorseful at what she realizes will be Desdemona's reaction to the handkerchief's loss, she pleads to have it returned, Iago's only response is to order his wife not to admit any knowledge of it. Although there can be no question that, in choosing to serve her husband rather than her mistress, Emilia makes a tragic mistake, there seems to be little more Shakespeare could have done to excuse her and make her sin against service as venial a one as possible.

Even if the audience still holds Emilia blameworthy at this point, however, she redeems herself in the final scene by her "heroic disobedience for which she pays with her life."[32] When Emilia realizes what has happened and why, she rejects the duty of wifely obedience, a choice with more than domestic implications: as Neely points out, "Emilia's confession is not just a refusal of obedience; it destroys Iago's plot and refutes his philosophy, which requires that she act according to her own self-interest." [33] By continuing to serve her dead mistress, Emilia not only reveals her part in causing the tragedy, but also defies her master as well as her husband. Though both threaten her, she refuses to be silenced until Iago kills her, too late to save himself. Servant to the play's most virtuous character and wife to its villain, Emilia is perfectly positioned to "report the truth" (5.2.132), but her utter fearlessness in doing so allows her to transcend (or expand) the period's expectations of women, wives, and servants. [34]

The Winter's Tale's equally fearless Paulina is, of course, the ringer in this group, the serving gentlewoman who chooses, immediately and unshakeably, to serve her lady and the truth in spite of anything men, including her husband and her king, can say against her. (Of course, Paulina repeatedly defines herself as the true servant of an erring king, as well as a supporter of Hermione; see chapter 9.) There is, therefore, no consistent pattern to be found in the behavior of such conflicted gentlewomen, except that service to one's mistress seems generally to be more approved in the worlds of these plays than loyalty to all-too-untrustworthy men. The differences in the choices made by these characters and the outcomes of those choices may be generic, or due to Shakespeare's desire to ring the changes on this situation, or simply coincidental. In any event, Shakespeare seems to have found the conflicts inherent in the role of a serving-woman who also must please or wants to please a man not her employer to be both a useful dramatic device and a complicating theme not unworthy of his attention.

In his article about the duel between Peter Thump and his master Horner, Craig A. Bernthal poses a question that sums up the tension that must often have been produced by such conflicts of service: "if loyalty to the crown and to the family were *both* required to make Elizabethan society work, is not the impossibility of satisfying both requirements the most upsetting conjecture that could have been set before Tudor audiences?" (54). No doubt it was upsetting, but the conflict between monarch and family was only one of a number of conflicts that early modern people had to negotiate. And, upsetting as they may have been, logically irresolvable as the situations may have been, such conflicts are highly dramatic, which suggests why they are so often highlighted in Shakespeare's plays. Perhaps the playwright also felt that these situations were not devoid of personal interest for his audience, many of whom—in a society so dependent on various kinds of service—must have encountered similar conflicts in their own lives.

9

"Every good servant does not all commands": The Duty to Disobey

Sᴇʀᴠɪᴄᴇ, ꜰᴏʀ ᴍᴀɴʏ ᴏꜰ ꜱʜᴀᴋᴇꜱᴘᴇᴀʀᴇ's ꜱᴇʀᴠᴀɴᴛ-ᴄʜᴀʀᴀᴄᴛᴇʀꜱ, ɪꜱ more than mere obedience to command. Nor is it surprising that this is so. Although it appears that all nondramatic writers who deal with "the servant question" in this period stress the need for servants to be obedient under virtually any circumstances, such writers often mention that servants are not bound to obey commands that violate a higher law. The writers of legal, religious, and conduct books, however, generally avoid exploring the implications of conflicts arising from the need to be obedient both to employers and to other authorities, such as God, the king or queen, the law, the truth, or a servant's own conscience.[1] Shakespeare, though, is less reluctant to explore this uncharted, and potentially dangerous, territory: the plays provide many representations of servants who are willing and able, despite threats to their lives and livelihoods, to resist or disobey their employers, a disobedience that is often defined as a higher kind of service. Although Richard Strier has discussed "virtuous disobedience" in *King Lear* and the romances, such disobedience is neither a late development nor particularly rare;[2] Shakespeare, in fact, represents virtuously disobedient servants resisting their employers' commands frequently enough to suggest that conflicts of service were of continuing interest to both the playwright and his audience.[3] Shakespeare's treatment of such conflicts indicates both that he was willing to dramatize potentially controversial issues that the prose writers of his era were unwilling to explore and that his concept of service transcended the conventional one of simple obedience.

On the general question of obedience to higher authority, some writers, like E. Nesbit, present the conventional argument that there can be no discrepancy between serving God and civil authority, "because *Caesar* hath not . . . *commaund* divided with God: but (for the Scriptures teach so) deputed of God";[4] other writers, however, suggest that true service is service to God and at least hint at the possibility of discrepancies between service to God and service to men. Heinrich Bullinger, for example, states, "Againe, the servant must lay a part all evyll condicions, pryde, unfaythfulnes, brawling and murmuring, piking & tale telling, remembring Paules exhortacion saying: Ye servants be obedient to your maisters with feare & trembling in singlenes of your hart, as unto Christ, not with eye service as men pleasers, but even as ye servants of Christ, y^t ye may do the wyll of God from your harts with love. Think that ye serve the Lord, and not men."[5] Some writers go further still; Nicholas Ling declares the need for total obedience: "Servants must be obedient to their masters, whether they be courteous or froward . . . Nature, and the lawes which preserve nature, bind men that will be servants, to strict obedience"; nevertheless, there is an exception: "Men are bound to obey Magistrates, although they command things contrary to publique profit, except it be in such things as are contrary to the lawes of God."[6]

Other writers also suggest that servants' obedience is not absolute. William Gouge maintains that servants must obey their masters despite disagreeing with them: *"Though [servants] cannot in their judgement thinke that fit to be done which their master will have done yet upon his peremptorie command they must yeeld to the doing of it"*; on the very next page, however, he implies an exception to this rule and suggests that servants must at times use their own judgment: "the *Obedience which servants yeeld to their master must be such as may stand with their obedience to Christ."*[7] William Perkins concurs, declaring that the master is "not to require more of [his servants], then their strength will beare. The master is to rule over the servant *in justice*. And then is his comandement unjust whe[n] it will not sta[n]d with the course of nature, with the abilitie of his servant, or with the word of God."[8] Most of these writers appear to be reluctant to state directly that servants have a right to disobey unjust commands. Even a writer bold enough to do so tucks his statement away in a parenthesis: "And that S. Peter had onely respecte to the rough condicions of Maisters, and not to their vnlawful commandement agaynst God and their conscience (which they are bownde to do for no mans pleasure) the wordes do playnelie witnesse."[9]

Apparently, many writers of conduct books and of religious and political tracts believed that servants had a duty to serve God and their own consciences as well as their employers. While directly stating that servants should disobey was probably too subversive an action to be countenanced by authorities who relied on obedience to preserve their power, depicting conflicts of service, which did not require using such words as "disobey" or "disobedience,"[10] seems not to have provoked official condemnation. As Catherine Belsey has pointed out, "the drama is less inhibited because, while the project of theory is to eliminate problems, narrative depends on them."[11] Because conflicts of service to God, conscience, nation, monarch, family, employer, and one's own material interests must have been common and because such conflicts are often inherently dramatic, it is hardly surprising that throughout his career Shakespeare often chose to depict such conflicts. What may seem surprising is how often servants or characters who describe themselves as servants disobey the commands of employers or authorities on the grounds that doing so is doing the best possible service.[12]

Various servants in the comedies disobey or deceive masters and mistresses to serve better ones, their own ideas of virtuous behavior, or their own self-interest. In some instances, as when Mrs. Quickly deceives her employer, Dr. Caius, in *The Merry Wives of Windsor*, or when Maria, Feste, and Fabian deceive Olivia regarding Malvolio's madness, the servants' actions are primarily self-serving, although they also serve the ends of comic justice, since Caius does not deserve Anne Page and Malvolio does deserve a comeuppance. The comedies also provide an earlier instance of the kind of virtuous (albeit, in this instance, belated) disobedience Strier discusses, when Borachio, touched with remorse, reveals Don John's villainy to Don Pedro and Claudio. Other servants deceive or desert bad masters to serve better ones, as when Launcelot Gobbo, leaving to serve Bassanio, helps Jessica deceive Shylock, Touchstone deserts the service of Duke Frederick to follow Rosalind and Celia to Arden, and Adam transfers his service from Oliver to Orlando. Such changes suggest a major difference between the service owed by servants to their masters and the service owed by subjects to their rulers: subjects were not free to choose whom they would serve, unless they dared risk accusations of treason; servants, on the other hand, generally had a legal, though limited, right to change employers, and historical evidence indicates that many of them did so with some frequency.[13] This fact alone suggests that the early modern audience may have felt that the service owed to an employer, with whom the servant usually entered into a voluntary, temporary contract, was quite different from the absolute, lifelong service required of a subject. Despite the frequent Elizabethan attempts to link by analogy all service owed to higher authority—religious, political, civil, and economic—as proceeding from and sanctioned by service owed to God, therefore, disobedience to a mere employer may have occasioned much less concern in an Elizabethan audience than disobedience to royal or civic authority. Although servants who deceive or betray evil employers, or desert them without warning, are, strictly speaking, treacherous to those employers, we applaud their "betrayals," acknowledging, as Shakespeare and his audience obviously did, the force of Gouge's complaint: "So prone are servants to sooth their masters, as there is no sinne so horrible which at their masters command they will not be ready to doe."[14] Shakespeare's servants often refuse to continue serving bad masters or participating in injustice, recognizing that good service in a bad cause, as, for example, Oswald's to Goneril or Sir James Tyrell's to Richard III, is wrong.

Similarly, we are not disturbed by the disobedience of the Provost in *Measure for Measure*, even though after explicitly declaring that he will obey the charge brought to him by Angelo's messenger (4.2.107), he proceeds to disobey his orders. The Provost is very reluctant to disobey, both because, as he says, "I may make my case as Claudio's, to cross this in the smallest" (167–68) and because such disobedience is against his oath, sworn to the Duke and his "substitutes" (182–86). Even after he allows the disguised Duke to persuade him to disobey, he fears the result of his disobedience (4.3.188–91). Officially, he has done wrong, but in fact he has done well, and we are pleased when the Duke acknowledges this at the end of the play:

> Thanks, Provost, for thy care and secrecy;
> We shall employ thee in a worthier place.
> Forgive him, Angelo, that brought you home
> The head of Ragozine for Claudio's;
> Th' offense pardons itself.
>
> (5.1.541–45)[15]

Many of the masters who are disobeyed by servants in Shakespeare's plays, however, are not corrupt, but are, rather, deluded or desperate, and in their delusion or despair give commands

that confront their servants with difficult dilemmas. In such situations, we often find that the servants question and ultimately
disobey their masters' direct orders to serve instead some combination of their masters' best interests, the servants' own consciences, and, ultimately, an ideal of truth and virtue.

One such instance of disobedience occurs in the final scene of
Romeo and Juliet, when Romeo gives his final orders to his servant Balthasar:

> Upon thy life I charge thee,
> Whate'er thou hearest or seest, stand all aloof
> And do not interrupt me in my course.
> ... hence, begone.
> But if thou, jealous, dost return to pry
> In what I farther shall intend to do,
> By heaven, I will tear thee joint by joint
> And strew this hungry churchyard with thy limbs.
> The time and my intents are savage-wild,
> More fierce and more inexorable far
> Than empty tigers or the roaring sea.
>
> (5.3.25–27, 32–39)

Understandably, Balthasar replies, "I will be gone, sir, and not
trouble ye," but he then proceeds to tell the audience, "For all
this same, I'll hide me hereabout. / His looks I fear, and his intents I doubt" (40, 43–44). Balthasar's disobedience ultimately
does his master no good, but the fact that he does disobey despite
his fear that his master will kill him for doing so (131–34, 275–77)
shows considerable courage and suggests that his definition of
service embraces well-motivated disobedience to command even
at the risk of his life.[16]

Like Balthasar, Horatio and Marcellus are given orders by a
master whom they believe to be "desperate"; both men even give
Hamlet the same order: "You shall not go [after the Ghost]"
(*Hamlet* 1.4.87, 80–81). Hamlet—through authority, struggle, or
threat: "Unhand me, gentlemen. / By heaven, I'll make a ghost
of him that lets me! / I say, away!" (84–86)—frees himself, but
Marcellus and Horatio determine to follow him because " 'Tis not
fit thus to obey him" (88). Clearly, it is acceptable to disobey employers who are not in their right minds or "not themselves," and
this excuse serves many ill-advised employers and disobedient
servants throughout the canon, although the excuse is seldom
made explicit.

This excuse, however, is not applicable to all of the employers who are deservedly disobeyed. Cymbeline's nameless queen is consistently disobeyed because her social inferiors recognize that she is an evil and dangerous person. When she tries to obtain poison, she is defeated by the virtue and cunning of the doctor, Cornelius, who, knowing the queen's bad nature, silently refuses to trust her with anything stronger than a sleeping potion (*Cymbeline* 1.5.31–42); as Cornelius notes, "She is fooled / With a most false effect, and I the truer / So to be false with her" (42–44). The queen then tries to bribe Pisanio to win Imogen away from his master Posthumus and persuade her to love Cloten (48–77); her description of Pisanio after he leaves is negative, but, coming from her, these statements are compliments: "A sly and constant knave, / Not to be shaked; the agent for his master, / And the remembrancer of her to hold / The handfast to her lord" (77–80). After she leaves, Pisanio returns and confirms her judgment of his loyalty by saying "when to my good lord I prove untrue, / I'll choke myself. There's all I'll do for you" (89–90).[17]

Though Pisanio disobeys the queen, he does so to be loyal to his master; no such easy excuse can be made for Hubert de Burgh, who is both King John's subject and servant. Hubert is not only in John's service, but has explicitly sworn to do anything the king orders him to do, specifically to kill Prince Arthur (*King John* 3.3.56–66). In the event, however, Hubert cannot bring himself to murder the child, although he leads the king to believe that he has done so.[18] John's response is to blame Hubert for obedience:

> It is the curse of kings to be attended
> By slaves that take their humors for a warrant
> To break within the bloody house of life,
> And on the winking of authority
> To understand a law, to know the meaning
> Of dangerous majesty, when perchance it frowns
> More upon humor than advised respect.
>
> (4.2.209–15)

When Hubert reveals that Arthur is still alive, King John is relieved to find himself disobeyed. Clearly, this is disobedience that is not only acceptable, but to be praised. Hubert's virtuous disobedience, however, can neither save Arthur, who dies attempting to escape from his prison, nor serve the king by preventing his nobles, shocked at what they believe to be Arthur's murder, from deserting to the French. Hubert's refusal "to be butcher of an innocent child" (260) is a good deed in a naughty world, but except in terms of Hubert's own soul it has little consequence.[19]

Before he is aware of Arthur's death, King John asserts that Hubert had a duty, if not to refuse or protest against his evil command, at least to show reluctance:

> Hadst thou but shook thy head or made a pause
> When I spake darkly what I purposèd,
> Or turned an eye of doubt upon my face,
> As bid me tell my tale in express words,
> Deep shame had struck me dumb, made me break off,
> And those thy fears might have wrought fears in me.
>
> (232–37)

Given all of the emphasis placed on obedience to one's social superiors, it seems fairly outrageous to suggest that servants have an obligation to make it plain to their employer that they disapprove of an order. Nevertheless, Shakespeare depicts servants who go much farther than pausing or head-shaking. Emilia, in *Othello*, is obviously not of the opinion that servants have a duty not to contradict their masters, since she shows no reluctance to argue with Othello:

> I durst, my lord, to wager she is honest,
> Lay down my soul at stake. If you think other,
> Remove your thought; it doth abuse your bosom.
> If any wretch have put this in your head,
> Let heaven requite it with the serpent's curse!
> For if she be not honest, chaste, and true,
> There's no man happy; the purest of their wives
> Is foul as slander.
>
> (4.2.13–20)

Nor is she quicker to agree with her mistress, who wishes that heaven may pardon any man who has slandered her, only to hear her waiting-woman reply, "A halter pardon him! and hell gnaw his bones!" (142–43) and who later disputes Desdemona's opinion that neither Emilia nor any other woman would betray her husband (4.3.63–88). Emilia's most blatant resistance to her master, of course, occurs after Desdemona's murder, when she denies Othello's accusations, calling him devil, liar, "rash as fire," a "filthy bargain," and unworthy of his wife (5.2.135, 137, 139, 164,

167–68).[20] When he orders her to be silent and apparently threatens her, she defies him:

> Thou hast not half that power to do me harm
> As I have to be hurt. O gull! O dolt!
> As ignorant as dirt! Thou hast done a deed—
> I care not for thy sword; I'll make thee known,
> Though I lost twenty lives. Help! Help, ho, help!
> The Moor hath killed my mistress! Murder, murder!
>
> (5.2.169–74)

Although it is too late for Emilia to save her mistress, her refusal to obey Othello ultimately restores her mistress's reputation, exposes Iago's villainy, and reveals Othello's errors. Her disobedience, which continues even after her husband also commands her to be silent (190, 201, 226, 230), and which brings about her own death, is clearly service of a different order than that required to master or husband. Emilia decides for herself that, as she has earlier stated, "I must needs report the truth" (129).

So much has been written on disobedience in *King Lear* that there seems little more to say, but perhaps a couple of points deserve emphasis.[21] Much of the virtuous disobedience by servants in this play as in others may be related not only to discussions of justified disobedience in political and religious writings, but also to popular expressions of the same idea, such as appear, for example, in ballads.[22] Cornwall's First Servant may have acted to avoid deserving the kind of rebuke the cuckolded Lord Barnard gives his servants after killing his wife and her lover:

> Wo worth, wo worth ye, my merrye men all,
>   You never were borne for my goode:
> Why did you not offer to stay my hande,
>   When you sawe me wax so woode?[23]

The speaker of these lines expresses a sense of possession toward his "merrye men," but he also suggests that his men have free will and a responsibility to resist him for his own good when they see him acting crazy. This is very similar to King John's argument to Hubert ("dangerous majesty . . . perchance . . . frowns / More upon humor than advised respect"), but it is not only the argument of the powerful; Emilia does not suggest that Othello is mad, but she does suggest that he is mistaken ("Remove your thought; it doth abuse your bosom"), and Kent goes much further in a similar vein:

> Be Kent unmannerly
> When Lear is mad. What wouldst thou do, old man?
> Think'st thou that duty shall have dread to speak
> When power to flattery bows?
> To plainness honor's bound
> When majesty falls to folly. Reserve thy state,
> And in thy best consideration check
> This hideous rashness.
>
> (*King Lear* 1.1.145–52)

What is rarely said explicitly—it does not need to be said, because everyone knows it—is that the employers can make their mutinous servants suffer for their disobedience, however well intended, and the more powerful the employer, the greater the suffering he or she can inflict. Knowing this, however, does not prevent servants from serving their employers' best interests rather than simply carrying out their commands. And only the very worst employers, such as Cornwall, physically attack their servants: Lear does not attack Kent, any more than he beats the Fool, though he threatens both; King John does not attack Hubert, nor does Othello strike Emilia. Ralph Berry is certainly correct to say that, for the relatively powerless characters of the plays, including servants, "This limitation of choice to yielding or taking the consequences is the disabling weakness of the social order that Shakespeare diagnoses."[24] Yet Shakespeare repeatedly suggests that the "honor" to which Kent appeals—the duty, responsibility, and love that constitute ideal service—can and does overcome that systemic weakness. No doubt it is grossly unfair to ask the most powerless members of society to bear the brunt of correcting the system's flaws, but what society throughout history has done otherwise? It can, of course, be argued that Shakespeare is ameliorating the audience's concern by suggesting that servants and other good people will heroically sacrifice themselves when necessary to compensate for society's failures. It can also be argued, however, that Shakespeare is simply depicting the fate of virtuous people in a corrupt system.

The resistance throughout *King Lear*, whether by servants, children, or earls, tends to be phrased in terms of family relationships. Kent links the feelings and duties of subject, child, servant, and dependent:

> Royal Lear,
> Whom I have ever honored as my king,
> Loved as my father, as my master followed,
> As my great patron thought on in my prayers. . . .
>
> (139–42)

Similarly, Cornwall's First Servant appeals to his master as a longtime retainer who has grown to adulthood in Cornwall's household and thus is a member of his extended family:

> Hold your hand, my lord!
> I have served you ever since I was a child;
> But better service have I never done you
> Than now to bid you hold.
>
> (3.7.75–78)[25]

In neither instance is the appeal to family connection recognized by the head of the household: Lear banishes Kent; Cornwall and Regan kill their servant. Although it is not specifically mentioned as one of "the sequent effects" of the eclipses that Gloucester meditates upon, the bond between employer and servant is one of those we see being transformed in the course of the play, giving weight to Stanley Cavell's assertion that Lear's "last legitimate act is to banish love and service from his realm."[26] However, unlike the bond between parents and children, the dissolution of the bond between servants and employers is one-sided: employers fail to respect and honor good service, while servants continue to offer their employers such service.

Similarly, in *Timon of Athens,* Timon's servants ultimately show more loyalty to their master than he does to them. Early in the play, Timon's Steward often obeys his master's commands because "there is no crossing him in 's humor" (1.2.160), but he makes it clear that his obedience is reluctant. The Steward's definition of service stretches to trying to warn his master against the ruin his generosity is bringing on (176–77), finally concluding "I must be round with him" (2.2.8).[27] When he is finally able to make it clear to Timon that he is bankrupt, Timon complains that the Steward has served him badly in not having "fully laid my state before me" (129); but we believe the Steward's protests that he has often tried to do so, even to the point of disobedience:

> When for some trifling present you have bid me
> Return so much, I have shook my head and wept;
> Yea, 'gainst th'authority of manners prayed you
> To hold your hand more close. I did endure
> Not seldom nor no slight checks when I have
> Prompted you in the ebb of your estate
> And your great flow of debts.
>
> (140–46)

Like a lesser Kent, the Steward risks his personal happiness to advise his erring master, because to do so is part of his definition of good service. He goes on to defend his past service and enlighten Timon as to the reality of his situation (although, as he notes at lines 146–47, it is now too late for advice to be helpful), even after Timon says, "Prithee, no more" (168). Timon does not seem to resent this disobedience, even though he tells the Steward, "sermon me no further" (177), but the Steward continues his disobedience in the final lines of this scene, when Timon orders him, "Ne'er speak or think / That Timon's fortunes 'mong his friends can sink," to which the Steward replies, "I would I could not think it" (236–38). His disobedience in this instance is arguably out of his control, since it is difficult if not impossible to control one's thoughts, but his line suggests that because he knows better than his master, he will continue to disobey.

Although the Steward is not the only one of Timon's servants to display virtue while asserting his own opinions, the other servants do so by following Timon's orders and disobeying other Athenian aristocrats. When Timon sends Flaminius to Lucullus to request fifty talents, Lucullus, ironically, twice refers to Flaminius as "honest" (3.1.7, 40) but then shows how empty this compliment is by attempting to bribe Flaminius to betray his master by reporting that he could not find Lucullus; when Flaminius demonstrates his honesty by contemptuously refusing the bribe, Lucullus, who has also twice referred to him as "wise" and as "a towardly prompt spirit . . . and one that knows what belongs to reason," calls him "a fool, and fit for [his] master" (32, 35–37, 41, 44–51). For Lucullus, honesty and wisdom are antithetical, and Flaminius is an appropriate servant for Timon because both master and man prefer "honesty"—whether defined as generosity or faithful service—to the avarice and ingratitude that Lucullus defines as "wisdom." After Lucullus leaves, Flaminius is given a soliloquy to continue expressing not only his disgust but his incredulity at Lucullus's baseness and to curse his master's false friend (52–64). Although Flaminius is a servant and Lucullus a lord, it is clear that the socially inferior man is morally superior.

Servilius, who is more smoothly refused by Lucius, does "urge [Timon's need] faithfully," and is also flattered and promised an unspecified bribe, but does not express the same indignation (3.2.25–63). However, Timon's nameless Third Servant, who has been sent to Sempronius and refused by him, is given a soliloquy to lament the villainy of man in general, though his obvious distaste for "politic love" suggests that he is morally superior to the play's wicked nobles (3.3.29–43).[28] Even the usurers' servants dislike dunning Timon and comment disparagingly on their masters' behavior and ingratitude (3.4.18–29).

Although the Steward states in the middle of the play that "my lord and I have made an end" (56), he continues to address Timon as "my lord" and "my dear lord," while also continuing to resist what he takes to be his master's folly: when Timon orders him to invite Lucius, Lucullus, Sempronius, and the others to another feast, the Steward replies,

> Oh, my lord,
> You only speak from your distracted soul;
> There's not so much left to furnish out
> A moderate table.
>
> (113–16)

Ultimately, however, it appears that he obeys Timon in this matter, and he declares after "Timon's last" feast that he will find Timon and "ever serve his mind with my best will; / Whilst I have gold, I'll be his steward still" (3.6.90; 4.2.51–52).

When he does find Timon in the woods, however, Timon's first word to him is "Away!"—although perhaps the Steward cannot be said to disobey this command, since the immediately following "What art thou?" (4.3.477) seems to indicate a change of mind on Timon's part. The Steward continues his attempts to advise Timon (516–27), but Timon orders him to "live rich and happy," but also to "Hate all, curse all, show charity to none" (530, 532). The Steward resists this command—"Oh, let me stay / And comfort you, my master"—but receives a final order:

> If thou hat'st curses,
> Stay not; fly, whilst thou art blest and free.
> Ne'er see thou man, and let me ne'er see thee.
>
> (539–41)[29]

Since the Steward has resisted so many of Timon's previous injunctions, it is not surprising that this one, too, is disobeyed, although it is not clear that the disobedience is willful. In any event, the Steward reappears for a final confrontation with Timon, apparently at the insistence of the two Senators, but Timon ignores him, and the Steward, having apparently accepted his former master's misanthropy, speaks to Timon only to announce their arrival. His final service to his master is to say to the Senators,

"Trouble him no further. Thus you still shall find him" (5.1.212). Although the Steward is "only a servant," his role is important: he is not merely the only kind and honest man Timon is aware of encountering,[30] but also the only one to try to bring him to an understanding of reality; Apemantus professes to do so, but his version of reality does not take into account such virtue as the Steward's. The Steward is clearly a representation of good service, but such service obviously means not simply obeying one's master's commands, but serving his best interests, even at the cost of disobeying orders.[31]

Another, more serious, act of disobedience by a servant who loves his master occurs in act 4, scene 14, of *Antony and Cleopatra,* when Antony commands Eros to kill him. Although Eros has apparently sworn to perform this command at Antony's bidding (4.14.62–67, 81–82), he first exclaims, "The gods withhold me!" and then begs, "Oh, sir, pardon me!" (69, 80). After further persuasion and orders by Antony to stab him, Eros disobeys by killing himself instead.[32] Rather than becoming angry at this disobedience, Antony takes it as a lesson:

> Thrice-nobler than myself!
> Thou teachest me, O valiant Eros, what
> I should, and thou couldst not. My queen and Eros
> Have by their brave instruction got upon me
> A nobleness in record. But I will be
> A bridegroom in my death, and run into't
> As to a lover's bed. Come, then, and Eros,
> Thy master dies thy scholar. To do thus
> I learned of thee.   [*He falls on his sword.*]
>
>   (95–103)

Unfortunately, Antony is a less-than-competent student and bungles his lesson, but his reaction to Eros's disobedience suggests that employers can recognize disobedience to their commands as a higher form of service.[33] Antony's willingness to learn from Eros's example, though it leads to his prolonged death-agony, also leads him to kill himself, a more suitable death for "the greatest prince o'th' world" (4.15.56) than being slain by another.

An inconceivable command is also given to Camillo, who, although a lord, characterizes himself as one of Leontes' servants (*Winter's Tale* 1.2.351–55; 4.4.511–16). Ordered by his king and master to commit a murder, Camillo attempts to dissuade Leontes from his suspicions that he has been betrayed by Hermione and Polixenes, then tries to make sure that Hermione will not be punished, and finally plays along until he can virtuously reveal the proposed murder to Polixenes, with whom he then must flee to avoid Leontes' wrath (1.2.283–442). His soliloquy after he pretends to agree to become Polixenes' assassin reveals his dilemma as man and servant:

> Oh, miserable lady! But, for me,
> What case stand I in? I must be the poisoner
> Of good Polixenes, and my ground to do't
> Is the obedience to a master—one
> Who in rebellion with himself will have
> All that are his so too. To do this deed,
> Promotion follows. If I could find example
> Of thousands that had struck anointed kings,
> And flourished after, I'd not do't; but since
> Nor brass, nor stone, nor parchment bears not one,
> Let villainy itself forswear't. I must
> Forsake the court. To do't or no is certain
> To me a breakneck.
>
> (350–62)

Although there is never any doubt that Camillo will disobey Leontes' order to kill Polixenes, he does so at the cost of risking Leontes' wrath and, even if he avoids punishment, losing his home and position. What Leontes describes as Camillo's betrayal (2.1.46–49) is, in fact, a service Camillo performs not only for Polixenes and for Camillo's own sense of virtue, but also for Leontes, whom Camillo continues to characterize as his "master," even after fifteen years in Polixenes' service (4.4.515); by betraying Leontes, Camillo saves him from the sin of killing an innocent man, who is also his longtime friend and fellow king. Camillo's later betrayals are less serious and more self-serving: he betrays Polixenes by helping Florizel and Perdita to flee, and then betrays the young lovers by setting Polixenes on their trail. Since Polixenes refuses to allow Camillo to return home to Sicilia and his original master, Camillo sees these manipulations as his only chance to get what he wants, although he also expresses a desire to help the lovers (*Winter's Tale* 4.4.510–16).

James Edward Siemon asserts that "We are assured by the testimony of the two kings and by the outcome of events that Camillo is a wise and deserving man. Were we to judge him by his actions alone, we might reach a different conclusion, for we see him as a schemer and as an accomplished equivocator."[34] These conclusions seem based on partial evidence, with little sympathy for Camillo's dilemma. We are not limited to outside testimony and a serendipitous outcome in our judgment of Camillo: we have seen him attempt to dissuade Leontes from his criminal plot and we have heard him agonize about what he should do. To obey his king is to imperil himself body and soul; simply to refuse to obey Leontes and not to warn Polixenes condemns Camillo and almost certainly condemns the Bohemian king. It is true, as Andrew Gurr points out, that "Camillo, putting love before duty and fleeing with Polixenes, merely confirms Leontes' suspicions,"[35] but what else could Camillo possibly do in this situation? Siemon is probably correct in declaring that "Camillo's dramatic ancestor is no doubt that wily slave of classical comedy whose devious schemes are the efficient cause of the comic resolution" (12), but Camillo's predicament is a reminder of why servants (even noble one), like slaves, find it necessary to be clever, scheming, and manipulative: without power, such people must use their wits to get them what they want, and sometimes even to survive. As Hermione and the other members of Leontes' court are about to discover, virtue will not afford them protection from the king's madness; Camillo's deception is no more blameworthy than Antigonus's attempt to flee the attacking bear.

Arguably the play's greatest exemplar of virtuous disobedience is Paulina, who is protected from Leontes' wrath by her gender, her innocence, and, perhaps, her audacity.[36] Not only does she attempt to change Leontes' mind and restore his reason, but she explicitly declares that this is her purpose. Addressing a servant who is apparently trying to obey Leontes' command that "None should come at him" by keeping her away from the king, she says,

> Not so hot, good sir.
> I come to bring him sleep. 'Tis such as you,
> That creep like shadows by him and do sigh
> At each his needless heavings, such as you
> Nourish the cause of his awaking. I
> Do come with words as medicinal as true,
> Honest as either, to purge him of that humor
> That presses him from sleep.
>
> (2.3.32–39)

Paulina's argument is that service to the king's commands is bad service if it encourages the king to continue pursuing his erroneous course. Her service, like a purge, may be temporarily uncomfortable, but will lead to the recovery of health. She alone is serving the king's true best interests.[37]

Paulina's perception of her duty as a wife is similar to that of her duty as Leontes' servant; she declares that her husband can rule her "from all dishonesty," but that nothing but physical force can prevent her from "committing honor" (46–50). She then returns to the idea that she more truly serves Leontes than those who simply obey his commands:

>   Good my liege, I come—
> And, I beseech you hear me, who professes
> Myself your loyal servant, your physician,
> Your most obedient counselor, yet that dares
> Less appear so in comforting your evils,
> Than such as most seem yours—I say, I come
> From your good queen.
>
> (52–58)

Undeterred by Leontes' threats and insults, Paulina continues to try to persuade the king of his error, until he commands one or more of the lords and servants on their allegience to eject her from the room; though Paulina leaves, she does so while still protesting that simple obedience may be poor service: "You that are thus so tender o'er his follies / Will never do him good, not one of you" (128–29).

Although Paulina's words appear to have no effect on the king, who is now threatening the life of his infant daughter, Antigonus and the other lords take up her plea after she leaves. An unnamed Lord says to Leontes,

> Beseech Your Highness, give us better credit.
> We have always truly served you, and beseech'
> So to esteem of us; and on our knees we beg,
> As recompense of our dear services
> Past and to come, that you do change this purpose,
> Which being so horrible, so bloody, must
> Lead on to some foul issue. We all kneel.
>
> (147–53)

Leontes, however, refuses to be moved and punishes Antigonus for his failure to control his wife by ordering him, under threat of his own death and Paulina's, to take the baby out of Sicilia and leave it to die of exposure, and Antigonus—reluctantly and perhaps more for the sake of Paulina's life than his own—obeys.

Paulina puts Hermione's interests ahead of her husband's commands (and, perhaps, even welfare, although she can hardly be blamed for not anticipating that Leontes' punishment of Antigonus will lead to his death by bear), but she is not just defending Hermione and Hermione's daughter, but also, as she says at some length, fulfilling her duty as a subject to advise her monarch when he is self-deluded. Thus she is disobeying the imperatives to obey her king and her husband to obey the imperatives of good service to an erring master and support to a female friend and superior.

Emilia, Timon's Steward, Camillo, Paulina, and perhaps, by example though not in words, Eros attempt to instruct their masters, and we acknowledge, as no doubt Shakespeare's original audience did, that these servants are in these situations superior to their masters. Yet it is hard to see that any of the masters—apart, perhaps, from the deluded Othello and delusional Leontes—are themselves corrupt or that any of these servants, other than Camillo, would be corrupted by obeying the commands they are given. The commands—to leave, to be silent, to fulfill a vow—are not in themselves unreasonable or evil. And, even beyond the duty servants have to obey their masters and mistresses, these servants have strong motives for doing as they are told: Balthasar and Emilia seem, to themselves at least, to be risking their lives by their disobedience; Camillo is certainly risking his life, and Leontes threatens Paulina's; the Steward is at least risking his master's disfavor, and perhaps his own livelihood, in the early part of the play; and Eros seems to feel that his only option other than obeying Antony is to take his own life. We could hardly blame these servants, certainly not judge them to be corrupt, if they obeyed. Despite these justifications, however, they do not obey: they choose to serve their masters' or mistresses' best interests or their own consciences rather than the letter of command, and in so doing they suggest that their concept of service differs from the conventional one. Furthermore, because the plays validate what they say and do as they dare to defy the conventional idea of service, as well as their employers, at considerable risk to themselves, their words and actions suggest that their concept of service represents a higher standard, a standard in which "virtuous disobedience" becomes a duty.

Although some of the employers disobeyed by virtuous servants are evil, most are like Leontes, whom Camillo describes as being "in rebellion with himself" (1.2.354)—suffering from grief, jealousy, disillusionment, or some other emotional anguish that

leads to irrational behavior. The employers' frequent irrational-
ity may explain why, although the servants' disobedience is virtuous and noble, it is also useless; such disobedience never
succeeds in saving an employer (or—again with the exception of
Camillo—anyone else) and often results in the servants' deaths.
Cornwall's First Servant succeeds in giving his evil master his
death-wound, Emilia tells the truth that reveals Iago's evil, and
Eros sets an example to Antony, but it is difficult to see that what
is gained is worth the lives that are lost.

Ironically, within Shakespeare's plays, the duty of virtuous disobedience often becomes, not a source of liberation for servants,
but a harsher form of bondage. Because these servants dare to
demonstrate moral or intellectual superiority to their masters,
they run the risk of losing their livelihoods, and sometimes even
their lives. Conventional servitude, these plays suggest, is safer
than true service to a higher ideal. From an authoritarian perspective, the message appears to be that the wages of disobedience is likely to be death. But if we regard these disobedient
servants as they seem to regard themselves—as human beings
who happen to be employed as servants—it is not surprising that
when they choose to redefine themselves and their obedience,
they run the same risks as other characters in Shakespeare's
tragic worlds. By redefining service, rather than simply following
the conventional definition, these servants become actors, rather
than tools, accepting risks to their bodies rather than to their
souls. Service to one's own conscience may be another form of
servitude, but it is one that these servants share with many of
their masters and mistresses.

Although Elizabethan prose writers generally appear to have
been unwilling to do more than hint at the implications of the
subversive Christian idea that all souls are equal in God's sight,
Shakespeare explores these implications by representing servants who are more virtuous or intelligent (or both) than their
masters and who redefine service for their own virtuous ends.
As Strier states, "Shakespeare . . . pushed the paradox of right
obedience as sometimes consisting of disobedience as far as it
would go. He adopted the most radical possible position on the
issue of obedience to wicked authority."[38] Shakespeare's radical
representations offer a more sophisticated and enlightened concept of service and the obligations it entails than the officially
sanctioned view presented by writers of religious tracts and conduct books. For the many members of the audience who were
servants or had been servants, and even for many of those who

employed servants (and it may be worth repeating that these were not necessarily mutually distinct classes), the theater may have afforded one of the few opportunities to experience artistic depictions of employer-servant relationships. It is difficult to judge the effect on Shakespeare's audience of seeing disobedient servants validated: the challenge to employers' expectations of obedience could be part of the reason the civic authorities were so opposed to theaters as well as part of the reason for the popularity of plays; on the other hand, the dangers to disobedient servants portrayed in many of the plays may have defused any trend toward censorship, but may also have limited servants' desire to risk disobedience. The fact that theatrical representations of disobedient servants seem to have occasioned no outrage may suggest that many members of the audience, as well as Shakespeare, were in advance of the official ideas about service, or merely that such representations were not regarded as serious social commentary. It does at least seem probable, however, that Shakespeare's propensity for representing disobedient but virtuous servants in many plays throughout his career—often as his own additions to his received plots, and without apparent dramatic necessity—indicates that such explorations of service may have interested and been welcomed by many members of his audience.

10

"Duty in his service perishing": Servants and Violence

Both the fictional and ostensibly nonfictional depictions of servants in the early modern era often suggested that servants were likely to be dangerous.[1] Certainly servants did commit crimes, although much of the violence by servants seems to have been rioting, often by apprentices, rather than premeditated assault or murder.[2] With apprentices and rioting, however, Shakespeare's plays have little to do, and perhaps this helps to explain why there is relatively little violence by the servants in his plays, particularly little of the violence that the servant-employing classes apparently most feared.

This is not, of course, to suggest that there is no violence by servants in the plays. Aufidius's servants order Coriolanus to leave their master's house and threaten him; however, when he refuses to leave, the upshot is that he beats the third servant rather than being beaten (*Coriolanus* 4.5.7–53). Perhaps we are supposed to view these servants as attempting to serve their master by ejecting a man they perceive to be a beggar, or perhaps we should see them as bullies; in any event, their attempt at violence is turned against them, and they look ridiculous. Duke Frederick's wrestler, Charles, told by Oliver that Orlando is a "villainous" young man who will try to kill Charles, declares that he will maim or kill Orlando (*As You Like It* 1.1.139–52); however, thanks to Orlando's skill at wrestling, it is Charles who is hurt. Throughout most of the plays, servants are more likely to threaten violence verbally than actually perform it. This is perhaps most obvious in *Twelfth Night*, in which Olivia's servants are continually at odds, but in which their only real violence is Malvolio's confinement (possibly bound) in a dark room, an action that seems ordered by Sir Toby.[3] The violence in the play is among the gentlemen—Sir Toby, Sir Andrew, Sebastian, and "Cesario" (although it is true that "Cesario" is a serving-gentleman, despite the fact that "he" is not a man at all).[4] A similar situation prevails in *Romeo and Juliet*: during an exchange of insults, the First Musician says to Peter, "Then will I give you the serving-creature" to which Peter replies, "Then will I lay the serving-creature's dagger on your pate" and apparently draws his dagger, although he does not use it (*Romeo* 4.5.115–24).[5] The servants threaten but do not act; the play's serious violence is the province of the gentlemen.

Of course (as some readers may already be objecting) there are servants who offer violence—however comically and ineffectually—in *Romeo and Juliet*. However, servants who are violent in their masters' quarrels are rather a special case.[6] In *Romeo and Juliet*, although the Capulets' servants Sampson and Gregory are reluctant to fight with the Montagues' servants Abram and Balthasar, they seem to feel compelled to quarrel for the honor of the house they serve; as Gregory says, "The quarrel is between our masters, and us their men" (1.1.19–20). Although it is the entrance of Benvolio that precipitates the quarrel into an actual fight, the language that inspires the fight has to do with which servants serve the better man (*Romeo* 1.1.52–61).[7] Joan Ozark Holmer sees the servants' behavior as deriving from a "chauvinistic code of violent insolency that the male servants embrace in emulation of their perverse patriarchs," while Jill L. Levenson argues that the servants' behavior parodies the era's fashionable duelling code.[8] Both critics may be correct, but in any event the servants are not violent without reason, and the reason—however irrational—for their proposed violence is, as Holmer indicates, the violence of their masters. Given the animosity and propensity to violence of Old Montague, Old Capulet, Tybalt, and Mercutio, it is hardly surprising that their servants are also prone to quarreling and fighting.

Servants' violent behavior in other plays also echoes the violence of their masters. Although the Warders of the Tower protest that "We do no otherwise than we are willed" (*1 Henry VI* 1.3.10) by the Bishop of Winchester, the Duke of Gloucester's men fight with and overcome the Cardinal's men (56 s.d.; another skirmish at 69 s.d.). The Mayor of London threatens to "call for clubs" if they do not cease fighting (84). The servants renew the battle by throwing stones at each other (3.1.74–87); the Mayor of London reports that "many have their giddy brains knocked out" and the servingmen "Enter . . . in skirmish with bloody pates" (85, 87 s.d.). Later in the play, Vernon and Basset, identified as York and Somerset's servants respectively, challenge each other to combat (4.1.78–120). In both instances, it is clear that the great lords' animosity is the cause of their servants' violence; Gloucester and Winchester threaten each other, and Somerset and York are only restrained from fighting by King Henry's intervention. The servants are violent only because their masters involve their employees in their quarrels and set an example of violence.[9]

Servants, however, do not always limit themselves to fighting other men's servants at their employers' behest; Shakespeare depicts some servants who are willing to commit murder for their masters, often because these employers are unwilling or unable to do it themselves.[10] Kingship, in particular, seems to debar employers—even those who themselves have been successful murderers before coming to the throne, such as Richard III, Claudius, and Macbeth—from doing their own killing, other than in battle (although Claudius, of course, continues to dabble in poison, perhaps fulfilling the common belief that poisoners are apt to get addicted to their crime).[11] King John orders Hubert de Burgh to kill Arthur and Peter of Pomfret; Antiochus orders Thaliard to kill Pericles; Leontes orders Camillo to kill Polixenes, and Antigonus to expose the infant Perdita; and Alonso orders Gonzalo to force Prospero and his young daughter Miranda to set sail in a leaky boat. Richard II, no longer king and no longer an employer of servants, is forced to do his own killing—in self-defense, to be sure—at the end of his play. Noblemen may or may not do their own killing. Posthumus orders Pisanio to kill Imogen, but Brutus and his conspirators, like Othello, perhaps because of their belief that they are committing "honorable" murders, do it themselves (although Othello, of course, sends Iago to kill Cassio). Aaron, Chiron, and Demetrius do their own killing, except when they are framing people, as does Titus.[12] Saturninus, on the other hand, orders the unfortunate Clown executed rather than killing him himself.

Women generally employ men to do their killing for them or at least to help them; whether or not they seek help, they frequently choose poison as their weapon. Lady Capulet declares that she will "send to one in Mantua" who will poison Romeo (*Romeo* 3.5.88–91), though it is not certain whether this "one" is a servant. Other cases are clearer: Dionyza hires Leonine to kill Marina; Cymbeline's queen tries to get poison from Cornelius. Regan will shed blood any way she can: she herself kills the servant who is fighting with her husband, but, unable to pursue the blinded Gloucester herself, she encourages Oswald to kill him. Goneril, however, who seems to have no very high opinion of most men, does her own killing, first poisoning her sister and then stabbing herself, although she writes to Edmund, urging him to murder her husband, subscribing herself Edmund's "affectionate servant" (*Lear* 4.6.266–73).

Some servants are more than willing to take on the task of murder: Oswald and Sir James Tyrrel are eager for reward; Menas actually comes up with the idea of killing the triumvirs and volunteers to be their murderer, although he is not anxious enough to serve his master Pompey to do the murders without first getting Pompey's permission, which he does not receive.[13]

Some servants do commit murder, although most of the hired murderers in Shakespeare's plays are not identified as servants, and those who are are rarely effectual. Bernard Beckerman points out differences between the two hired murderers in *Pericles* who are servants, or at least acting as servants: "Leonine and Thaliard are minor villains in *Pericles*. They are both commoners and servants, both are commanded to commit murder by their masters. Yet they differ from each other. In manner Thaliard is prompt, reflecting a cynical attitude toward his task. Leonine is reluctant, reflecting an innate gentleness."[14] More important than these differences, however, is their great similarity: both fail at their assigned task, as is common for Shakespeare's servant-murderers. Iago fails to fulfill his master's command to kill Cassio, although he manages (with some difficulty) to kill Roderigo for his own purposes. Oswald, though enthusiastic in the pursuit of Gloucester, and Rosencrantz and Guildenstern, delegated by Claudius to deliver Hamlet to his death, fail spectacularly; Laertes—who is serving Claudius as well as his own desire for revenge—does manage to mortally wound Hamlet, but he does it so inexpertly and takes so long doing it that the murder does Claudius no good. Similarly, Antigonus does expose Leontes' infant daughter, but fails to accomplish his master's desire for the baby's death, and Gonzalo fails to fulfill his master Alonso's wish for the deaths of Prospero and Miranda (as the reformed Leontes and Alonso are later pleased to discover). Often, servants refuse to commit murder: Hubert de Burgh, Camillo, Pisanio, and Cornelius are simply too virtuous to commit or assist in committing murder, and all take action to spare their assigned or assumed victims.

The greatest sin a servant could commit, of course, was to become violent, particularly murderous, toward his employer.[15] Just as few of Shakespeare's servant-characters betray their masters or mistresses, few of them offer violence toward their "superiors." Cornwall's First Servant is an obvious exception; another notable exception is Peter Thump, who accuses his master, the armorer Thomas Horner, of treasonous speech (*2 Henry VI* 1.3.181–92). Horner denies the charge and explains the accusation as being motivated by the resentment of a servant who had been punished: "My accuser is my prentice; and when I did correct him for his fault the other day, he did vow upon his knees he would be even with me" (198–200). However, Horner arrives at the combat drunk, and, despite Thump's fear that he will not be able to match his master's skill in fighting, he kills Horner, who confesses his treason with his last breath (2.3.59–95). Thump's accusation is thus proved justified, and he leaves the stage with King Henry promising him a reward.

Commentators have noted that in his representation of this episode Shakespeare alters his sources, in all of which, although the servant triumphs, the master is innocent and his servant is guilty.[16] Shakespeare, therefore, cannot have changed the story simply because "[a]llowing Peter to triumph is dramatically more effective"[17] than giving the victory to his master; the change is that the servant is virtuous and the master treasonous. Critics dispute whether the original audience would have attributed Thump's triumph more to Divine Providence or double beer, and discuss whether the virtuous servant defeating and killing the traitorous master would have made the original audience feel pleased or nervous.[18] Given, however, that servants made up at least a portion of the original audience and given that many of the employer-characters in the history plays behave very badly, it is not particularly surprising that Shakespeare gives not only the victory, but the virtue, to the apprentice, nor is there any particular reason to believe that Peter Thump's success worried most of the Elizabethan audience. Thump is a rarity in Shakespeare's plays, both as an apprentice and as a servant who engages in violence against his employer, but his honesty, weakness, comical reluctance to fight, and piety (1.3.216–19; 2.3.72–79, 98–99) suggest that his betrayal of his master could only have occurred because his master was a traitor; there is no suggestion that servants in general are treacherous or physically dangerous. The narrative of Thump's triumph, in which is embedded the ostensible "miracle" of Simon Simpcox, is truly a miracle, and the exposure of Horner, like that of Simpcox, is obviously intended to be a cause of rejoicing.

One of the few later attempts at violence toward a master is Caliban's plot to murder Prospero. Given that *The Tempest* depicts Caliban as less than human, that Caliban forms a conspiracy to kill his master, and that Caliban seems to revel in the possible kinds of violence that could be inflicted on Prospero, it seems likely that most of the original audience would have utterly disapproved of this rebellion, whatever modern critical opinion of Caliban's situation may be. Although this attack by a servant (or slave, which may be significant) upon his master may seem a harking back to earlier plays' violence between master and servant, it is interesting that in this late play neither master nor servant seems able to enact the violence in his own person. Prospero delegates his violence toward Caliban to spirits equally enslaved by his magic, while Caliban delegates his violence toward Prospero to Stephano. Although Caliban understands that Prospero's power derives from magic, the punishments Prospero inflicts upon him are Stephen Greenblatt's "invisible bullets," with magic standing in for colonialist technology. Since Prospero is a duke and a wizard, a dignified figure, it is easy to see why Shakespeare does not depict him as physically lambasting Caliban, but if the delegation of violence is intended to make Prospero less comic, the same device has the opposite cause and effect for Caliban. The consequence of putting the drunken Stephano in charge of Prospero's murder, as Francis E. Dolan, among others, has noted, is to make the plot comic and inevitably ineffectual;[19] but it may also have been necessary for Shakespeare to create this conspiracy lest Caliban—a slave with a grievance who is shown suffering physical and mental torment to which he reacts like a human being, not a cartoon—become a character like Shylock: a comic butt whose presence threatens to unbalance his play by becoming overly dramatic and sympathetic.[20] Caliban gloating over what his drunken "god" might do to Prospero is comic; Caliban himself, seriously intent on killing Prospero, is much more likely to succeed, and is, therefore, not at all amusing.

Throughout the canon, however, as many commentators have noted, servants are more likely to be the victims than the perpetrators of violence.[21] It should be emphasized that violence toward servants includes more than simply the infliction of physical pain. Often employers remind their servants of their inferior positions and rebuke them for failing to carry out their duties to the employers' satisfaction; these rebukes and reminders arguably fall under the heading of "symbolic violence."[22] Rebukes are so common throughout the canon that anything like an exhaustive list would be extremely tedious, but it may bear mentioning that servants can be rebuked for all sorts of behavior. Slender reprimands Simple for his absence; Olivia (having previously scolded her Clown for his absence) reproves Malvolio for his bad attitude; the Countess of Rossillion reproaches her Steward for not anticipating Helena's flight; Timon rebukes his Steward for supposedly failing to warn him of his waning fortune; Macbeth rages at a messenger for being pale, etc., etc., etc.[23]

Servants are not only rebuked, but often threatened: Celia tells Touchstone that he will "be whipped for taxation one of these days" (A.Y.L. 1.2.81–82). Sebastian threatens to strike Feste (Twelfth Night 4.1.18–19). Ajax repeatedly threatens—and sometimes beats—Thersites (Troilus 2.1.10–11, 14–15, 25, 40, passim). Other servants are threatened with death, sometimes improbably, as is Balthasar (Romeo 5.3.25–39), sometimes seriously, as are Thaliard (Pericles 1.1.163–66; 1.3.1–3) and Paulina (Winter's Tale 2.3.114). Some threats toward servants are obviously facetious: the audience never fears that the Host will kill Simple if he fails to reveal his questions for the wise woman (Merry Wives 4.5.42)—although, because Simple is uncommonly dim, it seems likely that he may believe this threat; nor, despite Maria's warning, is it probable that Olivia will have Feste hanged for being absent (Twelfth Night 1.5.3–4, 16). On the other hand, it is by no means unlikely that she could fire him, which, as Maria points out, could be "as good as a hanging" to Feste (17–18). Firing is a frequent threat in the plays, as is beating, and the former may well have been the more serious.[24] But as is often the case, the plays do not mirror the reality of the period: for example, sexual exploitation of female domestic servants, however common it was at the time, is only glanced at by Shakespeare.[25]

Relatively little of the violence in Othello is directed against servants, but the final scene of the play includes threats of violence against Desdemona's serving-woman, Emilia, and her husband, Othello's ancient, Iago, and Othello's justification of his own violence as a servant of the Venetian state. Emilia's speech to Othello at 5.2.169–74 is similar to Kent's speech to Lear (1.1.164–67) in its suggestion that the hearer is threatening serious, possibly fatal, physical violence against a servant-speaker who is telling an unwelcome truth. Although Othello does not harm Emilia, her speech suggests that he threatens to silence her by stabbing her, a reaction that suggests how far he has fallen from his former nobility, even as her defiance in the face of such a threat from a man she knows has just murdered his wife demonstrates her courage and devotion to the truth. The depths to which Othello has sunk in considering even for a moment drawing his sword upon Emilia are suggested when Iago later threatens her, producing Gratiano's reaction, "Fie, / Your sword upon a woman?" (230–31).

That Emilia is motivated by a desire to tell the truth is emphasized throughout act 5, scene 2. Her first statement to this effect, however, is arguably ambiguous, since it is not certain from her response to Desdemona's lie clearing Othello of guilt and his denial of responsibility—"She said so. I must needs report the truth" (132)—if she will truthfully report what her mistress said, or if she is contrasting Desdemona's lie with what she suspects to be the truth. Subsequently, she makes it clear that not even the threats of violence from Othello and Iago can keep her from speaking the truth that will both convict them and clear Desdemona: "I will not charm my tongue; I am bound to speak"; " 'Twill out, 'twill out! I peace? / No, I will speak as liberal as the north. / Let heaven and men and devils, let them all, / All, all, cry shame against me, yet I'll speak"; "Moor, she was chaste. She loved thee, cruel Moor: / So come my soul to bliss as I speak true" (191, 226–29, 258–59). Her devotion both to truth and to her dead mistress, though it leads to her death, is clearly the highest type of service.

The plays occasionally suggest that abuse of servants is so disdained that members of the servant-employing classes may criticize other employers, even their own friends or relatives, because of the way these employers treat servants.[26] For example, Prince Hal says of "the boy that [he] gave Falstaff" that Falstaff "had him from me Christian, and look if the fat villain have not transformed him ape" (2 *Henry IV* 2.2.66–68).[27] Although no one could imagine Falstaff as a suitable master for a child, Hal nevertheless expresses disgust at the employer's influence on his young servant. More seriously, Richard, Duke of Gloucester, orders the Duke of Buckingham to denounce to the citizens the late Edward IV's "hateful luxury / And bestial appetite in change of lust, / Which stretched unto their servants, daughters, wives, / Even where his raging eye or savage heart, / Without control, lusted to make a prey" (*Richard III* 3.5.80–84). Whether or not this charge is true, it is obvious that Richard believes that such abuse of servants, as well as other female family members, will turn the citizens against Edward's memory. The abuse and corruption of servants, although they may not be prevented or punished, do not proceed altogether unremarked in the plays and are not approved of by the society in the plays.

Violence toward servants naturally differs depending on a play's genre; it also seems to change over the course of Shakespeare's career. The early comedies depict considerable physical violence directed at servants by employers. For instance, the Dromios are beaten in *The Comedy of Errors*, although S. Dromio is only beaten once, his brother coming in for all of the other staged beatings; thus it is E. Dromio who is allowed a few lines to complain that his life seems to consist of nothing but beatings (4.4.29–39).[28] Furthermore, other servants are also abused: Luce is threatened with a beating (3.1.59) and we are told that when E. Antipholus and E. Dromio break their bonds, they "[beat] the maids a-row," although it is not clear that the maids have done anything to deserve punishment (5.1.170). However, it must be pointed out that the violence directed toward the servants is hardly unique: nearly every character in the play is threatened with violence. E. Antipholus plans to beat Adriana "and her confederates" and threatens to pluck out her eyes and otherwise "disfigure" her; he also strikes Dr. Pinch, whom he and E. Dromio subsequently torture (4.1.15–18; 4.4.104–5; 5.1.182–83; 4.4.53; 5.1.169–77). S. Antipholus and S. Dromio, feeling threatened, go through the streets with drawn rapiers; soon after this episode, S. Antipholus and the Second Merchant are on the point of duelling when Adriana interrupts them (4.4.144–46; 5.1.29–34). And, of course, Egeon is under threat of execution throughout most of the play. As Camille Wells Slights notes, "The quarrels between masters and servants and between husband and wife display the injustice and violence inherent in the hierarchical social order, but the play invites the audience to see them not as individual sins nor as symptoms of social injustice but, as the title directs, as errors."[29]

Similarly, in *The Two Gentlemen of Verona*, servants are threatened with and experience physical violence: Proteus threatens Speed (1.1.104–11); Speed reports that Valentine beat him for failing to clean his master's shoes (2.1.76–80); Lance sets Speed up for what he hopes will be a beating (3.1.373–75); and it is possible that Julia strikes or pinches Lucetta (1.2.89–95). However, again the upper-class characters are more likely to be the victims of violence, or at least threats of violence, than are their servants: Speed suggests that Valentine strike Thurio (2.4.7); Thurio suggests that he wants to shed Valentine's blood (26–27); Proteus says he would die fighting with anyone who belittled Sylvia (112); Proteus declares his intention to rape Sylvia (5.4.55–59);

and Valentine threatens to kill Thurio if Thurio challenges Valentine's right to claim Sylvia (126–31).

There is more actual, as opposed to threatened, violence in *The Taming of the Shrew*: Petruchio beats Grumio for failing to knock at Hortensio's gate despite being repeatedly ordered to do so (1.2.5–18);[30] Grumio later reports that Petruchio again beat him on the way home and we see Petruchio physically abuse other servants after his arrival (4.1.2, 68–69, 135–36, 143, 153–55). In addition, a hungry Katharina beats Grumio for teasing her with feigned offers of food and Vincentio beats Biondello for participating in what Vincentio must feel to be the theft of his identity (4.3.31; 5.1.45–55). And, of course, there are threats of further violence toward the servants by their employers (4.1.25–28; 5.1.123–24). Here again, though, it is not only the employers who inflict violence, nor is it only servants who are victims. Grumio cuffs his fellow-servant Curtis's ear, for no particular reason (4.1.52–59). Petruchio strikes the priest who marries him to Katharina, while Katharina strikes her sister (whom she has first bound), breaks a lute over Hortensio's head (having earlier threatened "to comb [his] noddle with a three-legged stool"), and hits Petruchio (3.2.158–65; 2.1.21–22, 153–54; 1.1.64; 2.1.219–20). Petruchio tortures Katharina by depriving her of food and sleep (4.1.176–99). Finally, Petruchio orders Katharina to "swinge . . . soundly" Bianca and the Widow if they refuse to come when summoned, and it seems likely that the "womanly persuasion" Petruchio later mentions alludes to physical force (5.2.108, 124).[31]

In these plays, servants are often beaten for what is accidental or not their fault at all, suggesting that their employers are either choleric or "not themselves" due to emotional disturbance. Servants are sometimes allowed to complain, but both the beatings and the complaints often seem intended to amuse. With regard to *The Comedy of Errors*, Ralph Berry remarks that "It is a given of the play that the beating-up of servants is funny," and this also seems true for *The Two Gentlemen of Verona* and *The Taming of the Shrew*, although it might be said with equal accuracy that in these plays the beating-up of anyone is funny.[32] Fortunately, Shakespeare seems quickly to have outgrown this concept of humor, and the servants in the later plays, while often threatened, are rarely subjected to physical abuse by their employers, Caliban being the notable exception. In contrast to the other early comedies, there is little suggestion of violence in *Love's Labor's Lost*, although Armado does suggest that he could "enforce [Jaquenetta's] love" (4.1.80–81, 88–93); not to minimize the threat of rape, it is hard to take this more seriously than any other aspect of Armado's character, or, for that matter, anything else in the play. By the time of *A Midsummer Night's Dream*, there is no violence committed on or threatened toward servants (although it is at least possible that this is due to the fact that most of the servants in the play are fairies and therefore presumably invulnerable to most punishments).

Rather than usually showing violence as a means by which employers keep their servants in line, Shakespeare often represents employers as capable of displacing their anger onto servants, through rebukes, threats, or physical mistreatment.[33] The most obvious example of this is perhaps Petruchio, who, however, is presumably putting on an act for Katharina, but many masters and mistresses are clearly depicted as using their servants as whipping boys. One clear instance of this is the Duchess of York, who, when her husband is about to go to the king to accuse their son, the Duke of Aumerle, of treason, addresses the servant who has been ordered by the Duke to bring him his boots: "Hence, villain! Never more come in my sight" (*Richard II* 5.2.86). As Leonard Barkan points out, "We are invited to forget about Aumerle, about rebellion, and even about York's journey to the king. Instead the focus is on a mute servant, involved in the action in a remote and inconsequential way. The Duchess, taking out her frustration on the servant and the boots, is all the more frustrated because she cannot induce her son to beat up the poor servant. The Duke, oblivious to the meaning of the boots, just continues wanting them."[34] At the end of the same play, Richard beats the Keeper of his prison, partly for refusing to taste his food, which task the Keeper has been forbidden to do by Sir Pierce of Exton, but principally out of displaced anger toward "Henry of Lancaster" (5.5.98–104). Constance doubts, threatens, and insults Salisbury because she is horrified at the news he brings of the marriage of Blanche and the Dauphin (*King John* 3.1.1–15, 37–41). Hector strikes his armorer, Alexander tells Cressida, because he is shamed over having been "struck down" in battle by Ajax, while Ajax beats Thersites because it is the only way he can respond to Thersites' insults (*Troilus* 1.2.6, 31–36; 2.1.11 s.d., 40 s.d., 53 s.d.). Orsino's threat to kill "Cesario" is at least partly motivated by anger at Olivia, who has refused his love (*Twelfth Night* 5.1.110–29). When the disguised Imogen attempts to reveal her identity to the distracted Posthumus, who thinks he has murdered his innocent wife, his reaction is "Shall 's have a play of this? Thou scornful page, / There lie thy part. [*He strikes her; she falls.*]" (*Cymbeline* 5.5.230–31).[35]

Saturninus, infuriated at Titus, hangs the Clown who delivers Titus's supplication (*Titus* 4.4.42–49). This slaughter of an utterly innocent man is the most obvious evidence in the play of Saturninus's tyranny; in fact, since Saturninus has nothing to do with the death of his brother and apparently truly believes that Titus's sons are guilty of that crime, and is apparently unaware of Lavinia's rape and mutilation until the final scene, it can be argued that the hanging of the Clown is necessary to justify Saturninus's death at the end of the play.[36]

In *Antony and Cleopatra*, the violence against servants is widespread and the protagonists' reactions to their servants, which often include threats and violence, do much to characterize them. The messenger who comes to Antony in 1.2 with news of Fulvia and Lucius's war against Caesar fears that Antony may be angry with him, but Antony reassures him and even encourages him to speak the whole truth, however harsh it seems. Antony's responses to the messengers early in the play clearly represent a man who is capable of recognizing his faults and assuming responsibility for them. He claims to welcome the servants who tell him not only the truth about himself but even rumors motivated by "malice" (1.2.114).

This gracious treatment of the messengers in the second scene could not be more sharply contrasted with his treatment of Caesar's messenger, Thidias, in the wake of the battle of Actium. Granted that Antony's immediate cause of anger is the sight of Thidias kissing Cleopatra's hand (and, perhaps, whatever Enobarbus is supposed to have told him of Thidias and Cleopatra's conversation), it is obvious that Antony here is displacing onto Thidias the anger he feels toward Caesar, Cleopatra, and himself:

> Now, gods and devils!
> Authority melts from me of late. When I cried "Ho!",
> Like boys unto a muss kings would start forth
> And cry, "Your will?"—Have you no ears? I am Antony yet.
> (3.13.90–93)

This ringing declaration, however, only emphasizes the change in the Antony who formerly commanded not only kings, but, to some degree, his own passions; now he is reduced to violating civilized protocol by having a messenger whipped. Interestingly,

Antony appears anxious to debase the status of Thidias, who seems to be a gentleman, to that of a servant and dependent, and then to use that debased status to excuse his anger: he refers to Thidias as "this jack," "this jack of Caesar's," a "feeder," and "a fellow that will take rewards / And say 'God quit you!'" (94, 104, 110, 125–26). Instead of inspiring noblesse oblige, Thidias's inferior social status and service to his master become justifications for ignoble violence against him. Further to excuse himself, Antony justifies his whipping of Thidias—to Caesar, not to Thidias—by suggesting that

> If [Caesar] mislike
> My speech and what is done, tell him he has
> Hipparchus, my enfranchèd bondman, whom
> He may at pleasure whip, or hang, or torture,
> As he shall like, to quit me.
>
> (150–54)

Although the editor of the Arden edition, M. R. Ridley, cites North's *Plutarch* in noting that "Antony is not abandoning an innocent man thus, but a revolter" (140 n. 149), it seems unlikely that Shakespeare relied on most of his audience to be so familiar with Plutarch as to remember this rather obscure point. Antony's casual offer of his former bondman as a sacrifice to his cruelty toward one of Caesar's servants can hardly be justified and only increases our feeling that the defeat at Actium is not the greatest of Antony's falls. He is "Antony yet," but, as Enobarbus notes, "'Tis better playing with a lion's whelp, / Than with an old one dying" (95–96). The dramatic change in Antony's treatment of his social inferiors suggests to what degree his judgment and nobility have deteriorated by the middle of the play.[37]

Cleopatra is more consistent, and also more violent, than Antony. Early in the play, she threatens Charmian for praising Julius Caesar above Antony, saying, "By Isis, I will give thee bloody teeth" (1.5.73), although this threat—certainly an indecorous one for a queen to make—does not appear to frighten Charmian and is probably not meant to be taken seriously. But her threats to the messenger who comes to her in act 2, scene 5, though equally rhetorical, are probably much more seriously intended. She begins her conversation with him by suggesting that his words have the power to kill her, should he say that Antony's dead, but immediately goes on to say that if his message that Antony is "well" means that Antony is dead, "The gold I give thee will I melt and pour / Down thy ill-uttering throat" (34–35). While she is first extracting news of Antony, offers of reward outnumber threats, although the messenger's intelligent hesitation inspires Cleopatra to remark, "I have a mind to strike thee ere thou speak'st" (43). As soon as the messenger reluctantly reports Antony's marriage to Octavia, Cleopatra's rage explodes:

> *Cleopatra*
> The most infectious pestilence upon thee!
> *Strikes him down.*
>
> *Messenger*
> Good madam, patience.
> *Cleopatra* What say you? *Strikes him.*
> Hence,
> Horrible villain, or I'll spurn thine eyes
> Like balls before me! I'll unhair thy head!
> *She hales him up and down.*
> Thou shalt be whipped with wire and stewed in brine,
> Smarting in ling'ring pickle.
> *Messenger* Gracious madam,
> I that do bring the news made not the match.
> (62–68)

So frantic is Cleopatra that she next attempts to bribe the messenger to change his story, as if this would change reality, suggesting, however, that "the blow" she has given him is just compensation for "moving [her] to rage" (69–73). When the messenger repeats the truth, Cleopatra draws a knife, declaring "Rogue, thou hast lived too long" (74). The messenger makes a hasty exit after the brief justification, "What mean you, madam? I have made no fault" (75). Charmian pleads with Cleopatra to control herself, but Cleopatra, like Antony, seeks to justify her behavior, though in her case by a suggestion that her passions are like a natural misfortune, and—again like Antony—displaces her anger, in her case onto Egypt and nature itself:

> *Charmian*
> Good madam, keep yourself within yourself.
> The man is innocent.
> *Cleopatra*
> Some innocents scape not the thunderbolt.
> Melt Egypt into Nile, and kindly creatures
> Turn all to serpents!
> (76–80)

But Cleopatra at this point regains her self-possession, at least enough to admit that she has behaved badly:

> Cleopatra   Call the slave again,
>   Though I am mad, I will not bite him. Call!
> Charmian
>   He is afeard to come.
> Cleopatra   I will not hurt him.
>   [*The Messenger is sent for.*]
>   These hands do lack nobility, that they strike
>   A meaner than myself, since I myself
>   Have given myself the cause.
>
>   (80–85)

She goes on, when the messenger returns, to advise him that "Though it be honest, it is never good / To bring bad news" (86–87), which certainly he should already have learned. Despite further threats and curses on her part, the messenger continues loyal to his duty to tell the truth; he is nevertheless dismissed without thanks, if without further physical violence.

Like much of *Antony and Cleopatra,* this scene is complex in its effects. The violence of Cleopatra's rhetoric, if not her actual physical violence, is amusing as well as pitiful: her behavior as queen is ignoble, as she herself recognizes, but her passionate response as a forsaken woman is understandable. The unfortunate messenger is given his own voice, and, however much we sympathize with Cleopatra's anger and grief, we must also sympathize with him, as Cleopatra's own attendant obviously does. The threats and beatings inflicted on the messenger suggest both the undeserved misfortunes visited upon innocent servants and how disasters can make great persons forget their duty to behave magnanimously.

Despite her acknowledgement of her ignobility in striking her inferiors, Cleopatra makes one more attempt to do just that—again, admittedly, under particularly trying circumstances and with justification lacking in her attack on the messenger. In act 5, scene 2, she calls upon her treasurer, Seleucus, to vouch for the honesty of the inventory of her possessions that she gives to Caesar. When Seleucus declares that she has kept back more than she has declared, she attacks him:

> The ingratitude of this Seleucus does
> Even make me wild.—Oh, slave, of no more trust
> Than love that's hired! [*Seleucus retreats from her.*]

What, goest thou back? Thou shalt
Go back, I warrant thee! But I'll catch thine eyes,
Though they had wings. Slave, soulless villain, dog!
Oh, rarely base!

(152–57)

Presumably Cleopatra is restrained or Seleucus manages to dodge her attack (in North's *Plutarch*, she pulls his hair and boxes his ears), but his betrayal of his mistress seems to justify her anger. Whether Seleucus really betrays her or does her a final service by pretending to betray her (thereby disarming Caesar's suspicion that she means to kill herself), Cleopatra's response at this point suggests her powerlessness: the Queen of Egypt, betrayed by one of her servants, can only threaten to scratch out his eyes.

A surprising number of Shakespeare's servants die as a result of their service, though their deaths vary considerably and the effects of these deaths are also variable. We are unlikely to weep for Bushy and Green, who die because of their service to Richard II, or the servants of Sir Pierce of Exton whom Richard kills while they are serving their master by trying to kill the king (*Richard II* 3.2.141–42; 5.5.105–7). Prior to Tom Stoppard, we would have paid just as little attention to Rosencrantz and Guildenstern, although they also play their parts as collateral damage attributable to Claudius's villainy.[38] The more retributive among us may even applaud the deaths of some servants. Loyal though he is to his evil mistress, it is hard to regret the death of Oswald or the uncommon level of violence with which the villain of *Othello* is punished. Iago is physically assaulted by his principal victim, although he has already been made a prisoner and is presumably helpless; furthermore, he is threatened not merely with death, but with torture. Gratiano promises him that "Torments will ope your lips" (5.2.314), but it is not clear that the only reason for torturing Iago is to force him to explain his motives.

Some servants die almost unremarked, sometimes offstage, as do Duncan's unfortunate guards and Macduff's equally unfortunate servants. Although she never appears onstage, Cornelia, the midwife who attends Tamora's labor, is doomed to be killed by Aaron (*Titus* 4.2.168–70). Even servants who die onstage are often overlooked by critics; given all of the bloodshed in *Titus Andronicus* and the fact that he is taken offstage to be hanged, it may be understandable that the Clown is usually forgotten, but this forgetting is surprising in the case of Tamora's Nurse, given that Aaron not only stabs her onstage, but literally adds insult to injury by comparing her dying cries to the squealing of "a pig preparèd to the spit" (146–48). Like Iago, Kent survives the end of his play, but does not expect to live much longer, since he tells Albany, "I have a journey, sir, shortly to go. / My master calls me; I must not say no" (Lear 5.3.327–28).

Interestingly but disturbingly, servants in the histories and tragedies are liable to die whether they faithfully serve their masters or mistresses or whether they betray them. This phenomenon is particularly evident in Lear, in which Cornwall's servant is killed for rebelling, Oswald dies while faithfully serving Goneril, the loyal Kent foresees his imminent death, and the faithful Fool simply disappears. Similarly, in Antony and Cleopatra, Enobarbus appears to die as a result of what might be called a self-induced broken heart, condemning himself, in his dying speech, as a "master-leaver and a fugitive" (4.9.25). Eros, who remains faithful to Antony, cannot bring himself to honor his vow to kill his master, choosing instead to kill himself (4.14.62–95). Iras dies unexplainedly, although not inexplicably, after kissing Cleopatra farewell, and Charmian follows her mistress in committing suicide by snakebite (5.2.290–98, 321–28). All of these servants choose to precede or closely follow Antony or Cleopatra in death, although the tragedy is not of the servants' making and is not, except as they choose to identify with it, their tragedy.[39]

Like the noble deaths of servants in King Lear and Othello, these suicides or otherwise self-willed deaths arguably elevate servants by allowing them to share the tragic fates of their masters and mistresses. Martha Tuck Rozett maintains that Charmian's last lines express triumph and adds that "the stage littered with bodies is thus not the tragic spectacle one would expect it to be, for it serves as a reminder that all the deaths in the play are voluntary and self-imposed acts which assert the individual's power over his or her own fate."[40] However, these deaths also suggest that there is no escape for servants, whether or not they truly serve their employers. Bad service, though as varied as that of Oswald or Iago or Enobarbus, will be punished by death; but good service, though as varied as that of Cornwall's First Servant or Emilia or Charmian and Iras, will also lead to death.

In The Politics of Shakespeare, Derek Cohen expresses a popular idea about violence in Shakespeare's plays: "Violence itself is a politically constructed concept in the plays. There are the violent acts of the rich and the violent acts of the poor. The violence of the rich and powerful is always hedged with a rhetoric of righteousness, with the anxious claim that it is necessary for the good of society—however phony that claim proves to be" (64). However, this is simply and demonstrably not true: even as early as *The Comedy of Errors,* Shakespeare is allowing a beaten servant to complain about the unfairness of his lot; as early as *Titus Andronicus,* he is demonstrating the evil of the play's villains by having them slaughter a Nurse and a clownish messenger. No defense of Regan or Cornwall for killing Cornwall's heroic servant or of Othello for threatening Emilia is attempted, nor is it likely that the original audience would have found such a defense (had Shakespeare been so foolish as to attempt one) acceptable.

Generally speaking, the violence toward servants in the earlier plays seems intended to amuse the audience while reaffirming the social hierarchy: servants who are cheeky, disobedient, or merely stupid, from their masters' and mistresses' viewpoints, are subject to threats and beatings. The incidence of actual beatings decreases sharply after the early plays, although threats continue to be made. In the later plays, servants—including serving-men, serving-women, and upper-class characters who disguise themselves as servants or define themselves as servants—play increasingly important roles; no longer primarily comic figures, they become subject to much more serious threats and violence. The actual and threatened violence they suffer often implies a criticism of the masters and mistresses who offer such violence. Furthermore, the servants' reactions often imply that they are not only morally superior to their oppressors simply as victims of injustice, but frequently superior in an active sense, recognizing but risking the danger of violence and even death. While faithful servants are often represented as the moral equals or superiors of their employers, they frequently gain that equality or superiority only by their deaths, involved in catastrophes not of their making. While the violence directed by employers against servants, particularly in the tragedies, seems in general designed to show a failure of nobility in the employers and the innocence and often nobility of the servants, it is hard to judge what effect Shakespeare expected the frequent message that "service = death" to have on his audience. Perhaps both the playwright and his audience saw these plays as simply representing the truth of Cleopatra's observation: "Some innocents scape not the thunderbolt."

11

"Remember I have done thee worthy service": Conclusion

IN DESCRIBING THE FIRST SCENE OF *KING LEAR*, DEREK COHEN PAUSES to consider the "attendants" who accompany France and Burgundy:

> one of their functions is clearly visual and symbolic. Their presence is normally and reasonably taken for granted by readers and audiences. They are simply appendages to the power politics onstage. But they are vivid reminders of the hierarchical structure of the world of the drama . . . Their tacit participation in the scene as attendants . . . speaks eloquently of the social order being realized onstage. It is a sign, I think, of the degree to which we are ideologically and historically linked to that social order that we hardly remark these attendants—they are virtually unnoted in reviews and criticism, and it is not expected in production that audiences will pay more than glancing attention to them.[1]

It is certainly true that the attendants in this scene, as in most of the many parallel scenes in Shakespeare's plays, have more of a "visual and symbolic" function than a usefulness in terms of action or accomplishment. It seems curious, however, that Cohen sees them as "vivid reminders" whose "participation . . . speaks eloquently" while simultaneously acknowledging that they are "normally and reasonably taken for granted" and "virtually unnoted." It may of course be that, as he suggests, our involvement in Shakespeare's social order renders us—and rendered Shakespeare's original audience—oblivious to these attendants. It seems more likely, though, that in this scene, as in many others, we—like the play's original audience—recognize that the attendants are simply status markers for the royalty and aristocrats (and thus, that they may themselves be aristocrats, and, almost certainly, are at least gentlemen, and not impoverished peasants). Michael Neill offers a different explanation for the frequent

237

critical disregard of servants: "a concern with the politics of master-servant relations is so pervasive in the drama of the period that it is paradoxically easy to overlook the phenomenon altogether—very much as the politics of gender were overlooked for so long—as if such matters were an unproblematic given of the preindustrial world."[2]

However easy it may be to overlook servants and whatever the explanation for that neglect, the almost complete absence of servants in twenty-first century Western life is one of the major differences between our world and that of our ancestors and for that reason alone it should arouse our curiosity. We should look particularly closely at servant-characters because they are depictions of people whose society expected them, ideally, at least, to be silent and invisible. Despite that cultural expectation, however, Shakespeare insistently—although not, to be sure, consistently—calls attention to these characters, giving them both heroic and villainous roles, making them both schemers and victims, active and passive, quiet and garrulous, foolish and wise. We can assume that Shakespeare believed, at least, that his depictions of servant-characters and his considerations of service concerns would not repel audiences; we might even go so far as to assume that he believed that these depictions and considerations would interest a significant segment of the audience.

The range of characters and kinds of service in Shakespeare's plays is extremely broad. Shakespeare's kings and queens declare themselves as serving God, their countries, their people, and other monarchs; aristocrats declare themselves the servants of their monarchs. Even among "official" servants, the range is considerable: ladies- and gentlemen-in-waiting, pages, messengers, agricultural workers, valets, slaves, professional fools, amateur fools, stewards, scullery maids, housekeepers, nurses, and anonymous "attendants," who could be practically anything. Servants are as treacherous as Iago and as loyal (finally) as Emilia; as absurd as Simple and as serious as Timon's Steward; as virtuous as Pisanio and as immoral as Oswald; as comic as Touchstone and as tragic as Lear's nameless Fool; as intimate with their employers as Charmian and Iras and as distant from their masters and mistresses as any of the many nameless servingmen who populate the plays. Servants embody the wealth and power of their employers, perform tasks both menial and otherwise, offer advice (requested or not) and commentary, enact loyalty and disloyalty, ponder questions of conflicting services, disobey as well as obey their employers, offer and receive violence. They demonstrate the difficulties of service for the lower classes and comment—directly or indirectly—on the failures of their "betters" to realize the ideal of service.

Although we often use the word "service" as if it referred to a single, simple concept, service in Shakespeare's era was anything but simple. Neill remarks that the plays "[hold] the ideology of service up to debate, and . . . [expose] its painful contradictions: as always, Shakespeare seems more interested in questions than in doctrine, more concerned to stretch his audience upon the rack of doubt and uncertainty than to instruct them."[3] Generally, the ideal of service was perceived as requiring absolute obedience to authority, but there was another, more democratic, ideal operative in early modern society: "Though for outward order a master be more excellent then a servant, yet as a man he ought to judge himself equall."[4] Those ideals, though technically not conflicting, must at times have seemed difficult to reconcile, as must have been the various services—to God, monarch, employer, and conscience, among others—required of the average Elizabethan. Because service—as a fact of life for the common people and an ideal for everyone—was so much a part of early modern culture, it seems natural that it was part of the period's popular entertainment, particularly since servants and people who had been servants constituted a significant portion of the audience.[5]

Service both unites and divides the classes in the plays: service consists, at a minimum, of one who serves and one who is served; it defines a relationship, and Shakespeare depicts many such relationships as warm and affectionate. Simultaneously, however, service separates people into different classes, almost automatically generating the resentment and distrust inherent in an inequitable and often arbitrary system; Shakespeare also depicts these aspects of service, creating not only Iago and Malvolio, but women such as Maria, Margaret, and Nerissa, who can escape service only through marriage, and sometimes scheme to obtain that freedom. Service can also be seen as a uniting factor in society because everyone owes service to one or more entities, linking all persons, high and low, in a great hierarchy of service. However, just as the ideology of service can be used by the upper classes to oppress the less fortunate, the less wealthy and powerful members of society can use that ideology to criticize—sometimes even to their faces—their "superiors." Many characters are depicted as being forced to try to contradict the biblical injunction that "No man can serve two masters," but no

characters except outright villains reject service outright—and
even villains may swear service to "Nature," as Edmund does,
or to another character, as Goneril does to Edmund. A complex
but near-universal ideology, with connections to the culture's
politics, religion, social structure, and economics, service provides a natural theme for drama.

Thus, it is not surprising that service underlies all of Shakespeare's plays. It is a vast and often confusing accumulation of
conflicting paradigms—ideal, insult, fact of life, source of conflict,
motivation for virtue and villainy. Its pervasiveness makes it an
extremely useful source of plots and characters: the servant who
betrays his master; the servant who risks her life to help her mistress; the fool who amuses his fallen lord; the steward who comments on his master's folly. Shakespeare's representations of
service develop from his early plays, in which he often follows
classical models depicting employers and servants in stereo-
typed ways, with a great deal of broad humor, often focused on
masters beating their servants and the servants complaining
about this mistreatment, to the much more various, complex,
and nuanced treatment of service and servants in the later plays.
Because service was such a complex and ubiquitous concept in
the early modern period, and because Shakespeare made so
much, and such varied, use of it, service gives us a perspective
for examining many aspects of his plays. We can ask what it
means that characters such as Othello and Coriolanus think of
themselves as servants of their respective city-states. We can in-
vestigate how it affects our understanding of Antony and Cleopatra to see them as employers of servants, on whom the "triple
pillar of the world" and the "lass unparalleled" are depicted as
being dependent. We can explore how it may change our interpretation of *Macbeth* if we think of the murderous thane and his
wife as rebellious servants who forswear their allegiance to their
royal master. We can attempt to resolve the dilemmas of such
female characters as Emilia and Cordelia, caught between duty
to men and service to the truth. There are, in fact, few of Shakespeare's major characters who cannot be usefully viewed
through the prism of service. In addition, of course, we can ex-
amine the host of minor characters who are "mere" servants; if
we do so, we may notice that they are often not as "voiceless" or
passive as is generally assumed, and what they do and say may
also provide new insights into the plays.

Although Shakespeare's depictions of servants may sometimes lack realism in the sense of being historically accurate,

they are nearly always emotionally true. If it is unlikely that real servants would defy their masters and mistresses, they must often have wanted to do so (and we know that, occasionally, some did so). Despite the assumption of superiority that the early modern class system encouraged among the rich and powerful, intelligence and virtue were not the exclusive prerogatives of the upper classes. A man of extraordinary genius born into a family of no particular distinction and little wealth in a society that prized family and wealth above everything, a man who had worked and schemed to have his family proclaimed gentry, a man who spent his working life officially designated a servant first of a nobleman and then of the king, would perhaps have been as aware of this as anyone. And perhaps it would not be surprising if that awareness manifested itself in his work. Nor, perhaps, is it a coincidence that his work took shape in the early modern public theater, which, as Steven Mullaney points out, "emerged from and appropriated a place within the fissures and contradictions of the cultural landscape" and "certainly served as a prominent affective arena in which significant cultural traumas and highly ambivalent events . . . could be directly or indirectly addressed, symbolically enacted, and brought to partial and imaginary resolution."[6] Because service was such a broad and flexible concept during Shakespeare's era, resolution concerning it could only have been temporary, since other situations, other characters, might well call for different resolutions; however, given the need to keep churning out plays comprised of dramatic situations of interest to a very heterogeneous audience, this may have been one of the attractions of service as a subject. Although perhaps not inexhaustible, service certainly lends itself to a great many variations.

Because service is so pervasive in Shakespeare's plays, I have only been able to write a kind of survey or overview; exploring the topic exhaustively would require multiple volumes. Although critics have done valuable work on service, many aspects of the subject remain to be investigated, both in Shakespeare's works and in those of his contemporaries. More attention needs to be paid to the intersection of service and class: among other considerations, how early modern writers used the common understanding that the upper classes owed service to the commonwealth to mock or censure members of those classes who failed in that duty. The similarities and differences between men's and women's services, and the complications inherent in women's duties toward men are also worth exploring, as are convergences among service and early modern political and religious theories. The topic of service is potentially as rich a field for modern critics as it was for Shakespeare.

Recent critical attention directed toward poor and working-class people in the early modern period has been reflected in increased attention toward poor and working-class characters, including servants. Much of this attention, however, has been focused on the relatively small number of Shakespeare's servant-characters who openly rebel against their servant-roles or against the very idea of service. Poor, silent, oppressed servants are a tidy paradigm, but they are not, exclusively, the servants that Shakespeare depicts. While such characters are certainly interesting, concentrating only on them unbalances our understanding of the plays, which are not only or primarily about such rebellion; in addition, concentration only on resistance to authority obscures the other aspects of service that Shakespeare explores through his many and varied depictions of servants. We cannot fully understand Shakespeare's plays without appreciating what a comprehensive, varied, and important concept service is; nor can we understand them without accepting that servants—the meek, quiet, and good, as well as the dangerous, vocal, and bad—have a place in the story.

Notes

PREFACE

1. Exceptions include Jonas A. Barish and Marshall Waingrow, "'Service' in *King Lear*," *Shakespeare Quarterly* 9 (Summer 1958): 347–55; Ralph Berry, *Shakespeare and Social Class* (Atlantic Highlands, NJ: Humanities Press International, 1988); Mark Thornton Burnett, *Masters and Servants in English Renaissance Drama and Culture: Authority and Obedience* (New York: St. Martin's Press, 1997); Ann Jennalie Cook, "Timon's Servant Takes a Wife," in *Shakespeare: Text, Subtext, and Context*, ed. Ronald Dotterer (Selinsgrove, PA: Susquehanna University Press, 1989), 150–56; John Draper, "Shakespeare's Rustic Servants," in *Stratford to Dogberry: Studies in Shakespeare's Earlier Plays* (n.p.: University of Pittsburgh Press, 1961), 11–23; Thomas Moisan, "'Knock me here soundly': Comic Misprision and Class Consciousness in Shakespeare," *Shakespeare Quarterly* 42 (Fall 1991): 276–90; Michael Neill, "Servant Obedience and Master Sins: Shakespeare and the Bonds of Service," in *Putting History to the Question: Power, Politics, and Society in English Renaissance Drama* (New York: Columbia University Press, 2000), 13–48; Michael Neill, "'Servile Ministers': *Othello, King Lear* and the Sacralization of Service" (Vancouver, BC: Ronsdale Press, 2004); Laura Quinney, "Enter a Messenger," in *William Shakespeare's "Antony and Cleopatra": Modern Critical Interpretations*, ed. Harold Bloom (New Haven: Yale University Press, 1988), 151–67; S. Schoenbaum, "Enter a Porter (*Macbeth*, 2.3)," in *"Macbeth": Critical Essays*, ed. S. Schoenbaum (New York: Garland, 1991), 367–75; and Richard Strier, "Faithful Servants: Shakespeare's Praise of Disobedience," in *The Historical Renaissance: New Essays on Tudor and Stuart Literature and Culture*, ed. Heather Dubrow and Richard Strier (Chicago: University of Chicago Press, 1988), 104–33. In addition, Charles Wells, in *The Wide Arch: Roman Values in Shakespeare* (New York: St. Martin's Press, 1992), chapter 9: "*Antony and Cleopatra*—Duty, Service and Betrayal" (138–49), touches upon a wide range of service-related topics, including the relative positions of slaves and servants, service to the state, virtuous disobedience, and violence toward servants, in a range of plays, including not only the Roman plays, but several histories, *King Lear, Othello, As You Like It,* and *The Comedy of Errors.*

2. Some readers may object to my frequent use of "employers" to mean "masters and mistresses"; while I acknowledge that "employer" is not an exact synonym for the older phrase and may suggest less subordination than is strictly appropriate, repeating "masters and mistresses" hundreds of times simply became awkward. In addition, I am not sure that "master" and "mistress," being on the whole foreign terms to modern readers, do not suggest more oppression than the average servant may have felt most of the time.

3. Bruce Robbins, *The Servant's Hand: English Fiction from Below* (New

243

York: Columbia University Press, 1986), 40. Neill seems much more accurate when he comments that "plays like *King Lear* and *The Changeling* may be relatively uninformative about the precise material conditions of domestic labor in the early seventeenth century, but they are remarkably illuminating about the ideology and experience of service in a society that imagined itself as a hierarchy of servants and masters" ("Introduction," in *Putting History to the Question: Power, Politics, and Society in English Renaissance Drama* [New York: Columbia University Press, 2000], 3).

4. *Discipline and Punish: The Birth of the Prison*, trans. Alan Sheridan (New York: Random House / Vintage, 1979), 137.

5. In her interesting book on *King Lear*, Judy Kronenfeld finds that one of the things the play does is to "[call] attention to the possibility that superiors misuse, or are unworthy of, their dignities" (*King Lear and the Naked Truth: Rethinking the Language of Religion and Resistance* [Durham, NC: Duke University Press, 1998], 160); as I hope to show, *Lear* is far from the only play that raises this issue.

6. Robbins, *The Servant's Hand*, x.

7. "Shakespeare's Rustic Servants," 15.

CHAPTER 1. "THE LIVES OF OTHER"

All quotations from Shakespeare are taken from *The Complete Works of Shakespeare*, 5th ed., ed. David Bevington (New York: Pearson/Longman, 2004).

1. 2nd ed. (London, 1608), Ti^r. On the "legal reality" of these analogies as expressed in the law against "petit treason," see Kronenfeld, *King Lear*, 307–8, n. 72.

2. Of the development of "service" from a "feudal ideal" to payment for labor, M. D. Jardine writes, "I would argue that it is in the Renaissance period in England that the strains resulting from this transition between divergent concepts of service are most apparent. Disguised by use of the same term these are not shared values and ideas, as historicism would have it, but are antagonistic" ("New Historicism for Old: New Conservatism for Old?: The Politics of Patronage in the Renaissance," in *Patronage, Politics, and Literary Traditions in England, 1558–1658*, ed. Cedric C. Brown [Detroit: Wayne State University Press, 1991], 306); see also Robbins, *The Servant's Hand*, 40.

3. *A Remedy for Sedition* (London, 1536), A2^r, A2^v, A3^v.

4. *Shakespeare's Comic Commonwealths* (Toronto: University of Toronto Press, 1993), 8.

5. William Gouge, *Of Domesticall Duties* (London, 1622), 691; see also B. P., *The Prentises Practise in Godlinesse, and his true freedome* (London, 1608), 39^v; and Neill, "'Servile Ministers,'" 13–16. On "Protestant dualism," see Kronenfeld, *King Lear*, 132–34.

6. Slights, *Shakespeare's Comic Commonwealths*, 13, citing *The Sermons of John Donne*, ed. George R. Potter and Evelyn M. Simpson, 10 vols. (Berkeley: University of California Press, 1953–62), 5:114.

7. On the varying ideas of what a servant was, see Burnett, *Masters and Servants*, 2–5. On service as a temporary stage in the lives of many people, see A. L. Beier, *Masterless Men: The Vagrancy Problem in England 1560–1640* (London: Methuen, 1985), 23; Frances E. Dolan, *Dangerous Familiars: Representations of Domestic Crime in England, 1550–1700* (Ithaca: Cornell Univer-

sity Press, 1994), 67; and Peter Laslett, *Family Life and Illicit Love in Earlier Generations* (Cambridge: Cambridge University Press, 1977), 34.

8. Dolan, *Dangerous Familiars*, 66. Kronenfeld quotes William Perkins complaining that servants were so well dressed that it was difficult to distinguish them from their employers (*King Lear*, 133–34).

9. Still another derogatory usage is suggested by the statement that "'servant' was a euphemism for a pimp or male whore" (Joan Hutton Landis, "'By two-headed Janus': Double Discourse in *The Merchant of Venice*," *The Upstart Crow* 16 [1996]: 23).

10. Pistol does, of course, tend to overreact much of the time, and, since he has "stolen" Quickly from Nym, it is just possible that he perceives an insult where none was intended. It is also the case that Pistol fails to react to the Boy addressing him as "mine host" (2.1.82). Pistol does, however, take "host" as an insult (and it is likely that Nym, who is looking for a fight, intends it as such), which suggests that to Pistol, at least, being identified as one who owns and runs a tavern is a less honorable occupation than being a gentleman's retainer—even for such a poor excuse for a gentleman as Falstaff.

11. As M. C. Bradbrook points out, many characters who are servants or who are performing services are "purely functional" (*Shakespeare and Elizabethan Poetry: A Study of his Earlier Work in Relation to the Poetry of the Time* [1951; repr., London: Chatto and Windus, 1965], 94); see also Susan Snyder, "Naming Names in *All's Well That Ends Well*," *Shakespeare Quarterly* 43 (Fall 1992): 268. Even servants with significant roles are not protagonists: Antony Sher, who played the Fool in the RSC production of *King Lear* in 1982 and 1983, notes that "in the end it is Lear's play, Lear's story, and seen in that context the Fool's disappearance is not difficult to explain at all—he has simply been absorbed by Lear, replaced by his madness, digested as fodder for his new perception of the world" ("The Fool in *King Lear*," in *Players of Shakespeare 2: Further Essays in Shakespearean Performance by Players with the Royal Shakespeare Company*, ed. Russell Jackson and Robert Smallwood [Cambridge: Cambridge University Press, 1988], 165). However, servant-characters occasionally seem to have dominated their plays, at least in the judgment of Shakespeare's original audience. For example, Andrew Gurr comments that for John Manningham, who witnessed a performance of *Twelfth Night* at the Middle Temple in February 1602, "the most noteworthy feature of the performance was the gulling of Malvolio" (*Playgoing in Shakespeare's London* [Cambridge: Cambridge University Press, 1987], 111). Even modern critics sometimes find servants central to their plays: James Edward Siemon attributes the relatively happy resolution of *The Winter's Tale* to "the two servant-meddlers" Camillo and Paulina and the former servant Autolycus (who still refers to Florizel as his master) ("'But It Appears She Lives': Iteration in *The Winter's Tale*," *PMLA* 89 [January 1974]: 12, 16 n. 9). In addition, of course, it is not only servants or other lower-class characters whose roles may be merely functional.

12. See, for example, the discussions of subversion by Jonathan Dollimore ("Introduction: Shakespeare, Cultural Materialism and the New Historicism," in *Political Shakespeare: New Essays in Cultural Materialism*, ed. Jonathan Dollimore and Alan Sinfield [Ithaca: Cornell University Press, 1985], 2–17); Stephen Greenblatt ("Invisible Bullets: Renaissance Authority and Its Subversion, *Henry IV* and *Henry V*," in *Political Shakespeare*, 18–47); and Paul Brown ("'This thing of darkness I acknowledge mine': *The Tempest* and the Discourse

of Colonialism," in *Political Shakespeare*, 48–71); and Greenblatt's "Murdering Peasants," in *Learning to Curse: Essays in Early Modern Culture* (New York: Routledge, 1990), 99–130.

13. "Invisible Bullets," 28–29.

14. See, among many others, J. Fit John, *A Diamond Most Precious, worthy to be marked: Instructing all Maysters and Seruauntes, how they ought to leade their lyves, in that Vocation which is fruitfull, and necessary, as well for the Maysters, as also for the Seruants, agreeable to the holy Scriptures* (London, 1577), 40; I. G., *A Refutation of the Apology for Actors* (London, 1615; repr., NY: Scholars' Facsimiles and Reprints, 1941), 46; Gouge, *Of Domesticall Duties*, 686–88; and Juan Luis Vives, *A verie Fruitfull and pleasant booke; called the Instruction of a Christian Woman*, trans. Richard Hyrde (London, 1592), X4ʳ. See also Laslett, *Family Life*, 61; and Lu Emily Pearson, *Elizabethans at Home* (1957; repr., Stanford: Stanford University Press, 1967), 453.

15. *The Wide Arch*, 139; on the importance of "the theme of loyal service and betrayal" (138) in *Antony*, among non-servants as well as servants, see also Janet Adelman, *The Common Liar: An Essay on "Antony and Cleopatra"* (New Haven: Yale University Press, 1973).

16. Even Burnett suggests that "In English Renaissance drama, the male domestic servant or 'servingman' is a familiar type . . . Invariably dramatic texts associate the male domestic servant with a set of recurring features. Deflating lofty attitudes with bawdy and skilled in disguise, he often takes delight in declaring physical needs, hatching ingenious schemes and confounding magisterial authorities" (*Masters and Servants*, 79). This description clearly does not apply to many of Shakespeare's representations of male domestic servants, including *As You Like It*'s Adam, Timon's Steward, the Balthasars of both *Much Ado* and *Romeo and Juliet*, *Twelfth Night*'s Malvolio, and *Cymbeline*'s Pisanio. For a discussion of female servants in both history and literature, see Burnett, *Masters and Servants*, chapter 4.

17. *The Politics of Shakespeare* (New York: St. Martin's Press, 1993), 75. On Shakespeare's supposed representation of the rich as "normal" and the poor (presumably including most servants) as "abnormal," see 58–59. Cohen does, however, acknowledge that "Commentary and criticism have been complicit in such [derogatory] constructions of Shakespeare's weak and working class. They are known as the low characters, the farce characters, the fools, the butts, the knaves and whores" (57). Margot Heinemann differs, noting of Shakespeare's lower-class characters, including servants, "they are, of course, often given the most searching comments on the heroic action. The Gravediggers, Pompey the bawd, the soldiers before Agincourt, represent one of the most important means of distancing the main action and enabling the audience to judge it. Often, however, in modern productions these characters are routinely presented as gross, stupid and barely human—rogues, sluts and varlets with straw in their hair, whose antics the audience can laugh at but whose comments it can't be expected to take seriously. Indeed, the combination of Loamshire dialect and dated jokes often makes the comments unintelligible anyway" ("How Brecht Read Shakespeare," in *Political Shakespeare*, 202–30, 225).

18. *The Art of Coarse Acting* (1964; rev. ed. New York: Drama Book Specialists, 1981), 20, 21. Green's reference to "even the groundlings," of course, suggests that the equation of intelligence and aesthetic judgment with exalted social status is not extinct. The success of modern theatrical troupes (such as Shenandoah Shakespeare) performing uncut or nearly uncut versions of

Shakespeare's plays suggests that the assumption that modern audiences cannot appreciate such performances may be another form of snobbery.

19. Such characters, obviously, can be silenced in production, though often not without doing violence to the play. Kenneth Muir notes that by omitting the lines of Cornwall's Second and Third Servants at the end of act 3, scene 7 from his stage production, "Peter Brook played down the humanity, love, and compassion which is called forth by the opposing evil. The evil and cruelty are made to seem the natural characteristics of man, and man's humanity to man is made to seem exceptional and unnatural" ("The Critic, the Director, and Liberty of Interpreting," in *The Triple Bond: Plays, Mainly Shakespearean, in Performance*, ed. Joseph G. Price, 21, [University Park: Pennsylvania State University Press, 1975]).

20. Cohen, *Politics of Shakespeare*, 83.

21. On Edgar as a therapist, and on other views of his character, see Winfried Schleiner, "Justifying the Unjustifiable: The Dover Cliff Scene in *King Lear*," *Shakespeare Quarterly* 36 (Autumn 1985): 337–43.

22. *The World We Have Lost: Further Explored*, 3rd ed. (London: Methuen, 1983), 5.

23. *The Servant Problem and the Servant in English Literature* (Boston: Badger, 1928), 5–6.

24. In this failure to acknowledge the presence of servants, we are perhaps emulating their employers, for, as Margaret Visser points out, "the gentry were taught to pretend that any members of the lower orders who were in their presence, and upon whom they depended, were not really there" ("Tipping," in *The Way We Are* [1994; repr., Boston: Faber and Faber, 1996], 75).

25. *Industry of Devotion: The Transformation of Women's Work in England, 1500–1660* (New York: Columbia University Press, 1987), 206 n. 2.

26. Dollimore, "Introduction," 12.

27. Perkins, *Servant Problem*, 7–8.

28. Ralph Berry notes that "Shakespearean drama tests these equations" of social class with moral worth (*Shakespeare and Social Class*, xv). As Stephen Orgel has observed, dramatists attempted to give "counsel" to monarchs at least as early as Sackville and Norton's *Gorboduc* (*The Illusion of Power: Political Theater in the English Renaissance* [Berkeley: University of California Press, 1975], 9). Orgel also comments that Ben Jonson and Inigo Jones devised "martial" masques for both Queen Anne and Prince Henry (60–61, 66–67), although King James "was an ardent and programmatic pacifist" (61); this suggests that some dramatists were willing to take chances, even with the most powerful of audiences. (King James's only response seems to have been to cancel a second martial masque commissioned by the prince in favor of another by the same authors.) Even more interesting is Orgel's account of the masque *The Triumph of Peace* and Charles I's response to it: "The legal profession was on the whole uncomfortable about royal prerogatives, and unsympathetic to the crucial principle of Divine Right, which made the king responsible only to God. In 1634 the Inns of Court took the remarkable step of retaining Inigo Jones and James Shirley in an attempt to speak to the king in his own language. The lawyers presented a masque at Whitehall that was, for all its courtly splendor, diplomatically but unequivocally critical of the royal policies, and undertook, through the power of poetry and the marvels of spectacle, to persuade the royal spectator to return to the rule of law" (79). The lawyers' attempt at advising their monarch, however, went for naught, since "the message failed to get

across. The masque was a huge success; the royal solipsist saw in it nothing but adulation, and was graciously pleased to order it repeated" (80, 83). Although Orgel attributes this failure to communicate to "the nature of the medium" (80), it seems at least possible that the nature of the auditor and the lack of direct criticism were equally responsible.

29. In another approach to "otherness," Karen Newman suggests that "Portia and Lancelot Gobbo . . . represent the 'other' in the play, those marginal groups that are oppressed under the Elizabethan class/gender system, but whose presence paradoxically is needed to insure its existence" ("Portia's Ring: Unruly Women and Structures of Exchange in *The Merchant of Venice*," *Shakespeare Quarterly* 38 [Spring 1987]: 30).

CHAPTER 2. "WHAT DUTY IS"

1. Nicholas Ling, *Politeuphuia. Wits Commonwealth* (London, 1608), 118[r].

2. Philip Stubbes, *The Anatomie of Abuses* (London, 1595), 5. Stephen Gosson offers another version of this general idea: "No man is borne to seeke private profite: parte for his countrie, parte for his friendes, parte for himselfe" (*The School of Abuse* [London, 1579], E2[v]); see also "Cuthbert Conny-Catcher," *The Defence of Conny-Catching* (1592), ed. G. B. Harrison (1922–26; repr., New York: Barnes & Noble, 1966), 11–12; Bartholomew Batty, *The Christian mans Closet*, trans. William Lowth (London, 1581), 31[r]; and William Lowth, "Epistle Dedicatorie" to Batty, 4[r]. Robert Crowley argues that "The ende why all men be create, / As men of wisdome do agre, / Is to maintaine the publike state / In the contrei where thei shal be" ("The Voyce of the laste trumpet: The Marchauntes Lesson," in *The Select Works of Robert Crowley*, ed. J. M. Cowper [London: Early English Text Society, 1872], 86); he includes merchants and scholars, as well as princes ("The Marchauntes Lesson," 86–87; "The Scholars Lesson," 72, 74; "The Yeomans Lesson," 67). Crowley also repeatedly declares that the rich owe service to the poor ("One and thyrtye Epigrammes," *Works*, 9); a marginal note reemphasizes, "Thus the poor are robbed by those who should serve them"; see also "The Yeomans Lesson," 64; "Pleasure and Pain," 113–14; and "An informacion and Peticion agaynst the oppressours of the pore Commons of this Realme . . . ," 157, 160, 163, and 164.

J. H. Hexter notes that Renaissance writers on the education of the aristocracy, including Sir Thomas Elyot, Thomas Starkey, Roger Ascham, Sir Humphrey Gilbert, and Francis Walsingham, all emphasize that the end is "education for service in the princely commonwealth" ("The Education of the Aristocracy in the Renaissance," in *Reappraisals in History: New Views on History and Society in Early Modern Europe* [1961; repr., New York: Harper & Row, 1963], 65).

3. *Measure* 1.1.30–41. In his note to these lines, the Arden editor, J. W. Lever, notes their "social aspect" and compares "T. Carew, *Sermons* (1603), P7[v]: 'It is reported of a king that had painted in his armes a candlestick with a candle burning, and this posie written. *In seruing other I waste my selfe*'."

4. *Shakespeare's Comic Commonwealths*, 73.

5. Writers of conduct books had much to say about the qualities of good servants, although William Gouge's comment that "there are so few good, and so many bad servants" is typical (*Of Domesticall Duties*, 630). On the other hand, Claude Desainliens writes, "It is a great treasure, of a good servant and a good

wife" (*The French Littleton: A Most Easy, Perfect, and Absolute Way to learne the French tongue: set forth by Claudius Holyband, Gentil-homme Bourbon-nois* [London, 1593], 82). The ideal servant should be, among other things, intelligent, meek, cheerful, loyal, honest, and industrious; see Stephen Bateman, *Batman uppon Bartholome* (London, 1582), 76ᵛ–77ᵛ, and Thomas Becon, *The Sicke Mans Salue* (London, 1604), 152. The principal virtue of a good servant, of course, is obedience: see Desainliens, 80, 82; and Ling, *Politeuphuia. Wits Commonwealth*, 118ᵛ, 119ᵛ. J. Fit John indicates that a master is required to give servants "their dutyes, and couenaunts, as meate, drinke, lodging, linnen, wollen, apparell, their occupation, and whatsoeuer is agreede vpon betwene them, that there be found no vnrighteous dealing in hym, but all iustice, all equi-tie and truth," adding that "He that is true and iust to his mayster, is lyke vnto a precious Jewell" (*Diamond Most Precious*, 40, 73). Gouge too insists that masters must be good to good servants (686–88); see also William Perkins, *Christian Oeconomie: or, A Short Survey of the Right Manner of erecting and ordering a Familie, according to the Scriptures* (London, 1609), 153–56.

6. Bruce Robbins (*The Servant's Hand*, 35) attibutes this phrase to Elliot Krieger, *A Marxist Study of Shakespeare's Comedies* (London: Macmillan, 1979), but does not give a page number. Thomas Moisan suggests that Adam "carries fidelity to the ideal of service to the master to the extreme" ("'Knock me here soundly,'" 280 n. 12).

7. "'Without the form of justice': Plainness and the Performance of Love in *King Lear*," *Shakespeare Quarterly* 42 (Winter 1991): 454. Judy Z. Kronenfeld suggests that "'The constant service of the antique world' that Adam exempli-fies is well repaid by Orlando, who carries Adam on his shoulders as Aeneas carried his father Anchises on the way to the founding of a new society. Or-lando's support of his servant is also a somewhat clearer image of pastoral hu-mility—and nobility—than the Duke's sententious celebration of equality in the wind and rough weather of Arden before an admiring audience" ("Social Rank and the Pastoral Ideals of *As You Like It*," *Shakespeare Quarterly* 29 [Summer 1978]: 340). Some critics see Adam as Orlando's temporary surrogate father, who is replaced by Duke Senior (Louis Adrian Montrose, "'The Place of a Brother' in *As You Like It*: Social Process and Comic Form," *Shakespeare Quarterly* 32 [Spring 1981]: 40; Kay Stanton, "Remembering Patriarchy in *As You Like It*," in *Shakespeare: Text, Subtext, and Context*, ed. Ronald Dotterer [Selinsgrove, PA: Susquehanna University Press, 1989], 143).

8. Ann Jennalie Cook, *The Privileged Playgoers of Shakespeare's London, 1576–1642* (Princeton: Princeton University Press, 1981), 14.

9. However, the figure of Christ as a servant seems to have been a fairly common one. Gouge comments that "Of *willingnesse* to doe that dutie which belongeth to a seruant, Christ Iesus (who *tooke vpon him the forme of a seru-ant*) hath made himselfe a worthy patterne" (*Of Domesticall Duties*, 618), while Lawrence Humfrey writes of Christ, "Nor wente hee garded with greate trayne of Seruaunts, but picked oute his Disciples, Fishermen and Publicanes: to whome as Seruaunt hee serued" (*The Nobles; or, Of Nobilitye* [London, 1563], K8ᵛ; see also K8ʳ). Christ is also described as a servant in an anonymous Eliza-bethan pamphlet entitled *Certayne short Questions and Answeres*:

> *Quest.* Howe knowest thou [Christ] is equall with his father?
> *Ans.* Bycause he sayth, *I and the Father are one*, also *Paule* sayth, *He being equall with his Father, tooke vpon hym the shape of a seruant.*
>
> ([London, 1580], n.p.)

10. A pamphlet entitled *The Prentises Practise in Godlinesse, and his true freedome* establishes the lower end of the natural hierarchy by describing how God "hath put all the creatures in subiection vnder our feet: so that from the glorious Sunne in the firmament to the little Emmet that creepeth vpon the dust, euery thing doth vs seruice"; the same pamphlet also, however, establishes the idea of service as appropriate to the upper end of the political hierarchy in a prayer that reads in part: "Wee pray thee (good Father) shew special mercy to our most Noble and gratious K. *James* thine anointed seruant" (B. P., *Prentises Practise in Godlinesse*, 29ʳ; 11th page of prayer 1). Cook states, "At all social levels, hierarchical arrangements prevailed, further subdividing both the minority and the majority. Indeed it has been suggested that England presented a mosaic of complex hierarchies" (*Privileged Playgoers*, 12).

11. On monarchs as God's servants, see Crowley, "The Voyce of the laste trumpet: The Yeomans Lesson," *Select Works*, 67; Humfrey, *Nobles*, I2ᵛ–I3ʳ, and [E. Nesbit], *Caesar's Dialogve or A Familiar Communication containing the first Institution of a Subiect in allegiance to his Soueraigne* (1601; repr., Amsterdam: Theatrvm Orbis Terrarvm / Da Capo Press, 1972), 12–13, 16. On Queen Elizabeth I as serving God, see Humfrey, B2ʳ, and Richard Barckley, "The Epistle Dedicatorie," in *A Discourse of the Felicitie of Man: Or, His "Summum bonum"* (London, 1598), 5ʳ; Humfrey also refers to Elizabeth as God's handmaiden (B1ʳ). In a speech to the Commons on February 4, 1559, Elizabeth referred to herself as "a servant of Almighty God" (Leonard R. N. Ashley, *Elizabethan Popular Culture* [Bowling Green, OH: Bowling Green State University Popular Press, 1988], 311), while "A Sonnet Addressed by King James to His Son Prince Henry" indicates that kings should serve God (Thomas Percy, *Reliques of Ancient English Poetry*, ed. Henry B. Wheatley [3 vols., 1886; repr., New York: Dover, 1966], 2:301).

12. *Richard II* 4.1.177. Donna B. Hamilton suggests that it is Richard's poor service to God that brings him into subjection to his cousin: "Richard's failure in stewardship to God and the law presages his expulsion from the sea-walled garden that is John of Gaunt's 'other Eden'" ("The State of Law in *Richard II*," *Shakespeare Quarterly* 34 [Spring 1983]: 14).

13. *All's Well That Ends Well*, Twayne's New Critical Introductions to Shakespeare, no. 10 (Boston: Twayne / G. K. Hall, 1989), 69; "Rabbits, Ducks, and *Henry V*," *Shakespeare Quarterly* 28 (Summer 1977): 287. On monarchs as servants of the commonwealth, see Edmund Dudley, *The Tree of Commonwealth* (1509; repr., ed. D. M. Brodie [Cambridge: Cambridge University Press, 1948]), 17, 31, 36. Robert Allott writes that "Antiochus told his sonne Demetrius, that their kingdome was a noble slavery," but does not indicate precisely who or what Antiochus thought they were serving (*Wits Theater of the little World* [n.p., 1599], 163ᵛ).

14. See *2 Henry IV* 3.1.4–31; 4.5.21–31; *Henry V* 4.1.228–82.

15. *Richard III* 3.2.54, 58 (see also 3.4.38–40); *All's Well* 4.5.71; *2 Henry IV* 5.2.40; *Henry VIII* 3.2.248, 274; 5.3.101; 1.2.25; *Winter's Tale* 4.4.515. Lord Talbot calls himself "Servant in arms to Harry King of England" (*1 Henry VI* 4.2.4).

16. *King Lear* 1.1.141; 1.4.6; 5.3.239, 272, 328; Kent makes other references to Lear as his master when he is disguised as Caius. Gloucester twice refers to Lear as his master, but he also refers to the Duke of Cornwall as his master (3.3.18; 3.6.85; 2.1.57). On Gloucester as a servant, see Richard Strier, *Resistant Structures: Particularity, Radicalism, and Renaissance Texts* (Berkeley: University of California Press, 1995), 189–92.

17. *King John* 3.3.72–73; 5.7.72–73, 104. On actual nobles acting as or being described by contemporaries as servants of or serving royalty, see William Roper, *The Mirrour of Vertue or The Life of Syr Thomas More Knight some-time Lo. Chancellour of England* (Paris, 1626), 10, 11, 13, 29–30, 80–81, 111, 149, and 167–68; see also Thomas Twyne, *The Schoolemaster or Teacher of Table Phylosophie* (London, 1583), N6ᵛ. Gervase Holles notes that Queen Elizabeth employed "the gentlemen of greatest hopes and of the best fortunes and families . . . to fill the most honourable rooms of her household servants" (*Memorials of the Holles Family 1493–1656*, ed. A. C. Wood [1937; repr. in *Social Change and Revolution in England 1540–1640*, ed. Lawrence Stone (New York: Barnes & Noble, 1965), 149]). Gentlemen-servants were, technically, serving-men rather than servants, but—to their dismay—this distinction was becoming obscured during the Elizabethan period (I. M., *A Health to the Gentlemanly profession of Seruingmen* [1598; repr., London: Oxford University Press / Shakespeare Association, 1931], C3ᵛ–C4ᵛ).

18. *Hamlet* 1.2.162–63; 2.2.267–70; see also 3.2.52. On the relationship between "servants" and "friends"—both in language and reality—see Michael Neill, "'He that thou knowest thine': Friendship and Service in *Hamlet*," in *A Companion to Shakespeare's Works, Volume 1: The Tragedies*, ed. Richard Dutton and Jean E. Howard (Malden, MA: Blackwell, 2003), 319–38; Neill comments that "The egalitarian bias of true friendship meant that it was, as Bacon observed, virtually unobtainable for princes (no matter how intensely they might desire it) because it demanded an equality inimical to their authority" (322).

19. *Richard III* 3.2.53–55. As Charles Wells points out, "Aristocratic privilege carried with it the essential concomitants of service and responsibility to a cause larger than the individual himself" (*Wide Arch*, 96).

20. Lawrence Manley notes that not only Shakespeare's *2 Henry VI*, but such chronicle plays as Heywood's *Edward IV* and the group effort *Sir Thomas More* "concerned themselves not only with England's history and heroes, but also with the official Tudor doctrines of service and obedience" (*London in the Age of Shakespeare: An Anthology* [University Park: Pennsylvania State University Press, 1986], 210).

21. *Coriolanus* 2.3.52–53; 3.1.307–10; 3.3.89–90. Coriolanus also says that he owes his "life and services" to the Senate, and is described by Brutus as "a petty servant to the state" (2.2.133–35; 2.3.179).

22. On service as an opportunity available to the younger sons of the gentry, see Cook, *Privileged Playgoers*, 45, 63.

23. See, for example, *Henry V* 4.8.564–65; *All's Well* 2.3.244–48; *Measure* 2.2.78–82; and *1 Henry IV* 3.2.4–5.

24. On the early modern period's "deep gerontological bias," see Stephen J. Greenblatt, "The Cultivation of Anxiety: King Lear and His Heirs," in *Learning to Curse: Essays in Early Modern Culture* (New York: Routledge, 1990, 80–98), 92. That children should serve their parents is emphasized by W. Averell, in "A Glasse for all disobedient Sonnes to looke in . . . ," rebuking "dallying Daddes" for spoiling their children: "you adore them lyke Saintes, which should serue you lyke Sonnes" (*A Dyall for dainty Darlings* [London, 1584], D1ᵛ). William Vaughan maintains that "The first duty of childre[n] towards their parents is, that they obey them in all things, for that is well pleasing unto the Lord" (*Golden-grove*, P1ʳ).

25. Contemporary writers who insist that servants be treated as part of the family, often as sons and daughters, include Gouge (*Of Domesticall Duties*, 589,

679); Perkins (*Christian Oeconomie*, 2–4); Vaughan (*Golden-grove*, N7ᵛ); and Juan Luis Vives (*Instruction*, X3ᵛ–X4ᵛ). That servants were considered as part of the family is confirmed by Peter Laslett, who, however, notes that "a servant did not enjoy permanent membership of the household in which he served. When a servant left, the relationship was over" (*World We Have Lost*, 2–3; and *Family Life*, 61). See also Susan Dwyer Amussen, *An Ordered Society: Gender and Class in Early Modern England* (Oxford: Blackwell, 1988), 40–41; Craig A. Bernthal, "Treason in the Family: The Trial of Thumpe v. Horner," *Shakespeare Quarterly* 42 (Spring 1991): 44–45; Cook, *Privileged Playgoers*, 13; Dolan, *Dangerous Familiars*, 66; and Cynthia B. Herrup, *A House in Gross Disorder: Sex, Law, and the 2ⁿᵈ Earl of Castlehaven* (Oxford: Oxford University Press, 1999), 13–14.

26. Brenda Bruce, who played Juliet's Nurse in the Royal Shakespeare Company's 1980 and 1981 productions of *Romeo and Juliet*, asserts that "She is in fact the Mother, the person in whom Juliet lays her trust and confides her secret love" ("Nurse in *Romeo and Juliet*," in *Players of Shakespeare: Essays in Shakespearean Performance by Twelve Players with the Royal Shakespeare Company*, ed. Philip Brockbank [Cambridge: Cambridge University Press, 1985], 91).

27. Berry, *Shakespeare and Social Class*, 40.

28. Ibid.

29. Although some conduct books urged masters to avoid fraternizing with servants (see, for example, Stephen Guazzo, *The civile Conversation of M. Stephen Guazzo*, trans. G[eorge] Pettie and Barth[olomew] Young [London, 1586], 171ʳ–171ᵛ), Lady Anne Clifford reports that in 1603 she "learned to sing & play on the Bass Viol of Jack Jenkins my Aunt's Boy." On March 8, 1617, Lady Anne notes, "After Supper I play'd at Glecko with the Steward & as I often do after Dinner and Supper." On March 20, 1617, she reports, "I spent most of my time in walking and playing at Cards with the Steward and [Peter] Baskett [Gentleman of the Horse], & had such ill luck that I resolved not to play in 3 months." However, "The 30th and 31st I spent in hearing of reading & playing at Tables with the Steward" (*The Diaries of Lady Anne Clifford*, ed. D. J. H. Clifford [Phoenix Mill, UK: Alan Sutton, 1990], 27, 50, 51, 82).

30. "Celia and Rosalind in *As You Like It*," in *Players of Shakespeare 2: Further Essays in Shakespearean Performance by Players with the Royal Shakespeare Company*, ed. Russell Jackson and Robert Smallwood (Cambridge: Cambridge University Press, 1988), 59.

31. *T.G.V.* 2.1.1–90; *Measure* 1.2.84–115; *Antony* 1.5.69–72. Although Shakespeare may take liberties in depicting servants' impertinence, Claude Desainliens's works, which give us purportedly representative dialogue of Elizabethans at home, often suggest that servants were familiar with their masters. A page is seen sneaking a drink of wine, to which his master's response is merely to laugh and ask his friends, "Doth he not well? It is not the first that hee hath swallowed up: hee knoweth well the trade of it"; and a servant inquires of her master's son, who is demanding water to wash: "Can you not wash in the baason? Shall you haue alwayes a seruaunt at your tayle? you are to wanton" (*Campo di Fior, or else The Flourie Field of Foure Languages of M. Claudius Desainliens, alias Holiband: For the furtherance of the learners of the Latine, French, English, but chieflie of the Italian tongue* [London, 1583], 112–14, 64).

32. "Viola in *Twelfth Night*," in *Players of Shakespeare 2*, 85.

33. A. L. Beier presents evidence that suggests that many servants were young, and Laslett simply states that "servants were young people" (*Masterless Men; Family Life*, 63); it appears that the Elizabethans commonly thought of service as a young person's profession. See also Ilana Krausman Ben-Amos, *Adolescence and Youth in Early Modern England* (New Haven: Yale University Press, 1994), 2; Burnett, "Masters and Servants in Moral and Religious Treatises, c. 1580–c. 1642," in *The Arts, Literature, and Society*, ed. Arthur Marwick (London: Routledge, 1990), 67; Dolan, *Dangerous Familiars*, 65–66; Montrose, "Place of a Brother," 38; Lena Cowen Orlin, *Elizabethan Households: An Anthology* (Washington, DC: Folger Shakespeare Library, 1995), 33; and Lawrence Stone, *The Family, Sex and Marriage in England 1500–1800* (New York: Harper & Row, 1977), 92, 107–108, 167. Civis, in *A Diamond Most Precious*, suggests that "The old Prouerbe is true. A yong Courtyer, an old Begger, for they say seruice is none heritage," and proceeds to tell "Esop's" story of the greyhound who is "much made of" when young and swift, but "set at liberty without comforte" when old (11). Apprentices, of course, were generally young, but the Elizabethans often did not discriminate between apprentices and other servants or between servants and other workers. For example, Civis in *A Diamond Most Precious* refers to "younglinges, which are seruauntes, or Apprentyses (vse the tearme of speech thereof, as it shall please you)" (3). However, Sue Wright notes the existence of older servants and states that "it would be wrong to assume that service was an option for the young alone" ("'Churmaids, Huswyfes and Hucksters': The Employment of Women in Tudor and Stuart Salisbury," in *Women and Work in Pre-Industrial England*, ed. Lindsey Charles and Lorna Duffin (London: Croom Helm, 1985), 104.

34. "J. Fit John's" characters makes this association:

> *Puer.* I gather much of your talk, but though you speake of children, is the meaning thereof by seruauntes lykewyse?
> *Civis.* Yea all is one, for where there is a child or a sonne named, or a seruaunt, all is as one thing. . . .
>
> (*Diamond Most Precious*, 52)

This idea also occurs in Richard Hyrde's translation of Juan Luis Vives' *Instruction of a Christian Woman*, which directs its audience that "if a seruant haue done long seruice in [a woman's] house, let her take him none other wise than as her brother or her son" (X4r).

35. "'Standing to the wall': The Pressures of Masculinity in *Romeo and Juliet*," *Shakespeare Quarterly* 48 (Fall 1997): 268. Greenblatt discusses "what was for Shakespeare's England the age that demanded the greatest attention, instruction, and discipline, the years between sexual maturity at about fifteen and social maturity at about twenty-six. This was, in the words of a seventeenth-century clergyman quoted by Keith Thomas, 'a slippery age, full of passion, rashness, wilfulness,' upon which adults must impose restraints and exercise shaping power. The Elizabethan and Jacobean theater returned almost obsessively to the representation of this age group, which, not coincidentally, constituted a significant portion of the play-going population. Civic officials, lawyers, preachers, and moralists joined dramatists in worrying chiefly about what Lawrence Stone in *The Family, Sex and Marriage in England 1500–1800* calls 'potentially the most unruly element in any society, the floating mass of young unmarried males,' and it was to curb their spirits, fashion their wills, and delay their full entry into the adult world that the educa-

tional system and the laws governing apprenticeship addressed themselves. But girls were also the objects of a sustained cultural scrutiny that focused on the critical passage from the authority of the father or guardian to the authority of the husband" ("Cultivation of Anxiety," 83–84). See also Keith Thomas, "Age and Authority in Early Modern England," *Proceedings of the British Academy* 62 (1976), 205–48.

36. Wells, *Wide Arch*, 142. Burnett points out that "From apprentices learning a trade to the officials of the great noble households, servants were perhaps the most distinctive socio-economic feature of sixteenth- and seventeenth-century society" (*Masters and Servants*, 1). As Mary Hallowell Perkins notes, "The playwrights . . . could hardly ignore the servant in attempting to represent the life of the time" (*Servant Problem*, 40; see also 46).

37. Wells, *Wide Arch*, 140. In a note, Wells lists the suicides as "Enobarbus, Eros, Charmian, Iras and (in *Caes.*) Titinius" (148 n. 7). I do not think that Enobarbus is properly regarded as a suicide, unless wishing oneself dead can be regarded as a suicidal act, but his importance as a character can hardly be doubted.

38. "Living-in, dependent workers were probably the largest element in the labour force. They formed about two-fifths of the population with occupations and status recorded in seventeenth-century villages, mainly working as servants in husbandry; and between a half and two-thirds in towns, most of them apprentices and domestics" (Beier, *Masterless Men*, 23). On the large number of servants in Shakespeare's England and their ubiquity, see William Harrison, *The Description of England* (1587; repr., ed. Georges Edelen [Washington, DC: Folger Shakespeare Library / Dover, 1994]), 231; Paul Hentzner, *A Journey into England* (1598; trans. Richard Bently, ed. Horace Walpole [Strawberry Hill, 1757]), 88; Humfrey, *Nobles*, I1^r, V5^v; I. M., *Health*, H1^r, H1^v; William Brenchley Rye, *England as Seen by Foreigners in the Days of Elizabeth and James the First, 1592–1610* (London: John Russell Smith, 1865), 13, 70; John Stowe, *A Survey of London, Reprinted from the Text of 1603*, ed. Charles Lethbridge Kingsford (2 vols. [1908; repr., Oxford: Oxford University Press, 1971]), 1:88–89; Beier, 23, 51; Peter Burke, "Popular Culture in Seventeenth-Century London," in *Popular Culture in Seventeenth-Century England*, ed. Barry Reay (London: Croom Helm, 1985), 33; Burnett, "Masters and Servants," 67; Paul V. B. Jones, *The Household of a Tudor Nobleman* (1918; repr., New York: Johnson Reprint Company, 1970), 9–22, 239–42; Laslett, *World We Have Lost*, 13, 92; Dorothy Marshall, *The English Domestic Servant in History* (London: Historical Association, 1949), 4–6; Orlin, *Elizabethan Households*, 21; Jeffrey L. Singman, *Daily Life in Elizabethan England* (Westport, CT: Greenwood Press, 1995), 16, 30; Stone, *Family, Sex and Marriage*, 6, 25, 27–28; Joy Wiltenburg, *Disorderly Women and Female Power in the Street Literature of Early Modern England and Germany* (Charlottesville: University Press of Virginia, 1992), 12; and Wright, "'Churmaids, Huswyfes and Hucksters,'" 102–3. For examples of the number and variety of servants in great houses in the early modern period, see Jones, 239–42. Another indication that Shakespeare was not exactly holding the mirror up to nature in his depictions of servants is pointed out by Harry Levin: "Servants tend to be indelibly anglicised; even in the homeland of Brighella and Arlecchino, they are named Potpan and Sugarsop, Hugh Oatcake and Susan Grindstone" ("Shakespeare's Italians," in *Shakespeare's Italy: Functions of Italian Locations in Renaissance Drama*, ed. Michele Marrapodi, et al. [Manchester, UK: Manchester University Press, 1993] 21).

39. On the preponderance of male servants in great households, see Jones, *Household*, 16, and Marshall, *English Domestic Servant*, 6–7. On the other hand, C. M. Woolgar argues that "Most servants and attendants in the great household were male, certainly in the thirteenth and fourteenth centuries. There was some blurring of the picture in the fifteenth century. A recent study of gentry wills in the period 1460 to 1530 has shown that twice as many male household servants as female received bequests. This indicates a substantial change in balance. The picture in the sixteenth and seventeenth centuries was very different, moving to a female preponderance in domestic service" (*The Great Household in Late Medieval England* [New Haven: Yale University Press, 1999], 34).

40. *World We Have Lost*, 13. See also Beier, *Masterless Men*, 23; and Leo Salingar, *Shakespeare and the Traditions of Comedy* (Cambridge: Cambridge University Press, 1974), 255.

41. In addition to Francis the drawer in *1 Henry IV* and Peter Thump in *2 Henry VI*, apprentices also appear in what is generally thought to be a Shakespearean addition to *Sir Thomas More*, but it is nevertheless true that apprentices figure very little in the canon. On apprentices, see Ian Archer, *The Pursuit of Stability: Social Relations in Elizabethan London* (Cambridge: Cambridge University Press, 1991), passim; Burnett, *Masters and Servants*, 14–53; and Mihoko Suzuki, *Subordinate Subjects: Gender, the Political Nation, and Literary Form in England, 1588–1688* (Aldershot, UK: Ashgate, 2003).

42. As Laslett points out, "service in England and the West was a stage in the life cycle for large numbers of people," not necessarily a permanent occupation or class definition (*Family Life*, 34); see also Carl Bridenbaugh, *Vexed and Troubled Englishmen, 1590–1642* (London: Oxford University Press, 1967), 174.

43. " 'The Force of Imagination': The Subject of Blackness in Shakespeare, Jonson, and Ravenscroft," *Renaissance Papers 1991*, ed. George Walton Williams and Barbara J. Baines (Raleigh, NC: Southeastern Renaissance Conference, 1992), 56; *Merchant* 3.5.38–40. That most of Shakespeare's servants are men rather than women and "upper" servants rather than drudges may be part of the explanation for the lack of African servants (Imtiaz Habib, "Reading Black Women Characters of the English Renaissance: Colonial Inscription and Postcolonial Recovery," *Renaissance Papers 1996*, ed. George Walton Williams and Philip Rollinson [Raleigh, NC: Southeastern Renaissance Conference, 1997], 77). Of Shakespeare's other African characters, Morocco is a prince, Othello a prince by birth (he tells us), though later a slave and a general in the service of Venice, and Aaron a member of Tamora's household, probably in her service (even apart from being secretly her lover), but not explicitly depicted as a servant.

44. On servants rising in the world, see Bridenbaugh, *Masterless Men*, 141; Jones, *Household*, 26–27; and Orlin, *Elizabethan Households*, 22. On the popularity of the topic "how the talented but low born have been able to rise in the world," see Ashley, *Elizabethan Popular Culture*, 93.

45. *Shakespeare and the Rival Traditions* (1952; repr., Bloomington: Indiana University Press, 1970), 272. While contemporary writers who claimed that servants were able to rise in the world may have been writing propaganda for the upper classes (consciously or unconsciously), certainly many writers made such claims. See, for example, Becon, *Sicke Mans Salue*, 153; Fit John, *Diamond Most Precious*, 21, 50, 54; Gouge, *Of Domesticall Duties*, 644 (see also 621–22, 639); and Ling, *Politeuphuia. Wits Commonwealth*, 118^v, 119^v. Whatever

the propaganda value of these statements, it seems unlikely that servants were the principal audience for the works in which these statements occur, and improbable that such statements would be made repeatedly if, in fact, servants never or only rarely became masters. However, for a much grimmer view of the servant's situation, see Beier, *Masterless Men*, especially 24–27; see also Laslett, *World We Have Lost*, 4.

46. *Twelfth Night* 2.5.23–44. As Malvolio states, "There is example for't"; for instances of historical upper-class persons who married servants, see Burnett, *Masters and Servants*, 168–69, 175–76; see also James H. Lake, "The Psychology of Primacy and Recency Effects Upon Audience Response in *Twelfth Night*," *The Upstart Crow* 15 (1995): 29. For examples of servants marrying their masters' widows, daughters, or other family members, see Thomas Whitfield Baldwin, *The Organization and Personnel of the Shakespearean Company* (1927; repr., New York: Russell & Russell, 1961), 148, 149, 154–55; M. C. Bradbrook, *The Rise of the Common Player: A Study of Actor and Society in Shakespeare's England* (Cambridge, MA: Harvard University Press, 1962) 195; Burnett, *Masters and Servants*, 31–33; Jeanne Jones, *Family Life in Shakespeare's England: Stratford-upon-Avon 1570–1630* (Stroud, UK: Sutton / Shakespeare Birthplace Trust, 1996), 31; Stone, *Family, Sex and Marriage*, 61, 549; see also Andrew Gurr, *Playgoing in Shakespeare's London*, 111; Manley, *London in the Age*, 272; and Sir Thomas Overbury's Character of "A Serving-Man" ("Characters, or, Witty Descriptions of the Properties of Sundry Persons," in *The Miscellaneous Works in Prose and Verse of Sir Thomas Overbury, Knt.*, ed. Edward F. Rimbault [London: Reeves and Turner, 1890]), 70. As the editor of the *Roxburghe Ballads* points out, "The subject of a serving-man marrying the Squire's daughter was one of the most popular with buyers of ballads" (*The Roxburghe Ballads*, ed. William Chappell, 8 vols. [1872; repr., New York: AMS Press, 1966], 3:420).

47. *1 Henry VI* 3.4.20–26; *1 Henry VI* 3.1.164–74. In a later play, Richard Duke of Gloucester uses the idea of reward for service to mock the Earl of Warwick (*3 Henry VI* 5.1.25–33). On rewards to actual upper-class servants, see Richard C. Barnett, *Place, Profit, and Power: A Study of the Servants of William Cecil, Elizabethan Statesman* (Chapel Hill: University of North Carolina Press, 1969), 14–150 passim; Cook, *Privileged Playgoers*, 56–57; Cynthia B. Herrup, *House in Gross Disorder*, 14; Alan G. R. Smith, *Servant of the Cecils: The Life of Sir Michael Hickes, 1543–1612* (Totowa, NJ: Rowman and Littlefield, 1977), 41, 44, 188 n. 51; and Leonard Tennenhouse, *Power on Display: The Politics of Shakespeare's Genres* (New York: Methuen, 1986), 32–33.

48. *A.Y.L.* 5.4.169–74; *Henry V* 2.2.32–35. Writers of conduct books and religious tracts often promised heavenly, as well as earthly, rewards for good service (see, for example, Crowley, "The Voyce of the laste trumpet: The Seruauntes Lesson" [London, 1550], 59–63); but Shakespeare does not offer such consolation.

49. *2 Henry VI* 5.1.76–80; Berry, *Shakespeare and Social Class*, 8.

50. Berry, *Shakespeare and Social Class*, 118–19; see also 121.

51. Recent theatrical productions have frequently depicted *Macbeth*'s Third Murderer (often Seyton) making away with the other two after Banquo's murder; there is certainly poetic justice in such staging, as well as additional violence suitable to the play, but it does not arise out of Shakespeare's text.

52. On the reciprocal duties between employers and servants, see Amussen, *Ordered Society*, 38. On servants' wages and "fees," see Gouge, *Of Domesticall*

Duties, 684; Paul V. B. Jones, *Household*, 52–57; and Marshall, *English Domestic Servant*, 11. On gratuities to servants, including "higher" servants, see Ashley, *Elizabethan Popular Culture*, 24; Barnett, *Place, Profit, and Power*, 16, 83–85, 96, 99–100, 124; Paul V. B. Jones, 37–39; Marshall, 16–19; and Smith, *Servant of the Cecils*, 58–80, 66, 141, 143–45.

53. *Troilus* 3.3.1–32; *Measure* 5.1.541–42; *Tempest* 1.2.301–2, 423–24, 445–46, 502–3; 4.1.266–67; 5.1.87, 95–96, 243, 320–22. Perhaps the most unusual and disgusting reward-for-service situation in the canon occurs when the Bawd offers Bolt the opportunity to rape Marina as a reward for his work in obtaining her for the brothel (*Pericles* 4.2.127–29).

54. *Pericles* 2.Cho.16.s.d.; *Macbeth* 2.1.12–17. Such generosity, of course, may have additional resonance, as when Lord Hastings gives his purse to a Pursuivant also named Hastings, thereby rewarding a man whose appearance at that moment Lord Hastings takes to be a good omen, when in fact it proves to be one of the several portents of the nobleman's fall (*Richard III* 3.2.106 s.d.).

55. *Shrew* 4.4.17; *Tempest* 1.2.499; see also 3.3.83–88; 4.1.142, 164; 5.1.95, 228; *Twelfth Night* 1.5.70–71; 2.3.19–25, 29–31, 45, 46, 53, 54, 71; 5.1.22, 31–32; in addition, Viola praises the Clown in his absence (3.1.60–68). Tranio also gives gives Biondello at least enough money to buy a drink. Ariel, of course, has no need of money, and some critics would argue that Prospero's praise is simply a device to reconcile the enslaved spirit to his lot, although one can imagine what they would say if Prospero never spoke kindly to Ariel. Of course, there are employers who cannot be given credit for praising their servants: it is, for example, unlikely to alter one's opinion of Richard, Duke of Gloucester, that he says to the men he has hired to murder his brother, "I like you, lads" (*Richard III* 1.3.354).

56. *Twelfth Night* 2.3.25, 31, 33; 2.4.67; 3.1.43, 53; 4.1.18; 4.2.80–83, 110–13, 119; 5.1.25, 31–32. The Duke also promises a possible additional reward (5.1.38–40). Berry notes the multiple payments to Feste, and suggests that Feste's begging in 5.1 irritates Orsino (*Shakespeare and Social Class*, 74). There is, however, no more reason to think that Orsino is angered by Feste's undoubted impudence than that he is amused, and Orsino's suggestion that he may later give Feste another gratuity does not suggest that Orsino is annoyed. Slights mentions "the idea of reward for service rendered" as being prominent in *Twelfth Night*, and not only among employers and servants (*Shakespeare's Comic Commonwealths*, 222).

57. Berry, *Shakespeare and Social Class*, 74.

58. *L.L.L.* 3.1.129–31; 168–71. Costard suggests at 1.2.145–46 that Armado pays his servants low wages. For a contemporary criticism of employers' injustices regarding wages, see Gouge, *Of Domesticall Duties*, 685; on employers' failure to pay agreed-upon wages, see Bridenbaugh, *Vexed and Troubled Englishmen*, 210. Although Shakespeare devotes little attention to this topic, it was of no slight interest during this period; even a ballad-writer, spelling out "A right Godly and Christian A. B. C.," thought the subject worth raising: "Keepe not thy hyre-ling's wages backe, / God will his cry regard: / In poore men's matters be not slacke—/ the Lord will thee reward," further exhorting, "you masters, kindly deale!" (*Roxburghe Ballads*, 3:160–63, 161, lines 37–40, 46).

59. *L.L.L.* 3.1.129–31. On the jokes about remuneration as "a relic of Greek and Latin comedy," see A. C. Partridge, "Shakespeare and Italy," *English Studies in Africa* 4 (1961): 123.

60. Marshall notes that "The fact that women servants, unlike the men, wore

no distinguishing livery was sometimes a source of social embarrassment," when servants were mistaken for their "betters" (*English Domestic Servant*, 20).

61. Speed (who believes that he gave the letter to Julia) ultimately persuades Proteus to pay him sixpence, but appears to feel that the pay is inadequate (*T.G.V.* 1.1.140–43). Lucetta's failure to pay a messenger does not reflect well on her; perhaps the idea is that servants are apt to be less generous, even with one another, than are aristocrats. One is inclined to feel that this failure is included simply to give Speed and Proteus the opportunity to ring the changes on the situation.

62. P. H. Davison argues that this passage does not show "petty corruption" or "dishonesty": "Shakespeare's point here is surely the reverse. Shallow is shown to be rather silly and very naïve, but basically kind and human; Davy is concerned only to ensure that his friend has a fair hearing—which Shallow grants" (*2 Henry IV*, ed. P. H. Davison, 1977; reprinted in *William Shakespeare: Four Histories* [London: Penguin, 1994, 423–665], 5.1.46n.).

63. Critics differ on their opinion of the importance of money in the relationship between employers and servants. Alfred Harbage argues that the servants are generally not mercenary and are even capable of being "magnanimous" (*As They Liked It: A Study of Shakespeare's Moral Artistry* [1947; repr., New York: Harper Torchbooks, 1961], 191); however, Derek Cohen views the relationship between Timon and his servants as a purely mercenary one (*Politics of Shakespeare*, 92).

64. William Perkins describes slaves or bond-servants as one of two types of servants, the other being "free" servants (*Christian Oeconomie*, 157).

65. Shakespeare is hardly the only contemporary writer who expresses skepticism about the ideal of service. In addition to his fellow playwrights (think of Kyd's Pedringano, Marlowe's Ithamore, Jonson's Face, and Webster's Bosola, among many possible examples), Stephen Guazzo, for example, suggests that servants "take singuler pleasure in . . . drinking, playing, and speaking ill," that this misbehavior proceeds of "lacke of love" for their masters, and that "the very servitude it selfe may also be a cause of this lacke of love (that I may not say hatred) of the servants towards the masters, for that men serve commonly rather of necessitie, then of free will: for so much as a man knowing himselfe to be borne free, when he putteth him selfe in service, he forceth his nature, & though voluntarilie he maketh himselfe a prisoner, yet it is not to be said, y^t he is content with it, or that he hateth not him which kepeth him in su[b]jection" (*civile Conversation*, 165^v). I. M., author of *A Health to the Gentlemanly Profession of Servingmen*, complains that "the poore Servingman" is "inhumanely intreated" and "hardly used" (I2^v). On early modern authorities' mistrust of servants, see Jonathan Dollimore, "Transgression and Surveillance in *Measure for Measure*," in *Political Shakespeare: New Essays in Cultural Materialism*, ed. Jonathan Dollimore and Alan Sinfield (Ithaca: Cornell University Press, 1985), 76; and Stone, *Family, Sex and Marriage*, 96–97.

66. Genesis 4:9–12; 9:24–27; 27:38–40. "The wofull Lamentation of William Purcas" tells us that "Cain branded was a slave / for murthering of his brother" (*Roxburghe Ballads*, 3:29–35, lines 125–26). Ling's definition emphasizes the baser of the meanings of service: "*Serving, or servitude, is a certaine slavish bond of constraint, by which, either for commodity or love, men bind themselves to the will of others: making themselves subject to controlement*" (*Politeuphuia. Wits Commonwealth*, 117^v). Greenblatt notes that according to

William Tyndale's *The Obedience of a Christian Man*, "Servants . . . must understand that they are the property of their masters, 'as his ox or his horse'" (*Renaissance Self-Fashioning from More to Shakespeare* [Chicago: University of Chicago Press, 1980], 89, citing William Tyndale, *The Obedience of a Christian Man*, in William Tyndale, *Doctrinal Treatises and Introductions to Different Portions of The Holy Scriptures*, ed. Henry Walter [Cambridge, UK: Parker Society, 1848], 172). For contemporary objections to service as base and despicable, see Michael Roberts, "'Words they are Women, and Deeds they are Men': Images of Work and Gender in Early Modern England," in *Women and Work in Pre-Industrial England*, ed. Lindsey Charles and Lorna Duffin (London: Croom Helm, 1985), 157.

67. "The Aspiring Mind of the King's Man," *The Upstart Crow* 11 (1991): 10.

68. At the October 27, 1601 opening of Parliament, the Lord Keeper addressed Parliament: "Our enemies, saith he, are enemies to God, the Queen and the peace of this Kingdom, conspired to overthrow Religion, to reduce us to a tyrannical servitude, which enemies he named to be the Bishop of Rome and the King of Spain" (G. B. Harrison, *A Last Elizabethan Journal, Being a Record of Those Things Most Talked of During the Years 1599–1603* [1933; repr., London: Routledge & Kegan Paul, 1974], 206).

69. Strier asserts that "Kent is not insulting Oswald for being poor and in service," because "A figure like Oswald, a steward in a major noble household, was not at all poor, but actually quite grand" (*Resistant Structures*, 186). However, much of the language of the passage would seem to suggest that Oswald's comparative poverty and status as a servant are among the aspects of his character that provoke Kent's contempt. Perhaps not even a grand steward would be likely to impress an earl. Burnett feels that "A general preoccupation with blood dominates in the speech" (*Masters and Servants*, 173).

70. John F. Andrews, the editor of the Everyman Shakespeare, prefers the 1599 Second Quarto spelling, "hartless," because it "more faithfully conveys Tybalt's primary accusation: that Benvolio is taking unfair advantage of the metaphorical equivalent of 'Weaker Vessels' by drawing on Capulet servants at a time when they are undefended by a Capulet master" (1.1.68n.).

71. Berry, *Shakespeare and Social Class*, 111. Wells states that "Only in the cases of Caliban and the Dromios do we find the word 'slave' employed by Shakespeare in anything like its normal Roman sense. Elsewhere, when used at all, it is generally as an insult, implying a servile, cringing cast of mind" (*Wide Arch*, 142). This, however, ignores Shylock's purely descriptive use of the words "slave" and "slaves" (*Merchant* 4.1.90–98).

72. Berry, *Shakespeare and Social Class*, xiv.

73. On Coriolanus's use of "boy," see Berry, *Shakespeare and Social Class*, 157. An oddly parallel incident is described in "The Honour of a *London* 'Prentice," dated by the editor "Elizabeth's reign, before 1598" (591): the King of Turkey's son says to the apprentice, who has defeated twenty Turkish knights while maintaining Queen Elizabeth's honor, "Thou art a traytor, *English* boy, and hast the traytor plaid." The apprentice's response is "I am no boy nor traytor, thy speeches I defie, / For which I'll be revenged upon thee by and by." After breaking the king's son's neck by boxing his ear, the apprentice adds, "I am no *English* boy, / That can with one small box o' th' ear the Prince of *Turks* destroy" (*Roxburghe Ballads*, 7:590, lines 20–22, 27–28).

74. Even when such terms are obviously being used in a derogatory sense, it is not always clear to whom they refer. Since Roderigo refers to both Cassio

and himself as "villain" during and immediately after his attack on Cassio, it is not clear to which of them his later "O wretched villain!" refers (*Othello* 5.1.23, 29, 41). Similarly, Othello's "O cursed, cursed slave!" may be either a reference to himself or to Iago (5.2.278).

75. Berry, *Shakespeare and Social Class*, 108; Cornwall and Regan also apply the term "villain" to the blinded Gloucester (3.7.90, 99). On Regan's "A peasant . . ." as representing "outraged decorum," see Strier, *Resistant Structures*, 192. A similar failure to make discriminations that might seem significant to us was shown by Elizabeth, Countess of Shrewsbury (commonly known as Bess of Hardwick), who wrote on September 19, 1594 to Richard Bagott, a county Justice of the Peace, to complain about "that lewd workman Tuft," whom, she claimed, she had paid in advance for work on Hardwick Hall that he had promised but had not finished (Orlin, *Elizabethan Households*, 17). Although Tuft was apparently an independent contractor of sorts, Bess refers to him as "my hired servant," because, clearly, that is how she conceived of a social inferior hired to do work for her.

76. On Shakespeare's neutrality in depicting characters who use class rhetoric as abuse, see Berry, *Shakespeare and Social Class*, xiv.

77. "Servant Obedience," 46.

CHAPTER 3. "THE NEED WE HAVE TO USE YOU"

1. William Gouge asserts that "Servants are of all other things (except wife and children) of best and greatest use" (*Of Domesticall Duties*, 647). Lawrence Humfrey describes the variety and importance of the services provided by the lower classes to their employers: "For of trueth, the commen people are the handes of the Nobles, sith them selves bee handlesse. They labour and sweate for them, with tillinge, say[l?]ing, running, toylinge: by Sea, by land, with hands, wᵗ feete, serue them. So as wᵗoute theyr seruice, they nor eate, nor drink, nor are clothed, no nor live" (*Nobles*, N7ʳ).

2. Since Caius is an unmarried and apparently childless doctor, rather than a great nobleman with a family, his household is a relatively modest one. For an example "of how complicated a business it was to run and provision a great household," see the entries for Mary Petway's 1628 account book for the household of Sir William Pope quoted in Orlin, *Elizabethan Households*, 55, 57.

3. While some of the plays do notice, generally in passing, some of the daily tasks servants were routinely involved in, such as the preparation and serving of food (*Errors, Merchant, Antony, Coriolanus, Romeo*), many household tasks—particularly, perhaps, those performed by women—such as brewing, baking, sewing, housecleaning, and taking care of domestic animals such as poultry, pigs, and cows—are generally ignored throughout the canon. On the number and variety of tasks performed by women engaged in housewifery during this period, see Cahn, *Industry of Devotion*, 86–93, 175–76.

4. Laundry: *Merry Wives* 3.3.1–16, 133–36; rushes: *2 Henry IV* 5.5.1–4; dress: *Richard II* 5.2.77, 84, 87; undress: *Shrew* 4.1.132–36; arm: *Macbeth* 5.3.50; *Antony* 4.4.1–17; disarm: *Troilus* 1.1.1; fetch: *Merry Wives* 1.4.63–64, 82–83; *Romeo* 5.1.25; torchbearers: *Romeo* 1.4.1 s.d.; 5.3.1, 25; horses: *Richard II* 5.2.74, 77; *1 Henry IV* 2.3.72; *Henry V* 4.2.2; time: *2 Henry VI* 2.4.5; *Merry Wives* 2.3.3; chamberpot: *2 Henry IV* 2.4.34.

5. For example, *Twelfth Night* 4.1.1–18; *Measure* 1.1.15–16; 2.2.20–21, 25;

2.4.17–19; *L.L.L.* 1.2.147; 3.1.48; *2 Henry VI* 1.3.34–36; 1.4.79–81; *Romeo* 1.2.34–37; *Timon* 3.4.111–19. Female servants, of course, are sometimes ordered to summon people within the house, as the Nurse frequently summons Juliet (*Romeo* 1.3.1–4; 1.5.112; 2.2.135 s.d., 137, 149, 151; 4.5.1–13).

6. "Invisible Bullets," 29–30; see also Neill, "Servant Obedience," 20, 29. The importance of a large retinue is suggested in a passage from Raimond de Sebonde's *Natural Theology*: "We must believe that the angels are there in marvellous and inconceivable numbers, because the honour of a king consists in the great crowd of his vassals, while his disgrace or shame consists in their paucity" (quoted by E. M. W. Tillyard, "The Elizabethan World Order," in *Shakespeare's History Plays* [New York: Macmillan, 1946], 10–20; reprinted in *Shakespeare: The Histories: A Collection of Critical Essays*, ed. Eugene M. Waith [Englewood Cliffs, NJ: Prentice-Hall, 1965], 37). Tillyard quotes from an abridgement "Originally in Latin, translated into French by Jean Martin 1550. Quotation translated from book IV chap. 42 of French version." On the large numbers of servants, often described as idle servants, in great early modern households, see Hentzner, *Journey into England*, 88; Humfrey, *Nobles*, I1ʳ; Rye, *England as Seen*, 70, 195–97n. 30; and Cahn, *Industry of Devotion*, 13, 99.

7. *Romeo* 1.1.81 s.d.; *All's Well* 1.2.1 s.d.; *Richard II* 1.1.1 s.d.

8. Similarly, the commoner Cardinal Wolsey attempts to elevate his status by employing many gentlemanly retainers; after his fall, he laments to Thomas Cromwell, "No sun shall ever usher forth mine honors, / Or gild again the noble troops that waited / Upon my smiles" (*Henry VIII* 3.2.411–13).

9. "*King Lear* and the Magic of the Wheel," *Shakespeare Quarterly* 35 (Autumn 1984): 279–80.

10. *Richard II* 4.1.282–84; earlier, Sir Henry Greene has reported to Richard's queen that "all the household servants fled with [the Earl of Worcester] / To Bolingbroke" (2.2.60–61), proof that it is not only noblemen who are in revolt, but even Richard's servants.

11. *Shakespeare and Social Class*, 95.

12. *Hamlet* 2.2.270. Derick R. C. Marsh states that although most critics take Hamlet's remark that he is "most dreadfully attended" as a reference to his retinue, "the case for the audience seeing it primarily as a reference to the Ghost is irresistible" ("A Note on Hamlet's 'I Am Most Dreadfully Attended' (II.ii.266)," *Shakespeare Quarterly* 33 [Summer 1982]: 181); Neill, however, insists that the phrase's "more immediate reference is to the corrupted service that we already know to be exemplified in Rosencrantz and Guildenstern themselves" ("'He that thou knowest,'" 330). Neill also remarks that Hamlet's "double isolation, as both royal heir and alienated malcontent, results in an even more profound estrangement from a world that is itself marked, from the very beginning, as 'strange' and 'unnatural' (1.1.75; 1.2.232; 1.5.31, 34, 185–6)" (326).

13. According to Esha Niyogi De, "Yorick with the child Hamlet on his back suggests the father-figure: the nurturer of a new generation; this generation continues—is even reaffirmed—now that the man Hamlet alone is alive, succeeding the death of old Yorick" ("'When Our Deep Plots Do Pall': Endings and Beginnings in the Graveyard Scene in *Hamlet*," *Shakespeare Yearbook* 1 [Spring 1990]: 75).

14. "'For O, for O, the hobby-horse is forgot': Hamlet and The Death of Carnival," *Renaissance Papers 1996*, ed. George Walton Williams and Philip Rollinson (Raleigh, NC: Southeastern Renaissance Conference / Camden House, 1997, 81–91), 86; "Introduction" to *Titus Andronicus* (Arden Shakespeare, 3rd series [London: Routledge, 1995]), 12.

15. See chapter 9, n. 12.

16. Among many possible examples of ballads in which this motif occurs: The heroines of the songs "Fair Rosamond" and "The Spanish Lady's Love" both propose dressing as pages so that they can follow their lovers (Percy, *Reliques*, 2:158–64, 248–51); the heroines of "Child Waters" and "The Lady's Fall" actually do dress as pages (Percy, 3:59–65, 140–45), as do the heroines of "The Merchant's Daughter of Bristol" and "The True Maid of the South" (*Roxburghe Ballads*, 2:87–95, 627–32). The heroine of "The Lady Turned Serving-Man" dresses as a male servant for protection after her husband is killed and her servants flee (Percy, 3:86–90).

17. *Politics of Shakespeare*, 45.

18. Servants are required to prepare even an ordinary dinner (*Merchant* 3.5.44–61), but their presence is even more important during parties and feasts, as, for example, in *Romeo* 1.2.34–37; 1.3.101–104; 1.5.1–16, 26–29, 88; 4.2.1–9; 4.4.1–6, 14–28. The need for servants at feasts provides Shakespeare with opportunities to have them comment on the behavior of their "betters," as in *Antony* 2.7.1–16 and *Coriolanus* 4.5.153–242.

19. Servants are not explicitly mentioned as participating in the hunting in *As You Like It*, where the lords in exile appear to be fending for themselves, or in *Merry Wives*, where the middle-class characters go "a-birding."

20. The queen's reluctance to hear music is not, however, unique, since Cleopatra, in a somewhat similar situation of worrying about the man she loves, rejects the idea of listening to Mardian singing (*Antony* 1.5.9–11). Other unhappy lovers, such as Orsino and Mariana, apparently find comfort in listening to music (*Twelfth Night* 1.1.1–7; 2.4.1–7, 42–48; *Measure* 4.1.10–13). Whether Queen Katharine is comforted by her Gentlewoman's song (*Henry VIII* 3.1.3–14) is not indicated in the text, although Richmond Noble states that "Practically every commentator is agreed that the whole of the scene in which this song is contained is Fletcher's and not Shakespeare's, and consequently we are relieved of the necessity for any argument in the matter" (*Shakespeare's Use of Song: With the Text of the Principal Songs* [1923; repr., Oxford: Clarendon Press, 1967], 112); this assignment of the scene to Fletcher is confirmed by Brian Vickers, *Shakespeare, Co-Author* (Oxford: Oxford University Press, 2002), 333–402 passim. Leslie C. Dunn notes that "most of the characters who sing in Shakespeare are marginalized in some way, either by their class (servants, fools, mechanicals) or their psychological state (drunks, lunatics, besotted lovers), or because they are a different sort of being altogether (spirits, fairies, 'monsters' like Caliban)" ("The Lady Sings in Welsh: Women's Song as Marginal Discourse on the Shakespearean Stage," in *Place and Displacement in the Renaissance*, ed. Alvin Vos [Binghamton, NY: Center for Medieval and Early Renaissance Studies, 1995], 57). On actual seventeenth-century servants singing ballads, see Bernard Capp, "Popular Literature," in *Popular Culture in Seventeenth-Century England*, ed. Barry Reay (London: Croom Helm, 1985), 204.

21. *A.Y.L.* 2.5.1–8, 35–42; 2.7.174–94; 4.2.10–19. Duke Senior is accompanied to the forest by two pages, but they sing, not for him, but for Touchstone, who declares their singing "untunable" (5.3.39–41).

22. For a discussion of why the dirge is not sung, see Noble, *Shakespeare's Use of Song*, 136–37. One other upper-class figure, Lady Mortimer, sings to please her husband (*1 Henry IV* 3.1.242 s.d.), but as Noble notes, "as [the song] is in Welsh, we are not made aware of its contents. It serves its purpose not

only in providing a Welsh atmosphere, but also in imparting an air of mystery to the doings of the uncanny Glendower, with his out-of-the-way superstitious lore and 'skimble skamble stuff'" (111). For a discussion of Lady Mortimer's singing as representative of both female power and marginalization, see Dunn, "The Lady Sings." Immediately following Lady Mortimer's song, Kate, Hotspur's wife, twice rejects her husband's suggestion (or order) that she also sing (243–56).

23. *Hamlet* 4.5. passim; *Othello* 4.3.43–59; *King John* 5.7.12–24; *Lear* 3.6.25, 41–44; *Merry Wives* 3.1.11–28. Benedick also sings a snatch of song while suffering, he says, for love; he notes that he is a poor singer (*Much Ado* 5.2.26–30).

24. Although Hamlet apparently does not sing, he quotes from the ballad "Jephthah, Judge of Israel," as part of his pretence of madness (2.2.403–20). Although his reference to Polonius as Jephthah is appropriate insofar as both are associated with daughters, we are perhaps to presume that Hamlet feels that a prince quoting from a common old song will seem crazy. Oberon and Titania seem to suggest that they will sing with their train at the end of their play (*Dream* 5.1.386–95); since they have servants and are no longer perturbed, this would seem an anomaly, but Oberon and Titania are, after all, fairies, and should not be expected to abide by human rules. Perhaps fairies are expected to sing, since the children disguised as fairies sing in *Merry Wives* (5.5.93–102).

25. For example, hired musicians appear or are mentioned in *T.G.V.* 4.2.24–52, *All's Well* 3.7.39–41, *Cymbeline* 2.3.11–32, and *Romeo* 4.5.96–145; it is not clear whether the musicians who play at the Capulets' feast are hired for the occasion or part of the household (*Romeo* 1.5.26). Groups of an individual employer's servants play, and sometimes sing, at *L.L.L.* 5.2.157 s.d. and 212 s.d.; *Dream* 2.2.9–30, 4.1.29 s.d., 82 s.d., and 5.1.395 s.d.; *Merchant* 5.1.51–68; *Twelfth Night* 1.1.1–7 and 2.4.1–14; and *Tempest* 4.1.106–17. Viola plans to disguise herself as a singing eunuch when she proposes her service to Orsino, although she never sings or plays music in the course of the play (*Twelfth Night* 1.2.56–59). It is not clear who sings the song while Bassanio is making his choice among the caskets (*Merchant* 3.2.63–72), but it seems far more likely to be one or more servants than Portia, particularly since "All" join in to sing the last line. It is also not obvious who sings the "wedding song" in *As You Like It* (5.4.140–45), although it appears to be a group production (136); as noted above, two of the Duke's pages sing a duet in this play, but not for their master.

26. For example: Armado twice orders Mote to sing, although Mote, typically, disobeys the first command (*L.L.L.* 1.2.118–20; 3.1.1–3); Queen Katharine orders one of her gentlewomen to play the lute and sing (*Henry VIII* 3.1.1–14); Don Pedro commands a song from Balthasar (*Much Ado* 2.3.61–76); Falstaff asks Bardolph for "a bawdy song," but does not get it (*1 Henry IV* 3.3.13–14); and Feste sings at the command of Sir Toby, Sir Andrew, and Orsino (*Twelfth Night* 2.3.30–52, 57–71; 2.4.42–66). It is not clear who sings the hymn at Leonato's family tomb; Leonato seems to be suggesting that Claudio should sing the epitaph for Hero, but Claudio commands someone else (editors and directors sometimes draft Balthasar) to sing a hymn (*Much Ado* 5.1.275–79; 5.3.11–21). The unnamed Boys who sing in *Measure* (4.1.1–6) and *Antony* (2.7.115–20) are presumably servants. Most of the music performed by Ariel is presumably at Prospero's command (*Tempest* 1.2.320–21, 378–90, 400–408; 2.1.299–307); even that which may be Ariel's own idea, as at 3.2.127 s.d., does not interfere with Prospero's plans.

27. While it may be true that Feste takes pleasure in singing, he also makes

a good deal of money out of singing and clowning for people other than his mistress, garnering gratuities from Sir Toby, Sir Andrew, Orsino (repeatedly), Cesario, and Sebastian, who pays him to go away (*Twelfth Night* 2.3.25, 31, 33; 2.4.67; 3.1.43, 53; 4.1.18; 5.1.25, 32).

28. *Othello* 2.3.65–69, 84–91; *Winter's Tale* 4.3.1–12, 15–22, 121–24; *Tempest* 2.2.42–54, 176–85; 3.2.123–25; 5.1.88–94; for insight into Stephano's character, I am indebted to Janis Lull. Although Autolycus is no longer in Florizel's service, he continues to refer to the prince as his master (*Winter's Tale* 4.3.13–14; 4.4.713, 837); some of his later singing, of course, serves as advertising for the songs he is peddling as he pursues his true trade of theft, but his earlier songs appear to be effusions of sheer happiness. The First Gravedigger in *Hamlet* is perhaps not precisely a servant in the same sense as the preceding characters, but he is certainly performing a service as he digs Ophelia's grave, singing as he does so (5.1.61–64, 71–74, 94–97, 120–21).

29. Women do not usually write poems to men in the plays, but the deceived and enamoured Phebe addresses a verse epistle to "Ganymede," who, naturally, mocks it and her (*A.Y.L.* 4.3.14–64), and Beatrice writes a poem "containing her affection unto Benedick," just as Benedick writes poetry to her (*Much Ado* 5.4.83–89); both lovers are mocked by their friends.

30. Gayle Whittier makes a number of critical remarks on Romeo, whom she characterizes as "an apprentice lover-poet" ("The Sonnet's Body and the Body Sonnetized in *Romeo and Juliet*," *Shakespeare Quarterly* 40 [Spring 1989]: 29).

31. *T.G.V.* 3.1.140–49; *L.L.L.* 5.2.6–54; *A.Y.L.* 3.2.153–54, 161–75. Critics are notably disparaging of Orlando's attempts at poetry: see Howard C. Cole, "Shakespeare's Comedies and their Sources: Some Biographical and Artistic Inferences," *Shakespeare Quarterly* 34 (Winter 1983): 412; Robert Kimbrough, "Androgyny Seen Through Shakespeare's Disguise," *Shakespeare Quarterly* 33 (Spring 1982): 24–25; and Maura Slattery Kuhn, "Much Virtue in *If*," *Shakespeare Quarterly* 28 (Winter 1977): 47. Thomas Kelly, however, notes that G. K. Hunter offers "an atypically generous assessment of Orlando's verse making" in *Shakespeare: The Late Comedies* (London, 1962), 37 ("Shakespeare's Romantic Heroes: Orlando Reconsidered," *Shakespeare Quarterly* 24 [Winter 1973]: 18 n. 8).

32. Gentlemen who criticize their own poetry usually do so in soliloquy, although Hamlet includes his criticism in a note to Ophelia and spoken criticism may be overheard by other characters. This is obviously quite different from "Balthazar's pretended reluctance to sing" which Noble suggests is intended "to disarm criticism from the audience" (*Shakespeare's Use of Song*, 64 n. 1) and which is more obviously intended by Balthazar to wring praise from his auditors-to-be and by Shakespeare to provide opportunities for Benedick to criticize Balthazar's singing in comic asides. Other sorts of poetry written by gentlemen do not come in for criticism, though they may be no more distinguished than the love poetry; for example, Claudio presumably writes the epitaph he reads for Hero, Jaques composes a verse mocking his colleagues in Arden, and Pericles encloses a rhymed "passport" in the chest in which he encloses Thaisa (*Much Ado* 5.3.3–10; *A.Y.L.* 2.5.47–54; *Pericles* 3.2.70–77).

33. Caius, of course, does have servants, and John Rugby accompanies him in at least a couple of scenes. His housekeeper, Mrs. Quickly, on the other hand, is usually gone from his house, running errands for Mrs. Ford and Mrs. Page, and finally playing the Queen of the Fairies in the wives' final trick on Falstaff.

34. On other foolish servants, see Janet Adelman, "'Anger's My Meat': Feed-

ing, Dependency, and Aggression in *Coriolanus*," in *Shakespeare: Pattern of Excelling Nature*, ed. David Bevington and Jay L. Halio (Newark: University of Delaware Press, 1978); reprinted in *Representing Shakespeare: New Psychoanalytic Essays*, ed. Murray M. Schwartz and Coppelia Kahn (Baltimore: Johns Hopkins University Press, 1980), 149 n. 26; and Thomas Moisan, "Rhetoric and the Rehearsal of Death: The 'Lamentations' Scene in *Romeo and Juliet*," *Shakespeare Quarterly* 34 (Winter 1983): 398. For servants' "self-ridicule" as representing either "a strategy of deference and appeasement" or "a stubborn refusal to conform fully to the elaborate requirements of an hierarchical society," see Michael D. Bristol, *Carnival and Theater: Plebeian Culture and the Structure of Authority in Renaissance England* (New York: Methuen, 1985), 126–29.

35. *Servant Problem*, 44; see also 68.

36. *The Bedford Companion to Shakespeare: An Introduction with Documents*, 2nd ed. (Boston: Bedford / St. Martin's, 2001), 39–40. On servants' literacy, see Cahn, *Industry of Devotion*, 97; Dolan, *Dangerous Familiars*, 8; and Gurr, *Playgoing in Shakespeare's London*, 55.

37. "Learning to Curse: Aspects of Linguistic Colonialism in the Sixteenth Century," in *Learning to Curse: Essays in Early Modern Culture* (New York: Routledge, 1990), 23.

38. G. L. Kittredge, "The Dramatic Function of the Porter's Scene," from his *Shakspere*, 1916; repr. in *"Macbeth": Critical Essays*, ed. S. Schoenbaum (New York: Garland, 1991), 82; Marvin Rosenberg, "From *The Masks of Macbeth*"; repr. in *"Macbeth": Critical Essays*, 353. Schoenbaum discusses and quotes Edward Capell, who was apparently the first critic to comment on the Porter's usefulness in giving Macbeth time to clean up before his reappearance ("Enter a Porter," 370–71).

39. Critics have found the Porter to be integral to the play's effect. Rosenberg argues that the Porter "exploits central motifs in the play" ("From *The Masks*," 354); Kenneth Muir maintains that "The gap between desire and performance, enunciated by the Porter, is expressed over and over again by Macbeth and his wife" ("Image and Symbol in *Macbeth*," *Shakespeare Survey* 19 [1966]: 45–54; repr. in *"Macbeth": Critical Essays*, 348); John B. Harcourt suggests that the Porter scene "deglamoriz[es]" Macbeth, indicates "the subsequent course of the action, the consequences of Macbeth's crime," and incorporates "certain recurrent themes of the tragedy" ("'I Pray You, Remember the Porter,'" *Shakespeare Quarterly* 12 [Autumn 1961]: 394, 395).

40. David Willbern describes Malvolio as "mistreated" (although also as a "gull") ("Malvolio's Fall," *Shakespeare Quarterly* 29 [Winter 1978]: 89); Lake thinks that he "has a sympathetic dimension" ("Psychology of Primacy," 28). Stephen Dickey sees Malvolio represented as a bear baited by a pack of dogs ("Shakespeare's Mastiff Comedy," *Shakespeare Quarterly* 42 [Fall 1991]: 265–73); Richard A. Levin sees him as the play's "scapegoat" for the sins of all of its ambitious, scheming characters (*Love and Society in Shakespearean Comedy: A Study of Dramatic Form and Content* [Newark: University of Delaware Press, 1985], 118, 131); see also Berry, *Shakespeare and Social Class*, 63–74; and Northrop Frye, "Comic Myth in Shakespeare," in *Discussions of Shakespeare's Romantic Comedy*, ed. Herbert Weil, Jr. (Boston: D. C. Heath, 1966), 136. For opposing views, see Bradbrook, *Shakespeare and Elizabethan Poetry*, 231–32; John Hollander, "*Twelfth Night* and the Morality of Indulgence," in *Discussions of Shakespeare's Romantic Comedy*, 124–26, 130; and Joseph H.

266   NOTES

Summers, "The Masks of *Twelfth Night*," in *Discussions of Shakespeare's Romantic Comedy*, 114–15. For a discussion of the duties of an Elizabethan steward and his dramatic representation, see Burnett, *Masters and Servants*, chapter 5. Neill, who describes the baiting of Malvolio as "vicious," insightfully notes that "the disaffections of service typically appear not as the anger of an oppressed underclass, but as the envy or resentment of marginal men—figures whose claims to gentility are felt as increasingly compromised by anything that smacks of a servile dependency" ("Servant Obedience," 41).

41. In his diary, John Manningham refers to the plot against Malvolio as "A good practice" (quoted in G. B. Harrison, *Last Elizabethan Journal*, 262); Bradbrook notes Manningham's judgment (*Shakespeare and Elizabethan Poetry*, 231–32). See also Desainliens (alias Claudius Holyband), who notes that "It is not good to trust . . . a proud servant" (*French Littleton*, 88, 90).

42. Willbern, "Malvolio's Fall," 89.

43. Bradbrook, *Shakespeare and Elizabethan Poetry*, 231, 271 n. 19; see, for example, Berry, *Shakespeare and Social Class*, 71–72; and Willbern, "Malvolio's Fall," 88. On Malvolio's lechery, see also Burnett, *Masters and Servants*, 168; and Willbern, 88.

44. Berry describes Malvolio as "honest and able" (*Shakespeare and Social Class*, 69); Charles Lamb sees "no reason why he should not have been . . . accomplished" ("The Virtues of Malvolio," in *Discussions of Shakespeare's Romantic Comedy*, 9).

45. See Berry, *Shakespeare and Social Class*, 72; and Burnett, *Masters and Servants*, 159–61.

46. Burnett, *Masters and Servants*, 170; see also Berry, *Shakespeare and Social Class*, 72–73.

47. Donald Sinden, "Malvolio in *Twelfth Night*," in *Players of Shakespeare: Essays in Shakespearean Performance by Twelve Players with the Royal Shakespeare Company*, ed. Philip Brockbank (Cambridge: Cambridge University Press, 1985), 50. Despite this insight into Malvolio's bullying, Sinden finds him "tragic" (43).

48. Bristol describes the principal action of *Twelfth Night* as being the conflict between Carnival, represented by Sir Toby and his crew of revellers, and Lent, represented by Malvolio (*Carnival and Theater*, 202).

49. On foreshadowing in *Romeo*, see Joan Ozark Holmer, "'Draw, if you be men': Saviolo's Significance for *Romeo and Juliet*," *Shakespeare Quarterly* 45 (Summer 1994): 177.

50. See, for example, Maurice Hunt, "Shakespeare's Tragic Homeopathy," in *Shakespeare: Text, Subtext, and Context*, ed. Ronald Dotterer (Selinsgrove, PA: Susquehanna University Press, 1989), 78; and D. Douglas Waters, "Fate and Fortune in *Romeo and Juliet*," *The Upstart Crow* 12 (1992): 83.

51. On the effect of the servants' conversation in *Coriolanus*, see Paul G. Zolbrod, "Coriolanus and Alceste: A Study in Misanthropy," *Shakespeare Quarterly* 23 (Winter 1972): 51–52.

52. "The Canker Within: Some Observations on the Role of the Villain in Three Shakespearean Comedies," *Shakespeare Quarterly* 23 (Autumn 1972): 442–43.

53. "How the Play of Julius Caesar Works to a Climax at the Centre: A Study in Passion and Movement," in *Shakespeare as a Dramatic Artist*, 3rd ed. (Oxford, 1906; repr., *Discussions of Shakespeare's Roman Plays*, ed. Maurice Charney [Boston: D. C. Heath, 1964], 49).

54. On Francis and Hal, see Alan C. Dessen, "Shakespeare's Theatrical *Italics*," *Renaissance Papers 1991*, ed. George Walton Williams and Barbara J. Baines (Raleigh, NC: Southeastern Renaissance Conference, 1992), 96; and Greenblatt, "'Invisible Bullets,'" 31–32. Edward I. Berry sees Touchstone (as well as Jacques) serving as a foil to Rosalind, "setting off her distinctive qualities" ("Rosalynde and Rosalind," *Shakespeare Quarterly* 31 [Spring 1980]: 43); Susan Snyder suggests that Lavatch acts as the voice for both Helena and Bertram, in their "unacceptable tendencies": "sexual display/desire in her, aggression in him" ("'The King's not here': Displacement and Deferral in *All's Well That Ends Well*," *Shakespeare Quarterly* 43 [Spring 1992]: 24).

55. *Common Liar*, 51; *Broken Nuptials in Shakespeare's Plays* (New Haven: Yale University Press, 1985), 108.

56. "Gloucester and Harry Hunks," *The Upstart Crow* 9 (1989): 109; "Kent and the Audience: The Character as Spectator," *Shakespeare Quarterly* 32 (Summer 1981): 148 (see also 152–53); "Major Scenes in Minor Key," *Shakespeare Quarterly* 21 (Winter 1970): 56; "The Role of the Audience in Shakespeare's *Richard II*," *Shakespeare Quarterly* 36 (Autumn 1985): 262–81.

57. On Enobarbus as commentator, see Adelman, *Common Liar*, 50. For an account of how Enobarbus is largely responsible for constructing the audience's perception of Cleopatra, see Allyson P. Newton, "At 'the Very Heart of Loss': Shakespeare's Enobarbus and the Rhetoric of Remembering," *Renaissance Papers 1995*, ed. George Walton Williams and Barbara J. Baines (Raleigh, NC: Southeastern Renaissance Conference, 1996), 81–91.

58. "'Knock me here soundly,'" 282.

59. *Politeuphuia. Wits Commonwealth*, 118ʳ. As Harry Levin comments, "Davy, that 'justice-like servingman,' influencing Shallow's decisions to 'bear out a knave against an honest man,' is a comic role-model for what Falstaff soon expects to be: a friend at court who has the ear of the ascendant King (V.i.68, 48–49)" ("Falstaff's Encore," *Shakespeare Quarterly* 32 [Spring 1981]: 16).

60. On dependence upon servants in *King Lear*, see Robert L. Reid, "Lear's Three Shamings: Shakespearean Psychology and Tragic Form," *Renaissance Papers 1996*, 96, 106.

61. On Prospero's "dependency on and vulnerability to those who serve him" (62), see Dolan, *Dangerous Familiars*, 62–71.

62. Quinney emphasizes that "[Antony and Cleopatra] never appear 'all alone,' but are always accompanied and observed by an audience of waiting-women, eunuchs, generals, and so on" ("Enter a Messenger," 160).

63. See, for example, Cynthia Marshall, "Man of Steel Done Got the Blues: Melancholic Subversion of Presence in *Antony and Cleopatra*," *Shakespeare Quarterly* 44 (Winter 1993): 393; Quinney, "Enter a Messenger," 154–55; and Wells, *Wide Arch*, 144.

64. Wells, *Wide Arch*, 140.

65. For overviews of common critical representations of Cleopatra's character, see L. T. Fitz, "Egyptian Queens and Male Reviewers: Sexist Attitudes in *Antony and Cleopatra* Criticism," *Shakespeare Quarterly* 28 (Summer 1977): 297–316, and Jonathan Gil Harris, "'Narcissus in thy face': Roman Desire and the Difference It Fakes in *Antony and Cleopatra*," *Shakespeare Quarterly* 45 (Winter 1994): 408–25. Wells does note the importance of servants in this play: "This relationship between servants and their master or mistress is crucially important in *Antony and Cleopatra*. A dozen or so have speaking parts and, between them, around three hundred lines to say" (*Wide Arch*, 140). Elizabeth

A. Brown discusses Cleopatra's relationship with Charmian and Iras, concluding that the servants' lack of powerful connections other than the queen, and their failure to engage in politics, leaves Cleopatra isolated and vulnerable ("'Companion Me with My Mistress': Cleopatra, Elizabeth I, and Their Waiting Women," in *Maids and Mistresses, Cousins and Queens: Women's Alliances in Early Modern England*, ed. Susan Frye and Karen Robertson (New York: Oxford University Press, 1999, 143–44).

66. Cleopatra appears in sixteen of the play's forty-two scenes (1.1, 1.2, 1.3, 1.5, 2.5, 3.3, 3.7, 3.11, 3.13, 4.2, 4.4, 4.8, 4.12, 4.13, 4.15, and 5.2). Antony appears in twenty-two scenes (1.1, 1.2, 1.3, 2.2, 2.3, 2.6, 2.7, 3.2, 3.4, 3.7, 3.9, 3.11, 3.13, 4.2, 4.4, 4.5, 4.7, 4.8, 4.10, 4.12, 4.14, and 4.15). The protagonists appear together in only eleven scenes (1.1, 1.2, 1.3, 3.7, 3.11, 3.13, 4.2, 4.4, 4.8, 4.12, and 4.15) and interact in only nine. Although both characters appear in act 1, scene 2, Cleopatra leaves as Antony enters, and they do not speak to each other; since Antony enters engaged in conversation, it is possible that he does not even see Cleopatra. In act 4, scene 2, Cleopatra speaks and is spoken to only by Enobarbus, while they watch Antony address his soldiers (although, presumably, Cleopatra is included in Antony's general invitation to dine with him).

In all but three of her scenes (the exceptions being 3.7, which opens with Cleopatra threatening Enobarbus, whom she often treats as a servant; 4.8, in which she promises to reward Scarus for his service; and 4.12), Cleopatra appears with servants. (Iras is not specified as present in 4.4, but may be among the "others attending.") In 1.1, however, Cleopatra does not address the servants, nor they her, unless "The messengers!" (1.1.34) is an order for the messengers to come or be brought in.

The play contains various suggestions that the protagonists may themselves be servants. Cleopatra suggests that Antony takes orders from Caesar and Fulvia (1.1.20–34; 1.3.20–23); Antony suggests that he serves Cleopatra (1.2.184–86; 1.3.66–71); Cleopatra refers to Antony as "our master" (3.13.50) and acts as Antony's squire (4.4.5–15), and twice addresses Caesar, in their only meeting, as "my master and my lord" (5.2.115; "my master, and my lord!" at 5.2.190).

67. Although Cleopatra earlier calls on her servants to help lift Antony into the monument, it is likely that these lines are an error. See note on 4.15.12–13 in the Arden edition, 182–83.

68. Even Cleopatra's suicide is largely passive. Although she has arranged for the asps to be brought, her arrangement has consisted of giving an order: "I have spoke already, and it is provided" (5.2.195); the asps and her regalia are brought to her, she is dressed by her women, and she takes up two snakes, which bite her.

69. This information, which confirms what Cleopatra already suspects, is brought by Dolabella, who is one of Caesar's men, but Dolabella describes himself in the next line as Cleopatra's servant (5.2.204).

70. Possibly the audience is expected to infer that Cleopatra hopes or expects that her words will be reported to Antony by one of the messengers she is continually sending (including Alexas, who presumably overhears 1.5.56–64) or another servant, but this seems improbable, and there is no evidence in the play that any messenger does this.

71. It is perhaps just possible that Cleopatra is here using the royal "we," as she occasionally does elsewhere (3.7.5–6, 15–18; 3.13.2; and probably 1.2.84 and 4.15.3–6), but it is difficult to see how an actor could make this clear to the audience. Rackin points out that "Early in the play (I. ii. 32), Charmian says, 'I love

long life better than figs.' Now she and her mistress will choose the deadly figs and by their choice transform themselves from comic characters devoted to the life and sensual pleasures of this world to tragic characters who have the nobility to choose a good higher than mere survival" ("Shakespeare's Boy Cleopatra, the Decorum of Nature, and the Golden World of Poetry," *PMLA* 87 [1972], 210).

72. William D. Wolf notes that "Charmian completes the theme of Cleopatra's escape from the world by finishing her 'What should I stay' with

> In this wild world? So, fare thee well.
> Now boast thee, death, in thy possession lies
> A lass unparalleled.
>
> (V. ii. 313–16)"

("'New Heaven, New Earth': The Escape from Mutability in *Antony and Cleopatra*," *Shakespeare Quarterly* 33 [Autumn 1982]: 335).

73. Harris, "'Narcissus in thy face,'" 417.

74. "Cleopatra Again," *Shakespeare Quarterly* 7 (Spring 1956): 228.

CHAPTER 4. "THE MERE WORD'S A SLAVE"

1. The word "serve" occurs frequently in catchphrases throughout the canon, including "time (or "the day") serves" (*Antony* 2.2.9–10; *Timon* 1.1.270; 5.1.42; *Coriolanus* 4.3.29; for variations, see, among others, *Henry V* 3.6.65–66; *T.G.V.* 3.1.252; *Macbeth* 2.1.23–24; and *Winter's Tale* 2.3.21–22); and "serve my/our/the turn" (*L.L.L.* 1.2.164–65; *Richard II* 3.2.89–90; *Titus* 3.1.164; for variations, see, among others, *Troilus* 3.1.73–74; *All's Well* 4.1.46–54; and *Coriolanus* 4.5.93). "Serve" is also commonly used to mean "be sufficient" (*Twelfth Night* 1.5.47; *Coriolanus* 1.7.2–4; 2.3.14–15) and "behave toward" (*Errors* 2.1.12; *Timon* 5.1.20), among other meanings, including "courses of a meal" and "the religious rite performed at a funeral" (*Hamlet* 4.3.23–24; 5.1.236–38).

2. There are relatively few references to serving God, and they are often comic or merely take the form of the conventional exhortation, "Serve God." Examples include *L.L.L.* 5.2.523; *Much Ado* 4.2.19; 5.2.87; *Merry Wives* 2.2.50–51; 4.5.119–20; 5.5.128–29; *All's Well* 2.3.245; *Measure* 2.2.90–91; *Henry V* 4.8.64–65; *Romeo* 2.5.44; and *Othello* 1.1.111–12. Two examples of serious references to serving God are *Richard II* 3.2.98–99 and *Henry VIII* 3.2.455–58.

3. Wells notes Shakespeare's "sympathy for the lot of the common soldier," mentioning "the 'band of brothers' at Agincourt," and "the anonymous English (*sic*) sentry at the siege of Orleans" [*1 Henry VI* 2.1.5], and Feeble (*Wide Arch*, 146). The sentry, of course, is French, which suggests that Shakespeare's sympathy for the common soldier extended even beyond the bounds of patriotism.

4. See, for example, *All's Well* 1.2.13–15, 26–28; *1 Henry IV* 4.2.22, 32; *2 Henry IV* 1.2.133–34, 147–48; 3.2.251–52; *Twelfth Night* 3.3.26–28; *Henry V* 3.6.3–4, 15, 71–72; 4.7.96–101, 144; and *Timon* 3.5.62–67.

5. This sense of even military service as personal is reflected in the Duke of Ephesus's statement to Adriana: "Long since, thy husband served me in my wars" (*Errors* 5.1.161) and the First Lord's statement to the Countess of Rossillion that her son has "gone to serve the Duke of Florence" (*All's Well* 3.2.52).

6. Wells, *Wide Arch*, 144, quoting from *Shakespeare's Rome* (Ithaca: Cornell University Press, 1976), 152.

7. Hartsock states, "Though Antony never really releases himself from the claims of duty (it tears him to pieces), love is the ultimate value to this aging man" ("Major Scenes," 59).

8. Coriolanus says, "I had rather be their servant in my way / Than sway with them in theirs" (*Coriolanus* 2.1.202–3); the antecedents of "their" and "theirs" are uncertain: he has last mentioned "the patricians," while his mother has just alluded to "Rome" (194–97, 199–201). Similarly, Aufidius says of Coriolanus, "I think he'll be to Rome / As is the osprey to the fish, who takes it / By sovereignty of nature. First he was / A noble servant to them" (4.7.33–36), again confusing the referent, unless this is a suggestion that even the aristocrats unconsciously agree that "the people are the city." Coriolanus later says that he owes his "life and services" to the Senate (2.2.133–34), notes that he "got [his wounds] in [his] country's service" (2.3.52–53; see also 4.5.73–76), and claims that he has performed his deeds for the Roman people's "voices" (2.3.126–30). Others note "what services he has done for his country" (1.1 28–29; see also 2.2.37–41; 3.3.89–90; 4.2.20–22), although one Roman objects that "he did [what he did] to please his mother and to be partly proud" (1.1.36–37). Brutus describes Coriolanus as "a petty servant to the state" (2.3.179; see also 2.3.223, 236; 3.3.53). Whether Coriolanus serves Rome, the Roman people, some (presumably aristocratic) portion of the population, or an idea of Rome, it is clear that he regards himself, and is regarded by others, as a servant. Similarly, his relationship with Aufidius (who also describes himself as a servant: 5.6.30–31, 145–47) and the Volscians is described in terms of service (4.4.26; 4.5.93–97, 103–6; 5.3.132–35). R. B. Parker notes that "Coriolanus can only understand 'service' in a military sense" (*Coriolanus*, World's Classics series [Oxford: Oxford University Press, 1994], 3.3.85–86 n.). On Coriolanus's Rome as an abstraction, see Zolbrod, "Coriolanus and Alceste," 57. On Coriolanus as a character who is willing to give, but not to take, see Zolbrod, 58, and Jarrett Walker, "Voiceless Bodies and Bodiless Voices: The Drama of Human Perception in *Coriolanus*," *Shakespeare Quarterly* 43 (Summer 1992): 175.

9. On Othello reminding his hearers of his past service, see Carol McGinnis Kay, "Othello's Need for Mirrors," *Shakespeare Quarterly* 34 (Autumn 1983): 262; and Wells, *Wide Arch*, 145. Michael Neill argues that Othello's suicide "takes the form of a reenacted slaughter of the Turk" and that European emphasis on purity of "race" "threatened to turn a phrase like 'Moor of Venice' into a hopeless oxymoron" ("'Mulattos,' 'Blacks,' and 'Indian Moors': *Othello* and Early Modern Constructions of Human Difference," in *Putting History to the Question: Power, Politics, and Society in English Renaissance Drama* (New York: Columbia University Press, 2000) 273, 274; see also his "'Servile Ministers,'" 21. I would argue, however, that at the end of Othello's life he is depicted as choosing to be remembered as being "of Venice," although some of the play's final lines may suggest that the Venetians would prefer to forget him. Neill also notes that at the end of the play Lodovico "orders the erasure of the unsettling spectacle on the bed, and . . . ceremoniously reasserts his own role as the official servant of Venice" ("'Servile Ministers,'" 27).

10. Laslett suggests that in early modern society, "in spite of the subordination, the exploitation and the obliteration of those who were young, or female, or in service, everyone belonged in a group, a family group. Everyone had his or her circle of affection: every relationship could be seen as a love-relationship" (*World We Have Lost*, 5).

11. Thomas Heywood notes that, among other subjects, comedy "intreates of loue, deriding foolish inamorates, who spend their ages, their spirits, nay themselues, in the seruile and ridiculous imployments of their Mistresses" (*"An Apology for Actors" (1612) by Thomas Heywood [and] A Refutation of "The Apology for Actors" (1615) by I. G.*, introductions and notes by Richard H. Perkinson [New York: Scholars' Facsimiles and Reprints, 1941], F4ʳ). The language was not confined to theater or literature, however, as Philip Gawdy demonstrates in a letter to his father dated March 13, 1589: "I heare my oncle Anthony is at Graves End and further I heard not from him, he attendethe vppon his Mistress a thing vsual amongst all good servants. Myne owne experyence hathe taught me, I have bene a servant and had a Mistress. And I ever found that the greater the service, the greater was the reward" (*Letters of Philip Gawdy of West Harling, Norfolk, and of London to Various Members of his Family, 1579–1616*, ed. Isaac Herbert Jeayes [London: J. B. Nichols, 1906], 48). On love represented as "unmanly servitude" in *Much Ado about Nothing*, see John A. Allen, "Dogberry," *Shakespeare Quarterly* 24 (Winter 1973): 42–43.

12. Nicholas Ling also links these concepts: "The onely fruite of service, is love and reward, and the pleasure thereof, humility and obedience" (*Politeuphuia. Wits Commonwealth*, 118ʳ). Neill notes that "the overwhelming preponderance of examples" of using "servant" to mean "lover" come from *T.G.V.* ("'He that thou knowest,'" 333–34 n. 4).

13. William Rockett argues: "The thought that in this unfit task he serves his mistress makes Ferdinand's pleasure spring from the work itself, not from the anticipation of a reward external to the task. . . . No other character in the play so clearly demonstrates the virtue of liberality as does Ferdinand in his ability to serve for the sake of service itself" ("Labor and Virtue in *The Tempest*," *Shakespeare Quarterly* 24 [Winter 1973]: 81–82). While this may be true, it does not lessen the incongruity of a prince hauling logs in the service of his love.

14. See the entries for "serve," "serve one's lust," and "service and services" in Eric Partridge, *Shakespeare's Bawdy: A Literary & Psychological Essay and a Comprehensive Glossary* (1948; repr., New York: E. P. Dutton, 1960), 185.

15. *Measure for Measure*, ed. J. W. Lever (The Arden edition [1965; repr., London: Methuen, 1985], 1.2.102; 3.2.116 nn.). Mihoko Suzuki describes Pompey as voicing a "trenchant critique" in defending prostitution against Vienna's reformers (*Subordinate Subjects*, 96).

16. Joan Hutton Landis argues that "A 'servant' was a euphemism for a pimp or male whore[,] so that Shakespeare could avail himself of this second meaning by virtue of the character's role as well as the actual word" ("'By two-headed Janus,'" 23). There is, however, little evidence that Shakespeare wanted his audience to make this association in *Merchant* or other plays.

17. An example of how broadly the idea of service could be applied is given by "I. G." in *A Refutation of "The Apology for Actors"*: "GOD, who in the beginning, Created all thinges for his owne Glorie; and next himselfe, for the seruice of Mankind, among other thinges hath Created many for the Recreation of mans wearied spirites, that after some refection, hee might the more dilengently and earnestly apply himselfe to the honest labours of his Calling" (3). For another example of how service and obedience connect every aspect of creation, see E. Nesbit, *Caesar's Dialogve*, 102–6).

18. Lawrence Humfrey writes, "Thus reasonles beasts performe their duties, and denie not the Noble man at due tymes, theyr woll, mylke, laboure, and Ser-

vice" *(Nobles,* I6ʳ). Stephen Gosson notes "the use of many creatures which God hath ordeined for the service of man" *(Playes Confuted in five Actions* [London, n.d], F8ᵛ-G1ʳ). Nesbit mentions horses as serving *(Caesar's Dialogve,* D1ᵛ); Pierre Boaistuau comments on the faithful service rendered by horses and dogs *(Theatrum Mundi,* trans. John Alday [London, 1581], 37–38); and Lod[owick] Br[yskett] refers to a mastiff as his master's "old servant" *(A Discourse of Civill Life: Containing the Ethike part of Morall Philosophe, Fit for the instructing of a Gentleman in the course of a vertuous life* [London, 1606], 237).

    19. Another appropriate, if not precisely animal, association in *Macbeth* is that between Macbeth's servant Seyton and Satan; see Alan C. Dessen, *Elizabethan Stage Conventions and Modern Interpreters* (New York: Cambridge University Press, 1984), 6; and Martin Wiggins, "*Macbeth* and Premeditation," in *The Arts, Literature, and Society,* ed. Arthur Marwick (London: Routledge, 1990), 23–47, 40.

    20. Humfrey comments, "The moone taketh charge of yᵉ night, & serveth men, plants, livinge creatures" *(Nobles,* I5ᵛ). On Thomas Middleton referring to springs as servants, see William Hardin, "'Pipe-Pilgrimages' and 'Fruitfull Rivers': Thomas Middleton's Civic Entertainments and the Water Supply of Early Stuart London," *Renaissance Papers 1993,* ed. Barbara J. Baines and George Walton Williams (Raleigh, NC: Southeastern Renaissance Conference, 1993), 71–72.

    21. Wells points out, "Edmund's 'services are bound' to Nature. In other words, he disclaims all obligation to others, dedicating himself to that same self-interest which the Fool in theory advocates but abjures in practice, loyalty constantly overriding common sense" *(Wide Arch,* 143). See also Neill, "'Servile Ministers,'" 29–30.

    22. What might seem to us literary language was not limited to literary writing, but was simply a common figure of speech. For example, in *A Remedy for Sedition* (London, 1536), Richard Morison suggests that "a payre of shoes" or a cap can do service (B4ʳ).

    23. Similarly, Queen Katherine says to Cardinal Wolsey, "your words, / Domestics to you, serve your will as't please / Yourself pronounce their office" *(Henry VIII* 2.4.111–13), although it seems unlikely that she expects to persuade Wolsey to change his position.

    24. For a discussion of the attribution of this statement, see Philip Brockbank's note in the Arden edition (1976; repr., London: Routledge, 1988), 214n. 303.

    25. Although Polixenes similarly reduces his spies to mere body parts when he says, "I have eyes under my service" *(Winter's Tale* 4.2.34), he is simply referring to his servants in terms of the body parts that are significant to the service they are performing. He is not redefining these servants as body parts in order to make them seem less significant.

    26. Gillian Murray Kendall, in "'Lend me thy hand': Metaphor and Mayhem in *Titus Andronicus,*" discusses the connections and discontinuities between violence and rhetoric in the play, noting of this scene that "[Titus's] language inevitably severs him from the situation at hand" *(Shakespeare Quarterly* 40 [Fall 1989], 301); Kendall's statement obviously adds support to the theory that it is impossible to discuss this play without punning.

    27. Fear is commonly defined as being servile; thus the Duke in *Measure for Measure* describes life as "Servile to all the skyey influences" that afflict the body and, ultimately, "Merely . . . death's fool" (3.1.8–11). See also *Caesar* 1.1.75.

28. Michael Neill comments that "in the Player King's allegory, Love is imagined as the *servant* of Fortune" ("'He that thou knowest,'" 335 n. 16).

29. Although this wish appears to come true, by the end of the play Coriolanus tells Menenius, "My affairs / Are servanted to others" (*Coriolanus* 5.2.83–84).

30. Although the editor of the Pelican edition glosses "fool" as "dupe, plaything," the parallel with "slaves" suggests that "fool" in this line may refer to the servant so called; "life" would thus be perceived as not simply inferior to time, but as serving in a way that amuses time.

31. Occasionally, servants are involved in a kind of echo effect where the echo, however, has a different meaning than the original line. Thus in *Timon of Athens*, when Caphis says, "I go, sir," his master replies, "Ay, go, sir" (2.1.33–34); in his note to line 34 in the Arden edition, H. J. Oliver compares this to Lucullus's echoing of Flaminius's "His health is well, sir" (*Timon* 3.1.13–14). In *Coriolanus*, the titular hero ends a scene with the line, "I'll do [Aufidius's] country service"; the following scene begins with one of Aufidius's servingmen calling out, "Wine, wine, wine! What service is here?" (4.4.26; 4.5.1–2). In his note in the Arden edition, Brockbank comments, "As [A. H.] King observes, there is a nice ironical recoil of *service* upon the last line of the previous scene—noticeable when the playing is virtually continuous" (250 n. 1).

32. Berners A. W. Jackson, (Pelican) note.

33. See, for example, *2 Henry VI* 4.2.120; *T.G.V.* 3.1.157; *Macbeth* 1.2.20; and *Cymbeline* 2.3.122–26.

34. On the analogies drawn by writers of the period among God's creation, the state, and the household, see Amussen, *Ordered Society*, 35–38; Dolan, *Dangerous Familiars*, chapters 1–3; and Lena Cowen Orlin, *Private Matters and Public Culture in Post-Reformation England* (Ithaca: Cornell University Press, 1994), 10.

35. p. 233.

Chapter 5. "If I last in this service"

1. "Is *King Lear* an Antiauthoritarian Play?" *PMLA* 88 (October 1973): 1034.

2. William Gouge suggests mutual but unequal duties between servants and masters: "Among many other meanes to make servants faithfull to their master, and carefull to performe other duties sincerely, willingly, cheerefully, and diligently, as hath before beene noted, this is one of the most generall, namely, that *servants, in all things they doe for their master, make their masters case their owne,* and so doe for him as they would for themselves, or as they would have their owne servants doe for them. The generall rule of the Law is, *Love thy neighbor as thy selfe; and whatsoever you would that men should doe to you, doe you even so to them.* If thus every man must respect another, yea though he be a stranger, then much more must servants respect their master, because all that they can doe is after an especiall manner as a debt due to their masters: in which respect Christ saith, that *when they have done all that is commanded, they have but done their dutie*" (*Of Domesticall Duties*, 634).

3. On actual employers' affection for their servants, see John Aubrey, *Aubrey's Brief Lives*, ed. Oliver Lawson Dick (1949; repr., Harmondsworth, UK: Penguin, 1982), 42–43; and Paul V. B. Jones, *Household*, 62–63. For examples of employers expressing affection or concern for their servants, see Clifford, *Dia-*

ries, 127, 180, 252, 257; Gawdy, *Letters*, 60; and Marshall, *English Domestic Servant*, 24. For examples of generosity toward servants, see Clifford, xi, 263, and passim; Paul V. B. Jones, 41–45; and Marshall, 26. For examples of servants being remembered in their employers' wills, see Barnett, *Place, Profit, and Power*, 15, 42, 58, 63, 94, 115, 136; Becon, *Sicke Mans Salue*, 96, 150–51; Gerald Eades Bentley, *The Profession of Player in Shakespeare's Time, 1590–1642* (Princeton: Princeton University Press, 1984), 19, 20, 94, 130, 132; Ivor Brown, *Shakespeare and the Actors* (London: Bodley Head, 1970), 115; Gurr, *Playgoing in Shakespeare's London*, 222; Jeanne Jones, *Family Life*, 16, 18–19, 31, 104, 123; Marshall, 26; and Alan G. R. Smith, *Servant of the Cecils*, 41. For examples of employers doing, or attempting to do, favors for their servants or former servants, see Aubrey, 55; Gurr, *The Shakespearian Playing Companies* (Oxford: Clarendon Press, 1996), 168–69; Sir Thomas Overbury, "Crumms Fal'n from King James's Table," in *The Miscellaneous Works in Prose and Verse of Sir Thomas Overbury, Knt*, ed. Edward F. Rimbault (London: Reeves and Turner, 1890), 256; and Alan G. R. Smith, 64, 121, 138.

4. On the respect the Countess of Rossillion shows her servants, see Zitner, *All's Well*, 132–33. Charles Wells notes "Brutus' concern for young Lucius" (*Wide Arch*, 141), which is certainly an accurate observation, but Brutus is never less than respectful to any of his men.

5. On this episode, see Wells, *Wide Arch*, 179.

6. With regard to still another instance of an upper-class intervention to save servants from punishment—Sir John Falstaff's on behalf of his men, Bardolph, Nym, and Pistol, who have robbed Slender in *The Merry Wives of Windsor*, Jan Lawson Hinely comments, "the nobility often interfered to save members of their retinues from deserved punishment by city officials" ("Comic Scapegoats and the Falstaff of *The Merry Wives of Windsor*," *Shakespeare Studies* 15 [1982]: 38).

7. "Timon's Servant," 153; and Gawdy, *Letters*, 117.

8. I. G., *Refutation of the Apology for Actors*, 46.

9. *Timon* 2.2.180–90, 220, 226–28, 236–37. Martin Holmes comments on this episode: "By this time, Timon has practically forgotten his own shock and the peril of bankruptcy that threatens him; his main concern is to comfort and encourage a faithful servant by assuring him of his continued confidence and lessen his sense of despair and impotence by giving him something practical to do" (*Shakespeare and His Players* [New York: Scribner's, 1972], 182).

10. However, sexual intimacy—forced or consensual—between servants and their masters and mistresses was both a fact and a common trope in popular culture. See Amussen, *Ordered Society*, 167–68; Beier, *Masterless Men*, 25; Ben-Amos, *Adolescence and Youth*, 200–201; Capp, "Popular Literature," 209; Thomas Dekker, et al., *The Witch of Edmonton: A Critical Edition*, ed. Etta Soiref Onat (New York: Garland, 1980), 1.1.75–87, 153–66; 4.1.5–7; David Farley-Hills, "A *Hamlet* Crux," *Notes and Queries* 240 n.s. vol. 42 (September 1995): 319–20; "An Amorous Dialogue between John and His Mistress," in *Merry Songs and Ballads prior to the Year A.D. 1800*, ed. John S. Farmer (5 vols. New York: Cooper Square Publishers, 1964) 2:65–69; Harrison, *Last Elizabethan Journal*, 7–8, 31; Overbury, "A Chamber-maide," in *Miscellaneous Works*, 101; Overbury, "The First and Second Part of *The Remedy of Love*," in *Miscellaneous Works*, 210; "The Bashful Batchelor," in *Roxburghe Ballads*, 3:421–22; "The Catalogue of Contented Cuckolds," in *Roxburghe Ballads*, 3:481–83; and "The Widdow of Watling Street," in *Roxburghe Ballads*, 8:8–13.

11. Evidence of loyal and loving service can be found in the historical record as well as being reflected in the popular culture of the period. For accounts of servants risking, and sometimes losing, their lives in defense of their masters, see Harrison, *Last Elizabethan Journal*, 10; and Stephen K. Land, *Kett's Rebellion: The Norfolk Rising of 1549* (Totowa, NJ: Rowman and Littlefield, 1977), 47; this idea also appears as a motif in ballads: see "King of Scots and Andrew Browne," in Percy, *Reliques*, 2:222–25 and "The Lady Isabella's Tragedy," in Percy, *Reliques*, 3:155–58. On servants remembering masters in their wills, see Barnett, *Place, Profit, and Power*, 26, 31–32, 38, 71, 115, 134; Bentley, *Profession of Player*, 130–32; Clifford, *Diaries*, 65, n. 49; and Orlin, *Elizabethan Households*, 155, 157. Aubrey reports a conversation he had with Francis Potter (1594–1678) in 1674: "I asked him why he did not get some kinswoman or kinsman of his to live with him, and looke to him now in his great age? He answer'd me that he had tryed that way, and found it not so well; for they did begrudge what he spent that 'twas too much and went from them, wheras his servants (strangers) were kind to him and tooke care of him" (*Aubrey's Brief Lives*, 249). Aubrey also notes, in his account of George Abbott (1562–1633), Archbishop of Canterbury, that "Old Nightingale was his servant, and weepes when he talkes of him" (4).

12. Orlin notes that the comparative lack of privacy, even in great houses, "militated against the clear articulation of master and servant classes" (*Elizabethan Households*, 22); see also Singman, *Daily Life*, 79. On servants and employers being of similar status, see Orlin, 21–22. On the advantages that could accrue to servants and on the close relationships that sometimes developed between masters and servants, see Ben-Amos, *Adolescence and Youth*, 171–75, 212.

13. The only exception to the play's rule that characters other than Henry and Alice speak about, rather than to, Katharine, is her mother's expressed wish: "God, the best maker of all marriages, / Combine your hearts in one, your realms in one" (*Henry V* 5.2.358–59). This, however, is a political, rather than a personal, wish, and Katharine seems included only because convention demands it.

14. See, for example, Thomas Moisan, who notes the Nurse's "vicariously . . . furtively . . . maternal relationship to Juliet" ("Rhetoric and the Rehearsal," 396.) Moisan's principal purpose in this essay, however, is to analyze the mourning rhetoric of the Nurse and Juliet's parents in act 4, scene 5.

15. Although we do not see Cornelia die, we cannot doubt that Aaron, who is depicted as enjoying killing to such an extent that he makes a joke of the Nurse's death-cry, would fulfill his promise to murder the midwife as well.

16. Carol Thomas Neely notes that "Emilia's and Desdemona's lack of competitiveness, jealousy, and class consciousness facilitates their growing intimacy, which culminates in the willow scene" ("Women and Men in *Othello*: 'What should such a fool / Do with so good a woman?'" in *The Woman's Part: Feminist Criticism of Shakespeare*, ed. Carolyn Ruth Swift Lenz, Gayle Greene, and Carol Thomas Neely [Urbana: University of Illinois Press, 1980], 224–25).

17. Paulina and Emilia also express their love and respect for Hermione at 2.2.2–4, 20–25.

18. It is, of course, true that Ariel could be said to have an ulterior motive for revealing Caliban's plot: he might hope that Prospero's gratitude will take the form of setting him free. On the other hand, if Caliban's plot were to succeed,

Ariel would certainly be free. Presumably, we are to assume that Ariel expects the plot to fail—as, with Stephano and Trinculo involved, seems probable—and hopes to get credit for the failure.

19. See, for example, Barish and Waingrow, "'Service' in *King Lear*"; Graham, "'Without the form'"; Reid, "Lear's Three Shamings," 102 n. 34; and Wells, *Wide Arch*, 143.

20. Mark Thornton Burnett sees Kent as a combination of faithful servant and trickster (*Masters and Servants*, 83–84), but despite Viola's warning (*Twelfth Night* 2.2.27), disguise is certainly not "a wickedness" in this play. Jeffrey Stern describes Kent, Gloucester, and the Fool as "maternal males," but it is not necessary so to redefine these characters when the definition of faithful, loving servant is available ("*King Lear*: The Transference of the Kingdom," *Shakespeare Quarterly* 41 [Fall 1990]: 306). On loyalty in *Lear*, see Kronenfeld, *King Lear*, 158–59; and Neill, "Servant Obedience," 25–26, 45.

21. *Shakespeare's Comic Commonwealths*, 203.

22. Burnett, *Masters and Servants*, 82–83; see also Agnes Latham, introduction to *As You Like It* (The Arden Shakespeare, 2nd ed. [1975; repr., London: Methuen, 1977]), lxxii–lxxiii; Alan Rickman, "Jacques in *As You Like It*," in *Players of Shakespeare 2: Further Essays in Shakespearean Performance by Players with the Royal Shakespeare Company*, ed. Russell Jackson and Robert Smallwood (Cambridge: Cambridge University Press, 1988), 78; and Wells, *Wide Arch*, 144–45.

23. In a section entitled "Of Ingratitude," Robert Allott suggests that even a great man deserves blame for mistreating faithful servants: "Cato the elder, solde his old servaunts that had served him a long time, in the market, so wee use to sell beastes; a foule blot in so famous a man" (*Wits Theater*, 227ᵛ).

24. As Philip Brockbank points out in his notes to *Coriolanus* 4.5.163–75, Aufidius's servants' defense of their master's reputation is tentative and confusing (The Arden edition [1976; repr., London: Routledge, 1988]). At 186–96, they directly admit that Coriolanus "was wont to thwack" Aufidius.

25. Paul Gaudet argues that in *Richard II*, Shakespeare portrayed Bushy, Bagot, and Green as "faithful servants of the King," rather than depicting them in the traditional fashion, as self-seeking parasites, to complicate the audience's response to the main characters, suggesting another purpose "service" characters fulfill in the plays ("The 'Parasitical' Counselors in Shakespeare's *Richard II*: A Problem in Dramatic Interpretation," *Shakespeare Quarterly* 33 [Summer 1982]: 154).

26. M. C. Bradbrook even maintains that "The groom who appears in the final scene is a fully dramatized character who 'quarrels' with [the] choric gardeners" who appear earlier in the play (*Shakespeare and Elizabethan Poetry*, 136). On the relationship between Richard and the Groom, and other considerations of friendship and service in *Richard II*, see Neill, "'He that thou knowest,'" 324–26.

27. "The Idea of Excellence in Shakespeare," *Shakespeare Quarterly* 27 (Spring 1976): 142–43.

28. "A Contemporary Playwright Looks at Shakespeare's Plays," in *Shakespeare: Text, Subtext, and Context* (212).

29. Thaliard has the additional motive that his master, Antiochus, threatens his life if he fails to fulfill the command to murder Pericles, whereas Leonine, not so threatened, is poisoned by his mistress Dionyza, although, ironically, he has lied about killing Marina (1.1.163–66; 4.3.9–10). See Strier, *Resistant Struc-*

tures, 200. Richard A. Levin sees Portia's servant Stephano as untrustworthy because, in serving Portia, he supports her false story about where she has been in Bassanio's absence (*Merchant* 5.1.28–33), but this is so venial a sin that it is hard to imagine that many readers or audience members have noticed, much less been disturbed by, it (*Love and Society*, 81).

30. "Delusion as Resolution in *King Lear*," *Shakespeare Quarterly* 21 (Winter 1970): 31–32. See also Strier, *Resistant Structures*, 194–98. Wells observes of Oswald, among other servant-characters, that "False service—*obsequium* in its negative sense . . . evokes Shakespeare's strongest detestation" (*Wide Arch*, 146).

31. Richard Morison comments on the corrupting effect of bad masters on their servants: "I longe haue supposed, that as the bringing vp of the nobles, is the saulfe garde of a comune welthe, soo theyr euil education is the ruyne therof. For as noble men be, so theyr seruantes are. The mayster gyuen to ryot, the seruant must nedes thynke, that there is no thriuing for hym, excepte he shewe hym selfe a ruffler. So that though the seruaunt be good of hym selfe, yet to wynne the fauour of his mayster, he must counterfaite their condicions, that his maister most lyketh. Thus in vsynge theym a monethe or two, he maketh theym his owne. He nowe dissembleth no lenger, he is as they be, whom he hath longe folowed" (*Remedy for Sedition*, D3r). For another description of masters, specifically merchants, corrupting their servants, see Boaistuau, *Theatrum Mundi*, 82–83.

32. See Linda Anderson, *A Kind of Wild Justice: Revenge in Shakespeare's Comedies* (Newark: University of Delaware Press, 1987), 181n. 68; and Levin, *Love and Society*, 148.

33. Burnett comments, "To Kent's admission of identity Lear fails to respond, and the servant's perfect services are qualified in this supremely anticlimactic moment" (*Masters and Servants*, 83). See also Stanley Cavell, *Disowning Knowledge in Six Plays of Shakespeare* (Cambridge: Cambridge University Press, 1987), 71n. 9; and William Ringler, "Exit Kent," *Shakespeare Quarterly* 11 (Summer 1960): 316.

34. "Spectacles of Torment in *Titus Andronicus*," *Studies in English Literature 1500–1900* 36 (Spring 1996): 320. Smith does go on to comment on the death of the Clown as one of the play's "gross miscarriages of justice" and "a grotesque parody of public punishment" (320).

35. "Unproper Beds: Race, Adultery, and the Hideous in *Othello*," *Shakespeare Quarterly* 40 (Winter 1989): 407.

36. Even when critics remember servant-characters, they are apt to make unwarranted assumptions about these characters. On the basis of no apparent textual evidence, Dennis R. Preston posits that "It is most likely that Curio is a serving man to the Count, older than Valentine, perhaps a follower of Orsino's father" ("The Minor Characters in *Twelfth Night*," *Shakespeare Quarterly* 21 [Spring 1970]: 169). Even less probable is W. B. Thorne's assumption that Marina's nurse, Lychorida, is an "old maid" ("*Pericles* and the 'Incest-Fertility' Opposition," *Shakespeare Quarterly* 22 [Winter 1971]: 52). Not only is there no evidence in the play for either Lychorida's advanced age or maidenhood, but it is unlikely that a nurse for a newborn baby would be either a maid or elderly. Juliet's nurse is no maid, and though she mentions her age, she does so only to complain; furthermore, we meet her more than a decade after she was first employed as Juliet's nurse. That Juliet refers to the Nurse as old (*Romeo* 2.5.16) is meaningless, given that Juliet is not quite fourteen, an age at which

anyone over the age of twenty-five is likely to belong to the category of "old folks." The Nurse's comment that she has only four teeth (1.3.13–14) cannot be taken as evidence of advanced age either, given the likelihood in the early modern period that young adults, or even children, would lose teeth. Moreover, women used to assume that the loss of calcium occasioned by pregnancy and nursing would result in tooth loss: "a child, a tooth" was a common saying in the United States even within the last fifty years. The physical stress of wet nursing may have made tooth loss a frequent work-related hazard.

37. On the actual (considerable) mobility of servants during this period, see Amussen, *Ordered Society*, 73; Beier, *Masterless Men*, 24; Burnett, *Masters and Servants*, 58–59; Laslett, *World We Have Lost*, 7, 94; and Wright, "'Churmaids, Huswyfes and Hucksters,'" 103–5. Gouge suggests that "lazie and negligent" servants who spend time "in prating about state, and Church-businesse ... make their masters weary of their service; and by reason thereof they are oft shifted from house to house, and as *rolling stones, gather no mosse*" (*Of Domesticall Duties*, 621). The ballad "Seldom Comes the Better" warns servants against changing employers, but also employers against seeking new servants merely for the sake of novelty (*Roxburghe Ballads*, 2:509–13); another ballad, "Wit's never good till 'tis bought," also warns against leaving "a good service" (*Roxburghe Ballads*, 3:63–68).

38. Gouge states that "for the time that the servant hath covenanted to be a servant with his master ... a servant is part of his masters goods and possessions" (*Of Domesticall Duties*, 663).

39. There seem to be no instances in the plays of female servants changing service or even considering such a change, except to leave service to get married. There are several possible reasons for this sex-linked difference, some historical, some dramatic, and some a combination of both. Female servants may have had less freedom to change service than male servants. Male servants may have been more likely to be treated harshly, particularly in terms of physical abuse (other than sexual exploitation), at least in the plays, and therefore may have had more incentive, as well as more freedom, to leave. (No female servant in the plays is certainly physically abused by her employer.) There may have been fewer opportunities for "gentlefolk" to serve, since such people could only be employed by great households, whereas many households could employ a maid or man of all work; additionally, gentlewomen and gentlemen in service may have had more personal attachment to their employers than did "lower" servants, and therefore may have been more reluctant to change services. Since many of Shakespeare's female servants are "waiting-gentlewomen," their failure to consider changing service may have had a factual basis. Furthermore, the female servants Shakespeare depicts usually serve women, with whom they often have close ties. Finally, Shakespeare may simply have been less interested in the condition of female servants, the relatively small number of whom, in comparison to the number of male servants, roughly parallels the paucity of women's roles in general in comparison to the number of men's roles. (Even counting ladies in attendance as servants, there are at least four times as many named male characters in service as named female characters; including all of the unnamed characters, among them messengers, officers, posts, pages, and "servant[s] to" the mostly male characters, would make the proportion of male servants very much larger.)

40. Norman N. Holland notes that Lancelot's change of masters makes him another of the play's risk-takers: "All he does is cease being Shylock's servant

and become Bassanio's, or as Bassanio puts it, 'Leave a rich Jew's service to become the follower of so poor a gentleman' (II.ii.135–36). Gobbo, too, takes a chance, and he, too, wins" (*The Shakespearean Imagination* [1964; repr., Bloomington: Indiana University Press, 1975], 104). Levin sees Lancelot not merely as a servant changing jobs, but as disloyal (*Love and Society*, 33–34, 48–49).

41. Despite his expressed contempt for his employers, the Boy is still serving Pistol in act 4, scene 4 (Bardolph and Nym having been hanged, 4.4.71–74). Since he says that he "must stay with the lackeys, with the luggage of our camp," and Gower later reports that after the French attack on the luggage train, "there's not a boy left alive," it appears that we are to assume that the Boy never has a chance to seek better service (4.4.76–77; 4.7.5).

42. Perhaps Lance is destined to lose his service, since he has earlier been slow to react to Panthino's warning that this will happen if he fails to get to the ship on which his master is sailing (2.3.32–43).

43. Whether we are supposed to believe Autolycus's account of his life since leaving service (4.3.91–100) is impossible to determine.

44. Interestingly, although both Autolycus and Timon's Steward have been dismissed, each continues to refer to his former employer as "master" and continues to try to do him service, although, to be sure, Autolycus does so at least partly in hope of reward (*Timon* 4.2.27, 50–52; 4.3.474–76, 492–94, 516, 538–39; *Winter's Tale* 4.4.712–13, 834–45). Berry and Robert S. Miola both make note of Timon's servants' virtue and powerlessness (*Shakespeare and Social Class*, 163; "Timon in Shakespeare's Athens," *Shakespeare Quarterly* 31 [Spring 1980]: 26–28).

45. *Common Liar*, 46. Wells, on the other hand, states that "The dutifulness and dependability shown by the many servants and followers shine out all the brighter against the dark background of their 'betters'' venality" (*Wide Arch*, 139). Arnold Stein notes, "Dercetas has already demonstrated one familiar human response to loss: he has run hopefully to Caesar with Antony's bloodied sword" ("The Image of Antony: Lyric and Tragic Imagination," *Kenyon Review* 21 [Autumn 1959]: 597).

46. Although the English prided themselves on the absence of slaves in their country (see Bridenbaugh, *Vexed and Troubled Englishmen*, 49 n. 6; and Camille Wells Slights, "Slaves and Subjects in *Othello*," *Shakespeare Quarterly* 48 [Winter 1997]: 381–83), "service" was sometimes indistinguishable from slavery; Bridenbaugh reports that the parents of a child named Richard Frethorne "sold him to the Virginia Company for a servant" (11). Gouge states that masters may sell or bequeath servants (*Of Domesticall Duties*, 664–65). For examples of buying boys as apprentices, or purchasing part of the time remaining on their apprenticeship contracts, particularly actors' apprentices, see Baldwin, *Organization and Personnel*, 36–38, and Bentley, *Profession of Player*, 128, 134, 145–46. On historical evidence of lending servants, see Alison Plowden, *Tudor Women: Queens and Commoners* (London: Weidenfeld and Nicolson, 1979), 106. Berry notes that "Caliban's role is grounded in the term by which Prospero (and the Folio) refers to him, 'slave'" (*Shakespeare and Social Class*, 182–83).

47. "Learning to Curse," 26.

48. See Beier, *Masterless Men*; Paul Brown, "'This thing of darkness,'" 52–55; Dollimore, "Introduction," 12; Dollimore, "Transgression and Surveillance," 77; Greenblatt, "Invisible Bullets," 30–31; Paul Griffiths, "Masterless

Young People in Norwich, 1560–1645," in *The Experience of Authority in Early Modern England*, ed. Paul Griffiths, Adam Fox, and Steve Hindle (New York: St. Martin's Press, 1996), 146–86; and Neill, "Servant Obedience," 20–28.

49. For a discussion of Timon's Steward, whom we do see after his release from Timon's service, see chapter 9.

50. John Rooks describes Trinculo and Stephano as "masterless men" who engage in "naked profiteering" ("Savages Old and New: Images of Wildness in *The Tempest*," *Renaissance Papers 1992*, ed. George Walton Williams and Barbara J. Baines [Raleigh, NC: Southeastern Renaissance Conference, 1993], 80). For parallels between Stephano and Antonio, see John D. Cox, *Shakespeare and the Dramaturgy of Power* (Princeton: Princeton University Press, 1989), 205–6.

51. On the conspiracy as representing "Elizabethan fears regarding masterless men" and its indebtedness "to a tradition of official scorn heaped upon commoners who would be king," see Curt Breight, " 'Treason doth never prosper': *The Tempest* and the Discourse of Treason," *Shakespeare Quarterly* 41 (Spring 1990): 17.

52. Beier notes that "the literature of roguery" describes "a highly organized vagrant underworld. In 1552 Gilbert Walker said vagabonds were a 'corporation'; to Awdeley they were a 'fraternity', a 'company' with orders; to Harman a 'fleeting fellowship' in which 'rufflers' and 'upright men' were top dogs. At an annual beggars' convention in Gloucestershire a Lord of the Fair was supposed to be elected; a Chief Commander and officers for regiments were also reported. A new recruit, Thomas Dekker wrote, had to 'learn the orders of our house'; to recognize that 'there are degrees of superiority and inferiority in our society.' Even women and children had their assigned places in the vagrant pecking order" (*Masterless Men*, 8). As Beier concludes, "To people living in a society obsessed with hierarchy, it was natural to assume that criminals had leaders and followers" (125). To what degree this literature had a factual basis is arguable; a recent book that takes it at face value and sees it as highly influential on the drama of the period—and vice versa—is Bryan Reynolds' *Becoming Criminal: Transversal Performance and Cultural Dissidence in Early Modern England* (Baltimore: Johns Hopkins University Press, 2002).

53. Laslett notes that "There is evidence, however, that subordinate persons could quite easily conceive of a society without their social superiors, or even of disposing of such persons" (*World We Have Lost*, 294n. 7), but this does not suggest that hierarchy itself would be eliminated. Earlier, he states that "Social revolution, meaning an irreversible changing of the pattern of social relationships, never happened in traditional, patriarchal, pre-industrial human society. It was almost impossible to contemplate" (5).

54. Because so many people were employed as servants and because servants generally lived in such proximity to their employers, some servants, inevitably, were disloyal in various ways. For example, in 1599, one of the Earl of Essex's former servants, John Daniel, stole some of the Earl's letters from the Countess of Essex and attempted to blackmail the Countess, from whom he demanded 3,000 pounds for the letters' return (Harrison, *Last Elizabethan Journal*, 184–86). Corrupt housekeepers of various noblemen were said to entertain "jugglers" who gave demonstrations of the casting out of devils and made the houses "sanctuaries for Popish treason" without the owners' knowledge (ibid., 322). When witches wanted to get items that would give them power over a prospective victim (such as hair, fingernail or toenail clippings, clothing,

etc.), "disloyal servants could play an important part in providing the possessions that would endanger their masters" (Dolan, *Dangerous Familiars*, 183 n. 26; Dolan provides examples). In 1618 Lady Markham was ordered to perform penance at Paul's Cross "for marrying one of her servants while her husband [Sir Griffin] was still alive" (Bridenbaugh, *Vexed and Troubled Englishmen*, 372). On theft by servants, see Paul V. B. Jones, *Household*, 99–100.

Betrayal by servants was a common theme in the popular writing of the time. Pedringano betrays his mistress in *The Spanish Tragedy*, Ithamore his master in *The Jew of Malta*, and (on a lighter note), Face his master in *The Alchemist*, among many others. Thomas Nashe writes that prostitutes encourage "prentices and poor servants . . . to rob their masters" (1592; quoted in Manley, *London in the Age*, 279). On a servingman cheating his master of his money, see Samuel Rowlands's epigram, "A Strange Sighted Traveller" (1608; *London in the Age*, 254–54). Boaistuau indicates that princes seem to have "All that maye bee wished for, to the contentation of man, be it in provision of eating and drinking, varietie in meates, in magnificence of service, in vestures, that which may tickle the memorie and flatter the concupiscense of the flesh, is prepared for them, even from their cradle, for to conduct the estate of their lyfe in more hap and felicitie," but then asks, "but wherfore serveth their costly ornaments and honourable services, or delicate meates, when that they are in continuall feare to be poysoned, seduced and beguyled by their servitours?" (*Theatrum Mundi*, 100–101).

Ballads often represent servants as treacherous; see, for example, "Sir Cauline," in Percy, *Reliques*, 1:76–81; John Skelton's "An Elegy on Henry Fourth Earl of Northumberland," Percy, 1:119–26; "Edom o' Gordon," Percy, 1:143–47; "Glasgerion," Percy, 3:45–49; "Old Robin of Portingale," Percy, 3:55–58; "The Lady Isabella's Tragedy," Percy, 3:155–58; "The Lady and the Blackamoor," *Roxburghe Ballads*, 2:49–55; "The Lord of Lorne and the False Steward," *Roxburghe*, 2:56–63; "The Spanish Tragedy," *Roxburghe*, 2:454–59 (though here, as in the play, Belimperia's servant is threatened with death before he reveals her secret). In "The Lady Turned Serving-Man," the title character's servants flee when enemies attack (Percy, 3:86–90). Possible treachery by "fals messengers" is suspected in "King Estmere," Percy, 1:87–96. The title character of "Sir Aldingar" is a steward who falsely accuses the queen of adultery after she rejects his advances (Percy, 2:61–67). See also "On Thomas Lord Cromwell," Percy, 2:73–75.

55. Given that Lennox knows about Macduff's "broad words" and that the unnamed Lord he gossips with knows that Macduff has fled to England before Macbeth declares that he intends to kill Macduff, it does not appear that Macbeth's spies are as effective as he hopes (*Macbeth* 3.6.21–37; 4.1.82–86).

56. Servants in the popular literature of the time are often depicted as cuckolding their masters, but this idea rarely appears in Shakespeare, except in *Lear*, and then only in Edgar's fiction as poor Tom that as a servant he "did the deed of darkness" with his mistress (unless we are to believe Regan's insinuation that Goneril and Oswald are intimate). For examples of servants who cuckold their masters, see *A Sackful of News* (quoted in Ashley, *Elizabethan Popular Culture*, 296–97).

57. For Menas's presence in the final scenes as a way of foregrounding "all the tangled issues of loving loyalty versus reasonable service," see Homer Swander, "Menas and the Editors: A Folio Script Unscripted," *Shakespeare Quarterly* 36 (Summer 1985): 185.

58. Cavell, *Disowning Knowledge*, 26. Wells comments perceptively that "So powerful is this scene of atonement that Enobarbus more than redeems himself in the audience's eyes and stands, despite his transgression, with Eros, Charmian and the others as a model of sterling service and proven constancy" (*Wide Arch*, 140)

59. *Power on Display: The Politics of Shakespeare's Genres* (New York: Methuen, 1986), 97.

60. On Iago's position as a servant, see Dolan, 112, and Neill, "Servant Obedience," 26–28, and "Changing Places in *Othello*," in *Putting History to the Question*, 207–36. Russ McDonald notes that like the intriguer of comedy, Iago "[descends] from the tricky servants of Roman and Italian comedy as well as from the Vice of the English morality" ("Othello, Thorello, and the Problem of the Foolish Hero," *Shakespeare Quarterly* 30 [Winter 1979]: 58). For characters trusting in Iago's honesty, see 1.3.286–90, 297–98; 2.3.6, 171–72, 249–50; passim (*Othello*); 2.3.305–29 (Cassio); and 3.3.5; 4.2.124–80 (Desdemona). When Othello tells Emilia that her husband has accused Desdemona, she cannot believe it: "I know thou didst not, thou'rt not such a villain" (5.2.181); while this is hardly a ringing affirmation of honesty, it is evidence that Iago has managed to conceal his true character even from his wife.

61. Of course, it is also true that other characters are sometimes suspicious with reason: Iago and Roderigo lead Brabantio to suspect Othello, who has, in fact, eloped with Desdemona, although he has not, as Brabantio suspects, been dabbling in witchcraft. Without any urging from Iago, Bianca comes to suspect Cassio, who, though he tells her the truth about the handkerchief, mocks her to Iago (3.4.170–204; 4.1.109–49). Trying to explain Othello's anger, Desdemona imagines "some unhatch'd practice," and trying to account for Iago's jealousy, Emilia imagines a "squire" who has put suspicion of Othello into his mind (3.4.143; 4.2.152–54).

Even beyond Iago's complex and wide-ranging plots, of course, the theme of deception pervades the play. The Venetians are confronted by Turkish stratagems designed to mislead them (1.3.14–45); Brabantio argues that Desdemona "is abus'd . . . and corrupted / By spells and medicines" employed by Othello (62–63); even the "willow song" is about betrayal (4.3.57–59).

62. Miola notes Iago's "cunning choice of auto-psychological warfare over outright physical violence" ("Othello *Furens*," *Shakespeare Quarterly* 41 [Spring 1990]: 53).

63. *Dangerous Familiars*, 113; Dolan's immediate reference is Iago's speech to Roderigo in the first scene, beginning, "Oh, sir, content you. / I follow him to serve my turn upon him" (43–44). On Iago's refusal to serve, see also Neill, "'Servile Ministers,'" 21–24.

64. "Making More of the Moor: Aaron, Othello, and Renaissance Refashionings of Race," *Shakespeare Quarterly* 41 (Winter 1990): 451. For a very different view of Iago, "as both [homo]sexual object and displaced black Other," see Ian Smith, "Barbarian Errors: Performing Race in Early Modern England," *Shakespeare Quarterly* 49 (Summer 1998): 183.

65. Interestingly, in the ballad "The Lady and the Blackamoor" (*Roxburghe Ballads*, 2:49–55), a Moorish servant avenges himself on the master who has rebuked him by forcing his master to mutilate himself, raping and killing his master's wife, and murdering his employers' children before forestalling punishment by committing suicide. The ballad thus combines the themes of service, race, revenge, and sex, although making the Moor the servant-villain, rather than the master-victim.

Chapter 6. "Good counsel"

1. *Family, Sex and Marriage*, 6. On the intimacy between "officers and higher servitors of rank" and their employers, see Paul V. B. Jones, *Household of a Tudor Nobleman*, 35–37. Michael Neill reminds us that "in the court world to *serve* is always to *observe*" ("'He that thou knowest,'" 330).

2. There are a few situations in which employers doubt servants without suggestions of villainy on the employer's part. For instance, the brothers Antipholus often doubt their slaves (and each other's slaves), but their situation is exceptional and extremely confusing (*Errors* 1.2.53–96; 2.2.159–63; 3.1.6–10). Juliet trusts her Nurse, but orders her to send her man, Peter, away; under the circumstances, which demand secrecy, and given that Peter might feel that his first loyalty is to Juliet's father, this seems only good sense (*Romeo* 2.5.19–20).

3. John D. Cox points out that "when Cressida converses with her servant, Alexander, they both discourse wittily, first in blank verse, then in prose, without making any social distinction between each other (1.2)"; he also notes that *Troilus* is "the only play Shakespeare wrote that contains no audibly distinguishable low-life characters at all" (*Shakespeare and the Dramaturgy*, 61).

4. Lawrence Humfrey states that "[A learned man] muste not entreate [his servants] rigorouslye. Tirannous was the *Romaines* power of lyfe and death, and therfore ryghtly reft. Otherwyse teacheth *Paule* in our law. To deale gently, mildely, familierlye, with the[m], least we have as many foes as servaunts. To admit them to [talk?] and councell[.] For they are not all slaves of nature . . . *Socrates* in *Phedrus*, cou[n]sayleth to learn of anye thynge. Yea, were it a speakynge Oke. For, we ought not attend who speaketh, but what is spoken. Be they therefore frendelye to theyr servaunts, and preferre the worthye" (*Nobles*, V7^r-V7^v).

Stephen Guazzo makes a similar argument: "Let not the Maister take scorne to heare his reasons sometimes to consult with him, and to governe himselfe according to his faithfull advise: for that there have bene found servauntes, who have more advaunced and profited their maisters house, then his brothers children have. To conclude, the Maister ought to use his servant familiarlie, remembring to intreate his inferiours, as he would be intreated by his superiours" (*civile Conversation*, 173^v).

Lively examples of the familiarity we might expect between live-in servants and the families they serve occur in dialogues in the language textbooks attributed to Claude Desainliens (alias Claudius Holyband). For instance:

> [*Emanuel*] I pray thee, If thou love me, trusse my pointes.
> [*Beatrice*, a hand-maiden] What? hast thou armes of haye, or of butter? . . .
> [*Emanuel*] Put on my shoes I pray thee.
> [*Beatrice*] Put them on thy selfe.
> (*Campo di Fior*, 13, 17; see also *French Littleton*, 20, 22)

5. "*Guaz.* And for my part I cannot away to make my servants my companions, in being to familier with them: I like well to love them, but not to imbrace them.

Annib. We must set bound and limits to all our doings, which we must not go beyond: I hold well with you that the maister keepe his state and degree, for being as you say haile fellow well met with his servant, he should shew himselfe to low minded, and not fitte to commaund, and to be as it were a servaunt with servaunts, which would redound to his reproch: besides, he should soone perceive that too much familiaritie would breede contempt. And therefore men of judgement behave themselves with their servants in such sorte, that they neither make them to saucie by overmuch familiaritie, neither to fearefull by over much severitie: for in no wise let a maister be terrible to his servaunt, least in frowning still upon him, he make him thinke that neither he loveth him, nor liketh of his service, which is the way quite to discourage him: And yet in giving good countenaunce to his servant, he must be wary to observe fit time and place, and if I may lawfully say it, he must have two faces in one personage, immitating yᵉ sunne, which running his course in the skie, one while sheweth a face covered with cloudes, and when those mistie vapours are blowne away, it sheweth it selfe cleare and bright. And as it beseemeth the maister, abroade & in the presence of strangers, to cast a grave and sadde looke upon his servants: so it is his part, being retired into his owne house, to looke more pleasantly uppon them, and to speake more familiarlie unto them: which is a thing they love of life, & are there by incouraged to doe him good service" (*civile Conversation*, 171ʳ–171ᵛ).

6. Philip Gawdy reports receiving information and taking advice from servants (*Letters*, 5, 32, 84). The Earl of Essex's secretary, Henry Cuffe, was thought by contemporaries to be one of the Earl's most prominent "ill advisers" and Essex named Cuffe as "a principal instigator to the violent courses which he had undertaken" (Harrison, *Last Elizabethan Journal*, 127, 161). As Stephen Orgel reminds us, "early in Elizabeth's reign two political theorists gave the young queen counsel through the dramatic example of *Gorboduc*" and, during James I's reign, dramatists on more than one occasion offered the court entertainments that glamorized military matters (*Illusion of Power*, 9, 60–61, 66–67). Neither monarch was persuaded by the advice.

7. Later in the play, however, when master and man are fleeing a group of people trying to capture them under the misapprehension that they are madmen, S. Dromio gives his master some advice—"Run, master, run; for God sake, take a house! / This is some priory. In, or we are spoiled!" (*Errors* 5.1.36–37)—that S. Antipholus accepts.

8. The Nurse's earlier comment—"Shame come to Romeo!" (3.2.90)—though unrequested, might be thought to echo the sentiments in Juliet's immediately preceding speech (73–85); but Juliet's response to it—"Blistered be thy tongue / For such a wish!" (90–91)—suggests the difficulty of a servant's lot, even when the servant is trying to say what she thinks her mistress wants to hear.

9. See Cox, *Shakespeare and the Dramaturgy*, 78–79.

10. In North's *Plutarch*, Caesar tells the Romans "that they that should make warre with them should be Mardian the Euenuke, Photinus, and Iras, a woman of Cleopatraes bedchamber, that friseled her heare, and dressed her head, and Charmion, the which were those that ruled the affaires of Antonius Empire" (quoted in the Arden edition, 261). It is not always clear whether a servant serves Antony or Cleopatra or both. In Cleopatra's palace, despite the presence onstage of Charmian, Iras, Alexas, and Mardian, Enobarbus orders up the banquet; he is also ordered by Cleopatra to find Antony and bring him to her, and exits with Cleopatra as Antony comes onstage (1.2.12–13, 88–90, 92 s.d.). Similar confusion appears in Enobarbus's report of the treachery of Cleopatra's attendant Alexas, who "went to Jewry on / Affairs of Antony, there did dissuade / Great Herod to incline himself to Caesar / And leave his master An-

tony" (4.6.12–15). Even if "his" refers to Herod rather than Alexas, Enobarbus suggests that Alexas's original service was to Antony, rather than to Cleopatra or both.

11. Daniel Stempel suggests that the "disturbance of order" is the "dominant theme of the play," although he discusses such disturbance only in terms of Cleopatra's dominance over Antony as a threat to "the safety of the state" ("The Transmigration of the Crocodile," *Shakespeare Quarterly* 7 [Winter 1956]: 62, 63). The Romans in this play, however, apparently feel that the threat to hierarchy is social as well as sexual. As J. Robert Baker points out in summarizing Philo's comment at 1.1.10–13, "the Romans see Antony reduced from a principal support of the world to the domestic servant of a whore" ("Absence and Subversion: The 'O'erflow' of Gender in Shakespeare's *Antony and Cleopatra*," *The Upstart Crow* 12 [1992]: 109).

12. Not only does Lafew refer to Bertram as Parolles' "lord and master," but, in Parolles' presence, Bertram is referred to as his "master" by Helena and the king (2.3.186–87, 241; 1.1.166; 5.3.237). Bertram sends Parolles on errands and asks him, "Where are my other men, monsieur?" (2.4.39–55; 2.5.15, 89). Diana refers to Parolles as "a gentleman that serves the Count," and her mother calls him "a ring-carrier" for Bertram (3.5.56, 92–93). In the final scene, Parolles admits that he has been the pander between Diana and Bertram, whom he refers to as "my master" (5.3.240). As G. K. Hunter points out on his note to this line in the Arden edition, "the word which Parolles objected to in II. iii is now accepted without demur."

13. Parolles has his defenders; see J. Dennis Huston, " 'Some Stain of Soldier': The Functions of Parolles in *All's Well That Ends Well*," *Shakespeare Quarterly* 21 (Autumn 1970): 431–38; and Jules Rothman, "A Vindication of Parolles," *Shakespeare Quarterly* 23 (Spring 1972): 183–96. However, most critics are inclined to agree with Sheldon P. Zitner's assessment that "the clever servant-figure turns out, in the case of Parolles, to be a fool" (*All's Well*, 14).

14. Writers insist that servants avoid flattery or other feigning; William Vaughan lists as servants' second duty "that they bee honest and faithfull unto their masters, and not (as many now a-dayes do) flatter & cologue with them, thereby thinking to get some bootie" (*Golden-grove*, P8ʳ). Guazzo's description of the good servant includes the stipulation "That he goe not about to creepe in credit with his maister by flatterie or hipocrisie, but to serve and obaie him with an unfaigned heart: for by faigned wordes men gather an argument of faithlesse deedes, whereby his maister beginneth to suspect him, and to think that he had more neede to be overlooked, then instructed: but in anie wise let him not forget to doe his faithful and true intent, not for feare, but for duties sake: like as a good wise fellow answered to one, who saide unto him, If I take thee to my service, wilt thou be an honest man? Yea, saide he, though you take me not" (*civile Conversation*, 174ʳ). For other condemnations of servants' flattery, see Humfrey, *Nobles*, F1ʳ and F1ᵛ, H3ʳ, and V5ᵛ. Michael Neill suggests that "In *Othello*, Iago uses a devious form of flattery to promote himself from servant to 'friend' (3.3.385)" (" 'He that thou knowest,' " 335 n. 14).

15. Thomas Kelly observes that "Touchstone . . . makes memorable sport of such gentlemanly exercises as poison, bastinado, faction, and policy, just as Oliver shows them in practice" ("Shakespeare's Romantic Heroes," 16).

16. Cox refers to this speech as a "social inversion" (*Shakespeare and the Dramaturgy*, 68).

17. On the absence of servility among the servants in *The Two Gentlemen of Verona*, see Ralph Berry, *Shakespeare and Social Class*, 18.

18. Ibid., 76–77.

19. On Enobarbus and Dollabella's comments as helping to define "the image of Antony," see Arnold Stein, "Image of Antony," 591–98. William Rossky suggests that the explanation for Enobarbus's line "Hush, here comes Antony" (1.2.79) when it is actually Cleopatra who is entering the room is "that Enobarbus is not mistaking an 'Herculean' Antony in Cleopatra's clothes for the Queen but rather is accurately, though ironically, assessing the relationship between the principals, making the familiar point that Antony has become effeminate, a leader led by a woman" ("*Antony and Cleopatra*, I.ii.79: Enobarbus's 'Mistake,'" *Shakespeare Quarterly* 35 [Autumn 1984]: 324–25).

20. So important is it for a servant to hold his or her tongue, that Vaughan defines it as the first of a servant's duties: "The first duty of servants towardes their master is, that they be subject unto them, *and please them in all things, not answering againe*, nor replying, although otherwhiles they know better what is to be done, then their masters" (*Golden-grove*, P7ᵛ–P8ʳ). Nicholas Ling does not give this duty pride of place, but has more to say about its importance than about that of such duties as willingness to learn, faithfulness, and carefulness, which he lists earlier:

> [T]he fourth [duty of a servant is], silence in tongue, in not replying against his masters speeches.
> There ought to be in a servant double silence, the one, in not replying, or contradicting; the other, in not revealing abroad what his master doth at home. . . .
> A servant once made malapert, and saucy, will alwaies after kick at his duty, and scorne the co[n]trolement of his master. Ana.[xagoras]
>
> (*Politeuphuia. Wits Commonwealth*, 118ᵛ)

Guazzo suggests that verbal (and apparently even mental) opposition to a master's desires is undesirable: "Let the servaunt also conforme all his thoughts and doinges to the will and pleasure of his Maister, and to tye the Asse (as they say) where his maister will have him tied, without any contradiction: for there is nothing that spites a man more, then to see him who is bound unto him, and who ought to obey him, to make resistaunce against him" (174ʳ). Even courtiers, Guazzo urges, should practice self-censorship: "*Before their Prince let Courtiers silent bee, / Or let their words be saust with pleasant glee*" (*civile Conversation*, 175ʳ). Despite all of this good advice, however, it appears that servants continued to express their views, since William Gouge, commenting on *Ephesians* 6.5–8, seems to suggest that expressing verbal resistance to their masters has been part of servants' nature since biblical times: "It seemeth by the Apostles expresse mentioning of it, that *answering againe* hath beene an old evill quality in servants" (*Of Domesticall Duties*, 613). For other condemnations of servants' "answering again," see William Perkins, *Christian Oeconomie*, 157; and Vives, *Instruction*, X4ᵛ.

21. Bradbrook notes that "[Valentine's] new role of despairing lover is set forth and most robustly mocked at by his servant"; she also comments upon another effect of servant commentary: "Launce's 'parting' from his family completely kills Proteus's parting with Julia (which it immediately follows) using even the same puns" (*Shakespeare and Elizabethan Poetry*, 148, 153).

22. The disputes between Malvolio and the rest of the household are, of course, conducted in a grimmer vein, and at the end of the play Malvolio, declaring, "'I leave my duty a little unthought of, and speak out of my injury'" (5.1.309–10), begins a dispute with his mistress. For a discussion of Feste as a subversive character who helps correct the folly of both Olivia and Orsino, see

John D. Cox, "The Politics of Stuart Medievalism," in *Patronage, Politics, and Literary Traditions in England, 1558–1658*, ed. Cedric C. Brown (Detroit: Wayne State University Press, 1991), 218–20.

23. Berry remarks of the Soldier that "his familiar way with his General is the sign of a long relationship and of the sort of man Antony is with his troops" (*Shakespeare and Social Class*, xix).

24. In contrast, both the Doctor of Physic and Lady Macbeth's Waiting Gentlewoman are clearly afraid to discuss, even with one another, what they have overheard Lady Macbeth say (*Macbeth* 5.1.10–17, 79). Berry observes that the Gentlewoman "reflects a whole hinterland of communal response to the great crime on which the ruling house is founded" (*Shakespeare and Social Class*, xix).

25. Ty F. Buckman points out that in counselling Elizabeth not to marry Alençon, John Stubbs and Philip Sidney "saw themselves rendering faithful service, as prophet and courtier, to their Queen and realm"; however, he also notes that Sidney's representation of his advice as private was probably largely responsible for keeping him out of the sort of trouble that Stubbs encountered ("The Perils of Marriage Counselling: John Stubbs, Philip Sidney, and the Virgin Queen," *Renaissance Papers 1995*, ed. George Walton Williams and Barbara J. Baines [Raleigh, NC: Southeastern Renaissance Conference, 1996], 141, 137–38). That Kent and Cordelia challenge Lear's judgment in public may be the height of their offending. The Fool generally makes his points in private conversations; however, not all of Shakespeare's servants are so discreet, and not all employers object to servants who "answer again," even in public. In reality, public criticism was sometimes tolerated; for examples of entertainers and patrons of the drama criticizing monarchs and other exalted persons with at least relative impunity, see Cook, *Privileged Playgoers*, 120, 138–39; and Orgel, *Illusion of Power*, 79, 80, 83.

CHAPTER 7. "A LOSING OFFICE"

1. An exception to the usual critical obliviousness toward messengers is Ralph Berry, *Shakespeare and Social Class*. In a discussion of "stock type" characters, Berry notes that "Even those transparent necessities, Messengers, can transmit something individual. They are not there merely to deliver oral telegrams" (xix). Martin Holmes, *Shakespeare and His Players*, devotes a chapter to "Messengers, and their Function." Holmes points out how significantly performance can affect our reactions: "In printed texts the words 'They fight' or 'Enter a Messenger' occur again and again, because there are not many other words in which one can say so, and we are not encouraged to differentiate one fight, or one messenger, from another. As soon as we see them in performance, however, we see how very different they can be, not only in their natures but in their relation to the story and their effect upon it" (5). Bernard Beckerman, on the other hand, maintains that "The formal messenger is an example of a purely conventional figure who is not symbolic," who "has no identity," and whose "manner is often theatrical rather than natural" (*Shakespeare at the Globe: 1599–1609* [1962; repr., New York: Macmillan / Collier Books, 1966], 206, 205). Whether Shakespeare is more or less likely than his contemporaries to use messengers is in dispute: M. C. Bradbrook (*Elizabethan Stage Conditions: A Study of Their Place in the Interpretation of Shakespeare's Plays*

[1932; repr., Cambridge: Cambridge University Press, 1968], 119) suggests that Shakespeare is less apt than such contemporaries as Chapman and Jonson to use messengers' speeches, while Beckerman estimates that Shakespeare's Globe plays use about five times as many messengers as the non-Shakespearean Globe plays (205).

2. A few examples among the many possible: the messenger who brings Don Pedro's letter to Leonato and stays to volunteer information and opinions and answer questions provides plot and character background (*Much Ado* 1.1.1–90); Montjoy informs Henry V that the English have won the battle and tells him the name of the nearby castle (*Henry V* 4.7.82–88); the messenger who reports Alcibiades' approach to the senators volunteers the information that he met a messenger sent to persuade Timon to join Alcibiades' side (*Timon* 5.2.6–13); the messenger from Angelo to the Provost says, "My lord hath sent you this note, and by me this further charge, that you swerve not from the smallest article of it, neither in time, matter, or other circumstance. Good morrow; for, as I take it, it is almost day" (*Measure* 4.2.102–6).

3. Similarly, see the future Richard III's reaction to the appearance of the messenger bringing him word of his father's death: "But what art thou, whose heavy looks foretell / Some dreadful story hanging on thy tongue?" (*3 Henry VI* 2.1.43–44). The Princess of France also anticipates a messenger's news, but this interpretation may be less a result of an ability to read expressions than the other examples, as Marcade is presumably wearing mourning for the death of the French king, her father and his master, although Holmes insists that the mere wearing of black would not indicate mourning (62); furthermore, the princess does not interpret Marcade's appearance until after he has spoken, saying, "I am sorry, madam, for the news I bring / Is heavy in my tongue. The King your father—" at which point she interrupts with "Dead, for my life!" (*L.L.L.* 5.2.714–16). The princess also differs from many of the male readers of messengers as texts in not having a guilty conscience. For another kind of "reading" of a messenger, see the nameless Lord's description of Macbeth's "cloudy messenger" (*Macbeth* 3.6.41–44).

It is not only messengers, of course, whose looks may be read by bystanders; King Henry dismisses Worcester, who has criticized and obliquely threatened him, referring to his looks, rather than his words: "Worcester, get thee gone, for I do see / Danger and disobedience in thine eye. / Oh, sir, your presence is too bold and peremptory, / And majesty might never yet endure / The moody frontier of a servant brow" (*1 Henry IV* 1.3.15–19). Although Worcester is not a messenger, he is dismissed with a reminder that, in the king's eyes, he is a servant.

4. The Dauphin also curses a messenger for bringing him bad news (*John* 5.5.14). Even upper-class characters who deliver bad news may, of course, suffer for it, as when Salisbury delivers bad news and Constance hates him for doing so (*John* 3.1.1–41, 65–69).

5. In maintaining this, I take issue with the statement by Michael Redgrave that "Antony is described as 'noble' on no less than eight occasions. But, excepting for his generosity towards Enobarbus, and possibly in his death-scene, Antony is never *shown* to do one noble thing" (*Mask or Face: Reflections in an Actor's Mirror* [London: Heinemann, 1958], 79; quoted in Hugh Dickinson, "The Reformation of Prince Hal," *Shakespeare Quarterly* 12 [Winter 1961]: 37, n. 8).

6. As Janet Adelman has pointed out, "the number of messengers [in *Antony*] is extraordinary" (*Common Liar*, 35); see also Holmes, *Shakespeare and*

His Players, 77; and Quinney, "Enter a Messenger," 157. Adelman suggests that in this play "the audience is continually bombarded with messengers of one kind or another, not so much to convey information as to convey the sense that all information is unreliable, that it is message or rumor, not fact" (35; see also 28). Quinney's discussion of the play's messengers, among whom she includes, as "'messenger-figures,'" such characters as Alexas, the Soothsayer, and the Clown, argues that "the messengers begin as messengers, but end as angelloi; they are at first merely representatives, but, for Antony at least, they finally develop an autonomous presence, ushering in a rapport that is anonymous and otherworldly" (157). Antony, of course, is only one of Shakespeare's characters whose reaction to a messenger reveals character change; on the change in Albany's character as demonstrated by his reaction to the news of Gloucester's blinding, see Richard Strier, *Resistant Structures*, 194–95.

7. Robert J. Lordi sees "Richard's contradictory commands" as marking his "decaying fortunes" ("Brutus and Hotspur," *Shakespeare Quarterly* 27 [Spring 1976]: 184), but surely we are intended to see them as a change in Richard's behavior rather than merely a change in his luck. Portia's order to Lucius to "run to the Senate House" without telling him why he should go or what he should do there is a similar demonstration of her inability to control her emotional turmoil, as she herself recognizes (*Julius Caesar* 2.4.1–12, 40–47).

8. While Cleopatra's attack is the most memorable instance of violence toward a messenger in the canon, it is not the most extreme: that would be Saturninus's execution of the Clown Titus Andronicus drafts as a messenger to the emperor (*Titus* 4.3.94–110; 4.4.42–49). However, whether because the Clown is so minor a character or because the violence against him (unusually for *Titus*) takes place offstage, almost no commentator on the play remembers the murder of the Clown.

9. Quinney, "Enter a Messenger," 165; see also Martha Tuck Rozett, who finds Cleopatra's treatment of the messenger "predictable" ("The Comic Structures of Tragic Endings," *Shakespeare Quarterly* 36 [Summer 1985]: 164). Similarly, the most extreme violence practiced on a messenger in the canon, Saturninus's summary execution of the unfortunate Clown the Andronici have sent to him as a messenger, merely confirms the tyranny we have already learned to expect from the emperor.

10. Suggestions by such critics as Laura Severt King that the messenger's description of Octavia is accurate seem questionable ("Blessed when they were riggish: Shakespeare's Cleopatra and Christianity's penitent prostitutes," *Journal of Medieval and Renaissance Studies* 22:3 [Fall 1992]: 446). Carol Thomas Neely suggests that the term "caricature" is appropriate (*Broken Nuptials*, 144); see also Adelman, *Common Liar*, 36–37. Keith Rinehart maintains that Queen Elizabeth was "clearly the model" for this scene, citing her 1564 questioning of Scottish ambassador Sir James Melville regarding the attributes of Mary Queen of Scots ("Shakespeare's Cleopatra and England's Elizabeth," *Shakespeare Quarterly* 23 [Winter 1972]: 81–83).

11. For a description of some of the subtleties to be found in Montjoy's character, see Gary Taylor's "Introduction" to his edition *Henry V* (The Oxford Shakespeare [Oxford: Clarendon Press, 1982], 59–60). For a discussion of the messages in this play, see Joseph A. Porter, *The Drama of Speech Acts: Shakespeare's Lancastrian Tetralogy* (Berkeley: University of California Press, 1979), 125–35.

12. Pleas of ignorance are not limited to messengers who bring written infor-

mation, however; the messenger who orally reports the arrest of Rivers, Grey, and Vaughan denies knowing why they have been imprisoned (*Richard III* 2.4.46–48). Since the imprisonment is presumably the worst of his news, it may be that his ignorance is real, although it is also possible that we are to infer that he realizes that the prisoners are innocent but fears to state this knowledge openly.

13. Cleopatra, who like Northumberland receives bad news from a messenger and makes an unsuccessful attempt to bribe him to change his story, makes a similar comment on those who deliver unwelcome news: "Though it be honest, it is never good / To bring bad news. Give to a gracious message / An host of tongues, but let ill tidings tell / Themselves when they be felt" (*Antony* 2.5.86–89).

14. An exception to the rule that Shakespeare's messengers never lie (but see note 20), according to Nevill Coghill, is the Doctor who appears in *Macbeth* 4.3 to announce to Malcolm and Macduff that Edward the Confessor is about to appear, although the king never does so. Coghill, however, attributes this "pointless Doctor with his lying announcement" to a cut in a scene that originally did contain an appearance by the Confessor ("*Macbeth* at The Globe, 1606–1616(?): Three Questions," in *The Triple Bond: Plays, Mainly Shakespearean, in Performance*, ed. Joseph G. Price [University Park: Pennsylvania State University Press, 1975], 231).

15. In discussing "Cesario," Berry points out another problem encountered by some messengers—maintaining their social standing while performing their service function: "Viola/Cesario is shocked at Olivia's attempt to tip her, 'I am no fee'd post, lady, keep your purse' (1.5.268), a gaffe that confuses a Duke's Messenger with a postboy" (*Shakespeare and Social Class*, 73). David Schalkwyk comments on a more unusual problem Viola encounters: "It is perfectly in order for Cesario to articulate Orsino's desires, but the beloved cannot be replaced by a similar understudy. To address the petition to a substitute, the substitute her/himself suggests, would be to 'cast away' the 'speech,' to waste both labor and spirit. It is for this reason, to create the very condition of possibility of her 'penn'd' and 'con[ned]' speech, that Viola maneuvers Olivia into revealing her face" (" 'She never told her love': Embodiment, Textuality, and Silence in Shakespeare's Sonnets and Plays," *Shakespeare Quarterly* 45 [Winter 1994]: 390).

16. Messengers sometimes add praise, rather than blame, to their messages, although such praise often concerns someone not present and is not always appreciated by characters who are present. The messenger who not only reports the arrival of Bassanio's "ambassador of love" but extravagantly praises him is merely laughed at by Portia—who, nevertheless, expresses eagerness to see "Quick Cupid's post that comes so mannerly" (*Merchant* 2.9.85–100). However, the messenger who reports the arrival of Florizel and Perdita to Leontes' court, and who adds to his message his opinion that Perdita's beauty is unequaled, earns a rebuke from Paulina (*Winter's Tale* 5.1.85–112). The messenger who tells the tribunes that they "are sent for to the Capitol" adds considerable information about Coriolanus and the enthusiastic reception that he has received, which is also unlikely to be welcomed by Brutus and Sicinius, although it only confirms what they already know (*Coriolanus* 2.1.259–67).

17. As Virginia Mason Vaughan notes, "This is a judgment on England's peers. Rather than trusting the action to prod the audience into this sentiment, however, the dramatist announces the message. When the moral comes from

a nameless character who immediately disappears, it almost seems as if delivered from on high" ("Between Tetralogies: *King John* as Transition," *Shakespeare Quarterly* 35 [Winter 1984]: 410). Holmes argues that this speech proves that its speaker is "no subordinate" (*Shakespeare and His Players*, 59); of course, he also argues that Cleopatra's reference to "the merchandise which thou hast brought from Rome" (2.5.106) proves that the messenger to whom it is addressed is a "trader" (74). This speech is presumably an example of the "imperious manner" that Beckerman finds characteristic of the "formal messenger," but to suggest that this "forthrightness of expression" is a trait found in all or most such messengers is an oversimplification (*Shakespeare at the Globe*, 206).

18. However, given the tendency of the messengers early in the play to criticize the behavior of the upper classes, one must question the certainty of editors who convert the Folio's "Second Messenger" in act 4, scene 3 to Sir William Lucy, so that an upper-class character comments on "the vulture of sedition." While Lucy might be the speaker, there is no textual evidence that he is, since the Duke of York's "Lucy, farewell" (43) only indicates that Lucy is present, not that he has been speaking.

19. See, for example, Derek Cohen, who maintains that Shakespeare generally represents the poor as possessed of every negative quality, including stupidity, whereas the upper classes are depicted as having both admirable and discreditable members, although he later astutely notes that "political stability . . . and moral direction" are usually lacking in the privileged characters of *2 Henry VI*, the only history play he discusses at length. (*Politics of Shakespeare*, 55, 60).

20. Mrs. Quickly, of course, is one of Shakespeare's rare messengers who actually tells lies. Although Elizabeth Pittenger refers to Quickly as "this servant of many" ("Dispatch Quickly: The Mechanical Reproduction of Pages," *Shakespeare Quarterly* 42 [Winter 1991]: 391), it seems clear that Shakespeare is depicting Quickly as an ostensible servant who is almost entirely out for herself. On the other hand, Taylor finds "her report of Falstaff's death perhaps the most moving and most widely acclaimed messenger speech in the canon" ("Introduction," 64), although it can certainly be argued that the Quicklys of these two plays are so different as to amount to distinct characters.

21. Kenneth Muir, ed. *Macbeth* (The Arden Shakespeare [1951; repr., London: Methuen, 1980]), 4.2.64–72 n.

22. Katherine A. Rowe, on the other hand, concentrates on the messenger's personal rather than social reaction, suggesting that "the messenger who returns [Titus's] hand to the stage construes it as a *memento mori*" ("Dismembering and Forgetting in *Titus Andronicus*," *Shakespeare Quarterly* 45 [Fall 1994]: 290). Another compassionate messenger is the one who brings the news of the Duke of York's death to York's sons: he expresses admiration for York (whom he refers to as Hector and Hercules) and grief for his death, refers to York as "my loving lord," and says that the dead man's head set on the gates of the city of York is "the saddest spectacle that e'er I viewed" (*3 Henry VI* 2.1.45–67).

23. Tennenhouse, *Power on Display*, 39.

24. As Alvin Kernan notes, "no playwright or player was actually mutilated or hanged in James's time for what he had written or performed on stage, and portrayals of corrupt courts and evil rulers seem to have been acceptable so long as they avoided treating particular policies, prominent courtiers, or the

Scots who were the close companions of James I" (*Shakespeare, the King's Playwright*, 16; see also 96; and Gurr, *Shakespearian Playing Companies*, 35, 290); or, as Robert Greene advised, "thou hast a libertie to reprooue all, and name none; for one being spoken to, all are offended; none being blamed no man is iniured" (*Greenes Groatsworth of Witte, bought with a million of Repentence*, 1592; repr., Bodley Head Quartos, ed. G. B. Harrison [London: John Lane, 1923], 45). On the other hand, in 1632 the then Master of the Revels, Sir Henry Herbert, commented on James Shirley's play *The Ball:* "there were divers personated so naturally, both of lords and others of the court, that I took it ill, and would have forbidden the play, but that [the players' company representative Christopher] Beeston promised many things which I found fault withal should be left out and that he would not suffer it to be done by the poet any more, who deserves to be punished" (quoted in Bentley, *Profession of Player*, 161–62). As David Bevington points out, "Personal libel against men in authority was viewed as a danger to the state" (*Tudor Drama and Politics: A Critical Approach to Topical Meaning* [Cambridge, MA: Harvard University Press, 1968], 12). For further contemporary objections to and restrictions on players dealing with contemporary events or living persons, see Bradbrook, "The Triple Bond: Audience, Actors, Author in the Elizabethan Playhouse," in *The Triple Bond*, 51; and Harrison, *Last Elizabethan Journal*, 180, 341 n. 12th May.

CHAPTER 8. "'TIS PROPER I OBEY HIM . . ."

1. E. Nesbit explains this ideal in a dialogue between a father and son:

> *Son.* . . . I pray you shew me since the son of God hath said, that *no man can serue two masters*, how I can serue both God and *Cesar?*
> *Father.* My *sonne*, as the souldiour may at one time, in the same seruice fulfill his dutie both to the *Captaine* of his band, and to the *Generall* of the field (the one of them beeing not diuided from the other, but deputed by the other) so the subiect may in his whole life serue his *Caesar*, and the *King* of kings, because *Caesar* hath not (though the Poet sung so) *commaund* diuided with God : but (for the Scriptures teach so) *deputed* of God.
>
> (*Caesar's Dialogve*, 5)

2. On the multiple authorities and allegiances that could create conflicts of service, see Mark Thornton Burnett, *Masters and Servants*, 70–73; Ruth Kelso, *The Doctrine of the English Gentleman in the Sixteenth Century, with a Bibliographical List of Treatises on the Gentleman and Related Subjects Published in Europe to 1625* (1929; repr., Gloucester, MA: P. Smith, 1964), 99; and Orlin, *Elizabethan Households*, 45–46.

3. The question is sometimes raised in conduct books and other writing, but it never seems to be seriously explored, merely closed off by a declaration that obedience to God is paramount. Nesbit's brief "discussion" is typical:

> *Sonne.* But what if the vngodly Prince commaund mee to doe that which is wicked and vngodly?
> *Father.* First bee sure that thou beest not mis-led either by those whom *Paul* and *Iude* describe, nor by such to whom Christ himselfe doth denounce a woe, and hereof being truly assured by the constant Harmonie, not priuate interpretation of that,

which thou oughtest to account a *Lanterne vnto thy feete, and a light vnto thy pathes*, Resolue with Saint *Peter*, we ought rather to obey God then men.

(Caesar's Dialogve, 48–49)

4. Burnett states that "Peter is a comic figure who mistakes a 'usurer' (I.iii.30) for a usurper: he is also a threatening force whose act of 'petty treason' (the murder of a master by a servant) is left neatly unresolved" (*Masters and Servants*, 21). Craig A. Bernthal asserts that "The episode suggests that . . . what appears to be a celebration of the containment of treason may have been, at least for some of the audience, an unsettling examination of ambiguous loyalties and questionable heroism" ("Treason in the Family," 54).

5. Of course, not all critics agree that the audience should identify with power simply because the text may seem to do so. Margot Heinemann quotes Brecht: "'What you cannot have is the audience, including those who happen to be servants themselves, taking Lear's side to such an extent that they applaud when a servant gets beaten for carrying out his mistress' orders, as happens in Act I Scene 4'" and quotes the *Messingkauf Dialogues*: "'Thus to emphasise Lear's tyranny, Oswald could be made to stagger out after Kent has beaten him "with every sign of having been hurt"'" (trans. John Willett [London: Methuen, 1977], 62) ("How Brecht Read Shakespeare," 216).

6. Brakenbury's principal concern is to avoid responsibility, although his private attempt to do so—"I will not reason what is meant hereby, / Because I will be guiltless from the meaning" (1.4.93–94)—only indicates that he knows exactly what is meant. His public attempt to excuse himself—"I'll to the King and signify to him / That thus I have resigned to you my charge"—will not bear scrutiny, since even though it appears that the king sent an order for Clarence's execution, he did not send this one, and the slightest questioning would presumably reveal Richard's involvement (1.4.96–97; 2.1.87).

7. Whether to serve one's master or one's mistress must have been a common dilemma for many servants. Orlin comments, "Everyone had difficulty drawing the lines: which activities was the wife to supervise? which purchases? which servants? which servants at some times and not others?" (39). This conflict is also depicted in ballads: the page in "Old Robin of Portingale" reveals his mistress's plot to kill his master (Percy, *Reliques*, 3:55–58); the page in the ballad "Little Musgrave and Lady Barnard," upon hearing the title characters make an assignation, declares, "thoughe I am my ladyes page, / Yet Ime my lord Barnardes manne" and hastens to tell his master of his mistress's proposed affair (ibid., 70–74).

8. *Broken Nuptials*, 137.

9. *Politics of Shakespeare*, 60; see also 65. Michael D. Bristol, on the other hand, thinks that "the speeches of Cade and his followers constitute a powerful political and discursive indiscretion" (*Carnival and Theater*, 89); Bristol does not directly address Cade's expressed desire for absolute power. Ronald Knowles asserts that "ultimately, Cade is an inverted image of authority, both its distorted representative and its grotesque critic," but also states that "In these scenes of the play everything is qualified and compromised by the comic mode of the presentation of Cade" ("The Farce of History: Miracle, Combat, and Rebellion in *2 Henry VI*," in *Patronage, Politics, and Literary Traditions in England, 1558–1658*, ed. Cedric C. Brown [Detroit: Wayne State University Press, 1991], 200, 205).

10. Paul Dean points out that the fate of the man who kills Cade is to be taken

into service: "[Alexander Iden] cannot shut himself away from the political tug-of-war, but must bear Cade's body to the King and (unlike George a Greene) accept a knighthood and be taken into the King's service (V.i.64–82). This prompts the reflection that Iden's situation in the garden and Henry [VI]'s in the park are parallel: both are men who thought to escape the exigencies of political responsibility but discover that monarchy of the mind is insufficient" ("Shakespeare's *Henry VI* Trilogy and Elizabethan 'Romance' Histories: The Origins of a Genre," *Shakespeare Quarterly* 33 [Spring 1982]: 47–48).

11. It appears that Williams's suspicions are well founded, since after the battle we hear no more talk of brotherhood from Henry, but rather a concern for the nobility: "What prisoners of good sort are taken, uncle?" (4.8.75); Henry also makes distinction among the dead, those "of name" and "all other men" (4.8.102–6). See Stephen Greenblatt, *Shakespearean Negotiations: The Circulation of Social Energy in Renaissance England* (Berkeley: University of California Press, 1988]), 174 n. 59. Lawrence Danson suggests that the scene in which Henry talks to Williams, Bates, Court, and Pistol shows "the effort and the cost" to Henry of being king ("*Henry V:* King, Chorus, and Critics," *Shakespeare Quarterly* 34 [Spring 1983]: 38).

12. Critical interpretation of this episode ranges all over the map. Anne Barton argues that "[Henry's bounty] provides not the ghost of an answer to the questions raised during this particular encounter between common man and king disguised . . . Henry is generous to Williams, but it is a dismissive generosity which places the subject firmly in an inferior position and silences his voice" ("The King Disguised: Shakespeare's *Henry V* and the Comical History," in *The Triple Bond: Plays, Mainly Shakespearean, in Performance*, ed. Joseph G. Price [University Park: Pennsylvania State University Press, 1975], 101). For a similar view, see Paul Dean, "Chronicle and Romance Modes in *Henry V*," *Shakespeare Quarterly* 32 (Spring 1981): 23–24. Brownell Salomon suggests that the enchange of gloves is "a social-bonding ritual" that "symbolizes the reciprocity and mutuality existing between Henry and his men" ("Thematic Contraries and the Dramaturgy of *Henry V*," *Shakespeare Quarterly* 31 [Autumn 1980]: 350; see also 352). Janet M. Spencer maintains that "Henry forces Williams to mouth his own representational view of majesty in order to escape martial law for offering violence to the king" ("Princes, Pirates, and Pigs: Criminalizing Wars of Conquest in *Henry V*," *Shakespeare Quarterly* 47 [Summer 1996]: 176). Norman Rabkin asserts that Henry "terrifies Williams" ("Rabbits, Ducks," 293); Dean maintains that Williams is not really frightened (23). Harold C. Goddard argues that the episode shows that Henry "is not an honest man" (*The Meaning of Shakespeare*, 2 vols. [1951; repr., Chicago: University of Chicago Press, 1965] 1:252), whereas Joel B. Altman claims that Henry appears godlike ("'Vile Participation': The Amplification of Violence in the Theater of *Henry V*," *Shakespeare Quarterly* 42 [Spring 1991]: 30–31).

13. For a somewhat different reading of this scene, see Burnett, *Masters and Servants*, 85–86. For a discussion of this episode as an example of "virtuous disobedience" representative of radical political thinking, see Strier, "Faithful Servants," 104–33; Judy Kronenfeld, citing Cicero, sees "the servant's act as tyrannicide provoked by emotional pain at witnessing unjust cruelty," but thinks it is in line with less radical Protestant thought (*King Lear*, 163).

14. The plebeians' distrust extends beyond Caius Marcius to the entire senatorial class, which they doubt is serving them at all. In the play's first scene, Menenius seeks to persuade the rebellious citizens that the senators serve the

people as the belly serves the body's other members. Whether he convinces them, we never learn, because Caius Marcius's entrance breaks off the discussion.

15. "*Coriolanus*: The Death of A Political Metaphor," *Shakespeare Quarterly* 22 (Summer 1971): 202.

16. "*Coriolanus*: Body Politic and Private Parts," *Shakespeare Quarterly* 41 (Winter 1990): 463; Jagendorf later describes Coriolanus as "this representative of the ruling class, who will serve Rome only as a form of self-service" (466).

17. The kindly Gonzalo, of course, does not curse the Boatswain, although his prediction that the man will be hanged shows a similar rejection of the Boatswain's theory that deference to social superiors is less important than service that ensures survival. On the "class resentment" in the scene, see Berry, *Shakespeare and Social Class*, 180–81. On the Boatswain as declaring "the impotence of hierarchical authority," see Stockholder, "Aspiring Mind," 9. Greenblatt declares that the nobles' "snarling refusal" to work, "far from securing their class superiority, represents them as morally beneath the level of the common seamen" (*Shakespearean Negotiations*, 156); see also Cox, *Shakespeare and the Dramaturgy*, 194–95. On the "cheerful, sturdy, independent" (not to say "jaunty and impudent") attitude of "Shakespeare's common people," see Harbage, *Rival Traditions*, 182.

18. "'Treason doth never prosper,'" 10. R. Morison explains how skillful people doing good service conduce to the general good: "A comon welthe is then welthy and worthy his name, when euery one is content with his degree, gladde to do that, that he may lawfully doo, gladder to do that, whiche he seeth shalbe for the quietnes of the realme, all be it his priuate profyte biddeth hym doo the contrary. The shypman sayleth for other mens profyt, as moche as for his owne, but yet he sturreth the sterne, and turneth the sayle as hym lusteth, he castethe the shote anker, when he wyll, and not when they bydde hym, that are in his shyp. The phisition is called to do more good to other, then to hym selfe, and in dede oftymes he saueth the sycke, and taketh the disease hym selfe, but yet he dieteth his pacient, not as the paciente desyreth, but some tyme kepethe hym from meate, when he is hungry, some tyme from drynke, when he is ful thursty, seldom geuynge hym that he calleth for. Gouernours in a comune welthe, muste loke to the comons proftye, but they muste rule, or elles howe can they gouerne?" (*Remedy for Sedition*, A4ʳ–A4ᵛ).

19. P. 75. Fiona Shaw and Juliet Stevenson suggest that Shakespeare's female friends almost invariably cross age and class boundaries: "[Shakespeare] writes of female friendship, but rarely between women of the same age and status" ("Celia and Rosalind," 56).

20. Something similar happens in *Merry Wives*: although Mrs. Quickly is not actually Anne Page's servant, she is performing services for her (as well as for several other characters in the play). Mrs. Quickly's attempts to serve all of Anne's suitors or the characters who are supporting their suits make her at least potentially disloyal to Anne, who is committed to Fenton. However, in both her case and that of Juliet's Nurse, it may be the older woman's loyalty to her own interests that is the primary barrier to faithful service to her young mistress.

21. See Catherine Belsey, *The Subject of Tragedy: Identity and Difference in Renaissance Drama* (London: Methuen, 1985), 165–71; Gouge, *Of Domesticall Duties*, 636, 650; Guazzo, *civile Conversation*, 174ʳ; Suzanne W. Hull, *Chaste, Silent & Obedient: English Books for Women 1475–1640* (San Marino,

CA: Huntington Library, 1982), 6, 47, 51–55, 82, 117–18, 141; Neely, *Broken Nuptials*, 2, 19; and Vaughan, P7ᵛ–P8ʳ.

22. See Amussen, *Ordered Society*, 35–38; Heinrich Bullinger, *The Christian state of Matrimony* (trans. Miles Coverdale [London, 1575]), F82ʳ; Gouge, 595–96, 641, 642; Greenblatt, *Renaissance Self-Fashioning*, 89; Hull, *Chaste, Silent & Obedient*, 209; Nesbit, *Caesar's Dialogve*, 23; and W[illiam] Perkins, *Christian Oeconomie*, 156. The most famous statement of this idea in Shakespeare is, of course, Katherine's speech at the end of *The Taming of the Shrew* (5.2.140–83), but see also *The Merchant of Venice* 3.2.157–71.

23. For an overview of early modern writing on what Strier terms "obedience to the wicked," see "Faithful Servants," 104–10. Although Gouge is not alone in declaring that "the *Obedience which servants yeeld to their master must be such as may stand with their obedience to Christ*" (637), that flat statement tends to be the limit of discussion for writers of educational works. No explanation is provided; no examples are given. It is left to writers of entertainments, like Shakespeare, to explore what it means for servants to have to deal with conflicting services. See also Nesbit, *Caesar's Dialogve*, 48–49, and W[illiam] Perkins, *Christian Oeconomie*, 153–54.

24. Although some critics have made much of Olivia's "I would not have him miscarry for the half of my dowry" (3.4.64–65), this should perhaps be considered an automatic response by a generous mistress toward an ailing servant rather than a mark of special regard, particularly given her failure to inquire after him until the final scene, when she remarks, "A most extracting frenzy of mine own / From my remembrance clearly banished his" (5.1.281–82).

25. Ralph Berry suggests Maria's probable background, which may suggest why she would be willing to marry even so unpromising a knight as Sir Toby: "She is on the border of upstairs and downstairs, my lady's gentlewoman. To the Elizabethans, this would signify an established pattern. The daughter of a gentleman who lacked dowry potential would find her best social chances in the great house. There she would be protected, given the opportunity to meet suitable young gentlemen, and enabled to see something of the world. Her duties would be those of lady-in-waiting" (*Shakespeare and Social Class*, 70); Berry also notes that Toby refers to Maria as "My lady's chambermaid" (1.3.47), which he points out could mean "'lady-in-waiting,'" "'lady's maid,'" or "'female servant'" (70). However, Olivia refers to her as "my gentlewoman" (1.5.160), and there seems little reason to think that Maria's position in the house is not a comparatively privileged one, though still one of service, and subject, of course, to Malvolio. Jessica Tvordi, however, asserts that Maria is involved in a homoerotic alliance with Olivia and that they "jointly run a household in which all male characters are figured as subordinate to them" ("Female Alliance and the Construction of Homoeroticism in *As You Like It* and *Twelfth Night*," in *Maids and Mistresses, Cousins and Queens: Women's Alliances in Early Modern England*, ed. Susan Frye and Karen Robertson [New York: Oxford University Press, 1999], 122). See also Burnett, *Masters and Servants*, 142; Angela Hurworth, "Gulls, Cony-Catchers and Cozeners: *Twelfth Night* and the Elizabethan Underworld," *Shakespeare Survey* 52 (1999): 122–23; and Richard A. Levin, *Love and Society*, 25, 118. However, Hurworth's suggestion that what motivates Maria is "innocent enjoyment of a ridiculous spectacle" (131) seems to overlook Maria's cold-blooded response to Sir Toby's expressed fear that their trick will truly drive Malvolio mad: "The house will be the quieter" (3.4.136).

26. Berry, *Shakespeare and Social Class*, xviii–xix.

27. Borachio's early suggestion that he will arrange for Don Pedro and Claudio to "hear Margaret term [Borachio] Claudio" (2.2.42) makes no sense and is not mentioned again. M. C. Bradbrook explains that Margaret intends to engage in a "court game" or "masquerade," but notes that "It would not help the plot to hear Margaret call [Borachio] Claudio" and concludes that "the whole point is left extremely vague" (*Shakespeare and Elizabethan Poetry*, 266–67, n. 20). Morriss Henry Partee points out the implausibility of much of the plot against Hero, noting that "Margaret in particular remains an enigma" ("The Comic Equilibrium of *Much Ado About Nothing*," *The Upstart Crow* 12 [1992]: 67–69, 69). For a psychoanalytic explanation of this passage, see Janice Hays, "Those 'soft and delicate desires': *Much Ado* and the Distrust of Women," in *The Woman's Part: Feminist Criticism of Shakespeare*, ed. Carolyn Ruth Swift Lenz, Gayle Greene, and Carol Thomas Neely (Urbana: University of Illinois Press, 1980), 86–87, 97 n. 18. For an interpretation that sees a possibly treacherous Margaret as part of the play's "dark background," see Levin, *Love and Society*, 113–15, 115.

28. Although Margaret and Borachio are not married at the end of *Much Ado*, Margaret is apparently not going to be punished, which seems to call into question Harry Berger, Jr.'s statement that "the regnant ideology of the play . . . is that women are responsible for their sins but men are not" ("Against the Sink-a-Pace: Sexual and Family Politics in *Much Ado About Nothing*," *Shakespeare Quarterly* 33 [Autumn 1982]: 307); perhaps the ideology is different for servants. The play offers no suggestion that Borachio is going to be punished severely and it seems not impossible that a reformed Borachio, whose repentance appears at least as sincere as Claudio's, might not be welcomed, or at least accepted, into the community at the end of the play. This seems to be what John A. Allen is suggesting when he rather slangily comments that Borachio "shows distinct signs of going straight after he has been caught red-handed in his dirty work" ("Dogberry," 37).

29. Berry, *Shakespeare and Social Class*, xviii. Carole McKewin refers to Margaret as a "trouble-maker" and describes "the counter-universe of women in *Much Ado about Nothing*" as "an uncomfortable landscape . . . where waiting women, impatient with keeping below stairs (v.ii.9), are not allies of their mistresses, but treacherous, if unwitting, imposters at midnight windows" ("Counsels of Gall and Grace: Intimate Conversations between Women in Shakespeare's Plays," in *The Woman's Part*, 124, 125–26). See also Burnett, *Masters and Servants*, 140–42.

30. Margaret cannot, in these lines, be referring only to sex, since that would not guarantee her release from service.

31. Neely defines Emilia as "dramatically and symbolically the play's fulcrum," adding that "Emilia, stealing (*sic*) the handkerchief, is the catalyst for the play's crisis; revealing its theft, she is the catalyst for the play's denouement" ("Women and Men," 211–39, 213, 231). However, as Caroline Patey points out, "it is interesting to note how Shakespeare has manipulated his source for [*Othello*]; the handkerchief which provides the reason for so many bloody consequences is deliberately stolen in the *Hecatommithi*, whereas in *Othello* it is originally lost by Desdemona, and Shakespeare makes sure that we understand that Iago's repeated intentions to steal it had long been defeated . . . (III.iii.296, 314–15)" ("Beyond Aristotle: Giraldi Cinzio and Shakespeare," in *Italy and the English Renaissance*, ed. Sergio Rossi and Dianella Savoia [Milan: Edizioni Unicopli, 1989], 179–80).

32. Greenblatt, 244. Greenblatt adds: "As Gabrielle Jackson pointed out to me, Emilia feels that she must explain her refusal to observe her husband's commands to be silent and go home:

> Good gentlemen, let me have leave to speak,
> 'Tis proper I obey him but not now:
> Perchance, Iago, I will ne'er go home.
>
> (5.2.196–98)

"The moment is felt as a liberating gesture and redeems her earlier, compliant theft of the handkerchief, but it is both too late and fatal. The play does not hold out the wife's disobedience as a way of averting tragedy" (302 n. 40). See also Andreas Mahler, "Italian Vices: Cross-Cultural Constructions of Temptation and Desire in English Renaissance Drama," in *Shakespeare's Italy: Functions of Italian Locations in Renaissance Drama*, ed. Michele Marrapodi, et al. (New York: Manchester University Press, 1993), 64.

33. Neely, "Women and Men," 232. Neely also notes that "Othello chooses Iago's friendship over Desdemona's love temporarily and unwittingly; Emilia's choice of Desdemona over Iago is voluntary and final" (225). On Emilia's "virtuous repudiation of patriarchal authority" (27), see Neill, "'Servile Ministers,'" 25–27. For a discussion of Emilia's insistance upon speaking the truth at all costs as an interrogation of the period's conventions for women's behavior, see Orlin, *Private Matters*, 226–28; see also Dolan, *Dangerous Familiars*, 115; and Elizabeth Wiley, "The Status of Women in *Othello*," in *Shakespeare: Text, Subtext, and Context*, ed. Ronald Dotterer (Selinsgrove, PA: Susquehanna University Press, 1989), 132–35.

34. The Emilia we see in the final scene is difficult to reconcile with Cox's insistence that "[Shakespeare's] most serious characters are invariably those with the greatest social prestige" (*Shakespeare and the Dramaturgy*, 67). Nina Rulon-Miller's description, "Emilia is a woman co-opted into patriarchy who will betray her beloved mistress to please her husband" ("*Othello*'s Bianca: Climbing Out of the Bed of Patriarchy," *The Upstart Crow* 15 [1995]: 110), also seems something of an over-simplification. Douglas E. Green, on the contrary, argues that "Emilia overturns the patriarchal power to which even in dying Desdemona submits" ("Staging the Evidence: Shakespeare's Theatrical Revengers," *The Upstart Crow* 12 [1992]: 35).

CHAPTER 9. "EVERY GOOD SERVANT . . ."

1. Richard Strier notes that this issue is raised, but not fully developed, in Baldassare Castiglione's *The Book of the Courtier* and Sir Thomas More's *Utopia* (*Resistant Structures*, 167–69). On the other hand, the author of a popular ballad was quite straightforward about the issue:

> If thou serve a lord of prise,
> Be not too boistous in thine servise:
> Damne not thine soule in none wise,
> For servise is non heritage. . . .
> Than serve we God in alle wise:
> He shall us quiten our servise,

And yeven us yiftes most of prise,
Hevene to ben our heritage.

Quoted in R. T. Davies, ed., *Medieval English Lyrics: A Critical Anthology* (n.p.: Northwestern University Press, 1964), 154–55. Davies dates the song "Earlier 15th c."; see his note, p. 334.

2. Strier, "Faithful Servants," 104–33; much of the material in this essay reappears in Strier's *Resistant Structures*, Essay 7, "Impossible Radicalism II: Shakespeare and Disobedience" (165–202). Although I generally agree with what Strier says about "virtuous disobedience" in *Lear* and the romances, and in the few earlier plays he mentions, such as *Hamlet, Richard III,* and *King John,* it seems to me that virtuous disobedience is considerably more common in Shakespeare's plays than Strier suggests and that the ideal of service Shakespeare represents often goes beyond a concern with "corrupt and corruption-inducing authority" (176).

3. Charles Wells observes, "Often Shakespearean servants are given orders which, if carried out, would violate the dictates of conscience," mentioning Leontes ordering Antigonus to throw Perdita in the fire (*Winter's Tale*), Pisanio being ordered first to betray Posthumus and then to kill Imogen (*Cymbeline*), and Clitus, Dardanius, and Volumnius's refusal to kill Brutus (*Caesar*) (*Wide Arch*, 145). Carol Thomas Neely notes that in the romances, "The murderous impulses of rulers and others are deflected by good servants who (unlike [Thaliard], who tries to murder Pericles lest he himself be murdered by his master, Antiochus) speak out against tyranny and, when deputized to do violence, mitigate its force" (*Broken Nuptials*, 187). Disobedience, of course, is not the only way to demonstrate servants' moral superiority to their employers. As Judy Z. Kronenfeld points out, Shakespeare depicts Corin in *As You Like It* as being more virtuous than his original master ("Social Rank," 344).

4. E. Nesbit, *Caesar's Dialogve*, 5. Similarly, William Gouge writes that "servants in performing duty to their master performe duty to Christ, and in rebelling against their master they rebell against Christ" (*Of Domesticall Duties*, 641).

5. Bullinger, *Christian state of Matrimony*, 82ʳ.

6. Ling, *Politeuphuia. Wits Commonwealth* (London, 1608), 118ʳ; 119ʳ. See also Greenblatt, *Renaissance Self-Fashioning*, 92, 272 n. 43; and Orlin, *Private Matters*, 116–17.

7. Gouge, *Of Domesticall Duties*, 636, 637. Robert Crowley expresses a similar view:

> But if thy maister be wicked,
> And would haue the do wickedlie,
> Then se that thy fayth be pitched
> On thy Lord God most constantly.
>   Call to thy mynde good Daniel,
> Who serued his prince fayethfully,
> Notwythstandynge he was cruel,
> And eke his Lorde Gods enemy.
>   Serue him trulye, I say, for why
> God hath bade that thou shouldest do so;
> But do thou nothinge wickedly,
>   Neyther for wel nor yet for wo.
> ("The Voyce of the laste trumpet . . . : The Seruauntes Lesson," 61)

8. W[illiam] Perkins, *Christian Oeconomie*, 153–54.

9. Christopher Goodman, *How Superior Powers O[u]ght to be Obeyd of their subjects: and wherin they may lawfully by Gods Worde be disobeyed and resisted* (1558; repr., Amsterdam: Theatrum Orbis Terrarum, 1972), 117–18; see also Roper, *Mirrour of Vertue*, 79–81.

10. In fact, these are comparatively rare words in the canon and are generally used in contexts that would hardly threaten established authority. "Disobedience" is used of the Earl of Worcester, in whose eye Henry IV says he sees disobedience; the French, whom Henry VI says will become disobedient if the English disagree among themselves; the Roman plebeians; and Anne Page, Hermia, Hermione, Imogen, and young women who want to remain virgins, with Fenton denying it on Anne's behalf and Hermione on her own (*1 Henry IV* 1.3.16; *1 Henry VI* 4.1.142; *Coriolanus* 3.1.120; *Merry Wives* 5.5.221; *Dream* 1.1.87; *Winter's Tale* 3.2.68; *Cymbeline* 3.4.89; *All's Well* 1.1.139–40). "Disobedient" is used of "appetites," Sylvia, and (twice) Juliet (*Troilus* 2.2.182; *T.G.V.* 3.1.69; *Romeo* 3.5.160; 4.2.18). "Disobey" is used three times, each time as a suggestion of something that would never be done (*1 Henry VI* 5.4.170; *Henry V* 4.1.146; *Tempest* 4.1.77); "disobeys" is used once, by Richard III: "I'll make a corpse of him that disobeys" (*Richard III* 1.2.37). The overall sense is that disobedience is something that almost never occurs except when headstrong young women become enamoured of young men their parents consider unsuitable. Given all of the actual disobedience in Shakespeare's plays—including disobedience by servants—it seems unlikely to be coincidental that these words are almost invariably used only in comparatively benign contexts.

11. *Subject of Tragedy*, 111.

12. While Strier points out that Martin Luther drew a distinction between resistance to evil commands, which he condemned as rebellious, and nonobedience, which "led to the glory of martyrdom" (*Resistant Structures*, 170), Shakespeare's characters generally seem uninterested in such a distinction. They tend to be actively disobedient and show no interest in winning the martyr's crown. The exception might seem to be Camillo, who refuses to obey Leontes' command to poison Polixenes, but Camillo not only flees, but warns Polixenes, both resistant, though perfectly virtuous, actions. See also Belsey, *Subject of Tragedy*, 110–11.

13. Marshall, *English Domestic Servant*, 27.

14. Gouge, *Of Domesticall Duties*, 638–39.

15. The issue of the Provost's disobedience becomes somewhat clouded in the final scene when the Duke dismisses him for ostensibly obeying Angelo's order because it came by "private message" rather than "special warrant" (5.1.453–57). Since the Provost is reluctant to execute Claudio, it is somewhat surprising that he does not raise this point himself when the order arrives. Whatever the legalities are supposed to be, the conversations between the Duke and the Provost at 5.1.458–65 and 474–85 raise puzzling questions. It would seem that, as soon as the Duke's identity is revealed, the Provost must know he is out of trouble, since it was the disguised Duke who persuaded him to deceive the deputy and save Claudio, yet the Provost tries to excuse his behavior. Either this is a prearranged skit between the Duke and the Provost, which raises the question of whether we are to believe that the Provost knows of the Duke's identity before its public revelation, or we must accept that the Provost recognizes what the Duke is up to and plays along in an inspired fashion, in which case it seems odd that such an intelligent man has not earlier been given a "worthier place."

16. Joan Ozark Holmer discusses Shakespeare's expansion of Balthasar's role, but also finds that "the partial abandonment of Romeo by the fearfully obedient Balthasar" is a partial cause of the play's ultimate tragedy ("No 'Vaine Fantasy': Shakespeare's Refashioning of Nashe for Dreams and Queen Mab," in Shakespeare's "Romeo and Juliet": Texts, Contexts, and Interpretation, ed. Jay L. Halio [Newark: University of Delaware Press, 1995], 62).

17. On how the choice of allegiances in the play establishes the characters as functioning in "a moral universe," see Judiana Lawrence, "Natural Bonds and Artistic Coherence in the Ending of Cymbeline," Shakespeare Quarterly 35 (Winter 1984): 446.

18. Virginia Mason Vaughan states that "Hubert is . . . divided between his affection for Arthur and his loyalty to John. The Bastard is torn too, choosing John's cause only after Hubert's assurance that the boy has not been murdered" ("Between Tetralogies," 418).

19. An even worse world and a much worse king and master can be viewed as inspiring virtuous disobedience among some of the characters in Richard III; however, even apart from the fact that Richard's power is illegitimate, most of the characters who attempt to take action against him—including Queen Elizabeth, Buckingham, and Stanley—seem motivated more by fear for themselves and their families than by any desire to do good service. Margaret, who can only curse Richard, is fueled by anger and hatred, and Hastings, who might seem to be the exception, opposes Richard because he refuses to see injustice done to the boys he calls "my master's heirs" (3.2.54); rather than virtuous disobedience toward Richard, therefore, Hastings's actions are motivated by loyalty toward the late King Edward IV and his sons.

20. Sharon Beehler sees the dying Desdemona as "turning over her voice to Emilia," even though she also notes that Othello "has no incentive to regard Emilia, unlike Desdemona, as the 'cunning whore of Venice;' Emilia is an unknown factor, one which must be understood as speaking a different language, a language whose openness must be allowed" ("'An Enemy in Their Mouths': The Closure of Language in Othello," The Upstart Crow 10 [1990]: 82).

21. In addition to Strier, see Allgaier, "Is King Lear Antiauthoritarian," 1033–39; Barish and Waingrow, "'Service' in King Lear," 347–55; Graham, "'Without the form,'" 456–57; and Walter S. H. Lim, "James I, the Royal Prerogative, and the Politics of Authority in Shakespeare's The Winter's Tale," The Upstart Crow 21 (2001): 32. Lim also discusses Paulina at length.

22. Strier discusses a number of political and religious tracts by such writers as Christopher Goodman, John Ponet, and George Buchanan, "to demonstrate that in both versions of King Lear Shakespeare dramatized and espoused the most radical of these ideas [about justifiable disobedience]," that "Lear [is] the culmination of a development in Shakespeare's political thinking from a focus on the problem of order to a focus on the problem of corrupt (and corruption-inducing) authority," and that "After Lear, in the Romances . . . the distinction between virtuous disobedience and improper loyalty becomes axiomatic for Shakespeare—something he believes" (Resistant Structures, 176, 177). Although there are certainly parallels, I'm not sure that it is absolutely necessary to find precedent for Shakespeare's praise of disobedience by servants in political writers, since the ideas are also present, if not fully explored, in religious tracts, ballads, and other popular literature. In contrast to Strier, Richard L. Greaves argues "that Elizabethan Protestants repudiated the ideology of active political resistance and returned to the views espoused in early Tudor En-

gland" ("Concepts of Political Obedience in Late Tudor England: Conflicting Perspectives," *Journal of British Studies* [1980]: 33).

23. "Little Musgrave and Lady Barnard," in Percy, *Reliques*, 3:70–74, lines 105–8. In the ballad "Gil Morrice," John Steward makes a similar statement to his servants after killing his wife and the man he thinks is her lover (ibid., 3:100–103, lines 117–20).

24. *Shakespeare and Social Class*, 111; see also Cohen, *Politics of Shakespeare*, 82–83.

25. Lawrence Stone suggests that, while a young servant's master and mistress might serve in some sense as a surrogate family and help socialize the child, that socialization consisted largely of enforcing the concepts of deference and obedience (*Family, Sex and Marriage*, 27, 118). On Cornwall's nameless servant standing up to his master and mistress, see Burnett, *Masters and Servants*, 85–86. Berry argues that the servant's death is punishment for killing Cornwall, because the servant is a member of Cornwall's family, one whom Cornwall had "bred" (4.2.74), and that Albany's reaction to the news of Cornwall's death proves this (*Shakespeare and Social Class*, 109). However, when Albany addresses the gods—"This shows you are above, / You justicers, that these our nether crimes / So speedily can venge!" (79–81)—he is surely reacting to the news not that one of Cornwall's own servants attacked him, but that Cornwall, who had blinded Gloucester, has died of the wound given him by the servant.

26. *Disowning Knowledge*, 49. Michael Neill argues that "however virtuous Kent's disobedience may seem to us, it nonetheless involves a kind of sacrilege for which the play will require him to do penance" ("'Servile Ministers,'" 34–35). Although I agree with Neill (and with several of *Lear*'s characters) that service in the play is a sacred duty, I think that service is conceived of as more than obedience to royal authority; Kent both disobeys and suffers in the name of service, but he does not appear penitent and I do not think we are supposed to see him as having sinned.

27. Although Robert S. Miola comments that "the faithful steward . . . speaks out against the riotous indulgence," he parallels the Steward with Apemantus as protesters against "the moral decadence of the entire feast" rather than foregrounding the Steward's concern for Timon's well-being ("Timon in Shakespeare's Athens," 24). H. J. Oliver also links the Steward with Apemantus as the two characters in the play who cannot be bought ("Introduction" to the Arden edition [1959], l). D. Douglas Waters, however, sees the Steward and Alcibiades as parallel in their love for Timon ("Shakespeare's *Timon of Athens* and Catharsis," *The Upstart Crow* 8 [1988]: 99). See also Anne Lancashire, "*Timon of Athens*: Shakespeare's *Dr. Faustus*," *Shakespeare Quarterly* 21 (Winter 1970): 38–39; and William O. Scott, "The Paradox of Timon's Self-Cursing," *Shakespeare Quarterly* 35 (Autumn 1984): 297–99.

28. Rolf Soellner mentions "The plain but poetic eloquence of the servant Flaminius [which] shows up the commonplace vulgarity of Lucullus," adding that "The [nameless third] servant's concluding comment on the refined villainy of Sempronius is even stronger in its recoil from villainy" (*Timon of Athens: Shakespeare's Pessimistic Tragedy* [Columbus: Ohio State University Press, 1979], 86).

29. "'How fain would I have hated all mankind', Timon cries (IV.iii.503)—but he cannot hate them all, for the Steward stands there to make such hatred impossible. The presence of the Steward among the characters, then, so far from

being the puzzle or contradiction that Chambers found it, is essential to the meaning of the play and expressly forbids us from identifying *our* judgment (or Shakespeare's) with Timon's" (H. J. Oliver, "Introduction," l-li). For a contrasting view, see Cohen, *Politics of Shakespeare*, 97.

30. Timon ultimately acknowledges his Steward's virtue, but he apparently never knows of his other servants' goodness; we, however, do. At 4.2.1–29, Timon's servants regret their master's fall and vow fellowship, even as they part; the Steward shares out his money among them. Clearly these servants are more virtuous than their social "betters": they have sympathy for Timon and for each other, and their lack of avarice is shown not only by the Steward's generosity, but by his apparent need to encourage his fellows to take his money, which they are reluctant to do. As Burnett comments, "In this scene, the steward distributes money in a demonstration of the sound principles that underpin his domestic government. The effect is to bind the servants in an equitable fellowship, a sharp contrast with the material acquisitiveness subscribed to by Titus's parasitical entourage. When they hesitate to accept Flavius's gifts, moreover, the servants display a magnanimity of spirit that recalls the qualities for which their master was originally venerated. Through Flavius, the slow decline of Titus's magisterial reputation is highlighted" (163).

31. The servants in *Timon* are often largely ignored by critics; when attention is paid to them, opinions differ sharply. Cohen classes servants with "slaves . . . beggars, and whores," a group he describes as having little or no importance (*Politics of Shakespeare*, 89). Berry sees the servants as "escaping the play's nihilism" (*Shakespeare and Social Class*, 163). A. D. Nuttall describes the servants as "pathologically loyal," and does not see their presence as influencing the overall effect of the play, which he describes as "purged of all natural relations of affection" (*Timon of Athens*, Twayne's New Critical Introductions to Shakespeare, no. 8 [Boston: Twayne, 1989], 88, xviii). Soellner remarks that "Timon's loyal servants, particularly Flavius, attract some sympathy; but since they have no major part in the action, they have only a limited influence on our moral bearings" (*Timon of Athens*, 83–84).

32. Janet Adelman comments, "Eros kills himself to avoid obeying his master's command; his magnificent disobedience may be seen as a commentary on the disobedience of all the unreliable servants in the play" (*Common Liar*, 47).

33. Cleopatra suggests a somewhat similar view when her attendant Iras precedes her in death. Although Iras has not been disobedient, it is arguably indecorous of her to die before her mistress, and Cleopatra professes a fear that if Iras is the first to meet Antony, "He'll make demand of her, and spend that kiss / Which is my heaven to have"; her first reaction to Iras's death, however—"This proves me base"—is similar to Antony's reaction to Eros's suicide in its suggestion that the servant is superior to the employer.

34. "'But It Appears,'" 12. Siemon later acknowledges that Camillo (in both halves of the play) is "a servant who serves his master's highest interests by betraying him" (13).

35. "The Bear, the Statue, and Hysteria in *The Winter's Tale*," *Shakespeare Quarterly* 34 (Winter 1983): 423.

36. Gillian Murray Kendall argues that Leontes "tells Paulina he will have her burned—but her reply again reveals his impotence. She says 'I care not' (2.3.114), and so, like Barnardine, robs him of authority by refusing to repent, show fear, or in any way connive and assist in the ceremonies of execution or the rituals of power" ("Overkill in Shakespeare," *Shakespeare Quarterly* 43 [Spring 1992]: 45).

37. On Paulina as "the guardian and spiritual therapist of Leontes' conscience," see Stockholder, "Aspiring Mind," 6. Neely has much of interest to say about Paulina, whom she describes as "a chaste nurturer," "mediator," "comic shrew," and "wise counselor" (*Broken Nuptials*, 199).

38. *Resistant Structures*, 165–66.

CHAPTER 10. "DUTY IN HIS SERVICE PERISHING"

1. See, for example, "A Lamentable Ballad of the tragical end of a Gallant Lord and a Vertuous Lady, with the untimely end of their two Children, wickedly performed by a Heathenish Blackamoor their servant: the like never heard of" (although this may be more representative of racism than of class antagonism) (*Roxburghe Ballads*, 2:49–55). In *Arden of Feversham*, Arden's servant Michael participates throughout the play in the plots to kill Arden and finally assists in the murder; the lost play *Page of Plymouth* also apparently depicted servants assisting in the murder of their master. In *The Spanish Tragedy*, Pedringano helps to kill Horatio and murders Serberine, although it could be argued in his defense that he has been threatened with death by Lorenzo. On servants committing murder because of desire for their masters' wives or daughters and resentment of their masters, see Dolan, *Dangerous Familiars*, 40–41. Dolan discusses infanticide and the period's tendency to attribute it to female servants (chapter 4, esp. 159–60), which is particularly appropriate to the Shepherd who finds the abandoned infant Perdita and "can read waiting-gentlewoman in the scape" (*Winter's Tale* 3.3.71), although the criminals who abandon the child are a king and a lord who does his bidding.

2. Philip Gawdy, in a letter to his brother (dated May 12, 1602), reports that "Mr Bowton was kylled wth a knyfe by a little boy my Lord of Canterberryes page being Sr Thomas Wylfordes sonne" (*Letters*, 121). Richard Wilson notes that the leader of the 1596 enclosure rising in the Midlands was one of the Lord Lieutenant's servants, Bartholomew Steer, and that "The nucleus of the rising consisted of servants, who were reputed to be 'kept so like doggs as they would be ready to Cutt their masters' Throates,' and its targets were houses of enclosing gentry such as Elizabeth's favorite, Sir Henry Lee of Woodstock" ("'Like the old Robin Hood': *As You Like It* and the Enclosure Riots," *Shakespeare Quarterly* 43 [Spring 1992]: 2–3). For numerous examples of apprentice disorder and violence in the 1590s, see Mark Thornton Burnett, "Apprentice Literature and the 'Crisis' of the 1590s," in *Patronage, Politics, and Literary Traditions in England, 1558–1658* (ed. Cedric C. Brown [Detroit: Wayne State University Press, 1991]), 54–57. For servingmen and apprentices as beginning or being involved in brawls, riots, and disorders in, outside, or associated with the playhouses, see Cook, *Privileged Playgoers*, 250–51; on similar disturbances not associated with theaters, but also involving apprentices and occasionally other servants, see Cook, 256–58. See also Ashley, *Elizabethan Popular Culture*, 15, and Onat, *Witch of Edmonton*, 274.

3. Although Toby says of Malvolio, "we'll have him in a dark room and bound" (3.4.137–38), it seems unlikely that Malvolio was actually intended to be bound. He is rarely, if ever, bound in performance, and it is hard to see how he could be perceived as being able to write his letter to Olivia if he were bound.

4. Throughout the canon, women who disguise themselves as servants run the risk of becoming objects of a violence they would be unlikely to experience

as upper-class women; as servant-boys, they often run greater risks, although, ironically, they usually don male attire because they fear being preyed on as unaccompanied women (*T.G.V.* 2.7.40–43; *Twelfth Night* 1.2.53–56; *Merchant's* Jessica, who is accompanied by Lorenzo and apparently disguises merely to aid in her escape from Venice, is an exception). Shakespeare, however, never lets any of these women come to serious harm.

5. On the insults exchanged between Peter and the musicians in *Romeo*, see Frank Fabry, "Shakespeare's Witty Musician: *Romeo and Juliet*, IV.v.114–17" (*Shakespeare Quarterly* 33 [Summer 1982]: 182–83).

6. Alexander Neville comments, "Dogges of the same Kennell seldome fight together, except at meate: Seruants of the same Family commonly make a side" (*Norfolkes Furies or A View of Ketts Campe* [1575; trans. Richard Woods (London, 1615)], A3ᵛ). On violence by servants in defense of their masters, see Michael Dalton, *The Countrey Justice, conteyning the practice of the Justices of the Peace out of their Sessions. Gathered for the better helpe of such Justices of Peace as have not beene much conversant in the studie of the Lawes of this Realme* (London, 1618), 178, 222; and Beier, *Masterless Men*, 131. An example occurs in "A new Ballad intituled, The stout Criple of Cornwall, wherein is shewed his dissolute life and deserved death" (*Roxburghe Ballads*, 2:532–35), in which two of Lord Courtney's servants are killed while protecting their master's purse against a gang of highwaymen.

7. It seems odd that Gregory, identified as being "of the house of Capulet" describes Benvolio, a Montague, as "one of my master's kinsmen" (1.1.60–61); perhaps he is to be understood as speaking of the approaching Tybalt, but Tybalt does not enter for another six lines, and it seems more likely that this is simply an error. When Tybalt does enter, he refers to the fighting servants as "heartless hinds" (63). John F. Andrews, the editor of the Everyman Shakespeare, prefers the 1599 Second Quarto spelling, "hartless," because it "more faithfully conveys Tybalt's primary accusation: that Benvolio is taking unfair advantage of the metaphorical equivalent of 'Weaker Vessels' by drawing on Capulet servants at a time when they are undefended by a Capulet master" (68 n.).

8. Holmer, "'Draw,'" 176; Jill L. Levenson, "'*Alla stoccado* carries it away': Codes of Violence in *Romeo and Juliet*," in *Shakespeare's "Romeo and Juliet": Texts, Contexts, and Interpretation*, ed. Jay L. Halio (Newark: University of Delaware Press, 1995), 89–90.

9. Other dramatists also represent servants becoming violent because their employers involve them in their quarrels. In John Ford's *'Tis Pity She's a Whore*, Soranzo orders his servant Vasques to "correct" the gentleman Grimaldi by provoking him to a swordfight (1.2.40–46). In the anonymous *Arden of Feversham*, Alice Arden involves the Ardens' servant Michael in her plot to murder his master. In John Webster's *Duchess of Malfi*, Bosola does the murderous bidding of his masters, the Cardinal and Ferdinand, until he turns on them.

10. Real-life servants were also involved in murders committed by their employers. One of Sir John Fites's men reportedly struck a man named Slanning "on the head from behind, enabling Fites to run Slanning through with his sword" (Orlin, *Private Matters*, 241, quoting *The Bloody Book, or the Tragical End of Sir John Fites (alias) Fitz* [1605]). Servants of the Earl and Countess of Somerset were accused of helping their employers murder Sir Thomas Overbury (Gawdy, *Letters*, 179).

11. For a psychoanalytic reading of Macbeth's murders (with a glance at

Richard III's), see Robert L. Reid, who finds it "tempting to believe that Macbeth is the 'third murderer'" since this would mean that "for the second murder Macbeth both is and is not an active participant, owing to his descent into psychic bifurcation" ("Macbeth's Three Murders: Shakespearean Psychology and Tragic Form," *Renaissance Papers 1991*, ed. George Walton Williams and Barbara J. Baines [Raleigh, NC: Southeastern Renaissance Conference, 1992], 86 n. 21).

Critics do not always make distinctions between killings done in person and those done by hired accomplices; see, for example, R. Chris Hassel, Jr., who writes of Richard III: "He has stabbed a king, butchered two princes, punched another king 'full of holes,' washed a brother to death, killed Rivers, Grey, Vaughan, Hastings, 'wretched *Anne*,' and Buckingham" ("Military Oratory in *Richard III*," *Shakespeare Quarterly* 35 [Spring 1984]: 55). The servants or hired men who actually commit most of these murders seem in this reading to become Richard's invisible tools.

12. Although Titus does his own killing, he may be representing himself as a servant in rebellion, given Alan C. Dessen's suggestion that "for the original audience," Titus's costuming of himself as a cook in the final scene "would have suggested (wrongly) a subservient Titus debasing himself in degree in order best to serve his Emperor and Empress" (*Titus Andronicus* [Manchester, UK: Manchester University Press, 1989], 84).

13. As Homer Swander notes, Pompey's subsequent "death is filled, then, with apparently sufficient irony when it comes at the hands of one of Antony's officers. But the irony is even greater, more complex; for the script raises the possibility that the officer acted exactly as Pompey, earlier, so insists that Menas should have acted: without first telling his superior—in this case, Antony—about it. Antony, however, fails to find such service, as Pompey says *he* would have, 'well done.' Instead, he 'threats the throate' of the man who has thus played out the risks of service in a way that, through contrast, reminds us of Menas—and proves again the near-impossibility of serving 'these great Fellowes'" ("Menas and the Editors: A Folio Script Unscripted," *Shakespeare Quarterly* 36 [Summer 1985]: 186).

14. *Shakespeare at the Globe*, 153.

15. For discussions of violence toward a master or mistress by a servant, see Dalton, *Countrey Justice*, 204–5; Dolan, *Dangerous Familiars*, chapters 1 and 2; Orlin, *Private Matters*, 51, n. 85. Nicholas Ling states, "It is treason against God and man, for the servant to offer violence to his master," suggesting that violence, even if not fatal, was regarded, in at least some quarters, as treasonable (*Politeuphuia. Wits Commonwealth*, 119ʳ). John D. Cox notes that "everyone . . . who possessed a degree of privilege or power [assumed] that the lower classes were unstable, dangerous, and threatening" ("Politics of Stuart Medievalism," 214).

16. See Bernthal, "Treason in the Family," 52; and Knowles, "Farce of History," 198.

17. Bernthal, "Treason in the Family," 53.

18. "The king may see it simply; the audience is more likely to see an irony: it sees the 'right' result produced by oddly circumstantial means, by Horner's incapacity through drink. If this is Providence, it is of a kind difficult to credit, except in the simple mind of this king" (Knowles, "Farce of History," 199); "[Thump] bravely and successfully upholds the social order, unlike Jack Cade" (Suzuki, *Subordinate Subjects*, 64); "Peter Thumpe's ideological function is ap-

parently to prove the divine sanction of Henry VI's kingship—and kingship in general—in that a weakling such as Peter could survive trial by combat only through divine intervention. (It was by this rationale, of course, that Tudor propagandists explained the victory of the 'weak' English fleet over the Armada.) On a less conscious level, however, Thumpe's victory also dramatizes Tudor England's prevailing social nightmare—betrayal to the authorities by friends, servants, family. The story thus tugs the audience in opposite directions: toward satisfaction about the victory of a loyal subject over a treasonous one, and toward dis-ease that such a victory is achieved by a servant against a master" (Bernthal, "Treason in the Family," 44).

On Thump and Horner, see also Burnett, "Apprentice Literature," 52, and *Masters and Servants*, 20–21. On apprentice violence and fear of apprentice violence and disorder, see Bernthal, "Treason in the Family," 51–52; Peter Burke, "Popular Culture in Seventeenth-Century London," in *Popular Culture in Seventeenth-Century England*, ed. Barry Reay (London: Croom Helm, 1985), 34, 36; Burnett, *Masters and Servants*, 18–28; and Manley, *London in the Age*, 20, 36, 170.

19. "Caliban is so consistently characterized as a servant that he appears to internalize that characterization and to construe his actions as petty treason rather than as the reclamation of his own usurped kingdom . . . The limited scope of Caliban's ambitions and the extent to which, despite his eloquent nostalgia for lost autonomy, he seems to agree with his positioning as a 'servant-monster,' neutralize the threat that his plot poses, making him and his conspiracy not just harmless but humorous" (Dolan, *Dangerous Familiars*, 68).

20. On the effect of violence on Caliban, see Cohen, *Politics of Shakespeare*, 42, 48. On Caliban's ability, by the end of the play, to acquire "moral wisdom," and "the dignified humanity that Prospero and Caliban come to share," see Cox, *Shakespeare and the Dramaturgy*, 204–5. On Ariel and Caliban as versions of New Comedy slaves, see Bernard Knox, "*The Tempest* and the Ancient Comic Tradition," *Virginia Quarterly Review* 31 (Winter 1955): 73–89; for a rebuttal of this position, see Lester E. Barber, "*The Tempest* and New Comedy," *Shakespeare Quarterly* 21 (Summer 1970): 207–11.

21. See Berry, *Shakespeare and Social Class*, xix; Dolan, *Dangerous Familiars*, 4, 25; and Wells, *Wide Arch*, 145–46. Directors and actors, of course, may add violence not indicated by Shakespeare. Marvin Rosenberg notes that "In the theatre, [Macduff] has seized the Porter, twisted his arm backwards, pulled his head back by the hair, thrown him down" ("From *The Masks*," 63). Rosenberg does not indicate whether these actions took place in one production or several. On the other hand, directors may also eliminate violence to make a particular point: Margot Heinemann explains that "in Peter Brook's famous production of *Lear* with Paul Scofield—a production often called Brechtian because it alienated our view of the king—the director deliberately cut out the servants who stand up to Cornwall and Regan and try to help the blinded Gloucester, because he wanted to prevent 'reassurance' being given to the audience. The world of *Lear* must be shown as *wholly*, unchangeably (not relatively) black and evil, and so the crucial turning point, when the oppressed common people begin to resist the bullies and torturers, has to go—which means the forces which, however feeble as yet, will one day alter this world have to go too. Cutting the contradictions like this is positively *anti*-Brechtian" ("How Brecht Read Shakespeare," 223).

Non-Shakespearean plays and ballads of the period are full of threats of violence toward and even the murder of servants. A few of many possible examples include threats of violence toward servants and the apprehension of the servant Nicholas that his honest service may have endangered his life in Thomas Heywood's *A Woman Killed with Kindness* (3.2.53–54, 68–74). Lorenzo threatens to kill Bellimperia's servant Pedringano unless he betrays his mistress in Thomas Kyd's *Spanish Tragedy*, an episode repeated in the ballad version of the story ("The Spanish Tragedy," *Roxburghe Ballads*, 2:454–59); subsequently, Lorenzo employs Pedringano to murder Balthazar's servant Serberine, but betrays Pedringano to ensure his execution (2.1.59–93; 3.2.70–90; 3.3.30–33; 3.6.104–13). In *A Yorkshire Tragedy*, the Husband throws downstairs a Maid who cries for help as he tries to tear his young son out of her arms and knocks down and tears with his spurs a male Servant who attempts to restrain him after he has attacked his wife and killed two of his sons (sc. 5, lines 8–12, 40–43); this dramatizes the account given in the anonymous source pamphlet "Two Most Unnaturall and Bloodie Murthers" (1605). In the ballad "Robin Hood Newly Reviv'd," Robin Hood's nephew flees to the forest after killing his father's steward (*Roxburghe Ballads*, 2:426–31), while "The Cries of the Dead" describes how a Southwark weaver named Price cruelly murdered various apprentices (quoted in Manley, *London in the Age*, 147–50). Even Dick Whittington came in for abuse, since, according to a 1605 ballad, "London's Glory and Whittington's Renown," while Whittington was a scullion, "A sharp Cook-maid there was, that beat him day by day" (*Roxburghe Ballads*, 7:583, line 15).

22. Paul Brown uses this term with regard to Prospero's frequent reminders to Ariel of the latter's "indebtedness to the master" ("'This thing of darkness,'" 60). On the concept of "symbolic violence," Brown refers readers to Pierre Bourdieu, *Outline of a Theory of Practice*, trans. Richard Nice (Cambridge: Cambridge University Press, 1977), 190–97.

23. *Merry Wives* 1.1.184–85; *Twelfth Night* 1.5.38–39, 87–93; *All's Well* 3.4.1–3, 19–20; *Timon* 2.2.128–36; *Macbeth* 5.3.11–19. The Countess of Rossillion has earlier rebuked Lavatch for being a knave and a fool (1.3.8–90), but it is not clear how seriously she intends her reprimand to be taken.

24. Since servants commonly lived in their employers' houses and fed at their employers' expense, dismissal also meant immediate homelessness and hunger, unless they had money saved. For those servants who wore livery, it meant the loss of at least some of their clothing. In an age with few social services, it meant loss of income with no immediate likelihood of finding other employment. In addition, harsh penalties could be imposed upon the jobless poor: see Beier, *Masterless Men*, 9. Though many of Shakespeare's servants are threatened with firing, few are actually fired. Characters threatened with loss of employment include Mrs. Quickly and Robin (*Merry Wives* 1.4.117–18; 3.3.24–27) and possibly Adam (*Twelfth Night* 1.1.78–81). A few characters, however, are "put . . . into everlasting liberty": Lance is apparently fired for losing the little dog that Proteus ordered him to give to Sylvia (*T.G.V.* 4.4.57–59); Falstaff fires Pistol, Nym, and Bardolph, although he finds the latter another job (*Merry Wives* 1.3.4–18, 78–83).

25. On sexual exploitation of female domestic servants, see Amussen, *Ordered Society*, 159–61; Bridenbaugh, *Vexed and Troubled Englishmen*, 367; Burnett, *Masters and Servants*, 122–25; Martin Ingram, "The Reform of Popular Culture? Sex and Marriage in Early Modern England," in *Popular Culture in Seventeenth-Century England*, 129–65, 151, 156; Laslett, *World We Have Lost*, 178–79; Manley, *London in the Age*, 191; Stone, *Family, Sex and Mar-*

riage, 519, 549, 550, 613, 642, 646–47; and D. L. Thomas and N. E. Evans, "John Shakespeare in the Exchequer," *Shakespeare Quarterly* 35 (Autumn 1984): 316–17. This situation is reflected in the plays only in such brief mentions as Lorenzo's statement (possibly in jest) that Launcelot has impregnated "the Moor" and the old Shepherd's comment upon finding the abandoned infant Perdita that he "can read waiting-gentlewoman in the scape" (*Merchant* 3.5.37; *Winter's Tale* 3.3.71). Costard accuses Armado of impregnating Jaquenetta, pressures him to marry her, and accepts his challenge to fight about it, but there is no suggestion that the affair was anything but consensual, and Armado is apparently prepared to marry Jaquenetta (*Love's Labor's Lost* 5.2.669–99, 718–20, 873–74). Sexual abuse of male servants is never an issue, although James O'Rourke sees Thersites as "a sexual slave" ("'Rule in Unity' and Otherwise: Love and Sex in *Troilus and Cressida*," *Shakespeare Quarterly* 43 [Summer 1992]: 142). Amussen also cites cases of neglect of servants and unjust withholding of wages (160–61), an abuse that in Shakespeare's plays is only reflected in such facetious comments as Costard's about Armado's underpaying his servants (*L.L.L.* 1.2.145–46).

26. Writers of contemporary conduct books are of two minds about masters beating their servants. (The question of whether mistresses should impose physical discipline seems to receive little attention, although Juan Luis Vives writes, "I will not bid the man so straightly to beware, that he make not his servant, over homely with him, as I will the woman, which I would should not bee much conversant among her servants, nor meddle much with them, neither rebuke & correct the men, but leave that for her husbande to doe" [*Instruction*, X5ʳ].) Often the opinion seems to be some version of Stephen Bateman's statement that "A servaunt that knoweth his Lords will, and will not do it, shall be beaten with many stripes" (*Batman uppon Bartholome*, 76ᵛ; see also 74ᵛ and 76ʳ.) Furthermore, servants were apparently expected to accept such beatings, as Ling asserts: "Servants ought with patience to beare the corrections of their Maister," presumably including physical correction (118ʳ). See also Marshall, *English Domestic Servant*, 23. On the other hand, while discussing the faults of masters, one of Stephen Guazzo's characters says, "Those [masters] are yet worse which speake to theyr servaunts with their hands: who belike have bene beaten by their maisters, if they have served, and therefore they will revenge it upon their servants: or else perchance they perswade themselves that their servaunts can not helpe themselves with their Poignadoes, wherof I saw an example at *Padua*, Truelie there is nothing that angreth me more then that, for I cannot but think verie ill of those which triumph tirannouslie over their poore servauntes, from injuring of whome, they ought rather to abstaine, then of their equals: for that it is an act of great bountie, to keepe ones selfe from oppressing those whome he may easilie oppresse. And therefore it behoveth wise maisters to forbeare beating their servants, remembring that the supreme maister is not well pleased with him, who will take revenge out of his hands, and not leave the punishment of his servants to his divine pleasure, unlesse it be for such offences as are punisheable by h[u]mane lawes" (*civile Conversation*, 168ʳ). Much of Guazzo's dialogue about servants, here and elsewhere, suggests that Marshall is correct in asserting, "Though some employers were inconsiderate or bad in the generality of homes the human factor was a powerful agent in bettering conditions" (24). See also "J. Fit John," *A Diamond Most Precious*, 70; Thomas Fossett, *The Servants Dutie, or The Calling and Condition of Servants* (London, 1612), 46; Christopher

Goodman, *How Superior Powers O[u]ght to be Obeyd of their subjects: and wherin they may lawfully by Gods Worde be disobeyed and resisted* ([1558]; repr., Amsterdam: Theatrum Orbis Terrarum, 1972), 117–18; Gouge, *Of Domesticall Duties*, 659, 661; and Humfrey, *Nobles*, V7^r, V8^r. One wonders whether a feeling that the English were peculiarly hard on their servants may have given English writers a particular sensitivity to the issue of physical punishment. As Rye notes, "[Fynes] Moryson (*Itin.* 1617, Pt. 3, pp. 53, 149), explains this proverb: 'England in generall is said to be the Hell of Horses, the Purgatory of Servants, and the Paradice of Weomen . . . because they ride their horses without measure, and use their servants imperiously, and their women obsequiously'" (*England as Seen*, 197 n. 31).

27. Hal's later comment, "Has not the boy profited?" (80), is presumably ironic. One wonders if this is meant to be the same character as "Robin," the little boy later "loaned" by Falstaff to Mrs. Page (*Merry Wives* 2.2.106–9, 114–21; 3.2.1–8).

28. On the Antipholi beating their slaves in *Errors*, see Linda Anderson, *A Kind of Wild Justice: Revenge in Shakespeare's Comedies* (Newark: University of Delaware Press, 1987), 26–28; Alberto Cacicedo, "'A formal man again': Physiological Humours in *The Comedy of Errors*," *The Upstart Crow* 11 (1991): 25–27; and Deborah Baker Wyrick, "The Ass Motif in *The Comedy of Errors* and *A Midsummer Night's Dream*," *Shakespeare Quarterly* 33 (Winter 1982): 441. On the possibility that the violence of *The Comedy of Errors* could have been inspired, at least in part, by the threats of beatings and other physical violence in *Menaechmi*, see Anderson, 28. Berry simply concludes that "in the early plays . . . Servants have to be thumped" (*Shakespeare and Social Class*, xix), which seems a fair assessment, although many nonservant characters are also thumped.

29. *Shakespeare's Comic Commonwealths*, 31.

30. See Moisan, "'Knock me here soundly,'" 276–90.

31. Other suggestions of violence include Petruchio ordering Grumio to draw his weapon immediately after the wedding; Petruchio and Grumio both threatening the tailor; and Vincentio suspecting Tranio of having murdered Lucentio (3.2.236; 4.3.110–12, 141–44; 5.1.82).

32. Berry, *Shakespeare and Social Class*, 22. Of the violence directed by masters toward servants in *The Taming of the Shrew*, Berry suggests that it "seems closer to dramatic intensification than to caricature" (28). Contemporary reports of servants suffering violence and even death, either at the hands of their employers or because of their connection with their employers, are common. On beatings of and other violence directed by employers toward servants, see Bridenbaugh, *Vexed and Troubled Englishmen*, 91, 172, and 356; Orlin, *Elizabethan Households*, 40–41; and Stone, *Family, Sex and Marriage*, 167. Michael Brennan reports that after the arrest of Thomas Howard, Duke of Norfolk, in 1569, "Sir Thomas Smith, who was in charge of questioning some suspects of lesser rank, stated that William Barker [who was employed by Norfolk] had been 'the most doer betwixt the Duke and other foreign practisers', extracting his information from Norfolk's secretary, Bannister, 'with the rack', and from Barker 'with the extreme fear of it'" (*Literary Patronage in the English Renaissance: The Pembroke Family* [London: Routledge, 1988], 36). John Aubrey recounts that "in Queen Maries dayes, the Lord Stourton was attainted by his murthering of Mr Hargill his Steward, whom he killed and buryed in his Cellar, for which he was hanged in a silken halter at Salisbury" (*Aubrey's Brief*

Lives, ed. Oliver Lawson Dick [1949; repr., Harmondsworth, UK: Penguin, 1982], 222). David Rizzio, secretary and musician to Mary Queen of Scots, was murdered in 1566 by Mary's husband, Henry, Lord Darnley, and a group of Scottish noblemen, possibly in the hope that killing Rizzio in her presence would induce premature labor in the pregnant queen and perhaps bring about her death. And, in a parallel to the slaughter of Macduff's family and servants, in the summer of 1601, Sir Arthur Chichester's forces slew not only Patrick O'Quin, one of Tyrone's followers, and his family, but also his servants (Harrison, *Last Elizabethan Journal*, 183).

33. Messengers often come in for such mistreatment, as is discussed in chapter 7.

34. "The Theatrical Consistency of Richard II," *Shakespeare Quarterly* 29 (Winter 1978): 13.

35. Given the anarchic nature of *Twelfth Night*, it is not too surprising that it depicts a servant displacing his anger against a pair of knights. Since Malvolio's position as a servant prevents him from doing any more to Sir Toby and Sir Andrew than threatening them in Olivia's name, he vents his anger by threatening Maria, which seems particularly unfair in view of her attempts to silence the revellers (2.3.120–23).

36. For discussion of the Clown's death as "a gross miscarriage of justice" and as "[reiterating] the hollowness of Roman authority as manifested through the figure of the emperor," see Molly Easo Smith, "Spectacles of Torment," 320. See also Kendall, " 'Lend me thy hand,' " 312.

37. Carol Thomas Neely attributes Antony's anger to "[His] new vulnerability [which] is apparent when, in the messenger scene, he is more enraged and humiliated by Caesar's imagined indirect sexual triumph than he was by his actual military one" (*Broken Nuptials*, 148).

38. "Claudius's betrayal of duty is deadly to those who do their duty to him: Laertes (1.2.53–54), Polonius (2.2.44), and Rosencrantz and Guildenstern (2.2.29, 3.2.322). Further, it is poignant and ironic that those subjects who do understand kingly duty—Laertes, Ophelia, Rosencrantz and Guildenstern—die because their ruler fails them" (Catherine Brown Tkacz, "The Wheel of Fortune, the Wheel of State, and Moral Choice in *Hamlet*," *South Atlantic Review* 57 [November 1992]: 23).

39. Northrop Frye asserts that "the vital thread of Enobarbus's life was the tie that bound him to Antony, not anything inside himself" ("The Tragedy of Order: *Julius Caesar*," in *Fools of Time* [1965; repr., *Twentieth Century Interpretations of* Julius Caesar: *A Collection of Critical Essays*, ed. Leonard F. Dean (Englewood Cliffs, NJ: Prentice-Hall, 1968)], 99). It might be argued that Charmian and Iras commit suicide to avoid the fate that Cleopatra outlines to Iras at 5.2.205–23: "Thou, an Egyptian puppet shall be shown / In Rome as well as I." There are suggestions, however, that Charmian and Iras have already decided upon suicide before this point. Cleopatra has earlier whispered to Charmian, presumably about bringing in the Clown who delivers the asps, and received, from the chatty and frequently argumentative Charmian, no comment but "Madam, I will"; even more convincingly, Iras has already stated, "Finish, good lady, the bright day is done, / And we are for the dark" (191–95). On the loyalty and heroism of Antony and Cleopatra's servants, see John Alvis, "The Religion of Eros: A Re-interpretation of *Antony and Cleopatra*," *Renascence* 30 (1978): 192–93; and Elizabeth A. Brown, " 'Companion Me,' " 138, 142–43.

40. However, Rozett argues that this triumph is very different from the endings of "*Romeo and Juliet* and the later tragedies, where death is violent, arbitrary, and caused by treachery and misunderstandings, abruptly cutting off the lives of characters who unwittingly find themselves caught up in the tragic momentum of the play" ("Comic Structures," 163–64). A similar point might be made about the death of the Nurse in the early tragedy *Titus Andronicus*, who, in delivering Tamora's baby to Aaron, says, "O gentle Aaron, we are all undone!" (*Titus* 4.2.55), linking her fate with those of Tamora and Aaron, and who is killed by Aaron to forestall the possibility that she will reveal his affair with her mistress.

CHAPTER 11. "REMEMBER I HAVE DONE THEE . . ."

1. *Politics of Shakespeare*, 77.
2. "Servant Obedience," 14.
3. "'Servile Ministers,'" 20.
4. Gouge, *Of Domesticall Duties*, 653.
5. On servants as playgoers, see Baldwin, *Organization and Personnel*, 17n. 39; Bradbrook, *Rise*, 50, 103–4, 106; Burnett, *Masters and Servants*, 51n. 65; Gurr, *Playgoing in Shakespeare's London*, 8, 19–20, 30, 41, 54, 59, 65–67, 69, 138, 198–99, 202, 203, 206, 216, 217, 225, 232, and 236, and *Shakespearian Playing Companies*, 203–4; Marshall, *English Domestic Servant*, 12; Montrose, "'Place of a Brother,'" 33–34, and *The Purpose of Playing: Shakespeare and the Cultural Politics of the Elizabethan Theatre* (Chicago: University of Chicago Press, 1996), 46–51; and Charles Whitney, "'Usually in the Werking Daies': Playgoing Journeymen, Apprentices, and Servants in Guild Records, 1582–92," *Shakespeare Quarterly* 50 (Winter 1999): 433–58. Even though Ann Jennalie Cook argues that most of the audience for drama consisted of "the privileged," she cites a variety of primary materials that indicate that servants were frequently members of the audience (*Privileged Playgoers*, 129, 134, 152, 154, 217, 226). She also cites complaints by London officials of servants and criminals resorting to plays (246–47), but discounts them as exaggerations motivated by fear of disorder.
6. "Mourning and Misogyny: *Hamlet, The Revenger's Tragedy*, and the Final Progress of Elizabeth I, 1600–1607," *Shakespeare Quarterly* 45 (Summer 1994): 143–44.

Bibliography

Adelman, Janet. "'Anger's My Meat': Feeding, Dependency, and Aggression in *Coriolanus.*" In *Shakespeare: Pattern of Excelling Nature*, edited by David Bevington and Jay L. Halio. Newark: University of Delaware Press, 1978. Reprinted in *Representing Shakespeare: New Psychoanalytic Essays*, edited by Murray M. Schwartz and Coppelia Kahn, 129–49. Baltimore: Johns Hopkins University Press, 1980.

———. *The Common Liar: An Essay on "Antony and Cleopatra."* New Haven: Yale University Press, 1973.

Allen, John A. "Dogberry." *Shakespeare Quarterly* 24 (Winter 1973): 35–53.

Allgaier, Johannes. "Is *King Lear* an Antiauthoritarian Play?" *PMLA* 88 (October 1973): 1033–39.

Allott, Robert. *Wits Theater of the little World.* n.p., 1599.

Altman, Joel B. "'Vile Participation': The Amplification of Violence in the Theater of *Henry V.*" *Shakespeare Quarterly* 42 (Spring 1991): 1–32.

Alvis, John. "The Religion of Eros: A Re-interpretation of *Antony and Cleopatra.*" *Renascence* 30 (1978): 185–98.

Amussen, Susan Dwyer. *An Ordered Society: Gender and Class in Early Modern England.* Oxford: Blackwell, 1988.

Anderson, Linda. *A Kind of Wild Justice: Revenge in Shakespeare's Comedies.* Newark: University of Delaware Press, 1987.

Andreas, James R. "'For O, for O, the hobby-horse is forgot': Hamlet and The Death of Carnival." *Renaissance Papers 1996.* Edited by George Walton Williams and Philip Rollinson, 81–91. Raleigh, NC: Southeastern Renaissance Conference / Camden House, 1997.

Andrews, John F., ed. *Romeo and Juliet.* The Everyman Shakespeare. London: J. M. Dent, 1993.

Anonymous. *Certayne short Questions and Answeres. Very profitable and necessarye for young Children, and such as are desirous to be instructed in the principles of the Christian Fayth.* London, 1580.

Appelbaum, Robert. "'Standing to the wall': The Pressures of Masculinity in *Romeo and Juliet.*" *Shakespeare Quarterly* 48 (Fall 1997): 251–72.

Archer, Ian. *The Pursuit of Stability: Social Relations in Elizabethan London.* Cambridge: Cambridge University Press, 1991.

Ashley, Leonard R. N. *Elizabethan Popular Culture.* Bowling Green, OH: Bowling Green State University Popular Press, 1988.

Aubrey, John. *Aubrey's Brief Lives.* Edited by Oliver Lawson Dick. 1949. Reprint, Harmondsworth, UK: Penguin Books, 1982.

Averell, W. *A Dyall for dainty Darlings.* London, 1584.

Baker, J. Robert. "Absence and Subversion: The 'O'erflow' of Gender in Shakespeare's *Antony and Cleopatra*." *The Upstart Crow* 12 (1992): 105–15.

Baldwin, Thomas Whitfield. *The Organization and Personnel of the Shakespearean Company*. 1927. Reprint, New York: Russell & Russell, 1961.

Barber, Lester E. "*The Tempest* and New Comedy." *Shakespeare Quarterly* 21 (Summer 1970): 207–11.

Barckley, Richard. *A Discourse of the Felicitie of Man: Or, His "Summum bonum.*" London, 1598.

Barish, Jonas A. and Marshall Waingrow. "'Service' in *King Lear*." *Shakespeare Quarterly* 9 (Summer 1958): 347–55.

Barkan, Leonard. "The Theatrical Consistency of *Richard II*." *Shakespeare Quarterly* 29 (Winter 1978): 5–19.

Barnett, Richard C. *Place, Profit, and Power: A Study of the Servants of William Cecil, Elizabethan Statesman*. Chapel Hill: University of North Carolina Press, 1969.

Bartels, Emily C. "Making More of the Moor: Aaron, Othello, and Renaissance Refashionings of Race." *Shakespeare Quarterly* 41 (Winter 1990): 433–54.

Barton, Anne. "The King Disguised: Shakespeare's *Henry V* and the Comical History." In *The Triple Bond: Plays, Mainly Shakespearean, in Performance*, edited by Joseph G. Price, 92–117. University Park: Pennsylvania State University Press, 1975.

Basse, William. *Sword and Buckler, or, Serving-mans Defence*. London, 1602.

Bate, Jonathan. Introduction. In *Titus Andronicus*, edited by Jonathan Bate, 1–121. The Arden Shakespeare, 3rd series. London: Routledge, 1995.

Bateman, Stephen. *Batman uppon Bartholome*. London, 1582.

Batty, Bartholomew. *The Christian mans Closet*. Translated by William Lowth. London, 1581.

Beckerman, Bernard. *Shakespeare at the Globe, 1599–1609*. 1962. Reprint, New York: Macmillan / Collier Books, 1966.

Becon, Thomas. *The Sicke Mans Salue*. London, 1604.

Beehler, Sharon. "'An Enemy in Their Mouths': The Closure of Language in *Othello*." *The Upstart Crow* 10 (1990): 69–85.

Beier, A. L. *Masterless Men: The Vagrancy Problem in England 1560–1640*. London: Methuen, 1985.

Belsey, Catherine. *The Subject of Tragedy: Identity and Difference in Renaissance Drama*. London: Methuen, 1985.

Ben-Amos, Ilana Krausman. *Adolescence and Youth in Early Modern England*. New Haven: Yale University Press, 1994.

Bentley, Gerald Eades. *The Profession of Player in Shakespeare's Time, 1590–1642*. Princeton: Princeton University Press, 1984.

Berger, Harry, Jr. "Against the Sink-a-Pace: Sexual and Family Politics in *Much Ado About Nothing*." *Shakespeare Quarterly* 33 (Autumn 1982): 302–13.

Bernthal, Craig A. "Treason in the Family: The Trial of Thumpe v. Horner." *Shakespeare Quarterly* 42 (Spring 1991): 44–54.

Berry, Edward I. "Rosalynde and Rosalind." *Shakespeare Quarterly* 31 (Spring 1980): 42–52.

Berry, Ralph. *Shakespeare and Social Class*. Atlantic Highlands, NJ: Humanities Press International, 1988.

Bevington, David. *Tudor Drama and Politics: A Critical Approach to Topical Meaning*. Cambridge, MA: Harvard University Press, 1968.

Boaistuau, Pierre. *Theatrum Mundi*. Translated by John Alday. London, 1581.

Boswell, John. *The Kindness of Strangers: The Abandonment of Children in Western Europe from Late Antiquity to the Renaissance*. New York: Pantheon, 1988.

Bradbrook, M. C. *Elizabethan Stage Conditions: A Study of Their Place in the Interpretation of Shakespeare's Plays*. 1932. Reprint, Cambridge: Cambridge University Press, 1968.

———. *The Rise of the Common Player: A Study of Actor and Society in Shakespeare's England*. Cambridge, MA: Harvard University Press, 1962.

———. *Shakespeare and Elizabethan Poetry: A Study of his Earlier Work in Relation to the Poetry of the Time*. 1951. Reprint, London: Chatto and Windus, 1965.

———. "The Triple Bond: Audience, Actors, Author in the Elizabethan Playhouse." In *The Triple Bond: Plays, Mainly Shakespearean, in Performance*, edited by Joseph G. Price, 50–69. University Park: Pennsylvania State University Press, 1975.

Breight, Curt. "'Treason doth never prosper': *The Tempest* and the Discourse of Treason." *Shakespeare Quarterly* 41 (Spring 1990): 1–28.

Brennan, Michael. *Literary Patronage in the English Renaissance: The Pembroke Family*. London: Routledge, 1988.

Bridenbaugh, Carl. *Vexed and Troubled Englishmen, 1590–1642*. London: Oxford University Press, 1967.

Bristol, Michael D. *Carnival and Theater: Plebeian Culture and the Structure of Authority in Renaissance England*. New York: Methuen, 1985.

Brockbank, Philip, ed. *Coriolanus*. The Arden Shakespeare. 1976. Reprint, London: Routledge, 1988.

Brown, Elizabeth A. "'Companion Me with My Mistress': Cleopatra, Elizabeth I, and Their Waiting Women." In *Maids and Mistresses, Cousins and Queens: Women's Alliances in Early Modern England*, edited by Susan Frye and Karen Robertson, 131–45. New York: Oxford University Press, 1999.

Brown, Ivor. *Shakespeare and the Actors*. London: Bodley Head, 1970.

Brown, Paul. "'This thing of darkness I acknowledge mine': *The Tempest* and the Discourse of Colonialism." In *Political Shakespeare: New Essays in Cultural Materialism*, edited by Jonathan Dollimore and Alan Sinfield, 48–71. Ithaca: Cornell University Press, 1985.

Br[yskett], Lod[owick]. *A Discourse of Civill Life: Containing the Ethike part of Morall Philosophe, Fit for the instructing of a Gentleman in the course of a vertuous life*. London, 1606.

Buckman, Ty F. "The Perils of Marriage Counselling: John Stubbs, Philip Sidney, and the Virgin Queen." *Renaissance Papers 1995*. Edited by George Walton Williams and Barbara J. Baines, 125–41. Raleigh, NC: Southeastern Renaissance Conference, 1996.

Bullinger, Heinrich. *The Christian state of Matrimony*. Translated by Miles Coverdale. London, 1575.

Burke, Peter. "Popular Culture in Seventeenth-Century London." In *Popular Culture in Seventeenth-Century England*, edited by Barry Reay, 31–58. London: Croom Helm, 1985.

Burnett, Mark Thornton. "Apprentice Literature and the 'Crisis' of the 1590s." In *Patronage, Politics, and Literary Traditions in England, 1558–1658*, edited by Cedric C. Brown, 47–58. Detroit: Wayne State University Press, 1991.

———. *Masters and Servants in English Renaissance Drama and Culture: Authority and Obedience*. New York: St. Martin's Press, 1997.

———. "Masters and Servants in Moral and Religious Treatises, c. 1580–c. 1642." In *The Arts, Literature, and Society*, edited by Arthur Marwick, 48–75. London: Routledge, 1990.

Cacicedo, Alberto. "'A formal man again': Physiological Humours in *The Comedy of Errors*." *The Upstart Crow* 11 (1991): 24–38.

Cahn, Susan. *Industry of Devotion: The Transformation of Women's Work in England, 1500–1660*. New York: Columbia University Press, 1987.

Capp, Bernard. "Popular Literature." In *Popular Culture in Seventeenth-Century England*, edited by Barry Reay, 198–243. London: Croom Helm, 1985.

Cavell, Stanley. *Disowning Knowledge in Six Plays of Shakespeare*. Cambridge: Cambridge University Press, 1987.

Clifford, Lady Anne. *The Diaries of Lady Anne Clifford*. Edited by D. J. H. Clifford. Phoenix Mill, UK: Sutton, 1990.

Coghill, Nevill. "*Macbeth* at The Globe, 1606–1616(?): Three Questions." In *The Triple Bond: Plays, Mainly Shakespearean, in Performance*, edited by Joseph G. Price, 223–39. University Park: Pennsylvania State University Press, 1975.

Cohen, Derek. *The Politics of Shakespeare*. New York: St. Martin's Press, 1993.

———. *Shakespeare's Culture of Violence*. New York: St. Martin's Press, 1993.

Cole, Howard C. "Shakespeare's Comedies and their Sources: Some Biographical and Artistic Inferences." *Shakespeare Quarterly* 34 (Winter 1983): 405–19.

"Conny-Catcher, Cuthbert." *The Defence of Conny-Catching*. 1592. Ed. G. B. Harrison. 1922–26. Elizabethan and Jacobean Quartos series. New York: Barnes & Noble, 1966.

Cook, Ann Jennalie. *The Privileged Playgoers of Shakespeare's London, 1576–1642*. Princeton: Princeton University Press, 1981.

———. "Timon's Servant Takes a Wife." In *Shakespeare: Text, Subtext, and Context*, edited by Ronald Dotterer, 150–56. Selinsgrove, PA: Susquehanna University Press, 1989.

Cox, John D. "The Politics of Stuart Medievalism." In *Patronage, Politics, and Literary Traditions in England, 1558–1658*, edited by Cedric C. Brown, 211–20. Detroit: Wayne State University Press, 1991.

———. *Shakespeare and the Dramaturgy of Power*. Princeton: Princeton University Press, 1989.

Crowley, Robert. *The Select Works of Robert Crowley*. Edited by J. M. Cowper. Early English Text Society, extra series, xv. London: Early English Text Society, 1872.

Dalton, Michael. *The Countrey Justice, conteyning the practice of the Justices of the Peace out of their Sessions. Gathered for the better helpe of such Jus-*

tices of Peace as have not beene much conversant in the studie of the Lawes of this Realme. London, 1618.

Danson, Lawrence. "*Henry V*: King, Chorus, and Critics." *Shakespeare Quarterly* 34 (Spring 1983): 27–43.

Davies, R. T., ed. *Medieval English Lyrics: A Critical Anthology.* n.p.: Northwestern University Press, 1964.

Davison, P. H., ed. *2 Henry IV.* 1977. Reprinted in *William Shakespeare: Four Histories.* London: Penguin, 1994.

De, Esha Niyogi. "'When Our Deep Plots Do Pall': Endings and Beginnings in the Graveyard Scene in *Hamlet*." *Shakespeare Yearbook* 1 (Spring 1990): 59–80.

Dean, Paul. "Chronicle and Romance Modes in *Henry V*." *Shakespeare Quarterly* 32 (Spring 1981): 18–27.

———. "Shakespeare's *Henry VI* Trilogy and Elizabethan 'Romance' Histories: The Origins of a Genre." *Shakespeare Quarterly* 33 (Spring 1982): 34–48.

Dekker, Thomas, John Ford, and William Rowley. *The Witch of Edmonton: A Critical Edition.* Edited by Etta Soiref Onat. New York: Garland, 1980.

Desainliens, Claude (Claudius Holyband). *Campo di Fior, or else The Flourie Field of Foure Languages of M. Claudius Desainliens, alias Holiband: For the furtherance of the learners of the Latine, French, English, but chieflie of the Italian tongue.* London, 1583.

———. *The French Littleton: A Most Easy, Perfect, and Absolute Way to learne the French tongue: set forth by Claudius Holyband, Gentil-homme Bourbonnois.* London, 1593.

———. *The French Schoole-maister.* London, 1573. Reprint, English Linguistics 1500–1800 (no. 315), selected and edited by R. C. Alston. Menston: Scolar Press, 1972.

Dessen, Alan C. *Elizabethan Stage Conventions and Modern Interpreters.* New York: Cambridge University Press, 1984.

———. "Shakespeare's Theatrical *Italics*." *Renaissance Papers 1991.* Edited by George Walton Williams and Barbara J. Baines, 93–104. Raleigh, NC: Southeastern Renaissance Conference, 1992.

———. *Titus Andronicus.* Shakespeare in Performance Series. Manchester, UK: Manchester University Press, 1989.

Dickey, Stephen. "Shakespeare's Mastiff Comedy." *Shakespeare Quarterly* 42 (Fall 1991): 255–75.

Dickinson, Hugh. "The Reformation of Prince Hal." *Shakespeare Quarterly* 12 (Winter 1961): 33–46.

Dolan, Frances E. *Dangerous Familiars: Representations of Domestic Crime in England, 1550–1700.* Ithaca: Cornell University Press, 1994.

Dollimore, Jonathan. "Introduction: Shakespeare, Cultural Materialism and the New Historicism." In *Political Shakespeare: New Essays in Cultural Materialism*, edited by Jonathan Dollimore and Alan Sinfield, 2–17. Ithaca: Cornell University Press, 1985.

———. "Transgression and Surveillance in *Measure for Measure*." In *Political Shakespeare: New Essays in Cultural Materialism*, edited by Jonathan Dollimore and Alan Sinfield, 72–87. Ithaca: Cornell University Press, 1985.

Donno, Elizabeth Story. "Cleopatra Again." *Shakespeare Quarterly* 7 (Spring 1956): 227–33.

Doran, Madeleine. "The Idea of Excellence in Shakespeare." *Shakespeare Quarterly* 27 (Spring 1976): 133–49.

Draper, John. "Shakespeare's Rustic Servants." In *Stratford to Dogberry: Studies in Shakespeare's Earlier Plays*, 11–23. Pittsburgh: University of Pittsburgh Press, 1961.

Dudley, Edmund. *The Tree of Commonwealth*. 1509. Reprint, edited by D. M. Brodie. Cambridge: Cambridge University Press, 1948.

Dunn, Leslie C. "The Lady Sings in Welsh: Women's Song as Marginal Discourse on the Shakespearean Stage." In *Place and Displacement in the Renaissance*, edited by Alvin Vos, 51–67. Binghamton, NY: Center for Medieval and Early Renaissance Studies, 1995.

Egan, Robert. "Kent and the Audience: The Character as Spectator." *Shakespeare Quarterly* 32 (Summer 1981): 146–54.

Fabry, Frank. "Shakespeare's Witty Musician: *Romeo and Juliet*, IV.v.114–17." *Shakespeare Quarterly* 33 (Summer 1982): 182–83.

Farley-Hills, David. "A *Hamlet* Crux." *Notes and Queries* 240 (n.s. vol. 42, September 1995): 319–20.

Farmer, John S., ed. *Merry Songs and Ballads prior to the Year A.D. 1800*. 5 vols. New York: Cooper Square Publishers, 1964.

Fit, John, J. *A Diamond Most Precious, worthy to be marked: Instructing all Maysters and Seruauntes, how they ought to leade their lyves, in that Vocation which is fruitfull, and necessary, as well for the Maysters, as also for the Seruants, agreeable to the holy Scriptures*. London, 1577.

Fitz, L. T. "Egyptian Queens and Male Reviewers: Sexist Attitudes in *Antony and Cleopatra* Criticism." *Shakespeare Quarterly* 28 (Summer 1977): 297–316.

Fosset, Thomas. *The Servants Dutie, or The Calling and Condition of Servants*. London, 1612.

Frye, Northrop. "Comic Myth in Shakespeare." In *Discussions of Shakespeare's Romantic Comedy*, edited by Herbert Weil, Jr., 132–42. Boston: Heath, 1966.

———. "The Tragedy of Order: *Julius Caesar*." 1965. Reprinted in *Twentieth Century Interpretations of "Julius Caesar": A Collection of Critical Essays*, edited by Leonard F. Dean, 95–102. Englewood Cliffs, NJ: Prentice-Hall, 1968.

G., I. *A Refutation of the Apology for Actors*. 1615. Reprint, edited by Richard H. Perkinson. New York: Scholars' Facsimiles and Reprints, 1941.

Gaudet, Paul. "The 'Parasitical' Counselors in Shakespeare's *Richard II*: A Problem in Dramatic Interpretation." *Shakespeare Quarterly* 33 (Summer 1982): 142–54.

Gawdy, Philip. *Letters of Philip Gawdy of West Harling, Norfolk, and of London to Various Members of his Family, 1579–1616*. Edited by Isaac Herbert Jeayes. London: J. B. Nichols, 1906.

Goddard, Harold C. *The Meaning of Shakespeare*. 2 vols. 1951. Reprint, Chicago: University of Chicago Press, 1965.

Goodman, Christopher. *How Superior Powers O[u]ght to be Obeyd of their subjects: and wherin they may lawfully by Gods Worde be disobeyed and resisted.* 1558. Reprint, Amsterdam: Theatrum Orbis Terrarum, 1972.

Gosson, Stephen. *Playes Confuted in five Actions.* London, n.d.

———. *The School of Abuse.* London, 1579.

Gouge, William. *Of Domesticall Duties.* London, 1622.

Graham, Kenneth J. E. "'Without the form of justice': Plainness and the Performance of Love in *King Lear.*" *Shakespeare Quarterly* 42 (Winter 1991): 438–61.

Greaves, Richard L. "Concepts of Political Obedience in Late Tudor England: Conflicting Perspectives." *Journal of British Studies* (1980): 23–34.

Green, Douglas E. "Staging the Evidence: Shakespeare's Theatrical Revengers." *The Upstart Crow* 12 (1992): 29–40.

Green, Michael. *The Art of Coarse Acting.* 1964; rev. ed. New York: Drama Book Specialists, 1981.

Greenblatt, Stephen J. "The Cultivation of Anxiety: King Lear and His Heirs." In *Learning to Curse: Essays in Early Modern Culture,* 80–98. New York: Routledge, 1990.

———. "Invisible Bullets: Renaissance Authority and Its Subversion, *Henry IV* and *Henry V.*" In *Political Shakespeare: New Essays in Cultural Materialism,* edited by Jonathan Dollimore and Alan Sinfield, 18–47. Ithaca: Cornell University Press, 1985.

———. "Learning to Curse: Aspects of Linguistic Colonialism in the Sixteenth Century." In *Learning to Curse: Essays in Early Modern Culture,* 16–39. New York: Routledge, 1990.

———. "Murdering Peasants." In *Learning to Curse: Essays in Early Modern Culture,* 99–130. New York: Routledge, 1990.

———. *Renaissance Self-Fashioning from More to Shakespeare.* Chicago: University of Chicago Press, 1980.

———. *Shakespearean Negotiations: The Circulation of Social Energy in Renaissance England.* Berkeley: Unversity of California Press, 1988.

Greene, Robert. *Greenes Groatsworth of Witte, bought with a million of Repentence.* 1592. The Bodley Head Quartos. Edited by G. B. Harrison. London: John Lane, 1923.

Griffiths, Paul. "Masterless Young People in Norwich, 1560–1645." In *The Experience of Authority in Early Modern England,* edited by Paul Griffiths, Adam Fox, and Steve Hindle, 146–86. New York: St. Martin's Press, 1996.

Guazzo, Stephen. *The civile Conversation of M. Stephen Guazzo.* Translated by G[eorge] Pettie and Barth[olomew] Young. London, 1586.

Gurr, Andrew. "The Bear, the Statue, and Hysteria in *The Winter's Tale.*" *Shakespeare Quarterly* 34 (Winter 1983): 420–25.

———. *Playgoing in Shakespeare's London.* Cambridge: Cambridge University Press, 1987.

———. *The Shakespearian Playing Companies.* Oxford: Clarendon Press, 1996.

Habib, Imtiaz. "Reading Black Women Characters of the English Renaissance: Colonial Inscription and Postcolonial Recovery." *Renaissance Papers 1996.* Edited by George Walton Williams and Philip Rollinson, 67–80. Raleigh, NC: Southeastern Renaissance Conference, 1997.

Hale, David G. "*Coriolanus*: The Death of A Political Metaphor." *Shakespeare Quarterly* 22 (Summer 1971): 197–202.

Hamilton, Donna B. "The State of Law in *Richard II*." *Shakespeare Quarterly* 34 (Spring 1983): 5–17.

Harbage, Alfred. *As They Liked It: A Study of Shakespeare's Moral Artistry*. 1947. Reprint, New York: Harper Torchbooks, 1961.

———. *Shakespeare and the Rival Traditions*. 1952. Reprint, Bloomington: Indiana University Press, 1970.

Harcourt, John B. "'I Pray You, Remember the Porter.'" *Shakespeare Quarterly* 12 (Autumn 1961): 393–402.

Hardin, William. "'Pipe-Pilgrimages' and 'Fruitfull Rivers': Thomas Middleton's Civic Entertainments and the Water Supply of Early Stuart London." *Renaissance Papers 1993*. Edited by Barbara J. Baines and George Walton Williams, 63–73. Raleigh, NC: Southeastern Renaissance Conference, 1993.

Harris, Jonathan Gil. "'Narcissus in thy face': Roman Desire and the Difference It Fakes in *Antony and Cleopatra*." *Shakespeare Quarterly* 45 (Winter 1994): 408–25.

Harrison, G. B. *A Last Elizabethan Journal, Being a Record of Those Things Most Talked of During the Years 1599–1603*. 1933. Reprint, London: Routledge & Kegan Paul, 1974.

Harrison, William. *The Description of England*. 1587. Reprint, edited by Georges Edelen. Washington, DC: Folger Shakespeare Library/Dover, 1994.

Hartsock, Mildred E. "Major Scenes in Minor Key." *Shakespeare Quarterly* 21 (Winter 1970): 55–62.

Hassel, R. Chris, Jr. "Military Oratory in *Richard III*." *Shakespeare Quarterly* 35 (Spring 1984): 53–61.

Hays, Janice. "Those 'soft and delicate desires': *Much Ado* and the Distrust of Women." In *The Woman's Part: Feminist Criticism of Shakespeare*, edited by Carolyn Ruth Swift Lenz, Gayle Greene, and Carol Thomas Neely, 79–99. Urbana: University of Illinois Press, 1980.

Heinemann, Margot. "How Brecht Read Shakespeare." In *Political Shakespeare: New Essays in Cultural Materialism*, edited by Jonathan Dollimore and Alan Sinfield, 202–30. Ithaca: Cornell University Press, 1985.

Hentzner, Paul. *A Journey into England*. 1598. Translated by Richard Bently. Edited by Horace Walpole. Strawberry Hill, 1757.

Herrup, Cynthia B. *A House in Gross Disorder: Sex, Law, and the 2nd Earl of Castlehaven*. Oxford: Oxford University Press, 1999.

Hexter, J. H. "The Education of the Aristocracy in the Renaissance." In *Reappraisals in History: New Views on History and Society in Early Modern Europe*, 45–70. 1961. Reprint, New York: Harper & Row, 1963.

Heywood, Thomas. *An Apology for Actors*. 1612. Reprint, edited by Richard H. Perkinson. New York: Scholars' Facsimiles and Reprints, 1941.

Hinely, Jan Lawson. "Comic Scapegoats and the Falstaff of *The Merry Wives of Windsor*." *Shakespeare Studies* 15 (1982): 37–54.

Holland, Norman N. *The Shakespearean Imagination*. 1964. Reprint, Bloomington: Indiana University Press, 1975.

Hollander, John. "*Twelfth Night* and the Morality of Indulgence." In *Discus-

sions of Shakespeare's Romantic Comedy, edited by Herbert Weil, Jr., 119–31. Boston: Heath, 1966.

Holles, Gervase. *Memorials of the Holles Family 1493–1656*. Edited by A. C. Wood, Camden Society, 3rd series, LV, 1937. Reprinted in *Social Change and Revolution in England 1540–1640*, edited by Lawrence Stone. New York: Barnes & Noble, 1965.

Holmer, Joan Ozark. "'Draw, if you be men': Saviolo's Significance for *Romeo and Juliet*." *Shakespeare Quarterly* 45 (Summer 1994): 163–89.

———. "No 'Vaine Fantasy': Shakespeare's Refashioning of Nashe for Dreams and Queen Mab." In *Shakespeare's "Romeo and Juliet": Texts, Contexts, and Interpretation*, edited by Jay L. Halio, 49–82. Newark: University of Delaware Press, 1995.

Holmes, Martin. *Shakespeare and His Players*. New York: Scribner's, 1972.

Hull, Suzanne W. *Chaste, Silent & Obedient: English Books for Women 1475–1640*. San Marino, CA: Huntington Library, 1982.

Humfrey, Lawrence. *The Nobles or of Nobilitye*. London, 1563.

Hunt, Maurice. "Shakespeare's Tragic Homeopathy." In *Shakespeare: Text, Subtext, and Context*, edited by Ronald Dotterer, 77–84. Selinsgrove, PA: Susquehanna University Press, 1989.

Hunter, G. K. *All's Well That Ends Well*. The Arden Shakespeare. 3rd ed., 1959. Reprint, London: Methuen, 1966.

Hurworth, Angela. "Gulls, Cony-Catchers and Cozeners: *Twelfth Night* and the Elizabethan Underworld." *Shakespeare Survey* 52 (1999): 120–32.

Huston, J. Dennis. "'Some Stain of Soldier': The Functions of Parolles in *All's Well That Ends Well*." *Shakespeare Quarterly* 21 (Autumn 1970): 431–38.

Ingram, Martin. "The Reform of Popular Culture? Sex and Marriage in Early Modern England." In *Popular Culture in Seventeenth-Century England*, edited by Barry Reay, 129–65. London: Croom Helm, 1985.

Jagendorf, Zvi. "*Coriolanus*: Body Politic and Private Parts." *Shakespeare Quarterly* 41 (Winter 1990): 455–69.

Jardine, M. D. "New Historicism for Old: New Conservatism for Old?: The Politics of Patronage in the Renaissance." In *Patronage, Politics, and Literary Traditions in England, 1558–1658*, edited by Cedric C. Brown, 291–309. Detroit: Wayne State University Press, 1991.

Jones, Jeanne. *Family Life in Shakespeare's England: Stratford-upon-Avon 1570–1630*. Stroud, UK: Sutton / The Shakespeare Birthplace Trust, 1996.

Jones, Paul V. B. *The Household of a Tudor Nobleman*. 1918. Reprint, New York: Johnson Reprint Company, 1970.

Kay, Carol McGinnis. "Othello's Need for Mirrors." *Shakespeare Quarterly* 34 (Autumn 1983): 261–70.

Kelly, Thomas. "Shakespeare's Romantic Heroes: Orlando Reconsidered." *Shakespeare Quarterly* 24 (Winter 1973): 12–24.

Kelso, Ruth. *The Doctrine of the English Gentleman in the Sixteenth Century, with a Bibliographical List of Treatises on the Gentleman and Related Subjects Published in Europe to 1625*. c. 1929. Reprint, Gloucester, MA: P. Smith, 1964.

Kendall, Gillian Murray. "'Lend me thy hand': Metaphor and Mayhem in *Titus Andronicus*." *Shakespeare Quarterly* 40 (Fall 1989): 299–316.

322 BIBLIOGRAPHY

———. "Overkill in Shakespeare." *Shakespeare Quarterly* 43 (Spring 1992): 33–50.

Kernan, Alvin. *Shakespeare, the King's Playwright: Theater in the Stuart Court 1603–1613*. New Haven: Yale University Press, 1995.

Kimbrough, Robert. "Androgyny Seen Through Shakespeare's Disguise." *Shakespeare Quarterly* 33 (Spring 1982): 17–33.

King, Laura Severt. "Blessed when they were riggish: Shakespeare's Cleopatra and Christianity's penitent prostitutes." *Journal of Medieval and Renaissance Studies* 22:3 (Fall 1992): 429–49.

Kittredge, G. L. "The Dramatic Function of the Porter's Scene." From his *Shakspere*, 1916. Reprinted in *"Macbeth": Critical Essays*, edited by S. Schoenbaum, 81–83. New York: Garland, 1991.

Knowles, Ronald. "The Farce of History: Miracle, Combat, and Rebellion in *2 Henry VI*." In *Patronage, Politics, and Literary Traditions in England, 1558–1658*, edited by Cedric C. Brown, 192–210. Detroit: Wayne State University Press, 1991.

Knox, Bernard. *"The Tempest* and the Ancient Comic Tradition." *Virginia Quarterly Review* 31 (Winter 1955): 73–89.

Kronenfeld, Judy. *King Lear and the Naked Truth: Rethinking the Language of Religion and Resistance*. Durham, NC: Duke University Press, 1998.

———. "Social Rank and the Pastoral Ideals of *As You Like It*." *Shakespeare Quarterly* 29 (Summer 1978): 333–48.

Kuhn, Maura Slattery. "Much Virtue in *If*." *Shakespeare Quarterly* 28 (Winter 1977): 40–50.

Lake, James H. "The Psychology of Primacy and Recency Effects Upon Audience Response in *Twelfth Night*." *The Upstart Crow* 15 (1995): 26–34.

Lamb, Charles. "The Virtues of Malvolio." In *Discussions of Shakespeare's Romantic Comedy*, edited by Herbert Weil, Jr., 9–10. Boston: Heath, 1966.

Lancashire, Anne. *"Timon of Athens*: Shakespeare's *Dr. Faustus*." *Shakespeare Quarterly* 21 (Winter 1970): 35–44.

Land, Stephen K. *Kett's Rebellion: The Norfolk Rising of 1549*. Totowa, NJ: Rowman and Littlefield, 1977.

Landis, Joan Hutton. " 'By two-headed Janus': Double Discourse in *The Merchant of Venice*." *The Upstart Crow* 16 (1996): 13–30.

Laslett, Peter. *Family Life and Illicit Love in Earlier Generations*. Cambridge: Cambridge University Press, 1977.

———. *The World We Have Lost: Further Explored*. 3rd ed. London: Methuen, 1983.

Latham, Agnes, ed. *As You Like It*. The Arden Shakespeare. 2nd ed. 1975. Reprint, London: Methuen, 1977.

Lawrence, Judiana. "Natural Bonds and Artistic Coherence in the Ending of *Cymbeline*." *Shakespeare Quarterly* 35 (Winter 1984): 440–60.

Levenson, Jill L. " '*Alla stoccado* carries it away': Codes of Violence in *Romeo and Juliet*." In *Shakespeare's "Romeo and Juliet": Texts, Contexts, and Interpretation*, edited by Jay L. Halio, 83–96. Newark: University of Delaware Press, 1995.

Lever, J. W., ed. *Measure for Measure*. The Arden Shakespeare. 1965. Reprint, London: Methuen, 1985.

Levin, Harry. "Falstaff's Encore." *Shakespeare Quarterly* 32 (Spring 1981): 5–17.

———. "Shakespeare's Italians." In *Shakespeare's Italy: Functions of Italian Locations in Renaissance Drama*, edited by Michele Marrapodi, et al., 17–29. Manchester, UK: Manchester University Press, 1993.

Levin, Richard A. *Love and Society in Shakespearean Comedy: A Study of Dramatic Form and Content*. Newark: University of Delaware Press, 1985.

Lim, Walter S. H. "James I, the Royal Prerogative, and the Politics of Authority in Shakespeare's *The Winter's Tale*." *The Upstart Crow* 21 (2001): 27–38.

Ling, Nicholas. *Politeuphuia. Wits Commonwealth*. London, 1608.

Lordi, Robert J. "Brutus and Hotspur." *Shakespeare Quarterly* 27 (Spring 1976): 177–85.

M., I. *A Health to the Gentlemanly profession of Seruingmen*. 1598. Reprint, Shakespeare Association Facsimiles No. 3. London: Oxford University Press / Shakespeare Association, 1931.

MacDonald, Joyce Green. "'The Force of Imagination': The Subject of Blackness in Shakespeare, Jonson, and Ravenscroft." *Renaissance Papers 1991*. Edited by George Walton Williams and Barbara J. Baines, 53–74. Raleigh, NC: Southeastern Renaissance Conference, 1992.

Mahler, Andreas. "Italian Vices: Cross-Cultural Constructions of Temptation and Desire in English Renaissance Drama." In *Shakespeare's Italy: Functions of Italian Locations in Renaissance Drama*, edited by Michele Marrapodi, et al., 49–68. Manchester, UK: Manchester University Press, 1993.

Manley, Lawrence. *London in the Age of Shakespeare: An Anthology*. University Park: Pennsylvania State University Press, 1986.

Marsh, Derick R. C. "A Note on Hamlet's 'I Am Most Dreadfully Attended' (II.ii.266)." *Shakespeare Quarterly* 33 (Summer 1982): 181–82.

Marshall, Cynthia. "Man of Steel Done Got the Blues: Melancholic Subversion of Presence in *Antony and Cleopatra*." *Shakespeare Quarterly* 44 (Winter 1993): 385–408.

Marshall, Dorothy. *The English Domestic Servant in History*. London: Historical Association, 1949.

McDonald, Russ. *The Bedford Companion to Shakespeare: An Introduction with Documents*. Boston: Bedford / St. Martin's, 1996.

———. "Othello, Thorello, and the Problem of the Foolish Hero." *Shakespeare Quarterly* 30 (Winter 1979): 51–67.

McKewin, Carole. "Counsels of Gall and Grace: Intimate Conversations between Women in Shakespeare's Plays." In *The Woman's Part:Feminist Criticism of Shakespeare*, edited by Carolyn Ruth Swift Lenz, Gayle Greene, and Carol Thomas Neely, 117–32. Urbana: University of Illinois Press, 1980.

Miola, Robert S. "Othello *Furens*." *Shakespeare Quarterly* 41 (Spring 1990): 49–64.

———. "Timon in Shakespeare's Athens." *Shakespeare Quarterly* 31 (Spring 1980): 21–30.

Moisan, Thomas. "'Knock me here soundly': Comic Misprision and Class Consciousness in Shakespeare." *Shakespeare Quarterly* 42 (Fall 1991): 276–90.

———. "Rhetoric and the Rehearsal of Death: The 'Lamentations' Scene in *Romeo and Juliet*." *Shakespeare Quarterly* 34 (Winter 1983): 389–404.

Montrose, Louis Adrian. "'The Place of a Brother' in *As You Like It*: Social Process and Comic Form." *Shakespeare Quarterly* 32 (Spring 1981): 28–54.

———. *The Purpose of Playing: Shakespeare and the Cultural Politics of the Elizabethan Theatre*. Chicago: University of Chicago Press, 1996.

Morison, R[ichard]. *A Remedy for Sedition*. London, 1536.

Mortimer, John. "A Contemporary Playwright Looks at Shakespeare's Plays." In *Shakespeare: Text, Subtext, and Context*, edited by Ronald Dotterer, 207–23. Selinsgrove, PA: Susquehanna University Press, 1989.

Moulton, Richard G. "How the Play of Julius Caesar Works to a Climax at the Centre: A Study in Passion and Movement." In *Shakespeare as a Dramatic Artist*. 3rd ed. 1906. Reprinted in *Discussions of Shakespeare's Roman Plays*, edited by Maurice Charney, 40–52. Boston: Heath, 1964.

Muir, Kenneth. "The Critic, the Director, and Liberty of Interpreting." In *The Triple Bond: Plays, Mainly Shakespearean, in Performance*, edited by Joseph G. Price, 20–29. University Park: Pennsylvania State University Press, 1975.

———. "Image and Symbol in *Macbeth*." 1966; reprinted in *"Macbeth": Critical Essays*, edited by S. Schoenbaum, 337–51. New York: Garland, 1991.

———, ed. *Macbeth*. The Arden Shakespeare, 1951. Reprint, London: Methuen, 1980.

Mullaney, Steven. "Mourning and Misogyny: *Hamlet, The Revenger's Tragedy*, and the Final Progress of Elizabeth I, 1600–1607." *Shakespeare Quarterly* 45 (Summer 1994): 139–62.

Neely, Carol Thomas. *Broken Nuptials in Shakespeare's Plays*. New Haven: Yale University Press, 1985.

———. "Women and Men in *Othello*: 'What should such a fool / Do with so good a woman?'" In *The Woman's Part: Feminist Criticism of Shakespeare*, edited by Carolyn Ruth Swift Lenz, Gayle Greene, and Carol Thomas Neely, 211–39. Urbana: University of Illinois Press, 1980.

Neill, Michael. "Changing Places in *Othello*." In *Putting History to the Question: Power, Politics, and Society in English Renaissance Drama*, 207–36. New York: Columbia University Press, 2000.

———. "'He that thou knowest thine': Friendship and Service in *Hamlet*." In *A Companion to Shakespeare's Works, Volume 1: The Tragedies*, edited by Richard Dutton and Jean E. Howard, 319–38. Malden, MA: Blackwell, 2003.

———. Introduction. In *Putting History to the Question: Power, Politics, and Society in English Renaissance Drama*, 1–9. New York: Columbia University Press, 2000.

———. "'Mulattos,' 'Blacks,' and 'Indian Moors': *Othello* and Early Modern Constructions of Human Difference." In *Putting History to the Question: Power, Politics, and Society in English Renaissance Drama*, 269–84. New York: Columbia University Press, 2000.

———. "Servant Obedience and Master Sins: Shakespeare and the Bonds of Service." In *Putting History to the Question: Power, Politics, and Society in English Renaissance Drama*, 13–48. New York: Columbia University Press, 2000.

———. "'Servile Ministers': *Othello, King Lear* and the Sacralization of Service." Vancouver, BC: Ronsdale Press, 2004.

——. "Unproper Beds: Race, Adultery, and the Hideous in *Othello*." *Shakespeare Quarterly* 40 (Winter 1989): 383–412.

[Nesbit, E.] *Caesar's Dialogve or A Familiar Communication containing the first Institution of a Subiect, in allegiance to his Soueraigne*. 1601. Reprint, Amsterdam: Theatrvm Orbis Terrarvm / Da Capo Press, 1972.

Neville, Alexander. *Norfolkes Furies or A View of Ketts Campe*. 1575. Translated by Richard Woods. London, 1615.

Newman, Karen. "Portia's Ring: Unruly Women and Structures of Exchange in *The Merchant of Venice*." *Shakespeare Quarterly* 38 (Spring 1987): 19–33.

Newton, Allyson P. "At 'the Very Heart of Loss': Shakespeare's Enobarbus and the Rhetoric of Remembering." *Renaissance Papers 1995*. Edited by George Walton Williams and Barbara J. Baines, 81–91. Raleigh, NC: Southeastern Renaissance Conference, 1996.

Noble, Richmond. *Shakespeare's Use of Song: With the Text of the Principal Songs*. 1923. Reprint, Oxford: Clarendon Press, 1967.

Nuttall, A. D. *Timon of Athens*. Twayne's New Critical Introductions to Shakespeare, no. 8. Boston: Twayne, 1989.

Oliver, H. J. Introduction. In *Timon of Athens*, edited by H. J. Oliver. The Arden Shakespeare, xiii–lii. 1959. Reprint, London: Methuen, 1986.

——, ed. *The Merry Wives of Windsor*. The Arden Shakespeare. 1971. Reprint, London: Routledge, 1990.

Orgel, Stephen. *The Illusion of Power: Political Theater in the English Renaissance*. Berkeley: University of California Press, 1975.

Orlin, Lena Cowen. *Elizabethan Households: An Anthology*. Washington, DC: Folger Shakespeare Library, 1995.

——. *Private Matters and Public Culture in Post-Reformation England*. Ithaca: Cornell University Press, 1994.

O'Rourke, James. " 'Rule in Unity' and Otherwise: Love and Sex in *Troilus and Cressida*." *Shakespeare Quarterly* 43 (Summer 1992): 139–58.

Overbury, Sir Thomas. *The Miscellaneous Works in Prose and Verse of Sir Thomas Overbury, Knt*. Edited by Edward F. Rimbault. London: Reeves and Turner, 1890.

P., B. *The Prentises Practise in Godlinesse, and his true freedome*. London, 1608.

Partee, Morriss Henry. "The Comic Equilibrium of *Much Ado About Nothing*." *The Upstart Crow* 12 (1992): 60–73.

Partridge, A. C. "Shakespeare and Italy." *English Studies in Africa* 4 (1961): 117–27.

Partridge, Eric. *Shakespeare's Bawdy: A Literary & Psychological Essay and a Comprehensive Glossary*. 1948. Reprint, New York: E.P. Dutton, 1960.

Patey, Caroline. "Beyond Aristotle: Giraldi Cinzio and Shakespeare." In *Italy and the English Renaissance*, edited by Sergio Rossi and Dianella Savoia, 167–85. Milan: Edizioni Unicopli, 1989.

Patterson, Annabel. *Shakespeare and the Popular Voice*. Oxford: Blackwell, 1989.

Pearson, Lu Emily. *Elizabethans at Home*. 1957. Reprint, Stanford: Stanford University Press, 1967.

Percy, Thomas. *Reliques of Ancient English Poetry.* Edited by Henry B. Wheatley. 3 vols. 1886. Reprint, New York: Dover, 1966.

Perkins, Mary Hallowell. *The Servant Problem and the Servant in English Literature.* Boston: Badger, 1928.

Perkins, W[illiam]. *Christian Oeconomie: or, A Short Survey of the Right Manner of erecting and ordering a Familie, according to the Scriptures.* London, 1609.

Pittenger, Elizabeth. "Dispatch Quickly: The Mechanical Reproduction of Pages." *Shakespeare Quarterly* 42 (Winter 1991): 389–408.

Plowden, Alison. *Tudor Women: Queens and Commoners.* London: Weidenfeld and Nicolson, 1979.

Porter, Joseph A. *The Drama of Speech Acts: Shakespeare's Lancastrian Tetralogy.* Berkeley: University of California Press, 1979.

Preston, Dennis R. "The Minor Characters in *Twelfth Night.*" *Shakespeare Quarterly* 21 (Spring 1970): 167–76.

Quinney, Laura. "Enter a Messenger." In *William Shakespeare's "Antony and Cleopatra": Modern Critical Interpretations,* edited by Harold Bloom, 151–67. New Haven: Yale University Press, 1988.

Rabkin, Norman. "Rabbits, Ducks, and *Henry V.*" *Shakespeare Quarterly* 28 (Summer 1977): 279–96.

Rackin, Phyllis. "Delusion as Resolution in *King Lear.*" *Shakespeare Quarterly* 21 (Winter 1970): 29–34.

———. "The Role of the Audience in Shakespeare's *Richard II.*" *Shakespeare Quarterly* 36 (Autumn 1985): 262–81.

———. "Shakespeare's Boy Cleopatra, the Decorum of Nature, and the Golden World of Poetry." *PMLA* 87 (1972): 201–12.

Reid, Robert L. "Lear's Three Shamings: Shakespearean Psychology and Tragic Form." *Renaissance Papers 1996.* Edited by George Walton Williams and Philip Rollinson, 93–112. Raleigh, NC: Southeastern Renaissance Conference / Camden House, 1997.

———. "Macbeth's Three Murders: Shakespearean Psychology and Tragic Form." *Renaissance Papers 1991.* Edited by George Walton Williams and Barbara J. Baines, 75–92. Raleigh, NC: Southeastern Renaissance Conference, 1992.

Reynolds, Bryan. *Becoming Criminal: Transversal Performance and Cultural Dissidence in Early Modern England.* Baltimore: Johns Hopkins University Press, 2002.

Rhodes, Hugh. *The Booke of Nurture for men seruauntes, and children: (with Stans puer ad mensam).* London, 1568.

Rickman, Alan. "Jacques in *As You Like It.*" In *Players of Shakespeare 2: Further Essays in Shakespearean Performance by Players with the Royal Shakespeare Company,* edited by Russell Jackson and Robert Smallwood. Cambridge: Cambridge University Press, 1988.

Ridley, M. R., ed. *Antony and Cleopatra.* The Arden Shakespeare. 1954. Reprint, London: Routledge, 1988.

Rinehart, Keith. "Shakespeare's Cleopatra and England's Elizabeth." *Shakespeare Quarterly* 23 (Winter 1972): 81–86.

Ringler, William. "Exit Kent." *Shakespeare Quarterly* 11 (Summer 1960): 311–17.

Robbins, Bruce. *The Servant's Hand: English Fiction from Below*. New York: Columbia University Press, 1986.

Roberts, Michael. "'Words they are Women, and Deeds they are Men': Images of Work and Gender in Early Modern England." In *Women and Work in Pre-Industrial England*, edited by Lindsey Charles and Lorna Duffin, 122–80. London: Croom Helm, 1985.

Rockett, William. "Labor and Virtue in *The Tempest*." *Shakespeare Quarterly* 24 (Winter 1973): 77–84.

Rooks, John. "Savages Old and New: Images of Wildness in *The Tempest*." *Renaissance Papers 1992*. Edited by George Walton Williams and Barbara J. Baines, 79–91. Raleigh, NC: Southeastern Renaissance Conference, 1993.

Roper, William. *The Mirrour of Vertue or The Life of Syr Thomas More Knight sometime Lo. Chancellour of England*. Paris, 1626.

Rosenberg, Marvin. "From *The Masks of Macbeth*." 1978. Reprinted in *"Macbeth": Critical Essays*, edited by S. Schoenbaum, 353–66. New York: Garland, 1991.

Rossky, William. "*Antony and Cleopatra*, I.ii.79: Enobarbus' 'Mistake.'" *Shakespeare Quarterly* 35 (Autumn 1984): 324–25.

Rothman, Jules. "A Vindication of Parolles." *Shakespeare Quarterly* 23 (Spring 1972): 183–96.

Rowe, Katherine A. "Dismembering and Forgetting in *Titus Andronicus*." *Shakespeare Quarterly* 45 (Fall 1994): 279–303.

Roxburghe Ballads, The. Edited by William Chappell. 8 vols. 1872. Reprint, New York: AMS Press, 1966.

Rozett, Martha Tuck. "The Comic Structures of Tragic Endings: The Suicide Scenes in *Romeo and Juliet* and *Antony and Cleopatra*." *Shakespeare Quarterly* 36 (Summer 1985): 152–64.

Rulon-Miller, Nina. "*Othello*'s Bianca: Climbing Out of the Bed of Patriarchy." *The Upstart Crow* 15 (1995): 99–114.

Rye, William Brenchley. *England as Seen by Foreigners in the Days of Elizabeth and James the First, 1592–1610*. London: John Russell Smith, 1865.

Salingar, Leo. *Shakespeare and the Traditions of Comedy*. Cambridge: Cambridge University Press, 1974.

Salomon, Brownell. "Thematic Contraries and the Dramaturgy of *Henry V*." *Shakespeare Quarterly* 31 (Autumn 1980): 343–56.

Schalkwyk, David. "'She never told her love': Embodiment, Textuality, and Silence in Shakespeare's Sonnets and Plays." *Shakespeare Quarterly* 45 (Winter 1994): 381–407.

Schleiner, Winfried. "Justifying the Unjustifiable: The Dover Cliff Scene in *King Lear*." *Shakespeare Quarterly* 36 (Autumn 1985): 337–43.

Schoenbaum, S. "Enter a Porter (*Macbeth*, 2.3)." In *"Macbeth": Critical Essays*, edited by S. Schoenbaum, 367–75. New York: Garland, 1991.

Scott, William O. "The Paradox of Timon's Self-Cursing." *Shakespeare Quarterly* 35 (Autumn 1984): 290–304.

Shaw, Fiona, and Juliet Stevenson. "Celia and Rosalind in *As You Like It*." In *Players of Shakespeare 2: Further Essays in Shakespearean Performance by Players with the Royal Shakespeare Company*, edited by Russell Jackson and Robert Smallwood, 55–71. Cambridge: Cambridge University Press, 1988.

Sher, Antony. "The Fool in *King Lear*." In *Players of Shakespeare 2: Further Essays in Shakespearean Performance by Players with the Royal Shakespeare Company*, edited by Russell Jackson and Robert Smallwood, 151–65. Cambridge: Cambridge University Press, 1988.

Siemon, James Edward. "'But It Appears She Lives': Iteration in *The Winter's Tale*." *PMLA* 89 (January 1974): 10–16.

———. "The Canker Within: Some Observations on the Role of the Villain in Three Shakespearean Comedies." *Shakespeare Quarterly* 23 (Autumn 1972): 435–43.

Sinden, Donald. "Malvolio in *Twelfth Night*." In *Players of Shakespeare: Essays in Shakespearean Performance by Twelve Players with the Royal Shakespeare Company*, edited by Philip Brockbank, 41–66. Cambridge: Cambridge University Press, 1985.

Singman, Jeffrey L. *Daily Life in Elizabethan England*. Westport, CT: Greenwood Press, 1995.

Slights, Camille Wells. *Shakespeare's Comic Commonwealths*. Toronto: University of Toronto Press, 1993.

———. "Slaves and Subjects in *Othello*." *Shakespeare Quarterly* 48 (Winter 1997): 377–90

Smith, Alan G. R. *Servant of the Cecils: The Life of Sir Michael Hickes, 1543–1612*. Totowa, NJ: Rowman and Littlefield, 1977.

Smith, Ian. "Barbarian Errors: Performing Race in Early Modern England." *Shakespeare Quarterly* 49 (Summer 1998): 168–86.

Smith, Molly Easo. "Spectacles of Torment in *Titus Andronicus*." *Studies in English Literature 1500–1900* 36 (Spring 1996): 315–31.

Snyder, Susan. "'The King's not here': Displacement and Deferral in *All's Well That Ends Well*." *Shakespeare Quarterly* 43 (Spring 1992): 20–32.

———. "Naming Names in *All's Well That Ends Well*." *Shakespeare Quarterly* 43 (Fall 1992): 265–79.

Soellner, Rolf. "*King Lear* and the Magic of the Wheel." *Shakespeare Quarterly* 35 (Autumn 1984): 274–89.

———. "*Timon of Athens*": *Shakespeare's Pessimistic Tragedy*. Columbus: Ohio State University Press, 1979.

Spencer, Janet M. "Princes, Pirates, and Pigs: Criminalizing Wars of Conquest in *Henry V*." *Shakespeare Quarterly* 47 (Summer 1996): 160–77.

Stanton, Kay. "Remembering Patriarchy in *As You Like It*." In *Shakespeare: Text, Subtext, and Context*, edited by Ronald Dotterer, 139–49. Selinsgrove, PA: Susquehanna University Press, 1989.

Stein, Arnold. "The Image of Antony: Lyric and Tragic Imagination." *Kenyon Review* 21 (Autumn 1959): 586–606.

Stempel, Daniel. "The Transmigration of the Crocodile." *Shakespeare Quarterly* 7 (Winter 1956): 59–72.

Stern, Jeffrey. "*King Lear*: The Transference of the Kingdom." *Shakespeare Quarterly* 41 (Fall 1990): 299–308.

Stockholder, Kay. "The Aspiring Mind of the King's Man." *The Upstart Crow* 11 (1991): 1–23.

Stone, Lawrence. *The Family, Sex and Marriage in England 1500–1800*. New York: Harper & Row, 1977.

Stowe, John. *A Survey of London, Reprinted from the Text of 1603*. Edited by Charles Lethbridge Kingsford. 2 vols. 1908. Reprint, Oxford: Oxford University Press, 1971.

Strier, Richard. "Faithful Servants: Shakespeare's Praise of Disobedience." In *The Historical Renaissance: New Essays on Tudor and Stuart Literature and Culture*, edited by Heather Dubrow and Richard Strier, 104–33. Chicago: University of Chicago Press, 1988.

———. *Resistant Structures: Particularity, Radicalism, and Renaissance Texts*. Berkeley: University of California Press, 1995.

Stubs (Stubbes), Philip. *The Anatomie of Abuses*. London, 1595.

Summers, Joseph H. "The Masks of *Twelfth Night*." In *Discussions of Shakespeare's Romantic Comedy*, edited by Herbert Weil, Jr., 111–18. Boston: Heath, 1966.

Suzuki, Mihoko. *Subordinate Subjects: Gender, the Political Nation, and Literary Form in England, 1588–1688*. Aldershot, UK: Ashgate, 2003.

Swander, Homer. "Menas and the Editors: A Folio Script Unscripted." *Shakespeare Quarterly* 36 (Summer 1985): 165–87.

Taylor, Gary. Introduction. In *Henry V*, edited by Gary Taylor, 1–74. The Oxford Shakespeare. Oxford: Clarendon Press, 1982.

Tennenhouse, Leonard. *Power on Display: The Politics of Shakespeare's Genres*. New York: Methuen, 1986.

Thomas, D. L., and N. E. Evans. "John Shakespeare in the Exchequer." *Shakespeare Quarterly* 35 (Autumn 1984): 315–18.

Thomas, Keith. "Age and Authority in Early Modern England." In *Proceedings of the British Academy* 62 (1976): 205–48.

Thorne, W. B. "*Pericles* and the 'Incest-Fertility' Opposition." *Shakespeare Quarterly* 22 (Winter 1971): 43–56.

Tillyard, E. M. W. "The Elizabethan World Order." In *Shakespeare's History Plays*. New York: MacMillan, 1946. Reprinted in *Shakespeare: The Histories: A Collection of Critical Essays*, edited by Eugene M. Waith, 32–41. Englewood Cliffs, NJ: Prentice-Hall, 1965.

Tkacz, Catherine Brown. "The Wheel of Fortune, the Wheel of State, and Moral Choice in *Hamlet*." *South Atlantic Review* 57 (November 1992): 21–38.

Tvordi, Jessica. "Female Alliance and the Construction of Homoeroticism in *As You Like It* and *Twelfth Night*." In *Maids and Mistresses, Cousins and Queens: Women's Alliances in Early Modern England*, edited by Susan Frye and Karen Robertson. New York: Oxford University Press, 1999.

Twyne, Thomas. *The Schoolemaster, or Teacher of Table Phylosophie*. London, 1583.

Vaughan, Virginia Mason. "Between Tetralogies: *King John* as Transition." *Shakespeare Quarterly* 35 (Winter 1984): 407–20.

Vaughan, William. *The Golden-grove, moralized in three Bookes: A worke very necessary for all such, as woould know how to governe themselves, their houses, or their countrey*. 2nd ed. London, 1608.

Vickers, Brian. *Shakespeare, Co-Author*. Oxford: Oxford University Press, 2002.

Visser, Margaret. "Tipping." In *The Way We Are*, 72–76. 1994. Reprint, Boston: Faber and Faber, 1996.

Vives, Lewes (Joannes Ludovicus). *A verie Fruitfull and pleasant booke; called the Instruction of a Christian Woman*. Translated by Richard Hyrde. London, 1592.

Walker, Jarrett. "Voiceless Bodies and Bodiless Voices: The Drama of Human Perception in *Coriolanus*." *Shakespeare Quarterly* 43 (Summer 1992): 170–85.

Waters, D. Douglas. "Fate and Fortune in *Romeo and Juliet*." *The Upstart Crow* 12 (1992): 74–90.

———. "Shakespeare's *Timon of Athens* and Catharsis." *The Upstart Crow* 8 (1988): 93–105.

Wells, Charles. *The Wide Arch: Roman Values in Shakespeare*. New York: St. Martin's Press, 1992.

Whitney, Charles. "'Usually in the Werking Daies': Playgoing Journeymen, Apprentices, and Servants in Guild Records, 1582–92." *Shakespeare Quarterly* 50 (Winter 1999): 433–58.

Whittier, Gayle. "The Sonnet's Body and the Body Sonnetized in *Romeo and Juliet*." *Shakespeare Quarterly* 40 (Spring 1989): 27–41.

Wiggins, Martin. "*Macbeth* and Premeditation." In *The Arts, Literature, and Society*, edited by Arthur Marwick, 23–47. London: Routledge, 1990.

Wiley, Elizabeth. "The Status of Women in *Othello*." In *Shakespeare: Text, Subtext, and Context*, edited by Ronald Dotterer, 124–38. Selinsgrove, PA: Susquehanna University Press, 1989.

Willbern, David. "Malvolio's Fall." *Shakespeare Quarterly* 29 (Winter 1978): 85–90.

Willson, Robert F., Jr. "Gloucester and Harry Hunks." *The Upstart Crow* 9 (1989): 107–11.

Wilson, Richard. "'Like the old Robin Hood': *As You Like It* and the Enclosure Riots." *Shakespeare Quarterly* 43 (Spring 1992): 1–19.

Wiltenburg, Joy. *Disorderly Women and Female Power in the Street Literature of Early Modern England and Germany*. Feminist Issues series, edited by Kathleen Balutansky and Alison Booth. Charlottesville: University Press of Virginia, 1992.

Wolf, William D. "'New Heaven, New Earth': The Escape from Mutability in *Antony and Cleopatra*." *Shakespeare Quarterly* 33 (Autumn 1982): 328–35.

Woolgar, C. M. *The Great Household in Late Medieval England*. New Haven: Yale University Press, 1999.

Wright, Sue. "'Churmaids, Huswyfes and Hucksters': The Employment of Women in Tudor and Stuart Salisbury." In *Women and Work in Pre-Industrial England*, edited by Lindsey Charles and Lorna Duffin, 100–21. London: Croom Helm, 1985.

Wyrick, Deborah Baker. "The Ass Motif in *The Comedy of Errors* and *A Midsummer Night's Dream*." *Shakespeare Quarterly* 33 (Winter 1982): 432–48.

Zitner, Sheldon P. *All's Well That Ends Well*. Twayne's New Critical Introductions to Shakespeare, no. 10. Boston: Twayne / G. K. Hall, 1989.

Zolbrod, Paul G. "Coriolanus and Alceste: A Study in Misanthropy." *Shakespeare Quarterly* 23 (Winter 1972): 51–62.

Index

Abbott, George, 275 n. 11

Adelman, Janet, 80–81, 132, 246 n. 15, 264 n. 34, 267 n. 57, 288–89 n. 6, 289 n. 10, 303 n. 32

Allen, John A., 271 n. 11, 297 n. 28

Allgaier, Johannes, 116, 301 n. 21

Allott, Robert, 250 n. 13, 276 n. 23

Altman, Joel B., 294 n. 12

Alvis, John, 311 n. 39

Amussen, Susan Dwyer, 252 n. 25, 256 n. 52, 273 n. 34, 274 n. 10, 278 n. 37, 296 n. 22, 308–9 n. 25

Anderson, Linda, 277 n. 32, 310 n. 28

Andreas, James R., 67

Andrews, John F., 259 n. 70, 305 n. 7

Appelbaum, Robert, 41

Archer, Ian, 255 n. 41

Arden of Feversham, 304 n. 1, 305 n. 9

Ascham, Roger, 248 n. 2

Ashley, Leonard R. N., 250 n. 11, 255 n. 44, 257 n. 52, 281 n. 56, 304 n. 2

Aubrey, John, 273–74 n. 3, 275 n. 11, 310 n. 32

Averell, W., 251 n. 24

Baker, J. Robert, 285 n. 11

Baldwin, Thomas Whitfield, 256 n. 46, 279 n. 46, 312 n. 5

Ballads: "An Amorous Dialogue between John and His Mistress," 274 n. 10; "The Bashful Batchelor," 274 n. 10; "The Catalogue of Contented Cuckolds," 274 n. 10; "Child Waters," 262 n. 16; "The Cries of the Dead," 308 n. 21; "Edom o' Gordon," 281 n. 54; "Fair Rosamund," 262 n. 16; "Gil Morrice," 302 n. 23; "Glasgerion," 281 n. 54; "The Honour of a *London* 'Prentice," 259 n. 73; "King Estmere," 281 n. 54; "King of Scots and Andrew Browne," 275 n. 11;

"The Lady and the Blackamoor," 281 n. 54, 282 n. 65; "The Lady Isabella's Tragedy," 275 n. 11, 281 n. 54; "The Lady's Fall," 262 n. 16; "The Lady Turned Serving-Man," 262 n. 16, 281 n. 54; "The Lamentable Ballad . . . ," 304 n. 1; "Little Musgrave and Lady Barnard," 207, 293 n. 7, 302 n. 23; "London's Glory and Whittington's Renown," 308 n. 21; "The Lord of Lorne and the False Steward," 281 n. 54; "The Merchant's Daughter of Bristol," 262 n. 16; "A new Ballad . . . ," 305 n. 6; "Old Robin of Portingale," 281 n. 54, 293 n. 7; "On Thomas Lord Cromwell," 281 n. 54; "A Right Godly and Christian A. B. C.," 257 n. 58; "Robin Hood Newly Reviv'd," 308 n. 21; "Seldom Comes the Better," 278 n. 37; "Sir Aldingar," 281 n. 54; "Sir Cauline," 281 n. 54; "The Spanish Lady's Love," 262 n. 16; "The Spanish Tragedy," 281 n. 54, 308 n. 21; "The True Maid of the South," 262 n. 16; "Two Most Unnaturall and Bloodie Murders," 308 n. 21; "A warning to those who serve lords," 298–99 n. 1; "The Widdow of Watling Street," 274 n. 10; "Wit's never good till 'tis bought," 278 n. 37; "The wofull Lamentation of William Purcas," 258 n. 66

Barber, Lester E., 307 n. 20

Barckley, Richard, 250 n. 11

Barish, Jonas A., 243 n. 1, 276 n. 19, 301 n. 21

Barkan, Leonard, 229

Barnett, Richard C., 256 n. 47, 257 n. 52, 274 n. 3, 275 n. 11

Bartels, Emily C., 141